D1369879

THE COMPLETE GOING PUBLIC HANDBOOK

*Everything You Need to Know
to Successfully Turn a Private Enterprise
into a Publicly Traded Company*

FREDERICK D. LIPMAN

PRIMA VENTURE

An Imprint of Prima Publishing

3000 Lava Ridge Court • Roseville, California 95661
(800) 632-8676 • www.primalifestyles.com

To my wife, Gail

PRIMA PUBLISHING and colophon are trademarks of Prima Communications Inc., registered with the United States Patent and Trademark Office.

Data for Table 3.1 and partial data for Appendixes 2 and 3 supplied by Global Securities Information, *www.gsionline.com,* (800) 669-1154.

Disclaimer

This publication is designed to provide accurate and authoritative information (as of September 1999, except as otherwise noted) in regard to the subject matter covered. It is sold with the understanding that neither the author nor the publisher is engaged in rendering legal, accounting, or other professional service. If legal advice or other expert assistance is required, the services of a competent professional person should be sought.

> **—From a Declaration of Principles Jointly Adopted by a Committee of the American Bar Association and a Committee of Publishers and Associations.**

Library of Congress Cataloging-in-Publication Data on file.

ISBN 0-7615-2406-1

00 01 02 03 HH 10 9 8 7 6 5 4 3 2 1
Printed in the United States of America

How to Order

Single copies may be ordered from Prima Publishing, 3000 Lava Ridge Court, Roseville, CA 95661; telephone (800) 632-8676. Quantity discounts are also available. On your letterhead, include information concerning the intended use of the books and the number of books you wish to purchase.

Visit us online at www.primalifestyles.com

CONTENTS

Acknowledgments   ix

Introduction   xi

1   The Advantages and Disadvantages
    of Going Public   1
    The Advantages   1
    The Disadvantages   7

2   Advance Planning   13
    Ten Suggestions   13

3   The World of Underwriters   33
    What You Should Know About Underwriters   34
    How to Attract Underwriters   44
    Selecting an Underwriter   45
    *Limits on Underwriter Compensation
    and Offering Expenses   52*

4   Registering and Marketing the Traditional IPO   57
    The Valuation of Your Company   57
    Letter of Intent   59
    Types of Underwritings   61
    The Cost of a Traditional IPO   62
    Due Diligence   65
    Press Releases and Publicity   67

Major Participants and Timetable   71
The Prospectus   72
The Registration Process   73
State Securities Laws   73
Road Shows   76
The Pricing Meeting   77
Execution of Underwriting Agreement, Lock-up
* Agreements, and Effective Date   78*
Directed Shares   80
Closing   80

5 Preparing the Prospectus for the Traditional IPO   81
SEC Registration Forms   82
Advantages of Forms SB-1 and SB-2   83
Legal Concerns   84
Sections of Form S-1 Prospectus   85
Plain English   98

6 Nontraditional Methods of Going Public   99
What Are Nontraditional IPOs?   99
Why Can't a Company Qualify for a Traditional
* IPO?   100*
Why Consider a Nontraditional IPO?   101
Are There Any Advantages of Nontraditional
* IPOs Over Traditional IPOs?   103*

7 Self-Underwritings and Best-Efforts Public
  Offerings   105
Marketing   105
Broker-Dealers   106
Officers and Employees
Aftermarket Trading   107
Direct IPOs Over the Internet   108
Legal Considerations   109
Protecting Your Personal Assets   111
How Does the Company Choose Which Offering
* It Wants?   111*

Summary of Public and Private Offering
  Choices   118
Text of NASAA Model Accredited Investor
  Exemption   121

8   Regulation A: The $5 Million Offering   127

   Testing the Waters   128
   Who Can File Under Regulation A?   130
   Bad Boy Disqualification   130
   How Much Money Can Be Raised?   131
   Offering Statement and Offering Circular   132
   Outline of Regulation A   133

9   SCOR: The $1 Million Do-It-Yourself Registered
    Offering   141

   Federal Registration Exemption   143
   State Securities Laws   144

10   Mergers with Publicly Held Shell Corporations
     and Spin-Offs   149

   Shell Mergers   150
   Spin-Offs   153

11   Trading on the NASDAQ Stock Market
     and National Securities Exchanges   157

   Initial Listing Requirements   159
   Over-the-Counter Market vs. Exchanges   159
   What Is Best?   169
   Tick Rule and Short-Selling   170
   Fees   172
   Maintenance Criteria   172
   Corporate Governance Requirements   174
   Getting Your Stock in the Newspaper   176
   The NASDAQ National Market Fee Schedule   177
   The NASDAQ SmallCap Market Fee Structure   178

12 Being Public 181

Brief Summary 183
Form 3, Form 4, and Form 5 Reports—
  Section 16(a) of the 1934 Act 185
Liability for Short-Swing Profits—
  Section 16(b) of the 1934 Act 187
Short Sales and Sales Against the Box—
  Section 16(c) of the 1934 Act 190
Personal Use of Inside Information—
  Rule 10b-5 Under the 1934 Act 191
Tipping of Material Confidential Information—
  Rule 10b-5 Under the 1934 Act 195
Schedules 13D and 13G—
  Sections 13(d) and 13(g) of the 1934 Act 196
Trading During Distribution of Securities—
  Regulation M Under the 1934 Act 198
Foreign Corrupt Practices of 1977—
  Sections 10A, 13(b)(2), and 30A
  of the 1934 Act 199
Participants, Aiders and Abettors,
  Conspirators, and Controlling Persons 204
Conclusion 206

13 Rule 144 of the 1933 Act 207

One-Year Holding Period for Restricted
  Securities 209
Amount Salable Under Rule 144 210
Adequate Public Information 212
Manner of Selling 213
Form 144 213
Exemption for Restricted Securities Held Two
  Years 214
Control Securities 214
Conclusion 214

14 The Story of an IPO 217

Appendixes

1   Excerpts from Drkoop.com, Inc.'s Prospectus
    Dated June 8, 1999   235

2   Firm-Commitment IPO Underwritings Filed
    with the SEC, Which Were Publicly Offered
    During 1999, Listed by Name of Lead Managing
    Underwriter   287

3   Underwriting Discount and Certain Expenses
    of Firm-Commitment IPOs Filed with the SEC,
    Which Were Publicly Offered During 1999,
    Listed by Name of Lead Managing Underwriter   315

4   Timetable for Traditional IPO   349

5   Excerpts from Regulation A Offering Circular
    of Real Goods Trading Corporation Dated
    June 21, 1993   357

6   Form U-7 (Contains the SCOR Form)   399

Index   439

About the Author   449

ACKNOWLEDGMENTS

I want to acknowledge the helpful comments of my partners at the Philadelphia office of the law firm Blank Rome Comisky & McCauley LLP, including, but not limited to, Fred Blume, Barry H. Genkin, Richard J. McMahon, Alan L. Zeiger, Lawrence R. Wiseman, Sol D. Genauer, and Jane Storero. I also appreciated the comments of Robert J. Mittman of our New York office, and those of Sonia Galindo of our Baltimore office, who recently joined our firm from the Securities and Exchange Commission. I would also like to thank my former partners, G. Michael Stakias, Arthur H. Miller and James J. Bowes, who contributed to the earlier version of this book. I take full responsibility for any errors in this book and absolve each of the commentators.

I want to specifically acknowledge the helpful comments of Lynn Naefach of the Pennsylvania Securities Commission on Chapter 9.

Representatives of the New York Stock Exchange, the American Stock Exchange, and the NASDAQ Stock Market were kind enough to give me comments on Chapter 11, which I gratefully acknowledge.

My son, L. Keith Lipman, suggested the final chapter of this book, which is probably the most readable since I did not write it.

Our librarians, Manny Paredes, Rebecca Stanley, and Alison T. Husted, were very helpful in researching portions of this book. Laila Kassis, a summer intern, assisted in preparing Appendix 2.

I also want to thank David Richardson of Prima Publishing for his ideas concerning this update of my Going Public book and the staff at Argosy for their tireless efforts at producing this book.

Finally, I want to acknowledge my secretary, Herkita Trueheart, who spent countless hours typing and retyping this manuscript.

INTRODUCTION

Going public is a milestone for a growing company. Public companies can typically raise capital more cheaply and easily than private companies, with far fewer operational restrictions. Founders of public companies can retain their control positions and still sell their own stock to diversify their investments. Upon death, the founder's estate has a liquid asset to pay death taxes, without being forced to sell the company.

Even if you cannot sell your personal stock in your company's initial public offering (IPO), you may have a secondary or follow-on offering in which you do sell your stock in as little as three months after the IPO. In addition, you can usually start selling your own stock under Rule 144 of the Securities Act of 1933 as early as six months after the IPO without incurring any new registration costs. Rule 144 permits you to personally sell at least 1 percent of the outstanding stock every three months.

Greater growth is possible for public companies than for private companies because of their access to larger pools of capital. It is no coincidence that most of the Fortune 500 companies are publicly traded. Nor is it an accident that many of the Fortune 300 families' fortunes resulted from their association with founders of public companies. William Gates, III, the founder of Microsoft, became at age 36 (according to Forbes) the richest man in America with a net worth in excess of $6 billion, rising to $90 billion in 1999.

Private companies, like public companies, can also raise growth capital through internally generated funds, bank loans, and private placements of their securities. However, unlike public companies, private companies cannot offer private placement investors the liquidity of the public market place. This lack of liquidity generally results in a lower valuation for the company than for a comparable public company and limits the overall amount of available growth capital.

There are, however, a number of significant disadvantages to going public. Chief among these are the pressure to show earnings growth and the additional management, accounting, legal, and printing costs of both the IPO and subsequent compliance with federal and state securities laws. A complete description of the advantages and disadvantages are contained in Chapter 1.

A successful IPO requires careful advance planning beginning as early as five years before the IPO target date. Most business people begin planning for the IPO shortly before the target date. This is too late. A wise entrepreneur will obtain advice from experienced SEC (Securities and Exchange Commission) professionals well in advance of the target date to maximize the benefits of the IPO. Suggestions for advance planning, such as adopting stock option plans, are contained in Chapter 2.

A successful IPO also requires the careful selection of an underwriter and clever marketing of the IPO (described in Chapters 3 and 4), as well as lucky timing to fit within an IPO "window" in the stock market. The stock market's appetite for IPOs is extremely variable. IPO windows tend to open and close quickly.

Chapter 5 discusses the preparation of a prospectus.

The traditional IPO is a strange process. A company may spend several hundred thousand dollars before an underwriter will legally commit itself to buy even one share of stock. Although underwriters estimate the price at which the securities can be sold early in the registration process, they will not legally commit themselves until the SEC declares the registration statement effective. This is after most of your out-of-pocket costs have been incurred. The public offering price is determined based on market conditions existing at the time the SEC declares the registration statement effective. These market conditions may be drastically different than those existing at the time the IPO process began.

Thus, even the best advance planning and the most prudent selection of an underwriter may not be sufficient to ensure a successful IPO. In IPOs, it is better to be lucky than smart.

Chapters 6 through 10 describe some nontraditional methods of going public, including self-underwritten and best-efforts offerings, mergers with public shells, and spin-offs.

Chapter 7 discusses self-underwritten and best-efforts offerings, including unregistered Rule 504 offerings to accredited investors, which permit early stage companies to raise up to $1 million using the Internet and e-mail.

Chapters 8 and 9 describe Regulation A and SCOR (Small Corporate Offering Registration) offerings, respectively. SCOR is the $1 million "do-it-yourself" offering that permits offers and sales even to unaccredited investors after state registration.

Chapter 11 describes the requirements for trading on SmallCap NASDAQ and the NASDAQ National Market as well as national securities exchanges.

Chapters 12 and 13 describe some of the consequences of being public and Rule 144, respectively.

Chapter 14 is the exciting story of the 1986 Microsoft IPO.

CHAPTER 1

THE ADVANTAGES AND DISADVANTAGES OF GOING PUBLIC

THE ADVANTAGES

The major advantages of being public are as follows:

1. Lower Cost of Capital

A public company has more alternatives for raising capital than a private company. A private company, once it has exhausted its bank lines, generally raises additional equity and subordinated debt capital from individual and institutional investors in so-called private placements. These investors, particularly venture capital funds, insurance companies, and others, usually require very stiff terms, including significant operational restrictions.

In contrast, a public company also has the alternative of going to the public market place. The public market place typically does not demand the same stiff terms. This results in less dilution to the existing shareholders if equity capital is raised. If debt securities are publicly sold, the public market place tends to be much more liberal in imposing operational restrictions.

Two identical companies, one private and the other public, are valued quite differently by investors. Investors in the private company discount the value of its equity securities by reason of their "illiquidity," that is, the inability to readily sell them for cash.

The availability of the public capital alternative also permits the public company greater leverage in its negotiations with individual and institutional investors. Most institutional investors prefer investing in public companies since they have a built-in "exit," that is, they can sell their stock in the public market.

Suppose the market price of your company's stock never rises above the IPO price (a so-called broken IPO). Even in this disaster scenario, the IPO has permitted you to raise what is probably the cheapest form of equity capital— even if you have not achieved your other IPO objectives.

2.   *Personal Wealth*

A public offering can enhance your personal net worth. Stories abound of the many millionaires and multimillionaires created through public offerings. Even if you don't realize immediate profits by selling a portion of your existing stock during the initial offering, you can use publicly traded stock as collateral to secure loans.

In as little as three months after your IPO, you may be able to have another registered underwritten public offering in which you sell a significant percentage of your personal holdings. These secondary or follow-on offerings are only possible if your company's earnings have grown and your market price had risen significantly since your IPO.

These secondary or follow-on offerings permit you to diversify your personal wealth without selling or otherwise losing control of your company. You can have your cake and eat it too!

For approximately six months after the IPO (the lock-up period), the underwriter will restrict you from selling your personal stock, except in a secondary or follow-on offering authorized by the underwriter. Thereafter, you can sell stock under Rule 144. Rule 144 permits you to personally sell up to 1 percent of the total outstanding stock of the company every three months, or one week's average trading volume, whichever is higher. The sales have to be in unsolicited brokerage transactions or transactions with brokerage firms that make a market in your stock. You also have to publicly report these sales. Thus, it may not be desirable for you to utilize Rule 144 too frequently for fear of giving the investment community the impression that you are bailing out.

3. Competitive Position

Many businesses use the capital from the IPO to enhance their competitive position. The additional capital resources permit greater market penetration.

Some businesses have only a short window of opportunity to make a move. For example, a technology-based company can use the IPO proceeds to achieve a dominant position in the market place well before its underfinanced competitors.

Customers like to deal with well-financed businesses. A strong balance sheet is a good marketing tool.

4. Prestige

You and your co-founders gain an enormous amount of personal prestige from being associated with a company that goes public. Such prestige can be very helpful in recruiting key employees and in marketing your products and services. For example, the publicity surrounding the Internet IPOs, such as eBay, Inc., significantly increased the visitors to their Web sites.

5.   Ability to Take Advantage of Market Price Fluctuations

The market price of the stock of public companies can fluctuate greatly. These fluctuations may relate to overall stock market trends and have nothing to do with your company's performance. The stock market from time to time tends to unreasonably overprice your stock or severely underprice it. So-called momentum investing, caused primarily by day-traders, can occasionally cause wild price gyrations.

During the period that your stock is severely underpriced, your company has the ability to repurchase its stock on the stock market at these depressed prices, provided you have been wise enough to retain a cash reserve. Likewise, during the period that your stock is unreasonably overpriced, you can sell stock on very favorable terms. None of these opportunities is available to a private company.

6.   Enhanced Ability to Grow Through Acquisitions

The cash proceeds from the IPO can be used to make acquisitions to help your company grow faster. Indeed, underwriters prefer companies that can use the IPO proceeds to grow the business. A publicly traded company also may grow by using its own stock to make acquisitions. This option is generally not available to a private company that is forced to use cash or notes for acquisitions. Private company stock is not an attractive form of consideration to a seller since it lacks liquidity.

The ability to grow through stock acquisitions may permit your company to use pooling-of-interest accounting for acquisitions—at least until the year 2001 when it is expected to be abolished. An acquiring company using the pooling-of-interest method can reflect, as part of its own reported income, the income of the acquired company earned even before the date of the acquisition. Pooling-of-interest accounting also avoids the reduction of your company's future income caused by goodwill amortization resulting from the acquisition and the extra depreciation resulting from writing fixed assets of the acquired company up to their current values. If pooling-of-interest accounting is available, no goodwill is created and no write-up of fixed assets is required.

Spectacular increases can occur in your company's reported earnings per share as a result of the pooling-of-interest method of accounting for acquisitions. This could occur, for example, where your company's stock is valued at 20 times earnings and you use your stock to effectuate mergers based on paying 10 times the acquired company's earnings. After the merger, your stock price will presumably reflect the acquired company's earnings multiplied by 20.

Since your company's stock will trade for a multiple of your reported earnings per share, significant increases in your reported earnings per share can, in turn, result in dramatic increases in your company's stock price.

Even after January 1, 2001, when pooling-of-interest accounting is scheduled to be abolished, your company's ability to use stock instead of cash as an acquisition currency will permit greater growth opportunities than are available to competing private companies.

7. *Enhanced Ability to Borrow: No Personal Guarantees*

When your company sells stock, it increases its net worth and improves its debt-to-equity ratio. This should allow your company to borrow money on more favorable terms in the future.

The principals of private companies are often required to personally guarantee bank loans made to their companies. Once your company is public, banks and other financial institutions are less likely to require any personal guarantees.

8. Enhanced Ability to Raise Equity

If your company continues to grow, you will eventually need additional permanent financing. If your stock performs well in the stock market, you will be able to sell additional stock on favorable terms.

9. Attracting and Retaining Key Employees

Stock options offered by emerging public companies have much appeal and can help you recruit and retain well-qualified executives and motivate your employee-shareholders.

10. Liquidity and Valuation

Once your company goes public, a market is established for your stock and you will have an effective way of valuing that stock. Subject to Rule 144 (see Chapter 13), you can sell whenever the need arises.

Your stock prices can easily be followed. Prices are quoted daily and many newspapers print them.

11. Estate Planning

Many private companies have to be sold upon the death of their founder in order to pay death taxes. This may prevent you from passing the ownership of your private company to your family or to key employees.

Founders of private companies sometimes fund death taxes by maintaining large life insurance policies. However, the premiums on these life insurance policies can be a significant drain on the business. These premiums are not deductible for federal income tax purposes.

If your company's stock is publicly traded, your estate will have a liquid asset with which to pay death taxes.

THE DISADVANTAGES

The major disadvantages of going public are as follows:

1. *Expense*

The cost of going public is substantial, both initially and on an ongoing basis. As for the initial costs, the underwriters' discount or commission can run as high as 10 percent or more of the total offering. Additionally, you can incur out-of-pocket expenses that typically range from $250,000 to $500,000 or more for even a small offering of $15 million of your securities. (These initial expenses are discussed at greater length in Chapter 4.) If your IPO is cancelled at the last minute, you are still liable for other substantial costs.

On an ongoing basis, regulatory reporting requirements, stockholders' meetings, investor relations, and other expenses of being public can run from $50,000 to $100,000 or more annually. This is in addition to your management time, which can be considerable. The cost of printing and distributing your annual and quarterly reports, proxy statements, and stock certificates can alone be extremely costly if you choose to use expensive glossy, colorful printing processes and first class mail.

You may also need to hire additional financial and accounting personnel to help prepare your company's financial disclosures. Likewise, you may be required to hire a shareholder relations employee and to upgrade the quality of existing financial and accounting employees. Director and officer liability insurance is a must for public companies. These are all additional hidden costs of going public.

A number of smaller public companies have developed methods to minimize their ongoing costs of being public. These methods include the judicious use of outside professionals, issuing bare-bones annual and quarterly reports to shareholders, using inexpensive techniques to reproduce and mail these shareholder reports (such as third class mail), avoiding expensive shareholders' meetings, etc. Minimizing such expenses can reduce your ongoing costs (exclusive of director and officer liability insurance) to as low as $40,000 per year.

2.   *Pressure to Maintain Growth Pattern*

You will be subject to considerable pressure to maintain the growth rate you have established, particularly from analysts who follow your company's stock. If your sales or earnings deviate from an upward trend, analysts may recommend that your stock be sold and investors may become apprehensive and sell their stock, driving down its price. These price declines can be severe as investors flee your stock en masse. You may not have the capital with which to buy back the stock at these depressed prices. As a result, you will have unhappy stockholders.

You must report operating results quarterly. People will thus evaluate the company on a quarterly rather than on an annual basis. This intensifies the pressure and shortens your planning and operating horizons significantly. The pressure may tempt you to make short-term decisions that could have a harmful long-term impact on the company.

3. *Disclosure of Information*

Your company's operations and financial situation are open to public scrutiny. Information concerning the company, officers, directors, and certain shareholders—information not ordinarily disclosed by privately held companies—will be available to competitors, customers, employees, and others. Such information as your company's sales, profits, your competitive edge, material contracts with major customers and the salaries and perquisites of the chief executive officer and certain highly paid executive officers must be disclosed not only when you initially go public, but also on a continuing basis thereafter.

The SEC staff has a procedure to authorize confidential treatment for documents you file. However, you must apply to the SEC early in the IPO registration process to avoid holding up the IPO. Very sensitive information can typically be excluded from public scrutiny.

The SEC-mandated disclosures should not be a major concern to most businesses. Your competitors may already possess a lot more information about you than you realize. This information have been revealed by customers, suppliers, and former employees. Many companies already provide some financial information to business credit agencies, such as Dun & Bradstreet. Although public companies disclose much more financial information than private companies, the additional information is not necessarily a competitive disadvantage.

In general, public companies are only required to disclose information that is material to investors. Information about specific customers for your products do not have to be disclosed unless the customers' purchases are such a high percentage of your total sales as to be material to investors. Likewise, the exact profitability of specific products does not normally have to be disclosed, provided the product lines do not constitute a separate industry segment for financial reporting purposes. Management is given reasonable discretion in determining whether its business includes separately reportable industry segments. Accordingly, it is usually possible to avoid disclosure of the exact profitability of separate product lines.

4.   *Loss of Control*

If a sufficiently large proportion of your shares is sold to the public, you may be threatened with the loss of control of the company. Once your company is publicly held, the potential exists for further dilution of your control through subsequent public offerings and acquisitions. Likewise, you may be subject to a hostile tender offer.

This disadvantage can be alleviated by the careful insertion of anti-takeover provisions in your charter or by creating two classes of stock with disproportionate voting rights. Although there are few, if any, anti-takeover defenses that are completely, legally foolproof, some defenses can in practice be very effective against raiders. Defenses that deprive the raiders of voting power or that otherwise penalize the raiders are particularly effective.

Many underwriters, particularly prestigious underwriters, object to anti-takeover defenses in the charter of IPO companies. Such defenses may make it more difficult to attract institutional investors. This may result in the IPO selling at a discount—ranging from 5 percent to 20 percent. The few underwriters who do not primarily sell to institutional investors are usually more relaxed about these clauses.

What is a "normal" anti-takeover defense and what is "unusual" is typically a matter of negotiation with the underwriter. For example, some underwriters object to staggering the terms of the members of the board of directors. Others do not. In general, anti-takeover provisions, which are part of state law and require special shareholder action to opt-out of, will usually be accepted by underwriters.

Even if anti-takeover defenses cannot be inserted into your charter prior to your IPO, you can usually amend your charter after your IPO to insert these defenses. This should be accomplished before your personal stock ownership falls below 50 percent of the outstanding stock.

5. Shareholder Lawsuits

Public companies and their directors, officers, and control persons are susceptible to being sued by their shareholders in lawsuits.

Shareholder class action lawsuits typically follow a significant drop in the market price of your company's stock caused by adverse news about your company. The theory of these suits is that your company knew or should have known of the adverse news and had a duty to publicize it at an earlier date than the date the news actually became public. The lawsuit will allege that failure to publicize the information earlier constitutes "fraud-on-the-market."

Overly optimistic or exaggerated statements contained in your company's reports to shareholders, or in press releases, are usually cited in these lawsuits to support their allegations. These statements are typically the result of a misguided attempt to generate interest in your company.

Public companies can prevent such lawsuits, or at least win them if brought, only by a careful program of promptly disclosing adverse news to the trading markets and by avoiding overly optimistic or exaggerated comments in shareholder and press releases. This requires you to be sensitive to the need for such disclosures.

Since everyone makes a mistake occasionally, it is a good idea to obtain directors and officers liability insurance. Such insurance can cost anywhere from $20,000 to $100,000 per year or more. Some private companies already maintain this insurance, but usually at lower cost. Thus, it is only the extra insurance premium costs of being public that should be considered the real disadvantage of an IPO.

6.   *Estate Tax Disadvantage*

One of the advantages of an IPO is to create sufficient liquidity to pay death taxes. However, there is a concomitant disadvantage. It is more difficult to obtain a low estate tax valuation for a publicly traded stock than for the stock of a private company. This is true because the public market tends to value stocks on a multiple of earnings basis, rather than a book value basis.

CHAPTER 2

ADVANCE PLANNING

TEN SUGGESTIONS

Long-term advance planning is absolutely essential for a successful IPO. The following are ten suggestions for companies considering a future IPO, although not all of them are appropriate for all companies.

1. *Develop an Impressive Management and Professional Team*

Underwriters look for companies with impressive management teams. Reputable underwriters shy away from one-man companies. They also avoid companies headed by inventors or technology experts who lack executive skills. It has been suggested that this was the reason Jim Barksdale became CEO of Netscape, rather than Marc Andreessen.

Your chief financial officer must be an impressive as well as competent person. This is particularly true if your

CFO will be the main contact person for investment analysts after your IPO.

The assembly of your management team should not occur on the eve of your IPO. If you have a weakness in management, the time to upgrade your key employees is several years before your IPO target date. It may be prudent to obtain an objective evaluation of you and your management team by a reputable management consultant.

Your auditor and your attorneys must also be impressive to the investment community. Hire accounting firms and law firms that have the SEC background and expertise to guide you up to and through the IPO.

2. Adopt a Stock Option Plan

A stock option plan should be adopted as early as five years before the target date for your IPO. There are three advantages to granting options this early:

- You can grant options to yourself and your key employees at low exercise prices. Options should be issued with exercise prices equal to the appraised market value of your shares on the grant date to avoid accounting charges to your earnings. The earlier the options are granted in your company's growth cycle, the lower the appraised market value of your shares and, consequently, the lower the option exercise price.

- The prospect (even long term) of an IPO provides an incentive to your existing key employees and permits you to attract new key employees with stock options. Many stories circulate about key employees who became instant millionaires with their stock options after an IPO.

- The options will reduce the dilution of your equity when the IPO occurs (especially if you grant yourself a stock option), since underwriters usually do not consider a reasonable number of outstanding options in valuing your company.

Most companies adopt a stock option plan on the eve of their IPO. This is the wrong time to so this, since the options then have to be granted at the higher "market value" caused by your earnings growth and the imminent IPO. Moreover, you have lost the golden opportunity to motivate your key employees and attract new key employees during the years preceding the IPO.

What if you never have an IPO? The company may make the granted stock options not exercisable unless and until there is a public offering. If your company never has a public offering, the options expire unexercised.

The disadvantage of not permitting options to be exercised unless and until there is an IPO is that your company will have an earnings charge in the fiscal quarter in which your IPO occurs. This earnings charge will probably not affect your IPO valuation, since it is a nonrecurring charge and IPOs are generally valued based on the twelve months' earnings projected after the IPO.

One way to avoid this earnings charge is to permit the option to be exercised after a lengthy period (e.g., nine years), whether or not you have an IPO, and accelerate the exercise date if there is an IPO. Since this area is very complicated, consult your accountant before establishing this type of plan.

A stock option is a great incentive device for key employees, whether your company is private or public. It gives key employees a proprietary interest in helping your company grow. It may lower the amount of cash compensation you pay to retain and attract key employees. If you desire to compensate your employee option-holders even if your company never has an IPO, you can, if you wish, provide for cash payments to cancel these options.

How is your market value determined? An independent appraiser should be used to determine the market value of a company whose stock is not publicly traded. The cost of such an appraisal can, with some shopping, be obtained for as little as $10,000 or possibly even less.

What should be the duration of the stock options? The stock options granted to your key employees can have a term of up to ten years and still have the benefit of incentive stock option treatment under the Internal Revenue Code. If you want incentive stock option treatment for your own options, you generally cannot give yourself an option having a term in excess of five years and your option price has to be 110 percent of market.

Since the duration of the option may be more important to you than the tax benefits, consider giving yourself a non-incentive stock option having a ten-year term issued at market value (not 110 percent of market). The loss of the tax benefits can be more than made up for by the additional five-year term and the lower option price.

What happens if key employees terminate their employment before the IPO? Any good stock option plan should contain a provision that terminates the option to the extent then unexercised upon an employee leaving, with or without cause, or after being fired. If employment terminates before the IPO and the option is not exercisable until the company goes public, the employee has no further rights upon his termination.

If your stock option plan permits the employee to exercise an option before the IPO, and the employee has exercised a stock option before the termination, the option should contain a "call" provision permitting the company to buy back the stock. To avoid an earnings charge, the call price should equal the appraised market value of the stock.

Why not grant stock options on the eve of the public offering with exercise prices that are below your proposed public IPO offering price? The problem with this strategy is that it raises the eyebrows of the underwriters and the investment community. Options issued on the eve of the

IPO below the IPO price reward management even if the investment community suffers because the market price never happens to rise above the IPO price.

Moreover, the issuance of a stock option on the eve of an IPO with an exercise price below your *proposed* public offering price may result in accounting charges against the income of the company that could reduce the *actual* public offering price of your stock.

The SEC accounting staff may require accounting charges for options issued within one year of the IPO at prices below the IPO price. The SEC typically requires the company to justify these price differentials by variations in the valuation of the company between the date of the option grants and the IPO date.

For example, assume that your *proposed* IPO public offering price is to be based on a valuation of your company equal to 25 times your company's projected income after taxes. If your company grants stock options on the eve of the IPO at an exercise price below your stock's current market value (which is presumably your *proposed* IPO public offering price), your projected income would be reduced as a result of the accounting charge arising from issuance of the below-market stock options. For each dollar of reduction in your projected income, your company's valuation could be reduced by 25 times the reduction. As a result, your company must either issue more shares to raise the same amount of money or issue the same number of shares at a lower *actual* IPO public offering price per share.

3. *Grow Your Business with an Eye to the Public Market Place*

Growing your business with an eye to the public market place requires you to become familiar with publicly held companies similar to your own business. If you are engaged in two or more businesses, become familiar with publicly held companies in each of your businesses.

You should pay particular attention to the price/earnings multiple of similar public companies. You can find the trailing price/earnings multiple by dividing the market price of the stock by the earnings per share for the prior four quarters. This figure is regularly published in most financial newspapers.

If the price/earnings multiple of one of your two businesses is very low and is much higher for the other business, focus your attention on growing the business with the higher price/earnings multiple. Currently, Internet revenues (there are usually no earnings) receive the highest multiplier when valuing a company that has both an Internet business and a non-Internet business. Your growth efforts will receive greater reward by concentrating on the business with the most potential.

Underwriters are particularly interested in businesses that are dominant in their fields. Again, focus your efforts in becoming dominant in a niche business.

How large must my company be? Do you think that the company whose summarized financial information is presented in Table 2.1 is a good or bad candidate for a traditional, firm-commitment IPO?

If you guessed that this company could not possibly qualify for a traditional IPO, you are wrong. This company, Drkoop.com, completed an $84 million public offering in June 1999. The lead underwriter was Bear,

TABLE 2.1

	Fiscal Year Ending in		
	1997	1998	First Quarter 1999
Product Revenues	$0	$43,000	$404,000
Net Loss	($622,000)	($9,117,000)	($4,264,000)

Stearns & Co., Inc. and the co-managers were Hambrecht & Quist and Wit Capital Corporation (as e-manager). Drkoop.com operates an Internet-based consumer health-care network.

Some would argue that the Internet offering mania of the late 1990s was an aberration in the IPO market. Although the new Internet IPO offerings had less substance than many traditional IPOs, there are many precedents.

Those who think that the IPO markets during the last years of the 1990s were unprecedented should consider the financial results of the following company, whose results are shown in Table 2.2.

In February 1993, five years before the start of the Internet craze, the company just described closed a $24 million IPO. The lead underwriters were Morgan Stanley Group, Inc. and Kidder, Peabody & Co., both prestigious underwriters. The company is named Cyberonics. Its business is to design, develop, and bring to market medical devices that provide a novel therapy, vagus nerve stimulation, for the treatment of epilepsy and other debilitating neurological disorders.

The larger underwriters generally require a minimum IPO of $25 million in order to permit them to earn a reasonable profit and they prefer a post-IPO market capitalization (outstanding shares multiplied by share price) of at least $100 million to attract institutional investors. To achieve that level, the valuation of your company before the IPO must be at least $75 million.

TABLE 2.2

| | Fiscal Year Ending in | | | |
	1989	1990	1991	1992
Net Sales	—	—	—	$53,890
Net Loss	$(837,064)	$(1,489,026)	$(3,363,188)	$(3,492,703)

Underwriters generally do not wish to sell more than 50 percent of your company stock in the IPO. Therefore, if the underwriter's minimum IPO is $25 million, your company would need a $25 million pre-IPO valuation to stay within the 50 percent limit.

Some underwriters *say* that they will not consider any company for an IPO other than an Internet company unless the company has income after taxes of at least $1 million during the last fiscal year. *The $1 million earnings level is really a rule of thumb that is often violated by those who advocate it.* In computing the $1 million earnings level, underwriters normally permit you to add to your income the interest you will save in paying off debt from the IPO proceeds.

Whether or not your company ever reaches the $1 million earnings level, it may still be a good IPO candidate. Many companies that have no earnings whatsoever, but great growth potential, go public with national underwriters. *Your future growth potential is much more important to an underwriter than your current earnings.* Many national, regional, and local underwriters will underwrite your offering without regard to your earnings level.

Even very large and prestigious national underwriters occasionally underwrite a company with minimal or no earnings or large losses, and great growth potential. This is particularly true in "hot" industries, such as Internet companies. But it is not limited to this industry.

Startup companies with proven management teams are also taken public by prestigious underwriters. A "proven management team" means that it has successfully grown another company. For example, do you think that Bill Gates would really have difficulty finding an underwriter if he started another company?

According to a 1992 SEC release, a significant percentage of public companies have a market capitalization, assets, and revenues of less than $5 million. Compare the following the SEC charts.

PUBLIC COMPANIES—CLASSIFIED BY MARKET CAPITALIZATION

Market Capitalization	Cumulative Number and Percentage of Public Companies
Less than $5 million	3,003 (38%)
Less than $10 million	3,909 (49%)
Less than $15 million	4,393 (55%)
Less than $20 million	4,756 (60%)
Less than $25 million	5,017 (63%)

PUBLIC COMPANIES—CLASSIFIED BY ASSETS

Assets	Cumulative Number and Percentage of Public Companies
Less than $5 million	2,325 (25%)
Less than $10 million	2,961 (32%)
Less than $15 million	3,326 (36%)
Less than $20 million	3,612 (39%)
Less than $25 million	3,769 (41%)

PUBLIC COMPANIES—CLASSIFIED BY REVENUES

Revenues	Cumulative Number and Percentage of Public Companies
Less than $5 million	1,845 (22%)
Less than $10 million	2,494 (29%)
Less than $15 million	2,937 (35%)
Less than $20 million	3,287 (39%)
Less than $25 million	3,562 (42%)

It is clear that many public companies are relatively small.

Growth Strategies Reaching a high earnings level does give your company access to many more underwriters and reduces the percentage of the company you must sell in the IPO. Therefore, you should develop a strategy to maximize your earnings.

Your growth strategy might include expanding your product lines or entering into related businesses. This takes time. Your strategy might also include a merger with another company in your industry. Some IPO candidates merge on the effective date of the IPO. They fund the merger with the proceeds from the IPO or possibly use stock that is registered in the IPO.

Underwriters like companies that are showing growth through acquisitions. Identifying potential merger targets and negotiating transactions with them is not something easily done on the eve of the IPO.

Associating with a prestigious, professionally managed venture fund that will finance your growth can be an excellent IPO strategy. Institutional investors are more comfortable investing in a venture-backed IPO. These IPO investors tend to believe that the venture capitalists have thoroughly investigated your company before risking their own funds, and therefore feel your company is a good IPO bet.

Obviously, it is better to grow through bank loans and internally generated capital since you avoid diluting your equity; however, that is not always possible. Identifying and negotiating with private capital investment sources takes careful advance planning. Your growth strategy might require you to obtain additional private capital several years before the IPO target date.

4. Show Earnings or Revenue Growth Before You Go Public

Private companies are typically operated in a manner to minimize income taxes. As a result, they tend to adopt policies that reflect the lowest possible taxable income.

If your company is in a "hot" market segment, such as Internet IPOs in the late 1990s, your current accounting earnings (if any) are probably irrelevant. Some of the Internet IPOs showed very little revenue, let alone earnings, and became successful IPOs as a result of the speculative fever generated by the growth prospects of the Web.

Investors are normally interested in the post-IPO growth of accounting earnings. If your company is not in a hot industry, your pre-IPO earnings growth is important to investors as a predictor of your post-IPO earnings growth. You may have the greatest business in the world, but if you do not show your accounting earnings because of your minimization of taxes, you will not get the best price for your stock when you do go public. You may not even be able to have an IPO at all if you do not show sufficient earnings.

Underwriters also look at earnings trends to make certain that a consistent history of earnings growth over several years is reflected prior to the IPO. The investment community is justifiably suspicious of companies that show earnings for only one fiscal year just prior to the IPO target date.

Therefore, for at least two to three year fiscal years prior to your IPO target date, you should begin showing earnings growth for financial accounting purposes. This is not always inconsistent with minimizing taxes, since different policies can be adopted for both tax and accounting purposes (e.g., taking accelerated depreciation for tax purposes but not for accounting purposes).

One method of reflecting accounting earnings is to reduce shareholder-officer salaries. If you do not want to reduce your lifestyle, you should consider paying a dividend to make up for the shortfall. A dividend can have adverse tax effects if your company has not made a Subchapter S election. Therefore, you should consider becoming a Subchapter S corporation as part of your IPO planning. (There are other advantages to a Subchapter S election mentioned in Recommendation 9.)

If you are primarily an Internet company with no or little earnings, it is important to show Internet revenue growth prior to your IPO.

5. *Obtain Audited or Auditable Financial Statements*

The SEC normally requires audited income statements for three years in order to go public, if you or a predecessor have been in business that long. It may not be possible, on the eve of the IPO, to retroactively obtain audited financial statements. This is particularly true if sales of inventory account for a significant portion of your revenues and no auditor has ever observed your inventory.

Therefore, it is preferable to obtain either currently audited financial statements or "auditable" financial statements, that is, financial statements that are capable of being audited retroactively at the time of your IPO. Waiting until the eve of your IPO to obtain audited financial statements can delay your IPO and cause you to lose an IPO window. Therefore, start your audit at least six months before your IPO filing date.

6. *Clean Up Your Act*

Public companies operate in a fish bowl. If you engage in illegal or other questionable practices as a private company, you may have created contingent liabilities for your company that may have to be publicly disclosed in the IPO registration statement. No one will buy the securities of a company that may have significant contingent liabilities resulting from questionable practices.

It is wise to stop any questionable practices many years before your IPO target date. Indeed, the statute of limitations on causes of action for commercial bribery or for understatement of federal income taxes (e.g., as a result of inventory cushions, paying relatives who do not work, etc.) may be as long as six years and could be even longer in certain cases.

It is strongly recommended that you stop any such questionable practices well before the date you plan to go public. Besides, you'll sleep better at night.

7. *Establish Two Classes of Stock or Other Anti-Takeover Defenses*

It is never too early to establish two classes of stock or to set up other anti-takeover defenses. The longer the company has operated with these anti-takeover defenses, the more likely the company will be able to retain them in the IPO. However, there is no guarantee that any anti-takeover defenses can survive the negotiations with the underwriter.

The best anti-takeover defense is having two classes of common stock. The first class of common stock, call it Class A common stock, is intended to be sold in the IPO and has the right to elect only a small percentage of the members of the board or perhaps none at all. The second class of stock, call it Class B common stock, would elect a majority of the board of directors and, at the option of the holder, be convertible to Class A common stock, usually on a one-for-one basis. Both Class A and Class B stock are issued to the founder, with the majority of the shares being Class A stock. If stock options are granted, the options should be granted in the Class A stock to avoid dilution of control.

In the Martha Stewart Living Omnimedia, Inc. IPO, offered in October 1999, approximately $130 million of Class A common stock was sold to investors in a very successful public offering managed by Morgan Stanley Dean Witter (book manger). Each holder of Class A common stock was entitled to one vote per share. Martha Stewart continued to own all of Class B common stock, which was entitled to 10 votes per share. As a result, Martha Stewart had 96% of the total voting power after the IPO even though approximately 15 percent of the equity was sold in the IPO.

Other anti-takeover strategies can also be set up. These include staggering the election of the directors by classifying the terms of the members of the board of directors, prohibiting removal of the board of directors except for cause, allowing multiple director votes to the founders, etc.

Particularly valuable are clauses that prohibit purchase of more than a specified percentage (e.g., 10 percent) of the company's stock without board permission and that permit the company to repurchase at a loss to the investor any excess shares acquired without board permission. Although these clauses have not been legally tested, their very appearance in your charter has a deterrent effect.

Even if the potential underwriter objects to anti-takeover clauses, almost none objects to changing your company's state of incorporation. Changing your state of incorporation to a state such as Pennsylvania can dramatically increase the protection given to management from unwanted offers. Contrary to popular opinion, some states, including Delaware, may not be as protective against unfriendly suitors as other states.

No underwriter likes to have anti-takeover clauses in the IPO. If your IPO is marginal, it is likely that few (if any) anti-takeover clauses will survive underwriter scrutiny since they add unneeded marketing problems.

If the IPO cannot be sold with major anti-takeover clauses, then you should consider installing such anti-takeover clauses at the first annual shareholders' meeting after the company has gone public. In many states, the shareholder votes of the founders can be counted to approve anti-takeover amendments to the charter. However, establishing two classes of stock is much more difficult, if not impossible, once the company has gone public.

When interviewing potential underwriters, ask whether the existence of two classes of stock or other anti-takeover clauses would prevent their underwriting the IPO. Most underwriters, in their eagerness to obtain the business, are willing to accept reasonable anti-takeover clauses if such provisions are contemplated at the time they are hired.

8.   *Select Your Own Independent Board Members*

Consider appointing independent directors to your board prior to the IPO. Such independent directors can, if they have outstanding credentials, help establish the credibility of your management team to potential underwriters. They can also be helpful in introducing you to potential underwriters and guiding you through the IPO process.

Public companies are expected (and are required by stock exchange and the NASDAQ Stock Market rules) to have an independent audit committee of their boards of directors. The underwriters insist upon the appointment of independent directors in order to "dress-up" the prospectus for the investment community.

You will need independent directors anyway for the IPO. Therefore, why not obtain the benefit of their knowledge even before the IPO? Appointing them to your board before the IPO also gives you a chance to evaluate them as directors. It may also forestall a request by the underwriters to have their own designees appointed to the board; however there is no assurance of this. Even if you never have an IPO, many private companies find that having independent directors on their board is helpful since they can give dispassionate advice in the operation of your business.

Some potential directors prefer to be appointed to an advisory committee, rather than to the board of directors, because of liability concerns. If the person has outstanding credentials and the company does not maintain liability insurance for directors and officers, you may wish to accommodate their request. However, it should be understood that the person will join your board of directors when the IPO occurs since, presumably, the company will then purchase directors and officers liability insurance for them.

Most outside directors will accept a small stock option if you do not wish to pay them in cash for their services.

9. Create Insider Bailout Opportunities

Underwriters of IPOs are very wary of permitting founders of the company to sell any significant amount of their stock in the IPO. It looks like a bailout.

Subchapter S and Other Tax Flow-Through Entities
A Subchapter S corporation or other tax flow-through entity creates unique bailout opportunities. A Subchapter S corporation is a corporation that has elected to be taxed pursuant to Subchapter S of the Internal Revenue Code of 1986 (as amended). The shareholders of a Subchapter S corporation are personally taxed on the corporation's income for federal income tax purposes. The same tax rules are true for equity holders of limited liability companies, limited partnerships, and other tax flow-through entities.

Underwriters typically do not object to the withdrawal of this previously taxed income from the corporation or other entity upon the closing of the IPO. Of course, the company must still be reasonably funded after the withdrawal.

The withdrawal is in reality a dividend to the insider. It is typically justified by the fact that the income was previously taxed to the shareholders or other equity holders.

Shareholders of non-Subchapter S corporations (so called C or regular business corporations) have much greater difficulty convincing underwriters to permit a dividend on the eve of an IPO. Yet, economically, such dividends are very similar to a Subchapter S withdrawal.

Insider Debt Underwriters are less concerned with the company using part of the proceeds of the IPO to pay debts or other obligations to an insider, provided the debt or other obligations is incurred in a legitimate transaction.

For example, the insider may enter into a long-term patent license or real estate lease with the company and use a portion of the IPO proceeds to fund the license or lease payments. Likewise, the insider may sell property to the company provided it is normally used in company operations.

Alternatively, if payments to the insider as a result of the license, lease, or sale were originally funded with bank debt, underwriters generally do not object to the repayment of the bank debt with the IPO proceeds. This may be true even if the insider is a personal guarantor of the bank debt.

However, the sale of insider stock to the company would raise eyebrows unless the sale resulted from the retirement or death of one of the founders of the company.

Obviously, if the debts or other obligations to the insider are incurred on or upon the closing of the IPO, it looks more like a disguised bailout. Therefore, any insider transaction should generally happen well before the IPO. Equally importantly, only a small portion of the IPO proceeds should be used for this purpose.

10. Take Advantage of IPO Windows, Fads, and IPOs of Similar Companies

IPO windows open and close quickly. Your short-term planning should take advantage of these windows. You may prefer to have your IPO in six months or a year.

However, in six months or a year there may be no market for IPOs. Your plans must be flexible enough to take advantage of these windows.

Table 2.3 shows the great variation in the number of firm-commitment IPO underwritings from year to year that are declared effective by the SEC.

Fads often develop in IPOs when investor interest is high. For example, Internet issues are currently popular; previously, environmental and biotechnology issues were popular, but are not currently. If your company has a product line that can fit within a fad, you may want to change your IPO target date to take advantage of it.

The history of IPO fads is that the highest valuations are given to the earliest companies who have IPOs. Ultimately, the supply of companies feeding the fad increases and begins to overwhelm investor demand. This results in lower valuations for the later fad companies. The history of Internet IPOs appears to be following this same trend. The moral is that the early bird catches the worm.

Particular attention should be paid to IPOs of other companies in your industry. If another company in your business recently had a successful IPO, underwriters will be eager to market your company's public issue. This is particularly true if the current market price of the stock of the similar company is above its initial public offering price. Your stock will be attractive to underwriters since they can market your IPOs to potential investors with the analogy of the prior successful IPO.

To keep track of IPOs in your industry, consider subscribing to a publication called *The IPO Reporter*. For subscription information call (212) 765-5311.

TABLE 2.3

Year	Number of IPOs	Dollar Value of IPOs (in millions)
1970	238	$583.7
1971	253	1,071.7
1972	495	2,201.0
1973	96	1,433.9
1974	9	98.8
1975	6	189.4
1976	40	337.2
1977	32	221.6
1978	38	225.4
1979	62	398.4
1980	149	1,387.1
1981	348	3,114.7
1982	122	1,339.1
1983	685	12,460.9
1984	357	3,868.9
1985	355	8,497.6
1986	728	22,251.8
1987	556	26,847.3
1988	291	23,807.5
1989	254	13,706.1
1990	213	10,117.4
1991	403	25,147.7
1992	605	39,947.1
1993	818	57,423.2
1994	647	33,842.5
1995	583	30,207.8
1996	875	50,041.2
1997	636	44,226.0
1998	395	43,657.2
1999	543	68,825.2

Data for this table supplied by Securities Data Co.

THE WORLD
OF UNDERWRITERS

T he major marketing steps of your company's IPO involve the following activities:

- Attracting an underwriter
- Selecting an underwriter
- Creating the prospectus
- Doing road shows

Marketing your IPO also requires understanding the following topics that are interwoven with the marketing process:

- The valuation of your company
- The underwriter's Letter of Intent
- Types of underwritings
- The cost of the IPO
- Due diligence
- Press releases and publicity

- The major participants and timetable
- The registration process
- The pricing meeting
- Execution of the underwriting agreement and the effective date
- Closing

Chapter 3 covers attracting and selecting the underwriter. Chapter 4 discusses the rest of the marketing process of a traditional IPO.

WHAT YOU SHOULD KNOW ABOUT UNDERWRITERS

National Underwriters

Firms that underwrite IPOs range enormously in size, prestige, and other characteristics. National underwriters fall into two categories.

The first category includes underwriters that have retail distribution capabilities around the country due to their widespread retail brokerage operations as well as an institutional sales capacity. These firms are colloquially called "wire houses." Examples of such national firms include Merrill Lynch; Morgan Stanley, Dean Witter; PaineWebber; Prudential Securities, Inc.; Salomon Smith Barney, and others.

The second category includes national underwriters that are primarily focused on institutional sales and have few (if any) retail brokerage operations. This category includes Goldman, Sachs & Co.; Credit Suisse First Boston Corporation; Deutsche Banc Alex. Brown; Donaldson, Lufkin & Jenrette, Inc.; Bear, Stearns & Co., Inc., and many other excellent firms.

There are two major divisions within national underwriting firms of interest to IPO candidates: the investment banking division, and the institutional sales and retail brokerage division. The investment banking division raises capital (both privately and publicly), arranges mergers and acquisitions, and provides financial consulting and valuation services, such as fairness opinions, offensive and defensive strategies in connection with tender offers, proxy contests, and the like. The investment banking division generates its revenues by charging a fee based on a percentage of the new capital raised or a percentage of the value of a merger or acquisition, or by charging a fee for its consulting or valuation services.

The institutional sales and brokerage division of these national underwriters generates its revenues primarily through commissions earned on institutional sales and trades of already outstanding equity and debt securities as well as new offerings. The investment banking divisions typically generate substantially more revenue per employee than the brokerage divisions.

The Chinese Wall

A so-called Chinese Wall is legally required to exist between the investment banking and institutional sales and retail brokerage division. Investment bankers receive confidential information about issuers of publicly traded securities and their acquisition and other targets. This confidential information, if publicly revealed, could significantly affect the market prices of the securities of these companies. The Chinese Wall is designed to prevent the disclosure of this market sensitive information by the investment banking division to the other parts of the firm.

The Institutional Bias

As an incentive to the institutional sales and retail brokerage division to sell an IPO underwritten by the investment banking division, larger brokerage fees are typically paid to the individual brokers who generate institutional and retail sales of the IPO securities. This is necessary because more selling effort and time is required to sell an untested IPO security than to sell normally traded securities.

A far larger percentage commission is paid to brokers who make retail sales (sales to individuals) of IPO securities than to brokers who make institutional sales. The commission percentage paid to brokers who make institutional sales is typically lower on sales of both IPO and non-IPO securities because of the greater bargaining power of these institutions.

Underwriters typically charge a discount equal to 6 percent to 7 percent of the IPO public offering proceeds. For example, for a $20 million public offering of common stock, $1,200,000 might be the underwriters' discount. This means that the underwriter purchases the company's common stock issue for $18,800,000 and resells the issue to the public for $20 million. Underwriters may also be given an expense allowance to cover their out-of-pocket expenses.

The gross profit of $1,200,000, less out-of-pocket expenses not covered by any expense allowance, is typically divided three ways:

1. Amounts paid to both retail and institutional brokers that sell the IPO securities (including brokers for underwriting syndicate members)

2. Amounts credited to the investment banking division of the underwriter and paid to its key employees, usually as year-end bonuses

3. Amounts paid to the underwriting firms themselves

The bias of underwriters toward institutional sales of IPO securities is evident from this profit division. Since institutional sales generate lower brokerage commissions, the more IPO securities that are placed with institutions, the greater the amount of the underwriting profit available to the investment banking division and to the underwriting firms themselves.

In addition, institutional sales tend to be in much larger dollar amounts than retail sales to individuals. Thus, it is far easier and quicker to sell an entire IPO to institutions than to individuals.

This built-in bias toward institutional sales means that, left unchecked, a high percentage of IPO securities winds up in institutional hands. This may or may not be a desirable result for the company. For example, if five institutional investors collectively own 35 percent of your company's outstanding stock, this could threaten control of your company if the founders own significantly less than 50 percent of the outstanding stock.

Niche Underwriters

There are many excellent small underwriters who specialize in specific industries and have a national reputation in that industry. The niche underwriters typically co-underwrite issues with other firms to lend strength and credibility to the underwriting syndicate.

All underwriters have certain industries in which they tend to specialize. A niche underwriter, however, usually just specializes in a single industry.

Regional Underwriters

There are many excellent regional underwriters. These are firms that have distribution capabilities in only one region of the country and do not have as strong a reputation outside of their regions as the national underwriters. These firms typically co-underwrite the IPO issue with some of the other regional firms with complementary distributional capabilities in other regions.

There is only a blurry line between regional and national underwriters. Many hot regional underwriters soon achieve a national reputation and national underwriters lose their national reputation after a few flops.

Local Underwriters

There are many very small local underwriting firms located throughout this country. They are characterized by distinct limits on the dollar size of the issue they can handle and their local distributional capabilities. Many of these firms underwrite securities only on a "best-effort" basis, that is, they never make a firm commitment to buy securities from the issuer and they receive a commission only on the securities they actually sell.

These local underwriters are particularly useful if you are considering a nontraditional IPO (see Chapters 6 through 10). Brokers in smaller cities and towns have proven extremely adept at raising amounts up to $5 million. They are usually well known in their local areas and socialize with groups of wealthy investors from their city or town. These wealthy investors tend to follow the local underwriter into investments that he sponsors.

Underwriting Syndicates

IPO underwriting is generally performed by a managing underwriter who forms a syndicate. Even national underwriters with strong national distributional capabilities form syndicates when they wish to hedge their financial risk or obtain a more diversified distribution capability. The syndication also helps create interest in other syndicate underwriters in making strong aftermarkets in the IPO securities.

It is currently typical to have two managing underwriters in an IPO and even more than two in a very large (over $500 million) IPO. The advantage of two managing underwriters is the creation of greater distribution and aftermarket interest. The disadvantage is that the underwriting profits have to be split between two firms, thereby decreasing the profit incentive to each managing underwriter. This can be a particular problem where the total dollar amount of the public issue is small. Since many IPOs have comanaging underwriters, it would seem that the advantage usually outweighs the disadvantage.

In the arcane world of investment banking, it is customary to have the lead managing underwriter's name on the left side of the face page of the prospectus and the other managing underwriter's name on the right side. The leading managing underwriter is responsible for maintaining the books for the syndicate and is sometimes called the "book manager."

An underwriting syndicate should be distinguished from a selling group. The underwriting syndicate includes all parties to the underwriting agreement that is signed by the company. Members of the selling group are not. Although members of the underwriting syndicate may sell a portion of the shares they underwrite, they are not necessarily expected to sell such shares. The agreement among underwriters compensates each underwriter for assuming the underwriting risk rather than for actually selling shares.

The underwriting syndicate may be organized before or after the registration statement has been filed, whereas the selling group can only be formed after the filing.

Prestigious vs. Nonprestigious Underwriters

A number of academic studies suggest that the investment banking industry is subject to a rigid hierarchy. These studies divide underwriters into two categories: prestigious and nonprestigious. The prestigious underwriters consist of "bulge bracket," "major bracket," and "sub-major bracket" underwriters. The studies base these upon a ranking scale established by comparing "tombstone announcements" of public offerings listed in *Investment Dealer's Digest* and *The Wall Street Journal* from January 1979 to December 1983.

According to these academics, the rank of the under-writer depends upon its position in these tombstone advertisements. Those underwriters closest to the top of the advertisement (excluding managing underwriters) are more prestigious than those at the bottom of the advertisement. They list underwriters of equal rank alphabetically.

Those in the upper brackets of the hierarchy enjoy a more prestigious and more lucrative position than their lower bracket counterparts. The hierarchy is reflected in the tombstone announcements of public offerings. Occasionally an underwriter will withdraw from a public offering in order to avoid being placed in too low a category in the tombstone.

Figure 1.1 is an example of a tombstone that reflects this hierarchy. Ignore the managing underwriters when determining the tiers. The first tier starts with ABN AMRO Rothschild, Inc. and ends with Thomas Weisel Partners (Weisel being the last of this tier in alphabetical order). The second tier begins with Gruntal & Co., LLC and ends with Sands Brothers & Co., Ltd. The third tier starts with Advest, Inc. and ends with B.C. Zeigler and Company.

Academics have used these tiers to determine who is and who is not prestigious. These scholars examined numerous tombstones over a period of time and use a prestige scale of 0 to 9 points, giving underwriters in the top tier of any tombstone 9 points and those in the bottom tier 0 points. The underwriters with the highest number of points are the most prestigious.

Unfortunately, all of the academic studies are out of date. However, a quick glance at a number of tombstone

FIGURE 1.1
TOMBSTONE ADVERTISEMENT

41

advertisements in *The Wall Street Journal* will quickly give you a good idea as to how underwriters rank themselves.

Academic scholars view underwriters as the certifiers of the quality of the information released by issuers. The investment banker is a reputational intermediary. The difference in prestige can affect the investor's confidence in a security according to these scholars. A 1992 study concluded that it is in the issuing company's best interest to engage an underwriter with the most prestigious reputation so that prospective investors will give more credence to the company's prospects.

A recent academic study concluded that IPOs led by more prestigious underwriters performed better relative to the market and were less likely to be underpriced.

Underwriter Track Records

Appendix 2 contains a list of the names and addresses of the lead managing underwriters on all firm-commitment IPO underwritings filed with the SEC that had a public offer date between January 1 and December 21, 1999 (approximately). You can use this list to determine the frequency of IPOs by any given underwriter, the dollar amount of each IPO (excluding overallotment options), and the business of the company that had the IPO.

You can use Appendix 2 to determine:

- Which underwriters are willing to serve as lead managing underwriters of an IPO
- The frequency with which these underwriters are willing to serve as lead managing underwriters
- The industries with which each lead managing underwriter has IPO experience
- Which investment bankers are willing to underwrite smaller IPOs

If an investment banker proposes to underwrite your company and has not in the recent past served as lead managing IPO underwriter, you should carefully inquire as to its prior experience. It is possible that the investment banker has frequently been a managing IPO underwriter but is not frequently in the lead. However, the fact that it has not frequently been in the lead may mean that you should continue your search for a good lead underwriter.

The fact that an underwriter has not had prior experience in your industry should not automatically disqualify it. However, all other things being equal, if the proposed investment banker has had a successful IPO in your industry, it is more likely that your company's offering will be successful as well. A "successful" IPO refers to an IPO that was completed and the current market price of the stock significantly exceeds the initial public offering price.

Table 3.1 reflects the lead managing underwriters of firm-commitment IPOs filed with the SEC that had an offering date from January 1 through December 31, 1999.

Since Appendix 2 does not reflect managing underwriter experience other than as the lead underwriter, avoid mechanical reliance upon this appendix.

TABLE 3.1
NUMBER OF IPOS BY LEAD MANAGING UNDERWRITERS
JANUARY 1 THROUGH DECEMBER 31, 1999

Lead Managing Underwriters (Top 7 Only)	Number of IPOs
1. Credit Suisse First Boston	55
2. Goldman, Sachs	51
3. Morgan Stanley, Dean Witter	44
4. BancBoston Robertson Stevens	44
5. Donaldson, Lufkin, & Jenrette	35
6. Deutsche Banc Alex. Brown	26
7. Merrill Lynch	36

Data for this table supplied by Global Securities information, www.gsionline.com.

HOW TO ATTRACT UNDERWRITERS

If you have taken the right steps in planning your IPO, you will have no difficulty attracting an underwriter. Investment bankers create and maintain their reputation by underwriting companies whose securities do very well in the market place. Therefore, underwriters are interested in growth companies with competent management teams that have special market niches. They generally seek companies that can use the proceeds of the offering to grow the business.

To be attractive to an investment banker, your company must have a growth plan that is thorough and impressive. Growth of 20 percent or more a year is expected by most underwriters.

The business plan should contain detailed projections of your growth and descriptions of your business (including its birth and development) and the background of its management. The major assumptions behind your projections should be articulated. The business plan should also identify risk areas and describe any methods by which your company can hedge these risks.

The company must have a "story" that is credible to the investment community. Every aspect of the story will be thoroughly investigated by any reputable underwriter. Major customers and suppliers and even competitors may be contacted. Your banker may be contacted. Key employees will be interviewed. You must be prepared to answer questions arising from this investigation in a convincing manner.

Companies considering an IPO should seek the advice of their accountants, attorneys, and investment advisors in order to create a business plan that will appeal to an investment banker. These specialists can help you anticipate what questions an underwriter will ask and assist you in preparing the responses. When underwriters ask you questions, they are also appraising your qualities as an executive. You must demonstrate a thorough grasp of your business and its problems. This cannot be overemphasized. If you appear not to have the answer to an obvious question, but must research the question, the underwriter will wonder about your competency as an executive.

From the underwriter's viewpoint, management quality is the most important attribute of a potential IPO candidate. The underwriter's judgment of your executive talents and those of your management team is crucial in the underwriting decision.

Underwriters are turned off by companies whose managements are looking to bailout of their investment in the IPO. They want management to assume the same investment risks as the new investors in the IPO. It is possible for management to sell a small portion of its holdings in the IPO. However, even such small sales must be justified by a reason other than the risks of the business. For example, underwriters would not usually object if management sold a small portion of its shares as a result of personal tax costs resulting from the IPO or other personal needs.

Occasionally, underwriters request principals of companies to sell personal shares in order to create a large enough offering to permit the IPO to be effectuated. This is possible when the company does not need for its growth plan the extra funds derivable from selling more company stock.

SELECTING AN UNDERWRITER

The right investment banker is a major factor in the success of your IPO. The following are some of the attributes you should look for.

- *Reputation.* The better the reputation of your underwriter, the greater confidence investors have in purchasing your securities.

- *Distribution Capability*. It is important to have a large and varied base of investors in your company. This helps generate interest in your securities.
- *Experience*. It is helpful if the managing underwriter has had successful experience with companies in similar industries. This is particularly helpful if the stock of these other similar companies rose significantly above the IPO offering price after their IPOs.
- *Market-Making Capability*. After the completion of your IPO, it is important that there be a strong aftermarket in your securities. This increases liquidity to investors. Generally, the managing underwriter will make such a market and you should inquire as to the amount of resources the underwriter will devote to this task. You should ask whether the managing underwriter has an analyst for your industry, what the analyst's reputation is, and whether research reports on your company's stock will be periodically distributed.
- *Flexibility in Accommodating Your Needs*. If you desire to sell a small percentage of your own stock in the IPO, you should inquire whether that would be acceptable to the underwriters. Likewise, if you desire to retain two classes of stock and sell only the lesser voting class in the IPO, you should inquire whether the underwriter will object.

Upon the effective date of your registration statement, the underwriter will execute an underwriting agreement with the closing typically within three business days after the effective date. Underwriters will not commit to buy your securities until they are reasonably convinced that they can resell them. Unfortunately, almost all of the out-of-pocket costs of the IPO are incurred *before* the underwriter ever signs the underwriting agreement.

Therefore, it is important to choose an underwriter in whom you have great confidence. An ideal underwriter should value its reputation so much that it would absorb some losses on the IPO rather than completely abandon the IPO under adverse market conditions.

There are underwriters for every type of company. Some underwriters do not ordinarily handle IPOs, whereas other underwriters prefer IPOs. Some underwriters specialize in specific industries. Some underwriters only handle companies that have revenues or earnings over certain minimum figures. One way to chose an underwriter is to find other companies in your industry that have gone public and identify their underwriters.

Ideally, the underwriter should be sufficiently large enough to be able to easily handle your IPO (either by itself or with a co-managing underwriter), but sufficiently small enough so that your business and goodwill are important to them. You should inquire whether the underwriter has a long-term commitment to research in your industry.

There are a variety of opinions as to whether "shopping" your IPO among underwriters is desirable. If you have only a marginally desirable IPO, you may have no choice but to shop your IPO. If you have a very desirable IPO, you may want to approach a few larger underwriters and create competition among them.

In general, it is best to select the most prestigious underwriter who is interested in your IPO and who has sufficient interest to treat you as an important client. An experienced securities lawyer or accounting firm may also be helpful in recommending an underwriter. You should carefully review the information on IPO underwriters contained in Appendix 2 of this book before making your selection.

Prior to finalizing your selection, check with at least five companies for which this same underwriter acted as lead IPO managing underwriter. Make certain at least two of the IPOs were very recent. Two of the IPOs should be one year and two years old, respectively, in order to determine the aftermarket support given by the underwriter under consideration.

Going Public vs. Private Equity Capital

Many companies are too small to qualify for a public offering with a top-tier (bulge bracket) underwriter. Your company would generally need a minimum pre-IPO valuation of $40 to $50 million to qualify for an IPO with top-tier underwriters. Suppose your company has a pre-IPO valuation of $20 to $40 million. You can still go public with a very reputable underwriter, but not necessarily the top tier. Alternatively, you can raise private equity capital through a private placement with a bulge bracket underwriter to bridge an IPO with them.

A company with a pre-IPO ranging from $20 to $40 million will obtain a significantly better valuation by using a second-tier underwriter than by raising private equity capital. Private placement investors typically discount pre-IPO valuations, sometimes by as much as 33 percent or more. In addition, if you choose an IPO you will escape the restrictions and controls typically imposed by private placement investors. The higher the pre-IPO valuation, the more bargaining power you have with private placement investors. For example, with a pre-IPO valuation of $30 million or more, it is likely that you can negotiate either no or minimal restrictions and controls. In addition, the higher your pre-IPO valuation, the greater the likelihood that the IPO will happen and the smaller the discount valuation that you can negotiate with private placement investors.

Pre-IPO Valuation
Below $10 to $20 million

Suppose your company has a pre-IPO valuation below $20 million. You can still find lower-tier underwriters to take you public. Indeed, IPOs can be accomplished with pre-IPO valuation even below $10 million. The problem with IPOs with pre-IPO valuations below $10 million is that you are limited to a small group of third-tier under-writers. The SEC and the NASDAQ Stock Market (NAS-DAQ) in recent years have been cracking down on third-tier underwriters who have investigations pending against them by refusing to list the stocks of companies they underwrite. You must carefully review the records on any proposed underwriter to ascertain whether there are any pending investigations of alleged infractions by the underwriter. The very existence of those investigations may prevent your company from obtaining a listing.

Even if the third-tier underwriter has obtained NAS-DAQ listings for other companies, it is no assurance that some new development in the investigation will not cause NASDAQ to change its mind just when your company's registration statement has been cleared by the SEC. In general, the exchanges will follow NASDAQ's lead and similarly refuse your listing. Since NASDAQ refuses to give you an advance ruling about its attitude toward a particular underwriter, you are at risk in using third-tier underwriters.

The advantage of a third-tier, underwriter-sponsored IPO over private equity financing is that you obtain a much higher valuation. Therefore, you suffer less equity dilution. In one case the author is familiar with, the pre-money valuation for private equity financing was $4 million and for the IPO was $8 to $10 million. The second major advantage of a third-tier underwriter IPO over private equity is the lack of any restriction on your company in an IPO. In contrast, private placement investors may impose more restrictive covenants on your operations, your compensation, and your control of your company. In addition, private placement investors purchase preferred stock, which is in reality quasi-debt, since the private placement investor usually requires redemption rights after five years if you are not then public and a sale has not occurred. The following are the major disadvantages of a third-tier, underwriter-sponsored IPO:

- The cost can be in excess of $300,000 even after negotiated discounts if the failure is late in the IPO process. Third-tier underwriters have a higher record of failure than higher-tier underwriters in successfully completing IPOs. If the IPO is unsuccessful, you can be stuck with substantial accounting, legal, and printing costs.

- Third-tier underwriters typically take large fees for their services in proportion to the amount raised and require the public sale of not only common stock but a large number of warrants. The warrants generally have an exercise price, which is a small premium over the IPO price. The market overhang from a large number of warrants held by the public (and usually the third-tier underwriter) may prevent your stock price from rising in the aftermarket.

- An IPO can cost $700,000 to well over $1 million, whereas a private equity transaction can usually be accomplished for less than $100,000.

- There is usually limited institutional interest in the IPO because of its small size, which decreases the liquidity of the stock in the aftermarket.

- Third-tier underwriters typically do a poor job in sponsoring the stock after the IPO (this is also sometimes true of first-tier underwriters). Therefore, you need to employ a financial public relations firm and even their activity may not be effective. Consequently your stock price may founder despite good earnings growth.

- Your stock price will be at the mercy of only a few market makers because of the lack of instututional interest and the small float. This makes your stock more susceptible to being manipulated.

- It is more likely that your IPO stock will be sold to "investors" who will hold it only a short time, even as little as one day, to profit from the aftermarket price increase.

- All of these factors can result in your post-IPO stock price falling below the IPO price, resulting in unhappy investors and a poor reputation for your company.

- Your company will be subject to the costs of being public, which generally range from $50,000 to $100,000 or more per year (plus the cost of directors and officers liability insurance).

- Even if your company grows nicely with the IPO proceeds, some first-tier underwriters may not be willing to underwrite a follow-on issue because of the taint of the third-tier underwriter. (The author believes that these disadvantages, particularly the last one, can be exaggerated. The exaggeration is usually made by first-tier underwriters who prefer that you use their private placement group.)

The decision to use a third-tier underwriter or private equity is a difficult one. Even after considering all of the disadvantages of a third-tier underwriter IPO, the author has had the client decide to use that route primarily because of the higher IPO valuation and fewer restrictions for the company. On occasion, these clients have been sorry for that choice and on other occasions they have been happy. The happy clients were typically those where the IPO was successful in raising capital. The unhappy clients were most often those where the third-tier underwriter never completed the IPO and the client had to pay the costs of the unsuccessful IPO. There is nothing to prevent you from proceeding with an IPO with a third-tier underwriter and then switching to a private placement if the IPO is unsuccessful and is terminated. Most of the accounting, legal, and printing costs can be discounted in the event of an unsuccessful IPO.

LIMITS ON UNDERWRITER COMPENSATION AND OFFERING EXPENSES

Practically all underwriters are members of the National Association of Securities Dealers (NASD), which is the largest self-regulatory organization in the United States. The NASD, through its subsidiary, NASD Regulation, Inc. (NASDR), prohibits its members from commencing a public offering until the NASDR issues an opinion that it has no objections to the proposed underwriting. The NASDR objects to any underwriter terms or arrangements that it considers "unfair or unreasonable."

The NASDR lists the following factors (among others) that it considers when determining the maximum amount of underwriter compensation considered fair and reasonable:

- The offering proceeds
- The amount of risk assumed by the underwriters and related persons, which is determined by (a) whether the offering is "firm-commitment" or "best-efforts," and (b) whether the offering is an IPO or secondary offering
- The type of securities being offered

The NASDR determines the maximum amount of underwriter compensation on a case-by-case basis, and the NASDR rules do not specify a specific maximum percentage. Under the NASD Corporate Financing Rule, it is "unreasonable" for an underwriter and "related persons" in a public offering to receive (among other things):

- Securities as underwriting compensation in an aggregate amount greater than 10 percent of the dollar amount of securities offered to the public (excluding the overallotment option, securities constituting underwriter compensation, securities underlying warrants, options, and convertible securities except where acquired as part of a unit, and the like)

- Any non-accountable expense allowance in excess of 3 percent

- Any accountable expense allowance that includes payment for general overhead, salaries, supplies, or similar expenses of the underwriter incurred in the normal conduct of business

- Options, warrants, or convertible securities exercisable or convertible for more than five years or that fail other tests

- A right of first refusal having a duration greater than three years

Underwriters and related persons include underwriters, underwriter's counsel, financial consultants and advisers, finders, members of the selling and distribution group, any member participating in the public offering, and any and all other persons associated with or related to, as well as members of the immediate family, of any of the aforementioned persons.

The NASDR rule also contains complicated formulas for valuing warrants given to underwriters by the company and regulates the terms of these warrants. The rule also deems unreasonable any overallotment option of more than 15 percent of the amount of securities offered in a firm-commitment underwriting.

The NASDR's Corporate Financing Department (Department) has direct responsibility for the review of underwriting compensation. To ensure compliance with the compensation guidelines, the Department reviews public offerings before their effective dates and aggregates all items of value proposed to be received by underwriters and related persons. The Department then compares the total compensation, expressed as a percentage of offering proceeds, to the appropriate guideline applicable to the offering. For the Department to issue an opinion expressing "no objections" to the underwriting compensation, such compensation must be equal to or less than the maximum applicable guideline.

To predict levels of underwriting compensation accurately, the Department analyzed the amount of compensation received, as disclosed in the final offering document or prospectus, for 874 corporate equity offerings filed with the Department during calendar year 1991. All items of underwriting compensation received by underwriters and related persons were considered, including: cash discounts or commissions; accountable and non-accountable expense reimbursements; warrants, options, cheap stock, and other securities and rights to acquire securities received by underwriters and related persons; finders' fees paid for introducing the underwriter and the issuer; rights of first refusal; financial consulting and advisory fees; and all other items of value received in connection with the offering.

The offerings were organized into three categories: 402 firm-commitment IPOs, 380 firm-commitment secondary offerings, and 92 best-efforts offerings. For each of the three categories, the staff performed a regression analysis to predict expected amounts of compensation for certain size offerings in each category.

Table 3.2 reflects the results of the Department's study and indicates the gross proceeds of the offering (in millions of dollars) and the typical predicted percentage of gross proceeds, exclusive of any overallotment option, that might be allocated to underwriting compensation for firm-commitment IPOs, firm-commitment secondary offerings, and best-efforts corporate equity offerings. The amounts shown do not represent the compensation actually received from any one offering or the mathematical average for all offerings of a particular size reviewed during 1991. Such amounts also do not reflect the compensation originally proposed to be received when the offerings were filed with the NASD. However, it does indicate the generally accepted level of compensation as determined by the Department.

TABLE 3.2
TOTAL UNDERWRITING COMPENSATION

Gross Dollar Amount of Offering (millions)	Firm Commitment Initial Offerings (%)	Firm Commitment Secondary Offerings (%)	Best Efforts Offerings (%)
$1	15.80	14.57	11.83
2	14.31	12.91	10.72
3	13.44	11.94	10.07
4	12.82	11.26	9.61
5	12.34	10.72	9.26
6	11.95	9.56	8.96
7	11.62	9.12	8.72
8	11.33	8.76	8.50
9	11.08	8.45	8.32
10	10.65	8.18	8.15
11	9.90	7.95	8.04
12	9.18	7.74	7.86
13	8.49	7.56	7.73
14	7.82	7.39	7.61
15	7.59	7.24	7.50
16	7.55	7.10	7.40
17	7.52	6.97	7.30
18	7.48	6.85	7.21
19	7.45	6.74	7.12
20	7.42	6.63	7.04
25	7.29	6.20	6.68
30	7.19	5.86	6.39
35	7.10	5.60	6.14
40	7.02	5.37	5.93
45	6.95	5.19	5.74
50 or more	6.89	5.00	5.57

Prior to the IPO, many underwriters will raise private investment capital for your company. Under the NASDR Corporate Financing Rule, all compensation and other items of value received within the six-month period prior to the filing of the IPO registration statement are presumed (subject to rebuttal) to be underwriting compensation. The NASDR also examines all items of value received more than six months, but within one year, of the filing of the IPO registration statement. Underwriters who raise private capital for your company will typically wait at least six months, and preferably one year, before commencing work on the IPO to avoid these rules.

A chart of underwriter compensation for IPOs effective during 1999 appears in Appendix 3.

State securities laws also impose varying limits on underwriting compensation and offering expenses for IPOs that are subject to state regulation (see "State Securities Laws" in Chapter 4). For the most part, the NASDR limits are more restrictive. However, unlike the NASDR limitations, some states' restrictions on "offering expenses" can include legal and accounting fees and expenses paid by the company. However, the total offering expense limits in these states (ranging from 15 percent to 20 percent of the aggregate offering price) are usually high enough to avoid bumping into them.

The NASDR has also adopted rules ("free riding rules") designed to restrict the purchase of "hot issues" by NASD members and their directors, officers, employees, and other related persons. The purpose of these rules is to require a bona fide public distribution of hot issues. A hot issue is an IPO in which trading opens at a premium above the public offering price.

The selection of an underwriter is a critical step in the process of raising public capital. Your selection will undoubtedly be affected by the valuation the underwriter initially gives to your company. The valuation of your company and the registration and marketing of your IPO are discussed next.

CHAPTER 4

REGISTERING AND MARKETING THE TRADITIONAL IPO

O nce you have selected an underwriter, preliminary discussions take place concerning the valuation of your company, an underwriter's letter of intent is signed, and the registration process commences. The process ends with a closing at which you issue the shares in the company.

THE VALUATION OF YOUR COMPANY

Underwriters do not usually value your company until the "pricing meeting," which is held on the effective date of your registration statement or a few days thereafter. However, the underwriters should be able to determine the procedure for the valuation at the beginning of the IPO.

Generally, underwriters look at comparable companies that are public and determine their price/earnings multiple (or for Internet companies, their price/revenue multiple) or their multiple of EBITDA (earnings before interest, taxes, depreciation, and amortization). If a comparable company has been public for a while and its market price is 14 times its projected earnings, for example, on the effective date of the IPO registration statement, you may expect that your company will probably be valued at a 10 percent to 15 percent discount below the 14 multiple.

This discount provides an incentive for the institutional investors to buy your stock (as opposed to the stock of more seasoned public companies in your industry) on the grounds that your stock is a bargain.

If your company is using IPO proceeds to discharge the company's bank debt or other indebtedness, the underwriter will typically permit you to increase your earnings or EBITDA by the pro forma interest savings resulting from such discharge of debt.

Your company's adjusted earnings or EBITDA are then multiplied by the appropriate multiplier to value your company. For example, if the company's adjusted earnings or EBITDA is $4 million and the discounted multiplier is 12, the company will have a $48 million valuation prior to adjustment for the IPO proceeds. If the company wishes to raise $24 million from the sale of stock in the IPO, the company's overall valuation will be $72 million ($48 million plus $24 million) and $33\frac{1}{3}$ percent of the outstanding stock of the company will be sold in the IPO.

There is a tendency of underwriters to underprice the stock in the initial public offering. Therefore, it may be wise to consider minimizing the total number of shares that you sell in the IPO. Obviously, you must balance this consideration against your capital needs at the time the offering goes into effect. A slightly underpriced IPO has the advantage of permitting IPO investors to enjoy a price rise in the aftermarket trading. This may stimulate investor interest in future public offerings by your company. This is particularly important if you plan a follow-on or secondary offering in the near future.

Underwriters generally tend to price the stock of initial public offerings between $10 and $20 per share. Occasionally, they use an IPO price of $20 or more to create prestige for the issue. If the stock is priced below $5 per share, it is considered "penny stock" and is subject to onerous SEC rules applicable to brokers. The institutional investment community also tends to shun "penny stock" issues.

To get to a price range of $10 to $20, you may need to change your stock capitalization (by stock splits or reverse stock splits) to achieve the desired IPO price, based upon the valuation of your company and the proportion of your company to be sold in the IPO.

In general, a minimum of 1.1 million shares is sold in an IPO, preferably more than 1.1 million shares. The purpose of this minimum number is twofold: to make certain there is a sufficient "float" to permit an active trading market after the IPO and to qualify for the public float requirement to list the stock on the NASDAQ National Market has a public float requirement of 1.1 million shares (see Chapter 11).

LETTER OF INTENT

Once you have selected an investment banker interested in an IPO, your company will sign a letter of intent. The letter of intent usually is not legally binding (except as noted below), but it does express the basic business understanding of the parties. The letter of intent typically covers the following topics, among others:

- The expected offering price per share or valuation
- The amount of the underwriter's discount (or commissions in the case of a best-efforts offering)
- Any warrants given to the underwriter
- Overallotment option

- Who is responsible for the payments of expenses, such as lawyers, accountants, printers, filing fees, and other expenses (is there an underwriter's expense allowance and is it accountable or non-accountable?)
- Any board members to be designated by the underwriter
- Preferential rights on future financings by the company

Unless your company has very strong bargaining power, it is probably wise to agree to give the underwriter, if requested, a preferential right on future financings. However, it is also wise to limit that right to a period not exceeding one year and possibly under the condition that the sale of the company's stock in the IPO be at or close to the price projected by the underwriter.

It is important for the company to designate counsel for the underwriter from a list of counsel approved by the underwriter. Since the company will ultimately pay the fees and costs of the underwriter's counsel, the company should have input into this decision. The company should also attempt to designate the financial printer from an approved list submitted by the underwriter.

There may also be a clause inserted into the letter of intent that requires the company to pay the underwriter's counsel fees and other out-of-pocket expenses in the event the company decides to withdraw from the offering. At a minimum, this clause should be amended to insert a "not to exceed" figure. In addition, you may vary the maximum figure by whether the withdrawal occurs early or late in the registration process.

Occasionally, underwriters attempt to insert a clause in the letter of intent providing that if the company is sold before the IPO effective date, and the company withdraws from the IPO, a commission on the sale price should be paid to the underwriter. Such clauses should be carefully reviewed with your counsel and, in appropriate cases, rejected.

Generally the letter of intent legally restricts any press releases or other publicity by the company concerning the offering without approval of the underwriter.

The letter of intent does not prevent the underwriter from withdrawing from the IPO. It should be made clear that the company will not reimburse the underwriter for its own counsel fees or other expenses if the underwriter withdraws without any breach by the company. The best safeguard to the company against the arbitrary withdrawal of the underwriter from the IPO is the underwriter's investment of time, counsel fees, and costs in the IPO project as well as the damage to its reputation caused by an arbitrary withdrawal.

TYPES OF UNDERWRITINGS

There are generally two major types of underwritings:

1. Firm commitment
2. Best efforts

In a firm-commitment underwriting, the underwriters agree to buy, at a fixed price, all the securities being sold at a discount from the public offering price. The underwriters then resell the securities to the public at the public offering price. If the underwriters do not resell all the securities, the underwriters assume the investment risk with regard to the unsold securities.

Under a best-efforts commitment, the underwriters agree to use their "best efforts" to sell the securities. However, if they do not sell the entire amount to the public, they have no obligation to purchase the balance from the company. The underwriters merely act as agent for the issuer of the securities. They are never at risk if the securities are not sold.

There are several variations of the best-efforts commitment. For example, the agreement may provide that a minimum number of securities must be sold or the purchase price returned to the investors, or alternatively, no minimum is required.

Most initial public offerings with national or regional underwriters are on a firm-commitment basis. This is the traditional IPO underwriting. Indeed, best-efforts initial public offerings are relatively rare and the financial markets would view them as a sign of weakness.

As previously noted, even a firm-commitment underwriting is not "firm" prior to executing the underwriting agreement on the IPO registration statement's effective date.

THE COST OF A TRADITIONAL IPO

The largest single cost of your IPO is the underwriter's discount from the public offering price. In a firm-commitment underwriting, this normally ranges from 6 percent to 7 percent of the public offering price. In a best-efforts offering, the underwriter is paid a commission based upon the public offering price, the economic equivalent of the discount. All other factors being equal, the commissions in a best-efforts underwriting should be slightly lower than the underwriter discount since the underwriter assumes less risk.

Some underwriters also require the company to pay an expense allowance, which may or may not be on an accountable basis. This is a negotiated figure.

The company will also incur out-of-pocket costs for legal fees, accounting fees, and printing and engraving. Legal fees for your own counsel in an IPO are typically between $250,000 and $600,000, but they can substantially exceed $600,000 for particularly complex offerings, such as real estate investment trust offerings. This figure does not include a certain amount of corporate housekeeping that your company may have deferred for a number of years.

Accounting fees generally run between $150,000 and $250,000. However, they can be much higher if there are significant issues related to the audit.

Printing costs can run $100,000 to $350,000 or more, depending upon the length of the prospectus, the number of copies required, whether you use pictures and color, and the extent of the revisions required. Since revisions can be very expensive, it is best not to commence printing until after you circulate a reasonably good draft to all parties.

Other out-of-pocket costs include SEC filing fees (.000264 of the maximum aggregate offering price), blue sky fees and expenses ($5,000 to $10,000), filing fees of the NASD ($500 plus .01 percent of the gross dollar amount of the offering with a maximum filing fee of $30,500), and registrar and transfer fees (generally $5,000 to $15,000).

If your stock is to be listed on the NASDAQ Stock Market, there is a $5,000 one-time initial listing fee for both NASDAQ markets, the NASDAQ National Market and SmallCap Market.

The NASDAQ National Market charges, in addition to the listing fee, an entry fee and annual fees based on the company's total outstanding shares. The entry fee ranges from $33,750 on 1 million to 2 million outstanding shares to as high as $90,000 for over 100 million shares. The annual fees range from $10,960 per year for 1 million to 2 million outstanding shares to $50,000 for over 100 million outstanding shares.

The NASDAQ SmallCap Market charges, in addition to the listing fee, an entry fee that cannot exceed $5,000 for all equity securities and annual fees of $4,000 for the first class of securities issued.

If the underwriter withdrew very close to the effective date of the offering, it is possible your company could lose anywhere from $300,000 to $500,000, even after professional fees have been discounted.

The underwriter is liable for its counsel fees and costs and incurs significant executive time in any underwriting. Therefore, the underwriter has a significant investment that it may lose if you or it abandons the offering at a late stage.

The following is the cost breakdown (excluding underwriters' discount and expense allowance) contained in the $33 million IPO of Rubio's Restaurants, Inc., on May 21, 1999:

SEC Registration Fee	$ 10,071
NASD Filing Fee	4,123
NASDAQ National Marketing Listing Fee	17,000
Legal Fees and Expenses	250,000
Accounting Fees and Expenses	200,000
Printing and Engraving	150,000
Transfer Agent Fees	5,000
Miscellaneous	58,806
TOTAL	$700,000

The underwriters' discount totaled $2,315,250. The overall aggregate offering costs of $3,015,250 ($700,000 plus $2,315,250) were approximately 9.1 percent of the $33 million offering (disregarding the 15 percent overallotment option).

Contrast the relatively low expenses of the Rubio's Restaurant, Inc., IPO with the following expenses of the $84 million Drkoop.com, Inc. IPO on June 8, 1999:

SEC Registration Fee	$ 26,975
NASD Filing Fee	10,204
NASDAQ National Market Listing Fee	94,000

Legal Fees and Expenses	600,000
Accounting Fees and Expenses ...	195,000
Printing and Engraving	350,000
Blue Sky Fees and Expenses (Including Legal Fees)	10,000
Transfer Agent Fees	7,500
Miscellaneous	61,321
TOTAL	$1,355,000

The underwriters' discount in the Drkoop.com, Inc., IPO totaled $5,906,250. The overall aggregate expenses ($1,355,000 plus $5,906,250) were approximately 8.6 percent of the $84 million offering (disregarding the 15 percent overallotment option).

Appendix 3 contains underwriting discounts and expense breakdowns from recent IPOs.

DUE DILIGENCE

Under the Securities Act of 1933 ("the 1933 Act"), the company is absolutely liable if there are material misstatements or omissions contained in the registration statement at the time it becomes effective (unless the purchaser knew of the untruth). In addition, the following persons are also liable to investors in such an event, subject to the due diligence defense:

- Directors
- Officers who sign the registration statement (the principal executive, financial and accounting officers)
- The underwriters
- Experts (independent accountants and the like)

The due diligence defense permits these persons (excluding the company) to defend themselves from such liability if they have performed a reasonable investigation and have no reason to believe (and do not believe) that there were any material misstatements or omissions. With regard to the "expertized" portions of the registration statement (like audited financial statements), it is sufficient to establish a due diligence defense if these persons have no reason to believe (and do not believe) that there are any material misstatements or omissions.

The underwriters and their counsel spend much time and effort, both prior to filing the registration statement and after filing and prior to its effective date, in an attempt to establish this due diligence defense.

The most famous case on the due diligence defense is *Escott v. Barchris Construction Corporation*. This case arose out of a public offering by a company engaged in the construction of bowling centers, the growth industry of the late 1950s and early 1960s. The investors sued the company and its directors, its officers who signed the registration statement, its auditors, and its underwriters. The court found material misstatements and omissions in both the financial and nonfinancial portions of the prospectuses (e.g., the backlog).

The court held that none of the defendants had established a due diligence defense. The court created different standards of due diligence based upon (a) whether a director was or was not an officer and (b) each defendant's background and expertise.

The decision in Barchris is also noteworthy in rejecting due diligence defense claims by the following directors with respect to the portions of the registration statements other than the audited financial statements:

- Two founding directors and officers—"each men of limited education" for whom the "prospectus was difficult reading, if indeed they read at all"—had no diligence defense. The court stated that, "the liability of a director who signs a registration statement does not depend upon whether or not he read it or, if he did, whether or not he understood what he was reading."

- An outside director was liable even though he just became a director on the eve of the IPO and had little opportunity to familiarize himself with the company. The court found that the 1933 Act imposed liability on a director "no matter how new he is." The outside director was not permitted to rely on the statements of other directors and officers of the company who were "comparative strangers" without making further inquiry.

- An outside lawyer director who failed to check on his client's statements to him, which could "readily have been checked," including his client's overstatement of the company's backlog, was held personally liable.

PRESS RELEASES AND PUBLICITY

The following is a discussion of the restrictions on publicity during each of the following three time periods:

- Prior to filing the registration statement (the "gun jumping" prohibition)
- After filing the registration statement and prior to its effective date
- After the effective date of registration statement and during the continuation of public distribution

Prior to Filing Registration Statement ("Gun Jumping" Prohibition)

Section 5(c) of the 1933 Act generally makes it unlawful to offer to sell any security prior to the filing of a registration statement. This is the "gun jumping" prohibition. The purpose of this prohibition is to prevent issuers and other persons from arousing public interest in a securities offering prior to the filing of a registration statement.

The term "offer to sell" is broadly defined in Section 2(3) of the 1933 Act to include "every attempt to dispose of a security, for value." Publicity that a company does not express as an offer may, nevertheless, be construed by the SEC as an offer if it is deemed to involve such an "attempt."

The SEC has taken the position that the release of publicity in advance of a filing that has the effect of conditioning the public mind or arousing public interest in an issuer or in its securities constitutes an offer in violation of Section 5 of the 1933 Act. Upon discovery of such a violation, the SEC will usually delay the effective date of a registration statement in order to allow the effect of such publicity to dissipate.

The SEC has also taken the position that the prohibition against "offers" of securities prior to filing is not intended to restrict normal communications between issuers and their stockholders or the public with respect to important business or financial developments, provided such communications are consistent with the issuer's prior practice, are in the customary form, and do not include forecasts, projections, predictions, or opinions as to value. Nor does the prohibition affect discussions with underwriters.

In order to determine whether a particular activity or statement by an issuer would constitute an unlawful offer, the facts and circumstances surrounding each activity or statement, including its content, timing, and distribution must be analyzed. Since this determination often involves difficult legal issues, it is imperative that the company clear any proposed public disclosure with its counsel before its release. Such disclosures would include, but not be limited to, letters to shareholders, press releases, interviews, speeches, and advertisements. The

SEC is particularly concerned with publicity that artificially stimulates the markets by whetting the public appetite for the security. Your company's Internet site must be carefully checked by your counsel.

If your offering is a Regulation A offering (discussed in Chapter 8), you can "test the waters" before filing provided that you comply with certain disclosure requirements, submit the offering material to the SEC, and do not accept any money. However, you may not raise more than $5 million.

After Filing Registration Statement and Prior to Its Effective Date

After the filing of a registration statement and before its effective date, you may make verbal offers to sell securities. Thus, the underwriters may conduct "road shows" during this period. However, during this period, no written offers may be made except by means of a statutory prospectus (the "red-herring" prospectus). The underwriters may also place tombstone advertisements during this period.

Any verbal statements made by or on behalf of the company or its proposed underwriters must be consistent with the information contained in the filed registration statement.

You may not consummate any sales of securities during this period. The prohibition of sales includes a prohibition on contracts of sale as well as the receipt of any portion of the securities' purchase price.

The release of publicity (particularly in written form) during this period also raises a question about whether the publicity is a selling effort by an illegal means, that is, other than by means of a statutory prospectus. Therefore, the company should continue to clear any proposed publicity with its counsel prior to its release.

After Effective Date of Registration Statement and During Continuation of Public Distribution

After the effective date of the registration statement, you may make both written as well as verbal offers. However, during the period of the public distribution of the security, a copy of the final statutory prospectus must be delivered in connection with any written offer or confirmation or upon delivery of the security, whichever occurs first. You may use supplemental sales literature if you accompany it or precede it by a final statutory prospectus. You may consummate sales during the post-effective date period.

The release of publicity after the effective date and prior to completion of the public distribution likewise raises issues as to whether the publicity is a written offer or supplemental sales literature that must be accompanied or preceded by a final statutory prospectus. Therefore, your company should continue to clear any proposed public disclosure with its counsel until it completes the public distribution.

Prior to the completion of the public distribution, any verbal or written statements must be consistent with the information contained in the prospectus. Although it is not clear exactly when a public distribution has been completed, most lawyers believe that the public distribution period includes, at a minimum, the period after the IPO, during which securities dealers must deliver a prospectus (25 days for securities listed on a national securities exchange or the NASDAQ Stock Market) and, if there is an overallotment option, until that option has been exercised or expired.

The period from immediately before the IPO filing until the post-IPO completion of the public distribution of your company's securities is sometimes called the "quiet period."

MAJOR PARTICIPANTS AND TIMETABLE

The major participants in the IPO are as follows:

- Company: typically, the CEO and CFO
- Company Counsel
- Underwriter
- Underwriter's Counsel
- Independent Auditors

Table 4.1 is a typical timetable for an IPO, once a letter of intent with an underwriter has been signed.

TABLE 4.1
KEY STEPS IN THE IPO PROCESS

Stages		Week 1	2	3	4	5	6	7	8	9	10	11	12	13	14
Phase 1	Due diligence	•	•	•											
	Draft registration statement		•	•	•	•									
Phase 2	Initial filing with SEC				•										
	Preparation of road show and marketing materials						•	•							
Phase 3	Receiving of comments from SEC								•	•	•	•			
	Printing and distributing of red herrings										•	•			
	Road show presentations											•	•		
Phase 4	Pricing of IPO													•	
	Filing of final prospectus with SEC													•	
	Closing of IPO														•

However, the table is misleading because Phase 1 does not begin until a letter of intent is signed, and obtaining an executed letter of intent can take several months to several years. During this period, you must put your corporate house in order and market your company to potential underwriters. You should implement the advance planning steps outlined in Chapter 2, resolve shareholder issues, and prepare a marketing plan.

Underwriters typically take several months to better understand the company before entering into a letter of intent. Therefore, your IPO planning should normally assume that a minimum period of approximately nine months will elapse between your deciding to go public and actually receiving the funds. A more detailed timetable is contained in Appendix 4.

THE PROSPECTUS

Usually, the company's securities counsel drafts the IPO registration statement and then distributes it to the underwriter, the underwriter's counsel, the independent auditors, and the executives of the company. The prospectus is Part I of the registration statement. Part II contains other information, which although filed with the SEC, is not distributed to investors, such as a breakdown of the costs of the offering, indemnification rights of directors and officers, lists of exhibits, and certain financial statement schedules.

Generally the underwriters and others "wordsmith" the initial draft of the prospectus until it tells a convincing story to potential investors. This process is sometimes laborious and time-consuming, and typically occurs at various meetings of all the parties. These "all hands" meetings may last through the night, especially those meetings held at the printer immediately prior to filing.

Of most concern to the underwriters are the prospectus summary, the business description section, the management discussion and analysis section, and the use of proceeds section. These sections must present a cohesive and convincing story to investors. Chapter 5 describes these sections in greater detail.

THE REGISTRATION PROCESS

Once you file the original IPO registration statement with the SEC, there is generally a quiet period (no marketing or advertising) until the SEC issues its letter of comment. Typically this occurs within 30 days after the filing. Although the SEC may decide not to review the IPO registration statement, this is relatively rare.

Once you receive the comment letter, you prepare revisions to the registration statement, along with supplemental explanations where required, and file an amendment to the registration statement. The SEC may require several amendments before it is willing to declare the registration statement effective. All IPO filings with the SEC (as well as most other SEC filings) are required to be made electronically.

In general the prospectus is not distributed and the road shows are not held until the prospectus has been amended to reflect the SEC's comments.

STATE SECURITIES LAWS

If your company's securities will be authorized for listing on any of the following exchanges or automated quotation systems, they are exempt from state registration requirements:

- New York Stock Exchange
- National Market System of the NASDAQ Stock Market
- American Stock Exchange
- Tier I of the Pacific Exchange, Incorporated
- Tier I of the Philadelphia Stock Exchange, Incorporated
- The Chicago Board Options Exchange, Incorporated

The overwhelming number of IPOs meet these requirements. If your IPO satisfies these tests, you can skip this section. If your company's securities will be listed or traded elsewhere, such as on the NASDAQ SmallCap Market, the Bulletin Board, or the so-called Pink Sheets, this section is applicable to you.

Unless your company is exempt as provided above, the registration statement also has to be filed and ultimately cleared in the states in which offers and sales will be made. Almost all of the states have securities (blue sky) laws. Some states will not clear IPOs that they consider too speculative or risky. This can occasionally cause serious problems for the marketing of the IPO.

The most common blue sky problem is the prior sale by the company to insiders and promoters of stock at prices substantially below the IPO price ("cheap stock"). The states generally deem prior sales at 85 percent or less of the IPO price to be "substantially" below the IPO price. The cheap stock issue is typically raised with respect to companies that have no significant earnings or are in the development stage. The usual justifications for cheap stock include:

- The value of the company has increased since the date of issuing the cheap stock
- The low price for the stock results from resale restrictions

- Shares were sold to officers and employees at low prices in lieu of normal compensation
- The number of shares involved is *de minimis*

If the state securities administrator does not agree with the justification, some states require that the shares be escrowed until the achievement of certain earnings objectives by the company and canceled if those earnings objectives are not satisfied in five or six years.

The IPOs, particularly of promotional or developmental stage companies, can also suffer from some of the following blue sky problems:

- Some states may not register the stock if the company's existing capital is less than 10 percent of the aggregate offering price of the stock sold in the IPO, or if the total cash invested by promoters is less than 10 percent of the aggregate offering price.

- Some states look with disfavor on excessive numbers of warrants or stock options given to promoters and insiders.

- Some states object to excessive dilution (the difference between the IPO price and the pro forma net tangible book value per share after giving effect to the IPO) if the dilution to new investors exceeds 50 percent.

- Some states object to insider loans.

- Some states will not register IPOs if the class of stock offered to the public has either no voting rights or less than proportional voting rights. Justifications for the unequal treatment include giving the IPO stock a dividend or liquidation preference.

- Some states object to "blank check" preferred stock, that is, where the board of directors sets the terms of the preferred stock without shareholder approval.

- Some states object to a company having a negative net worth unless the company projections expect to show profits in a reasonable period of time.
- Some states limit the amount of expenses that you may incur in a public offering.

Most of these blue sky problems surface in states that have merit review laws. These laws permit a state administrator to determine the substantive merits and fairness to investors of the IPO. This contrasts with the SEC review of IPOs under the 1933 Act, which (theoretically at least) considers only the adequacy of the disclosures.

ROAD SHOWS

Sometime after the initial filing date and before the effective date, the underwriter will organize and schedule road shows that showcase the company's executives. These involve marketing meetings at various cities in the United States and possibly abroad with potential underwriting syndicate members, portfolio managers, securities analysts, brokers, and institutional investors.

A presentation is usually made by the company (with the underwriter providing assistance) and the audience is given the opportunity to ask questions. The underwriters will rehearse you on expected questions and the disclosure guidelines to which you must adhere.

The road shows (including one-on-one meetings with institutional investors) are usually hectic times for both the underwriter and the company's executives. They involve substantial traveling over a compressed time period, generally ranging from one to two weeks. Be prepared for a physically grueling schedule. The road shows educate the financial community about your company and generate interest in your IPO.

The following is a list of some of the mutual funds that purchase IPO securities and whom you may expect to meet on your road shows:

- IPO Plus Aftermarket
- Blackrock Micro-Cap
- Oppenheimer Enterprise
- William Blair Value Discovery
- ASAF Janus SmallCap Growth
- Hancock SmallCap Growth
- Neuberger & Berman Millennium
- Founders Discovery
- Northstar Special
- Phoenix SmallCap

A few firms broadcast road shows over the Internet, including Bloomberg LP (over its proprietary terminals), and NetRoadshow, a unit of Yahoo! Inc. Almost all of the road shows are prerecorded. However, live road shows over the Internet are emerging as a possible alternative.

THE PRICING MEETING

The pricing meeting firmly establishes the public offering price for your securities. This meeting typically occurs after the close of the market on the day prior to the effective date of the registration statement or within a few days thereafter.

The investment banker will recommend a public offering price based upon a number of factors. The most important factor is the price/earnings multiples (or for Internet companies, the price/revenue multiple) or EBITDA multiples of companies in the same industry that are of comparable size and capitalization and market conditions in general at the time of the pricing meeting. The feedback from the road shows is also seriously considered by the underwriter.

It is important that you do your own homework in preparing for the meeting. You should be aware of the price/earnings multiple and EBITDA multiple of comparable companies (including both the trailing and the projected

12 months), and you should be prepared to negotiate with the underwriters. However, your bargaining power is usually very limited. It is generally better to sell your company's stock slightly too cheaply than to have unhappy IPO investors because the aftermarket price falls below the IPO price.

Once the IPO valuation is established, it is common practice to split the outstanding pre-IPO common stock to obtain the correct ratio of new IPO shares to all outstanding shares. For example, assume that the underwriter intends to sell 3 million shares at $15 per share (a total of $45 million) and that your company is valued at $135 million, including the $45 million gross IPO proceeds. The 3 million new IPO shares should equal $\frac{1}{3}$ of all outstanding shares after the IPO, since $45 million gross IPO proceeds equals $\frac{1}{3}$ of your $135 million valuation. Therefore, a total 6 million shares should be owned by all pre-IPO shareholders. If you only have 1 million pre-IPO shares outstanding, you would immediately declare a 6 for 1 stock split. Thus, after the IPO, there would be 9 million shares outstanding; the public would own 3 million shares for the gross proceeds of $45 million, and all pre-IPO shareholders would own 6 million shares.

In the event that a holding company is being formed that will become the parent of your existing operating company on the IPO effective date, a similar result can be obtained by adjusting the exchange ratio for exchanging holding company stock for your own stock in your existing operating company.

EXECUTION OF UNDERWRITING AGREEMENT, LOCK-UP AGREEMENTS, AND EFFECTIVE DATE

The underwriters and your company execute the underwriting agreement on the date (or the evening before the date) you expect the SEC to declare the IPO registration statement effective.

This is the first time the underwriters legally bind themselves to purchase your securities. They must purchase securities at a closing generally held three business days after the date of execution. The underwriting agreement is a complicated agreement and contains a number of "outs" for the underwriter. The most important outs are:

- A breach by the company of the warranties, representations, or covenants set forth in the underwriting agreement
- The failure to deliver legal opinions, the accountant's "cold comfort" letter (a highly qualified accountant's letter to the underwriter), or other similar documents at the closing
- An order issued by the SEC suspending the effectiveness of your registration statement
- The closing of the major trading markets

The underwriting agreement may also contain an overallotment option, also sometimes called a "green shoe." This option typically permits the underwriter to purchase up to a maximum of an additional 15 percent of the number of shares included in the basic offering. The underwriter can only exercise the option within 30 days of the public offering date. This option permits the underwriter to sell to the public more shares than it must purchase under the underwriting agreement, and to cover its short position by exercising the overallotment option.

You and your directors and officers will be required to execute a so-called lock-up agreement with the underwriters at or prior to the date of executing the underwriter agreement. These agreements require that you not sell or otherwise transfer your securities for a period of time, usually six months. However, more than six months may be required for weaker or unusual IPOs. The prohibition on the sale of your securities typically also includes a prohibition on short selling, acquiring puts, or other hedging devices.

On the date the SEC declares your IPO registration statement effective, you may list the stock or the stock may qualify for trading on an exchange or on NASDAQ. Chapter 11 contains the requirements your stock must meet for listing on the NASDAQ Stock Market and the major stock exchanges.

You will typically also register your securities under Section 12 of the Securities Exchange Act of 1934. This registration is required as a condition for listing your securities on the NASDAQ Stock Market, the national securities exchanges, and the NASDAQ Bulletin Board. This registration makes your company subject to various periodic reporting requirements, proxy rules, tender offer rules, short-swing profit rules, and the like. For more information, see Chapter 12.

DIRECTED SHARES

Most underwriters will permit 5 to 10 percent of the total number of shares to be sold in the IPO to be directed to family and friends. Care should be taken in directing shares to customers or their purchasing agents, since this could result in public disclosure and possible embarrassment. Some underwriters are considering making you liable if some of these directed shares are not paid for by your family and friends and cannot otherwise be easily sold.

CLOSING

The closing is generally held three business days after the execution of the underwriting agreement. At the closing, the company and other selling shareholders receive the check (typically in next-day funds) and the underwriter receives the company's securities.

CHAPTER 5

PREPARING THE PROSPECTUS FOR THE TRADITIONAL IPO

The company, its counsel, and its accountants prepare the initial draft of the prospectus for the traditional IPO (as noted in Chapter 4). They submit this draft to the underwriters and their counsel for comment. Subsequently, they resubmit redrafts incorporating the comments to all parties. At all-hands meetings, everyone reviews the redrafts to hone them into shape.

The preparation of a prospectus for the traditional IPO reflects the tension between two objectives: creating a good marketing document and avoiding legal liability.

You can often reconcile these conflicting objectives by tilting the disclosure in the Prospectus Summary and Business sections more toward the marketing objective. Although from a legal viewpoint it may be better to scatter risk factors throughout the document, marketing considerations typically prevail when drafting those two sections.

You can compromise the marketing/legal liability objectives by creating a separate section of the prospectus entitled Risk Factors, which explains those risk factors related to the business. Frequent cross references are then made throughout the prospectus to the Risk Factors section. Thus, you will notice prospectuses that contain a Risk Factors section having the cross-reference words "See Risk Factors" liberally sprinkled throughout the prospectus, particularly in their marketing-oriented Business section.

SEC forms and rules dictate the contents of the prospectus for the traditional IPO. These forms and rules are elaborate and complicated. Here are the highlights.

SEC REGISTRATION FORMS

You register the traditional IPO on a Form S-1 Registration Statement. It applies if no other registration statement form is applicable.

In 1992, the SEC adopted a special registration statement form for a "small business issuer." A small business issuer refers to a company and other issuer that:

- Has revenues of less than $25 million
- Has a public float of less than $25 million (if the issuer is publicly held, the aggregate market value of the securities held by noncontrolling persons is less than $25 million)
- Is a U.S. or Canadian issuer
- Is not an investment company
- If a majority owned subsidiary, the parent corporation is also a small business issuer

Any small business issuer can use Form SB-2 to register its securities. If, as a small business issuer, you have not previously registered more than $10 million in securities offerings in any continuous 12-month period (including the present transaction), you can use Form SB-1 to register up to $10 million of securities to be sold for cash.

ADVANTAGES OF FORMS SB-1 AND SB-2

The big advantages of Forms SB-1 and SB-2 over Form S-1 are that they require less specified disclosure and only two years of audited financial statements. Form S-1 requires three years of audited financial statements.

The purported advantage of Form SB-1 over Form SB-2 is that it permits a question and answer format (Form SB-2 requires a narrative format). For an example of the question and answer format, see the offering circular in Appendix 5.

The lesser disclosure requirements of Forms SB-1 and SB-2 may decrease overall preparation costs. However, it is not yet clear how material this cost reduction will actually be.

There are two major problems with Forms SB-1 and SB-2:

- It is unclear whether the professional investment community will accept the question and answer format of Form SB-1 and the fewer disclosures of both Form SB-1 and Form SB-2.

- Legal liability considerations may cause Forms SB-1 and SB-2 to look more like Form S-1, thereby destroying any cost savings.

Institutional investors and other members of the professional investment community are accustomed to a narrative format, not a question and answer format. Likewise, these investors may not be satisfied with the lesser disclosures of Forms SB-1 and SB-2. This is especially true for Form SB-2, which a small business issuer could use for a large dollar offering normally presented on Form S-1. For example, a non-small business issuer must register a $15 million offering on the more elaborate Form S-1, whereas a small business issuer can register the same $15 million offering on Form SB-2, with fewer specified disclosures.

Just as a company tries to please customers with its marketing material, so must an underwriter accommodate the desire of the professional investment community. This community is used to the Form S-1 format. Old customs die hard!

LEGAL CONCERNS

Although the SEC made a good faith attempt to simplify disclosure for small business issuers, it did not modify its anti-fraud and other legal liability rules. Thus, Rule 408 under the 1933 Act still requires the disclosure of all other material information necessary to make the disclosures in Forms SB-1 and SB-2 not misleading. Merely complying with the explicit disclosure requirement of these forms does not insulate the company from liability.

Likewise, Sections 11 and 15 of the 1933 Act still make the company and its directors, officers, and other control persons liable for material misstatements or omissions in Forms SB-1 and SB-2. The liability of the company is absolute (unless the investors knew of the falsity). The personal liability of directors, officers, and other control persons applies even to material misstatements or omissions made in good faith, unless such persons can prove that in the exercise of reasonable care they could not have known of the material misstatements or omissions.

For example, Form S-1 requires the disclosure of products contributing more than 15 percent of the company's annual consolidated revenues (10 percent if total consolidated revenues exceed $50 million per year). Forms SB-1 and SB-2 do not specifically require that disclosure.

If sales of a particular product constitute a disproportionately high amount of the company's revenues (say 25 percent of annual revenues) and such contribution is not disclosed, reasonable arguments can be made that the omission is material and creates legal liability. This is true even though neither Form SB-1 or SB-2 specifically requests that information.

SECTIONS OF FORM S-1 PROSPECTUS

The following are the headings found in a typical IPO prospectus that are part of the Form S-1 Registration Statement and distributed to investors.

Prospectus Summary

The Company

Risk Factors

Dividend Policy and Prior S Corporation Status [if applicable]

Use of Proceeds

Dilution

Capitalization

Selected Financial Data

Management's Discussion and Analysis of Financial Condition and Results of Operations

Business

Management

Certain Transactions

Principal Shareholders

Description of Capital Stock

Shares Eligible for Future Sale

Underwriting

Legal Matters

Experts

Additional Information

Financial Statements

From the viewpoint of the professional investment community, the sections entitled Business, Management Discussion and Analysis ("MD&A"), and Use of Proceeds are among the more important sections of the nonfinancial disclosures in the prospectus.

Business

The following are some of the information you must have in the Business section of the prospectus. (The "registrant" in the SEC rules refers to the company or other entity registering the securities.)

General Development of the Business This is a description of the general development of the business, its subsidiaries, and any predecessor(s) during the past five years, or such shorter period as the registrant may have been engaged in business. You must disclose information for earlier periods if material to understanding the general development of the business.

No Prior Revenues If the company has not received any prior revenues from operations during each of the past three fiscal years, you must provide a detailed description of your plan of operation.

Industry Segments For each of the registrant's last three fiscal years or for each fiscal year the registrant has been engaged in business, whichever period is shorter, the company must state the amounts of revenues from external customers, a measure of profit or loss, and total assets attributable to each of the registrant's industry segments.

Principal Products The principal products produced and services rendered by the registrant in the industry segment and the principal markets for, and methods of distribution of, the segment's principal products and services must be described. In addition, for each of the last three fiscal years, the company must state the amount or percentage of total revenue contributed by any class of similar products or services that accounted for 10 percent or more of consolidated revenue in any of the last three fiscal years or 15 percent or more of consolidated revenue, if total revenue did not exceed $50 million during any of such fiscal years. The description should include the following information.

- *The Product or Segment.* A description of the status of a product or segment (whether in the planning stage, whether prototypes exist); the degree to which product design has progressed or whether further engineering is necessary; if there has been a public announcement of, or if the registrant otherwise has made public information about, a new product or industry segment that would require the investment of a material amount of your company's assets or that otherwise is material. You are not required to disclose otherwise nonpublic corporate information that would, if known, adversely affect the your competitive position.
- *Raw Materials.* The sources and availability of raw materials.
- *Patents, etc.* The importance to the industry segment and the duration and effect of all patents, trademarks, licenses, franchises, and concessions held.

- *Seasonality.* The extent to which the business of the industry segment is or may be seasonal.

- *Working Capital Items.* Tell how your company's and the industry's practices relate to working capital items (e.g., if the registrant is required to carry significant amounts of inventory to meet rapid delivery requirements of customers or to assure itself of a continuous allotment of goods from suppliers; if the registrant provides rights to return merchandise; or if the registrant has provided extended payment terms to customers).

- *Dependence on Customers.* Disclose how dependent the segment is upon a single customer or a few customers, the loss of any one or more of which would have a material adverse effect on the segment. According to the guidelines, "The name of any customer and its relationship, if any, with the registrant or its subsidiaries must be disclosed if sales to the customer by one or more segments are made in an aggregate amount equal to 10 percent or more of the registrant's consolidated revenues and the loss of such customer would have a material adverse effect on the registrant and its subsidiaries taken as a whole." You may include the names of other customers unless it would be misleading.

- *Backlog.* Give the dollar amount of backlog orders believed to be firm as of a recent date and as of a comparable date in the preceding fiscal year. Indicate what portion of this you reasonably expect you will not fill within the current fiscal year and give seasonal or other material aspects of the backlog.

- *Competition.* Describe the competitive conditions in the business including, where material, the identity of the particular markets in which your company competes, an estimate of the number of competitors, and your company's competitive position (if known or reasonably available). Identify the principal methods of competition (price, service, warranty, product performance, or the like) and explain the positive and negative factors pertaining to your competitive position.

- *R&D.* If it is material, give the estimated amount your company spent during each of the last three fiscal years on research and development activities. Use generally accepted accounting principles.

- *Effects of Environmental Laws.* You must disclose the material effects that compliance with federal, state, and local provisions regulating the discharge of materials into the environment, or otherwise relating to the protection of the environment, may have upon the company and its subsidiaries' capital expenditures, earnings, and competitive position.

You should carefully review the Business section of the Drkoop.com prospectus in Appendix 1.

Management Discussion and Analysis

The SEC views the MD&A section as one of the most important sections of disclosure documents because it helps explain the financial results to the reader. As a result, enforcement actions have been brought by the SEC based upon defective MD&As.

Underwriters also are concerned with the MD&A, but for different reasons. The MD&A and Business sections must dovetail. A reader of the MD&A must be able to understand the financial results of the company's business as discussed under the Business section. In addition, the MD&A should explain the selected financial information that precedes it.

The MD&A must provide the reader with information with respect to the liquidity, capital resources, and results of company operations. It includes other information necessary to understand the company's financial condition and the results of its operations. The following are some of the highlights from the SEC rules as to what must be contained in the MD&A section of the prospectus.

Liquidity The SEC requires the identification of any known trends or any known demands, commitments, events, or uncertainties that will result in or that are reasonably likely to result in the registrant's liquidity increasing or decreasing in any material way. If a material deficiency is identified, the course of action that the registrant has taken or proposes to take to remedy the deficiency should be indicated. Also, the company is required to identify and separately describe internal and external sources of liquidity, and briefly discuss any material unused sources of liquid assets.

Capital Resources This section should detail the registrant's material commitments for capital expenditures as of the end of the latest fiscal period, the general purpose of such commitments, and the anticipated source of funds needed to fulfill such commitments should be described.

The registrant must describe any known material trends, favorable or unfavorable, in the registrant's capital resources. Any expected material changes in the mix and relative cost of such resources should be indicated. The discussion must consider changes between equity, debt, and any off-balance sheet financing arrangements.

Results of Operations The information required by the SEC about the results of operations includes the following disclosures. The registrant should describe any unusual or infrequent events or transactions or any significant economic changes that materially affected the amount of reported income from continuing operations and, in each case, indicate the extent to which income was so affected. In addition, any other significant components of revenues or expenses that, in the registrant's judgment, should be described in order to understand the registrant's results of operations:

- Any known trends or uncertainties that have had or that the registrant reasonably expects will have a materially favorable or unfavorable impact on net sales or revenues or income from continuing operations should be described. If the registrant knows of events that will cause a material change in the relationship between costs and revenues (such as known future increases in costs of labor or materials or price increases or inventory adjustments), the change in the relationship must be disclosed.

- The discussion and analysis must focus specifically on material events and uncertainties known to management that would cause reported financial information not to be necessarily indicative of future operating results or of future financial condition. This would include descriptions and amounts of matters that would have an impact on future operations and have not had an impact in the past, and matters that have had an impact on reported operations and are not expected to have an impact upon future operations.

SEC Example of MD&A Disclosure: Liquidity The SEC has given companies examples of what it expects the MD&A to contain. The following is an example of liquidity disclosure by a financially troubled company.

"The Company has violated certain requirements of its debt agreements relating to failure to maintain certain minimum ratios and levels of working capital and stockholders' equity. The Company's lenders have not declared the Company in default and have allowed the Company to remain in violation of these agreements.

Were a default to be declared, the Company would not be able to continue to operate. A capital infusion of $4,000,000 is necessary to cure these defaults. The Company has engaged an investment banker and is considering various alternatives, including the sale of certain assets or the sale of common shares, to raise these funds.

"The Company frequently has not been able to make timely payments to its trade and other creditors. As of year-end and as of February 29, 1988, the Company had past due payables in the amount of $525,000 and $705,000, respectively. Deferred payment terms have been negotiated with most of these vendors. However, certain vendors have suspended parts deliveries to the Company. As a result, the Company was not always able to make all shipments on time, although no orders have been canceled to date. Were significant volumes of orders to be canceled, the Company's ability to continue to operate would be jeopardized. The Company is currently seeking sources of working capital financing sufficient to fund delinquent balances and meet ongoing trade obligations."

SEC Example of MD&A Disclosure: Capital Resources The following is an example of proper disclosure of planned capital expenditures necessary to maintain sales growth:

"The Company plans to open 20 to 25 new stores in fiscal 1988. As a result, the Company expects the trend of higher sales in fiscal 1988 to continue at approximately the same rate as in recent years. Management estimates that approximately $50 to $60 million will be required to finance the Company's cost of opening such stores. In addition, the Company's expansion program will require an increase in inventory of about $1 million per store, which is anticipated to be financed principally by trade credit. Funds required to finance the Company's store expansion program are expected to come primarily from new credit facilities with the remainder provided by funds generated from operations and increased lease financings. The Company recently entered into a new borrowing agreement with its primary bank, which provides for additional borrowings of up to $50 million for future expansion. The Company intends to seek additional credit facilities during fiscal 1988."

SEC Example of MD&A Disclosure: Results of Operation In the following example, the company analyzes the reasons for a material change in revenues and in so doing describes the effects of offsetting developments.

"Revenue from sales of single-family homes for 1987 increased 6 percent from 1986. The increase resulted from a 14 percent increase in the average sales price per home, partially offset by a 6 percent decrease in the number of homes delivered. Revenues from sales of single-family homes for 1986 increased 2 percent from 1985. The average sales price per home in 1986 increased 6 percent, which was offset by a 4 percent decrease in the number of homes delivered.

The increase in the average sales prices in 1987 and 1986 is primarily the result of the Company's increased emphasis on higher priced single-family homes. The decrease in homes delivered in 1987 and 1986 was attributable to a decline in sales in Texas. The significant decline in oil prices and its resulting effect on energy-related business has further impacted the already depressed Texas area housing market and is expected to do so for the foreseeable future. The Company curtailed housing operations during 1987 in certain areas in Texas in response to this change in the housing market. Although the number of homes sold is expected to continue to decline during the current year as a result of this action, this decline is expected to be offset by increases in average sales prices."

SEC Example of MD&A Disclosure: Known Uncertainty The following is an example of a "known uncertainty" that you must disclose in the MD&A.

"Facts: A registrant has been correctly designated a PRP by the EPA with respect to cleanup of hazardous waste at three sites. (A PRP is a potentially responsible party as designated by the Environmental Protection Agency under the Superfund Law). No statutory defenses are available. The registrant is in the process of preliminary investigations of the sites to determine the nature of its potential liability and the amount of remedial costs necessary to clean up the sites. Other PRPs also have been designated, but the ability to obtain contribution is unclear, as is the extent of insurance coverage, if any. Management is unable to determine that a material effect on future financial condition or results of operations is not reasonably likely to occur.

"Based upon the facts of this hypothetical base, MD&A disclosure of the effects of the PRP status, quantified to the extent reasonably practicable, would be required. For MD&A purposes, aggregate potential cleanup costs must be considered in light of the joint and several liability to which a PRP is subject. Facts regarding whether insurance coverage may be contested, and whether and to what extent potential sources of contribution or indemnification constitute reliable sources of recovery may be factored into the determination of whether a material future effect is not reasonably likely to occur."

The preceding example illustrates just how difficult MD&A disclosure can be.

SEC Example of MD&A Disclosure: General An example of a typical MD&A section can be found in the Drkoop.com prospectus dated June 8, 1999, which appears in Appendix 1.

As described earlier under Business, if a company has separate business segments, revenues and profits of each segment must be separately disclosed. This disclosure can be harmful competitively. The accounting criteria for what constitutes a separate segment are fairly vague and most companies successfully take the position that they do not have any significant separate segments apart from their main businesses.

Use of Proceeds

The SEC rules require the disclosure of the use of proceeds from the offering. The following are some of these SEC rules:

- The registrant must state the principal purposes for which the net proceeds to the registrant from the securities to be offered are intended to be used and the approximate amount intended to be used for each such purpose. Where the registrant has no current specific plan for the proceeds, or a significant portion thereof, the registrant must so state and discuss the principal reasons for the offering.

- Where less than all of the securities to be offered may be sold and more than one use is listed for the proceeds, the registrant must indicate the order of priority of such purposes and discuss the registrant's plans if substantially less than the maximum proceeds obtained.

- If any material amounts of other funds are necessary to accomplish the specified purposes for which the proceeds are to be obtained, the registrant must state the amounts and sources of such other funds needed for each such specified purpose and the sources thereof.

- If any material part of the proceeds is to be used to discharge indebtedness, the registrant must set forth the interest rate and maturity of such indebtedness. If the indebtedness to be discharged was incurred within one year, the registrant must describe the use of the proceeds of such indebtedness other than short-term borrowings used for working capital.

- If any material amount of the proceeds is to be used to acquire assets (other than in the ordinary course of business), the registrant must describe briefly and state the cost of the assets, where such assets are to be acquired from affiliates of the registrant or their associates, the names of the persons from whom they are to be acquired and the principal followed in determining the cost to the registrant.

- Where the registrant indicates that the proceeds may be, or will be, used to finance acquisitions of other businesses, the identity of such businesses, if known, or, if not known, the nature of the businesses to be sought, the status of any negotiations with respect to the acquisition, and a brief description of such business must be included.

An example of the use of proceeds section can be found on page 252 of the Drkoop.com prospectus.

Other Important Sections of the Prospectus

The following are the more important SEC Regulation S-K disclosure items (excluding financial statements and information) to include in an IPO prospectus on Form S-1:

Item 103	Legal proceedings
Item 202	Description of registrant's securities
Item 304	Changes in and disagreements with accountants on accounting and financial disclosure
Item 401	Directors, executive officers, promoters, and control persons
Item 402	Executive compensation

Item 403   Security ownership of certain beneficial owners and management

Item 404   Certain relationships and related transactions

Item 503   Summary information, risk factors, and ratio of earnings to fixed charges

Item 505   Determination of offering price

Item 506   Dilution

Item 509   Interest of named experts and counsel

The executive compensation disclosures required by Item 402 apply to the chief executive officer at the end of the last completed fiscal year, regardless of compensation level. It also applies to the company's four most highly compensated executive officers (other than the CEO) at the end of the last completed fiscal year whose total annual salary and bonus exceeds $100,000. The executive compensation rules are complex and a delight to insomniacs and anyone who enjoys completing *The New York Times* crossword puzzle.

The only major exclusion from these compensation disclosures is perquisites (fringe benefits) provided they do not exceed the lesser of $50,000 or 10 percent of the total annual salary and bonus. In addition, nondiscriminatory group medical, life, and similar group insurance plans generally made available to all salaried employees escape disclosure.

Particular attention should also be paid to Item 404, which requires extensive disclosure of transactions (or series of similar transactions) with or involving the company or any of its subsidiaries in which a director, executive officer, 5 percent stockholders, and members of their immediate family had a direct or indirect material interest. "Immediate family" includes a person's spouse, parents, children, siblings, mothers and fathers-in-law, sons and daughters-in-law, and brothers and sisters-in-law.

Complying with Item 404 requires a very careful review of all transactions that involve insiders or their immediate families during the prior three years. There are limited exclusions from the required disclosures (such as transactions involving $60,000 or less) that are narrowly interpreted by the SEC and conservative securities lawyers.

A prospectus is a complicated and exhausting document to prepare. It requires relentless attention to detail. Hundreds of hours of time will be required to be spent by your chief financial officer and your attorneys and accountants.

Your involvement will also require a significant time commitment. You must be prepared to continue to manage and operate your business while spending inordinate amounts of time on the prospectus preparation process.

Plain English

Effective October 1, 1998, the SEC adopted new rules requiring companies to write and design the cover page, summary, and risk factors section of their prospectus in plain English. Prior to October 1, 1998, prospectuses contained complex legal jargon in these sections that was difficult for the average reader to understand. The new rules (among other things) require companies to use short sentences, definite, concrete, and everyday language in these prospectus sections, and to design these sections to make them inviting to the reader.

Unfortunately, the SEC staff has occasionally applied the new rule with excessive zeal, causing the SEC staff to be dubbed the "grammar police." We hope that a more reasonable approach will be used in the future by the SEC staff to avoid unduly burdening smaller businesses. An example of the "plain English" requirements is contained in the Drkoop.com, Inc. prospectus in Appendix 1.

CHAPTER 6

NONTRADITIONAL METHODS OF GOING PUBLIC

A traditional IPO is underwritten on a firm-commitment basis and filed with the SEC. Many companies that cannot qualify for a traditional IPO can still raise growth capital through a nontraditional IPO.

WHAT ARE NONTRADITIONAL IPOS?

Non-traditional IPOs include several categories of IPOs:

- Self-underwritten offerings and offerings taken on a best-efforts basis through broker-dealers
- Mergers with a publicly held shell corporation
- Spin-offs

Chapters 7 through 10 discuss each of these nontraditional offerings. Chapter 7 covers self-underwritten and best-efforts offerings. Two special types of self-underwritten and best-efforts offerings, namely Regulation A and SCOR offerings, are covered in Chapters 8 and 9, respectively. Turn to Chapter 10 to read about mergers with a publicly held shell corporation and spin-offs.

WHY CAN'T A COMPANY QUALIFY FOR A TRADITIONAL IPO?

Companies may not qualify for traditional IPOs because they are too small, they are not in a "hot" industry, or they have unproven management or growth potential. Although many small or startup companies in hot industries can qualify for a traditional IPO even if they have no revenue, a small company that is in an unexciting business will have difficulty finding a willing underwriter.

At various times, the market has considered Internet, software, environmental, biotechnology, and healthcare companies hot. However, a small company with management that has proven successful in prior businesses may still be a candidate for an IPO, even though its industry is not "hot." Other major reasons for a company being disqualified from a traditional IPO include the following:

- Your industry's growth prospects are questionable.
- The company cannot use the minimum amount of proceeds raised from the traditional IPO (typically a minimum of $20 million less IPO costs). Institutions are typically not interested in investing in IPOs in which the post-IPO market valuation is less than $100 million.
- The management of the company is not impressive to the investment community.

- There are problems with the background of the promoters of the company (SEC or other governmental investigations are pending, civil fraud suits are unresolved, criminal convictions, and the like).
- Other traditional IPOs in the same industry performed poorly.
- The public markets are saturated with public offerings of similar businesses.
- There is no market for IPOs.

The market for traditional IPOs is very cyclical. At the height of the cycle, many more companies can qualify for a traditional IPO than at its low point. If your company is a questionable candidate for a traditional IPO, it may be best to time your IPO to correspond with the high point in the cycle. This is easier said than done.

The cycles in traditional IPOs also affect the marketability of nontraditional, self-underwritten, or best-efforts offerings. However, the cycle effect is not as direct. The IPO cycles do not significantly affect shell mergers and spin-offs.

WHY CONSIDER A NONTRADITIONAL IPO?

Some financial consultants advise companies, if they cannot qualify for a traditional IPO, to not go public. Some consultants go so far as to say that, if you cannot attract a prestigious underwriter, you should not go public. The primary objections to a nontraditional IPO are:

1. If the company waits until it is large enough to qualify for a traditional IPO, it will receive a better price for its stock.
2. There is not an active and liquid market for the stock after a nontraditional IPO.

The soundness of this advice depends upon the company's other alternatives. If the company has no other method of raising needed growth capital than a nontraditional IPO, it is certainly bad advice not to explore that alternative.

However, even companies that can raise growth capital privately should explore nontraditional IPOs. The low valuation placed on the company by private investors may result in too great an equity dilution of the founders. In some cases, the "illiquidity discount" is so large that the founders lose control of the company. This loss of control may occur on the first round of private financing, but it is more likely lost as subsequent rounds of needed financing are sought from venture capitalists or other private investors. Even companies that can generate growth capital through internal earnings should consider a nontraditional IPO.

If your business is technology based, that technology may only have a limited lifespan until someone improves on the technology. The capital generated from a nontraditional IPO can assist such a company by immediately exploiting the technology and becoming a significant market force. Staying private may merely result in losing an opportunity that has a short window.

Many companies fade because their competition is much better capitalized. Staying private when your competitors are raising public capital may result in weakening your market position. This has proven especially true in retail businesses. Consider companies such as Blockbuster Video that have dominated their market against gigantic, retail stores. Levitz Furniture is a good 1970s example of this same phenomenon. Capital is a key weapon in competition.

It is true that nontraditional IPOs sometimes result in weak or non-existent public markets. However, even traditional IPOs occasionally suffer from the same problems. It is therefore extremely important to be certain that there will be an active and liquid marketplace after the nontraditional IPO.

ARE THERE ANY ADVANTAGES OF NONTRADITIONAL IPOS OVER TRADITIONAL IPOS?

Even companies that qualify for a traditional IPO may decide that they do not want to risk the large expenditures required prior to obtaining a firm commitment from an underwriter. Until the underwriter makes a firm commitment, there is no assurance as to what the valuation of the company will be. Thus, the company does not have any guarantee as to the minimum proceeds of the IPO.

Many underwriters tend to give a company too high a valuation estimate when the company is selecting an underwriter. The underwriters know they are competing with other underwriters for the IPO, and that the valuation estimate given by an underwriter is a major factor in determining whether that underwriter is ultimately selected by the company. Hence, there is an inherent tendency to inflate the valuation estimate.

A nontraditional IPO, such as a shell merger, permits the company to precisely know its valuation prior to incurring substantial expenditures. Hence, the company knows how much equity it must give up to the promoter of the shell prior to incurring major expenditures. There are, however, other disadvantages to a shell merger you must weigh against this particular advantage.

A self-underwritten or best-efforts offering permits the company to establish its own valuation within reasonable limits. The market will determine whether that valuation is correct. If it is too high, the securities will not sell.

In a traditional IPO, sophisticated institutional investors, to whom the underwriter markets the securities, play a crucial role in determining valuation. This is because a significant portion of the underwritten offering is typically sold to such institutional investors.

A self-underwritten or best-efforts offering is typically marketed to retail buyers. Retail buyers tend to be less sophisticated than institutional investors. As a result, self-underwritten or best-efforts offerings can generally be marketed at higher valuations, resulting in less equity dilution.

Notwithstanding this advantage of self-underwritten and best-efforts offerings, very few companies that qualify for a traditional IPO will seek this alternative. Marketing your company's securities is difficult and time consuming. Most executives are better off using their time to run their own business instead of marketing their company's securities.

CHAPTER 7

SELF-UNDERWRITINGS
AND BEST-EFFORTS
PUBLIC OFFERINGS

S ome companies go public by registering and selling their own stock. Such companies may also pay commissions to broker-dealers to sell their stock. In some cases, broker-dealers enter into formal best-efforts underwriting arrangements with the company and agree to use their best efforts to sell the company's stock.

MARKETING

Self-underwriting requires a very significant marketing effort by management, which can interfere with the normal business operations of the company. The success of these offerings is far from assured. However, where alternative capital sources are not available, or are available at too steep a price, this route should be seriously considered.

Any company that attempts a nontraditional IPO must have a thoughtful marketing plan to sell its securities. The absence of a firm-commitment underwriting makes such a marketing plan imperative. Marketing efforts may be performed by licensed broker-dealers, or by officers and full-time employees of the company, or both.

BROKER-DEALERS

Many local and regional brokers are willing to assist companies in marketing their IPOs. No prestigious underwriting firm, whether national or regional, is likely to be interested in such marketing, however.

It is in your best interest to make certain that the broker pays the most attention to your offering. The sales commissions negotiated with local and regional brokers must be sufficiently high to provide incentive for their marketing efforts. Your IPO will typically compete with other IPOs and securities offerings for the attention of the broker, so it is usually not wise to unduly reduce sales commissions. Brokers tend to concentrate their efforts where their reward is the highest.

It is a truism that securities are sold, not bought. Someone has to induce the customer to buy your securities. The customer will not call you, except in unusual circumstances. The broker's endorsement of your offering is an effective selling technique. It is much more effective than touting your own company's investment merits. The third-party endorsement, which the broker brings to your securities offering, is an essential part of the marketing plan.

As noted, NASDR and state securities laws place limits on the amount brokers can charge for securities offerings. The brokers must clear the amount of sales commissions and other compensation (warrants and others) with the NASDR prior to commencing their selling efforts. The harder the marketing effort for the broker, the closer the overall compensation will approach the maximum permitted by the NASDR.

OFFICERS AND EMPLOYEES

Officers and employees can be effective spokespersons for the company in its self-marketing efforts. If the company suffers from a severe capital shortage, officers and employees are motivated by the desire to sell securities in order to retain their jobs. Thus, they tend to be much more energetic in their selling efforts. However, officers and employees must be carefully trained to avoid statements not contained in the prospectus.

Care must be taken to comply with applicable federal and state registration and licensing requirements for brokers, dealers, and securities salespersons. To avoid federal registration, the officers and employees doing the selling should be full-time employees primarily performing duties other than selling securities and no portion of their compensation should be based on such sales.

States vary as to their licensing requirements. Merely being exempt from federal licensing does not exempt the officer and employee from state licensing. Since the federal exemption (contained in Rule 3a4-1 under the Securities Exchange Act of 1934) and any applicable state exemptions are complicated, the company should seek advice from a securities lawyer.

AFTERMARKET TRADING

You must structure a nontraditional IPO so that your company's stock will qualify for trading on the NASDAQ Stock Market, a national securities exchange, or the NASDAQ Bulletin Board (see Chapter 11). Brokers willing to make a market in your stock must be lined up in advance of your nontraditional IPO. Such brokers must have an incentive to continue as active market-makers.

Special SEC rules apply to brokers in connection with the sale of penny stock. A penny stock is a stock selling for less than $5 per share. Many brokers prefer not having to comply with the recordkeeping provisions of these SEC rules. Accordingly, it is preferable to structure your company's capitalization to avoid having to sell the stock for less than $5 per share.

To avoid unreasonable spreads between the Bid and Asked prices (the brokers' profit) for your stock, at least three brokers should be making an active market in your stock.

DIRECT IPOS OVER THE INTERNET

Direct IPOs over the Internet are becoming increasingly popular for small growth companies as vehicles for raising capital. These offerings generally fall under Regulation A, which allows small companies with offerings under $5 million to conduct a public offering that is exempt from registration requirements under Section 3(b) of the Securities Act (see Chapter 8). Using the Internet for such offerings provides several advantages. First, companies seeking to raise capital over the Internet may be able to avoid the expensive brokerage fees that they otherwise would have to pay to underwriters. Second, companies may reach wider audiences of potential investors than they otherwise could reach through paper-based offerings. Finally, the time and costs involved in the delivery of offering materials may be reduced by electronic transmission.

In March 1995, the New York based Spring Street Brewing Company (Spring Street), a microbrewer, successfully used the Internet to raise $1.6 million from 3,500 investors in a direct IPO pursuant to Regulation A. In its IPO, Spring Street sold over 870,000 shares at $1.85 a share. Spring Street opted for this route of raising capital mainly because of the high costs associated with conducting a traditional IPO with the help of underwriters.

Spring Street was the first company to publicly sell shares of common stock through the Internet. In doing so, Spring Street paved the way for other small companies that may similarly wish to attempt to raise capital directly via the Internet. Keep in mind, however, that many states prohibit a direct public offering without the use of a registered agent.

In 1996, the North American Securities Administrators Association (NASAA) passed a resolution, which if followed by states, would exempt Internet offers (but not sales) where (i) the Internet offers states that securities are not being offered to residents of a particular state and (ii) the offer is not otherwise specifically directed to any person in a state. The resolution also permits securities to be offered on the Internet where (i) no sales are made until registration and prospectus delivery have been effected, or (ii) an exemption is available.

Approximately 32 states have adopted the NASAA resolution, but with certain bells and whistles (see NASAA Web site at *www.nasaa.org/bluesky/guidelines/resolu.html*). For example, California implemented the NASAA Internet Resolution, except that California adds a condition that the Internet offer must originate outside California. Thus, corporations located in California may not post offers on the Internet *unless* some other exemption is available.

LEGAL CONSIDERATIONS

The sale of securities is a highly regulated transaction. You must comply with both federal and state securities laws. These laws regulate the necessity of registering the securities and the registration and licensing of brokers, dealers, and agents. They also create remedies and penalties for material misstatements and omissions in connection with the offer and sale of securities. Criminal penalties apply to flagrant violations.

The company is absolutely liable for material misstatements or omissions in offerings registered under the 1933 Act (unless the investor knew of the material misstatement or omission). The 1933 Act typically also makes directors, officers, and other controlling persons of the company personally liable if the company violates the law. For example, under Section 15 of the 1933 Act, controlling persons can be personally liable for material misstatements and omissions made by the company in connection with the offer or sale of securities. The liability can extend even to honest mistakes unless the company and the controlling persons can prove that they exercised reasonable care.

Nontraditional IPOs tend to be more dangerous than traditional IPOs. In a traditional IPO, the underwriter is very sophisticated and represented by knowledgeable counsel. This is not always true in nontraditional IPOs. Many local underwriters and brokers are not terribly sophisticated and do not seek advice from securities lawyers. As a result, these local underwriters and brokers have a higher risk of inadvertently violating the myriad of rules applicable to them than are sophisticated national and regional underwriters.

To protect itself, the company should enter into a selling agreement with a local underwriter or broker-dealer that contains (among others) the following clauses:

- Warranties and representations by the broker-dealer of its compliance with federal and state securities laws and NASD rules
- Covenants that the broker-dealer will continue to comply with during the period of the securities offering
- Indemnification rights for the company if the broker-dealer fails to do so

All parties typically prepare the disclosure documents (the prospectus, offering circular, etc.) in a traditional IPO with greater care than in a nontraditional IPO. This is due partly to the discipline imposed by counsel for underwriters of the IPO who are highly adverse to risk. You should employ sophisticated securities lawyers to prepare the disclosure documents and monitor the offering. You should use the same care as is typical in the traditional IPO.

PROTECTING YOUR PERSONAL ASSETS

In view of the potential personal liability of control persons under federal and state securities laws, consider doing the following:

- If state law exempts jointly owned property from creditors of either spouse, transfer the assets of the control person into the names of the control persons and the control person's spouse.
- Transfer assets of the control person to his or her spouse (provided the marriage is strong).
- Take great care in preparing disclosure documents and in selling securities.
- Use sophisticated professionals to assist the company. The company's auditor must be trained in securities law and be a member of the SEC Practice Section of the American Institute of Certified Public Accountants. The company's lawyer should be an experienced securities lawyer.

HOW DOES THE COMPANY CHOOSE WHICH OFFERING IT WANTS?

The type of offering you choose depends on the following factors:

- Does your marketing plan require you to solicit investors who are strangers or to advertise publicly for investors?
- How much money do you wish to raise?
- Where do you wish to sell the securities?

If you want to be able to approach potential investors who are strangers or to advertise publicly in the United States, you must either register the securities, exempt them under Regulation A, or qualify for a federal and state exemption that permits "general solicitation" or "general advertising." The terms "general solicitation" and "general advertising" are defined in SEC Regulation D to include the following:

- Any advertisement, article, notice, or other communication published in any newspaper, magazine, or similar media or broadcast over television or radio
- Any seminar or meeting whose attendees have been invited by any general solicitation or general advertising (subject to a minor exception)

If you do not have to solicit investors who are strangers and you do not have to advertise publicly for investors, you should, if possible, tailor your marketing plan to comply with SEC Rule 506 to avoid the hassle and delay of dealing with federal and state regulatory agencies. An offering under Rule 506 avoids the necessity of complying with the registration provisions of state securities laws and the amount of capital you can raise is not limited. However, offerings under Rule 506 can only be sold to "accredited investors" (unlimited in number) and up to 35 sophisticated and experienced investors with whom you or your solicitor have a preexisting relationship. If you or your solicitor have no "preexisting relationship" with a potential investor (whether or not he or she is an accredited investor), your solicitation of that potential investor could constitute a "general solicitation" and your sale to that investor would not qualify under Rule 506.

According to SEC Rule 501, adopted under the 1933 Act, an accredited investor includes, among others, the following individual investors:

- Any natural person whose individual net worth, or joint net worth with that person's spouse, at the time of his purchase exceeds $1,000,000

- Any natural person who had an individual income in excess of $200,000 in each of the two most recent years or joint income with that person's spouse in excess of $300,000 in each of those years and has a reasonable expectation of reaching the same income level in the current year

If you need to approach strangers or advertise publicly, but are willing to offer and sell securities to investors in only one state, you should consider an intrastate offering. This offering must be registered with the state, unless the offering is confined only to accredited investors and the state recognizes this exemption from its registration requirements. In addition, state advertising rules must be complied with. If you need the ability to solicit investors in more than one state, then an intrastate offering is inappropriate for your company.

Most self-underwritten and best-efforts offerings are for less than $5 million. Accordingly, your practical choices are to use a Regulation A or an intrastate offering registered with one state. If your offering is for $1 million or less (over a 12-month period), you can use the SEC Rule 504 exemption together with a SCOR registration (see Chapter 9) or an all accredited investor offering in states that exempt that offering (see "Rule 504/Accredited Investor Exemption," in the next section).

If your offering is wholly or partly outside of the United States, the amount offered and sold outside of the United States can, in certain circumstances, avoid being integrated with the U.S. offering. Thus, under certain circumstances, you could sell $1 million of securities under Rule 504 in the United States and concurrently sell $1 million abroad without violating the $1 million limit under Rule 504 provided you comply with SEC regulations.

Offerings Permitting General Solicitation or Advertising

General solicitation and general advertising are only permitted in the following types of initial public offerings:

- Offerings registered with the SEC, typically on Form S-1 or on Form SB-1 and Form SB-2 (limited to small business issuers)
- Regulation A offerings filed with the SEC and the states in which the offering is made (see Chapter 8)
- Intrastate offerings registered in one state and offered and sold only to residents of that state
- Offerings outside of the United States (typically pursuant to SEC Regulation S) in countries that do not prohibit general solicitation or advertising
- Offerings under SEC Rule 504 (limited to $1 million over a 12-month period) that are also registered with the states on a SCOR Registration form (see Chapter 9)
- Offerings under SEC Rule 504 (limited to $1 million over a 12-month period) that are sold only to accredited investors in states in which such accredited investor offerings are exempt

Rule 504/Accredited Investor Exemptions

Offerings conducted under Rule 504 (limited to $1 million over a 12-month period) permit general solicitation and general advertising only in connection with a SCOR Registration (Form U-7) (see Chapter 9) or an all accredited investor offering exempted from registration by state law. Rule 504 does not apply to public companies, investment companies, or development stage companies with no specific business plan or purpose, or companies that have a business plan to engage in a merger or acquisition with an unidentified company.

If you want to generally solicit only accredited investors and you are willing to limit your offering to $1 million over a 12-month period, you can avoid the costs of registering your offering under the federal or state law provided you comply with SEC Rule 504 and state accredited investor exemptions. Approximately 30 states have adopted an accredited investor exemption. A copy of the model accredited investor exemption appears at the end of this chapter and is reproduced on the NASAA Web site. However, many states have adopted changes to the model and many states still require the use of a registered agent to conduct an accredited investor offering.

As of June 30, 1999, the following states permit a company to generally solicit accredited investors under SEC Rule 504 without using a registered agent and without registering the securities being offered: Arkansas, California, Colorado, Delaware, Iowa, Maine, Minnesota, Ohio, Pennsylvania, Utah, Washington, West Virginia, and Wisconsin. However, some of these states place restrictions that must be carefully examined before conducting a Rule 504 public offering limited to accredited investors. For example, in California, the issuer must be either a California corporation or another business entity organized under the laws of California; a general announcement of the offering can be made only by a written document; a filing is required both before and after the securities are offered.

In most states that have adopted the accredited offering exemption, a public trading market cannot immediately develop because the securities can only be sold to persons whom the issuer believes are purchasing for investment only, and unregistered resales within one year are presumed to violate this provision. Pennsylvania has not adopted this requirement.

There is a "bad boy" disqualification from the state accredited investor exemptions. In addition, no telephone solicitation is permitted unless prior to placing the call, the company reasonably believes that the prospective purchaser to be solicited is an accredited investor.

Unlimited Dollar Amount Offerings

You can register self-underwritings and best-efforts offerings in an unlimited dollar amount on Form S-1. If the company is a small business issuer, it can register these offerings in an unlimited dollar amount on Form SB-2 in the same manner as traditional IPOs. As you may recall, the primary requirements for a small business issuer are that the company have revenues of less than $25 million and a public float of less than $25 million.

Alternatively, a company can register an unlimited dollar amount of its stock with a state securities commission in an intrastate offering (offers and sales limited to one state) if the company otherwise legally qualifies. No federal registration is required for intrastate offerings.

A company can also sell an unlimited dollar amount of its stock to accredited investors (unlimited in number) and up to 35 sophisticated and experienced investors pursuant to Rule 506 of SEC Regulation D, provided there is no general solicitation or advertising. Rule 506 is a so-called safe-harbor, which if complied with will automatically satisfy the private placement exemption [Section 4(2)] from the registration provisions of the 1933 Act. If you comply with Rule 506, you avoid the necessity of complying with the registration provisions of state securities laws because the 1933 Act preempts these state registration provisions (provided you comply with any notice filing requirements of the states)

Even if you don't comply with Rule 506, your private placement may still be exempt from registration under the private placement exemption contained in Section 4(2) of the 1933 Act. However, unlike a Rule 506 offering, a private placement under Section 4(2) must still comply with the registration or exemption provisions of state securities laws. Unlike intrastate offerings and Forms S-1 and SB-2, you cannot use general solicitation or general advertising in either a Rule 506 offering or in a private placement under Section 4(2).

Limited Dollar Amount Offering

Companies can also raise limited dollar amounts of funds according to the following federal forms and rules:

- Form SB-1 Registration Statement (up to $10 million) for small business issuers
- Regulation A (up to $5 million, including not more than $1.5 million to be received by selling security holders) (Regulation A is not limited to small business issuers.)
- Rule 505 of Regulation D (up to $5 million), but limited to certain accredited investors plus up to 35 nonaccredited investors
- Rule 504 of Regulation D (up to $1 million over a 12-month period)

Regulation A offerings and Rule 504 offerings, under certain limited circumstances, permit general solicitation or advertising as previously noted, unlike Rule 505 offerings, which never permit general solicitation or advertising.

Federal offering exemptions under Regulation A, Rule 505 and Rule 504 require either registration or an exemption from applicable state securities laws. Thus, if your company wishes to take advantage of these dollar limited federal exemptions, your company must choose states to market company securities that have hospitable securities laws.

SUMMARY OF PUBLIC AND PRIVATE OFFERING CHOICES

The following is a summary of the public offering choices and the private offering choices for raising capital in the United States in self-underwritten and best-efforts offerings.

The Public Offering Choices

General solicitation is permitted and there is no investor qualification for the following public offerings:

1. Public Offerings Registered with SEC

    Primary Advantages: Better terms for founder than private placements; Unlimited marketing where blue skied or if state law preempted; No investor qualification

    Primary Disadvantages: Cost (typical range: firm-commitment underwriting, $700,000 to over $1 million; self-underwritten, $200,000 to $500,000; plus any underwriting or commissions and expense allowance); Audited financials required

2. Public Intrastate Offerings Registered in One State (exempt from federal but not state registration)

   Primary Advantages: Same as Public Offering Registered with SEC; No federal review required

   Primary Disadvantages: Can only be marketed in one state; Must comply with state registration requirements

3. Public Regulation A Offerings (exempt from federal registration, but federal review required)

   Primary Advantages: Can "test the waters" before filing in some but not all states; Audited financial statements not required for federal review unless otherwise available (however, states may still require audited financials); Less disclosure required than in SEC-registered offerings; Can use question-and-answer format; Unlimited marketing where blue skied

   Primary Disadvantages: Limited to $5 million in rolling 12 months, including no more than $1.5 million in non-issuer resales; Must be reviewed by both federal and state regulators; Professional help required; Cost (typical range: $200,000 to $300,000)

4. Public Rule 504/SCOR Offerings

   Primary Advantages: Same as Regulation A, except no federal review required, no offers prior to registration effective date, and unaudited financial statements permitted in most states; Can be completed without professional help; Typically costs approximately $30,000

   Primary Disadvantages: Limited to $1 million in rolling 12 months; Must be reviewed by state regulators; Audited financial statements required after offering if more than 100 securityholders; Higher risk of defective disclosure and personal liability if prepared without professional help

5. Public Rule 504/Accredited Investor Offerings

Primary Advantages: Same as Regulation A, except no federal review required and exempted by states that have adopted accredited offering exemption; No specific disclosure requirements; Probably the least expensive of all offerings (typically $15,000 to $30,000)

Primary Disadvantages: Limited to $1 million in 12 months; Can only be sold to accredited investors; Most states do not permit immediate trading market to develop

The Private Offering Choices

In the following offerings in the United States, no general solicitation or general advertising is permitted, and marketing is limited to qualified investors with whom there is a preexisting relationship with the company or broker soliciting the sale:

1. Rule 505

Primary Advantages: Can sell to 35 unsophisticated persons and unlimited number of accredited investors; No federal review required

Primary Disadvantages: Limited to $5 million in rolling 12 months; No general solicitation or advertising permitted; Professional investors may extract onerous terms because of illiquidity; Registration provisions of state securities laws not preempted

2. Rule 506

Primary Advantages: Unlimited dollar amount can be sold to 35 sophisticated and experienced investors in financial and business matters and an *unlimited* number of accredited investors; No federal review is required; Registration provisions of state securities laws are preempted, provided notice is given (if required by state).

Primary Disadvantages: No general solicitation or advertising is permitted; Professional investors may extract onerous terms because of illiquidity.

The following other requirements must be satisfied under both Rule 505 and 506:

1. Disclosure of certain information (unless all purchasers are accredited investors)
2. Restrictions on resale of the securities
3. Notice filed with the SEC and state blue sky regulators

Antifraud provisions of the securities laws require disclosure even in an all accredited investor offering.

Private placements may also be effectuated under the judge-made case law decided under Section 4(2) of the 1933 Act and also under Section 4(6) of that law (dealing with sales solely to accredited investors). Angel offerings to individuals under the case law of Section 4(2) are infrequent because of the conflicting court decisions and the lack of any preemption of state securities law. Section 4(6) of the 1933 Act is likewise infrequently used because it is more restrictive than Rule 506.

TEXT OF NASAA MODEL ACCREDITED INVESTOR EXEMPTION

Any offer or sale of a security by an issuer in a transaction that meets the requirements of this rule is exempted from [Sections requiring registration and filing of advertising materials].

(A) Sales of securities shall be made only to persons who are or the issuer reasonably believes are accredited investors. "Accredited investor" is defined in 17 CFR

230.501(a) [amendment or successor rule] [some states may elect to include the entire text of SEC Rule 501(a) in lieu of an in corporation by reference].

(B) The exemption is not available to an issuer that is in the development stage that either has no specific business plan or purpose or has indicated that its business plan is to engage in a merger or acquisition with an unidentified company or companies, or other entity or person.

(C) The issuer reasonably believes that all purchasers are purchasing for investment and not with the view to or for sale in connection with a distribution of the security. Any resale of a security sold in reliance on this exemption within 12 months of sale shall be presumed to be with a view to distribution and not for investment, except a resale pursuant to a registration statement effective under sections [insert registration sections] or to an accredited investor pursuant to an exemption available under (state securities act).

(D) (1) The exemption is not available to an issuer if the issuer, any of the issuer's predecessors, any affiliated issuer, any of the issuer's directors, officers, general partners, beneficial owners of 10% or more of any class of its equity securities, any of the issuer's promoters presently connected with the issuer in any capacity, any underwriter of the securities to be offered or any partner, director or officer of such underwriter:

(a) within the last five years, has filed a registration statement which is the subject of a currently effective registration stop order entered by any state securities administrator or the United States Securities and Exchange Commission;

(b) within the last five years, has been convicted of any criminal offense in connection with the offer, purchase or sale of any security, or involving fraud or deceit;

(c) is currently subject to any state or federal administrative enforcement order or judgment, entered within the last five years, finding fraud or deceit in connection with the purchase or sale of any security; or

(d) is currently subject to any order, judgment or decree of any court of competent jurisdiction, entered within the last five years, temporarily, preliminarily or permanently restraining or enjoining such party from engaging in or continuing to engage in any conduct or practice involving fraud or deceit in connection with the purchase or sale of any security.

(2) Subparagraph (D) (1) shall not apply if:

(a) the party subject to the disqualification is licensed or registered to conduct securities related business in the state in which the order, judgment or decree creating the disqualification was entered against such party;

(b) before the first offer under this exemption, the state securities administrator, or the court or regulatory authority that entered the order, judgment, or decree, waives the disqualification; or

(c) the issuer establishes that it did not know and in the exercise of reasonable care, based on a factual inquiry, could not have known that a disqualification existed under this paragraph.

(E) (1) A general announcement of the proposed offering may be made by any means.

    (2) The general announcement shall include only the following information, unless additional information is specifically permitted by the [Administrator]:

        (a) The name, address and telephone number of the issuer of the securities;

        (b) The name, a brief description and price (if known) of any security to be issued;

        (c) A brief description of the business of the issuer in 25 words or less;

        (d) The type, number and aggregate amount of securities being offered;

        (e) The name, address and telephone number of the person to contact for additional information; and

        (f) A statement that:

            (i) sales will only be made to accredited investors

            (ii) no money or other consideration is being solicited or will be accepted by way of this general announcement; and

            (iii) the securities have not been registered with or approved by any state securities agency or the U.S. Securities and Exchange Commission and are being offered and sold pursuant to an exemption from registration.

(F) The issuer, in connection with an offer, may provide information in addition to the general announcement under paragraph (E), if such information:

    (1) is delivered through an electronic database that is restricted to persons who have been prequalified as accredited investors; or

(2) is delivered after the issuer reasonably believes that the prospective purchaser is an accredited investor.

(G) No telephone solicitation shall be permitted unless prior to placing the call, the issuer reasonably believes that the prospective purchaser to be solicited is an accredited investor.

(H) Dissemination of the general announcement of the proposed offering to persons who are not accredited investors shall not disqualify the issuer from claiming the exemption under this rule.

(I) The issuer shall file with the [Commission/Division] a notice of transaction, a consent to service of process, a copy of the general announcement, and a [$fee/fee language] within 15 days after the first sale in this state.

CHAPTER 8

REGULATION A:
THE $5 MILLION OFFERING

egulation A is an exemption from registration requirements of the federal Securities Act of 1933. Complying with Regulation A does not exempt the company from having to meet state securities law requirements. Do not assume that because you have qualified your company's offering under Regulation A, that you can sell it in any state you want. There is little comfort in being arrested by the state police instead of the FBI.

Regulation A offerings are exempt from federal registration, but not from federal review. You must submit an offering statement to the SEC. You must wait for comments and comply with such comments prior to the SEC declaring the offering statement effective. In this respect, there is very little difference between a traditional IPO registered with the SEC and a Regulation A offering. The primary advantages of a Regulation A over a registered offering are:

- You can "test the waters" prior to going to the expense of preparing the offering statement (where permitted by state law.

- Audited financial statements are not required for federal review, unless otherwise available (however, states may still require audited financials to satisfy state securities laws).

- Less disclosure is required.

- You can use a question-and-answer format in the offering circular.

TESTING THE WATERS

The major advantage of the Regulation A offering is that you can determine if there is any investor interest prior to incurring significant legal, accounting, and printing costs. Unlike a registered offering, you may solicit indications of interest prior to preparing or filing a Regulation A offering statement with the SEC.

This testing-the-waters rule permits the company to publish or deliver a simple written document or make a scripted radio or television broadcast to determine if there is investor interest. The company can say anything it wishes in the test-the-waters document or script, with two exceptions:

- The document or script cannot violate the anti-fraud laws.

- The document or script must contain certain required disclosures.

The written document or script of the broadcast must identify the chief executive officer of the company and identify briefly and in general its business and products. The document or script must also state that no money is being solicited and, if sent, will not be accepted. Moreover, the document or script must indicate that an indication of interest involves no obligation or commitment of any kind by the investor and that no sales will be made until a completed offering circular is delivered.

The inability to legally bind investors, or to even escrow their money, is a serious drawback to the utility of the test-the-waters rule. A period of three or more months may pass between the date the investors express their interest until the date the complete offering circular has cleared the SEC and become available for distribution. Investors who initially express an interest in the investment may change their minds in the interim.

The utility of using radio, television, or newspaper marketing is also questionable. Traditionally, securities are sold by personal recommendation of brokers, friends, barbers, and the like. Investors typically follow these recommendations because they are theoretically given privately to the proposed customer. The customer has a sense of being favored with exclusive information not available to the public. The public nature of radio, television, or newspaper marketing may detract from the investor appeal of the company's securities.

Despite these handicaps, the ability to solicit indications of interest without incurring major expense can be very useful. The rule permits any written document provided to the potential investor to contain a coupon, returnable to the company. The coupon would reveal the name, address, and telephone number of the prospective investor. This permits the accumulation of a potential investor list, which can be useful after the offering circular has cleared the SEC.

Once the company submits the written document or script to the SEC, the company can orally communicate with the potential investor. This permits a sales pitch by telephone. Obviously, all communications are subject to the anti-fraud provisions of federal and state securities laws.

Any solicitation to purchase a security must satisfy state as well as federal securities laws. You must check with the state in which any offer is to be made to see if testing the waters is legal. If an investor who lives in Michigan is vacationing in Maine when you solicit the investor, you must check securities laws of both Michigan and Maine.

Apart from testing-the-waters rules, the rules relating to when offers and sales of securities under a Regulation A offering may be made are similar to those applicable to a traditional IPO.

WHO CAN FILE UNDER REGULATION A?

The following are the major requirements for any company that wishes to file a Regulation A offering statement:

- The company must be organized in the United States or Canada.
- The company must not be a public company (it must not file reports under Section 13 or 15(d) of the Securities Exchange Act of 1934).
- The company must not be a development stage company that either has no specific business plan or purpose or has indicated that its business plan is to merge with an unidentified company.

It should be noted that development stage companies that do have a specific business plan (other than merging with some unidentified company) do qualify for Regulation A.

BAD BOY DISQUALIFICATION

Rule 262 of Regulation A contains a "bad boy" provision disqualifying certain companies from filing under Regulation

A. The provision is waivable by the SEC upon a showing of good cause. The bad boy provision is very broad and denies use of Regulation A in the following situations, among others:

- If any director, officer, 10 percent shareholder, promoter, underwriter, or any partner, director, or officer of an underwriter:
  - was convicted within 10 years prior to filing of certain felonies or misdemeanors relating generally to securities
  - is subject to a court, SEC, or U.S. postal service order enjoining certain activities relating to securities or use of the mails to make false representations
  - is suspended or expelled from membership in certain securities associations
- If the company, or any of its predecessors, or any affiliated issuer, or any underwriter have had certain problems with the SEC or others within the past five years

HOW MUCH MONEY CAN BE RAISED?

Your company may raise a maximum of $5,000,000 in cash and other consideration under Regulation A. In computing the $5,000,000 figure, you must subtract the aggregate offering price for all securities sold within 12 months before the start of the Regulation A offering. Thus, you may raise a maximum of $5,000,000 every 12 months (plus the time necessary to offer and sell the securities).

Regulation A also permits the receipt of up to $1,500,000 in cash or other consideration by all selling securityholders. However, your company may not make affiliate resales if it has not had net income from continuing operations in at least one of its last two fiscal years.

You must subtract the amount sold by selling securi-tyholders in computing the $5,000,000 limit. Thus, if sell-ing securityholders sell $1,500,000 of their securities, the company can only sell $3,500,000 during the relevant 12-month period.

There are complicated rules for computing the $5,000,000 limit, particularly the "integration" rules. For example, securities sold in a private placement within six months after the completion of the Regulation A offering may have to be integrated with the Regulation A, thereby destroying the exemption. An experienced securities lawyer can assist you in navigating these complicated rules.

OFFERING STATEMENT AND OFFERING CIRCULAR

You file a Regulation A offering statement with the SEC's national office in Washington, DC. The Regulation A offering statement is analogous to a registration state-ment for a fully registered offering. The Regulation A offering circular is analogous to the prospectus, which you would include in a registration statement for a fully registered offering.

The offering circular must include a balance sheet as of the end of the most recent fiscal year and statements of income, cash flows, and other stockholders' equity for each of the two fiscal years preceding the date of the bal-ance sheet. You must prepare financial statements in accordance with generally accepted accounting principles in the United States, but these do not need to be audited; however, if audited financial statements are available, you must provide them.

The company has the option of preparing the offering circular in a question-and-answer format. If the company has audited financial statements and does not need to test the waters, the company should consider the alternative of filing a Form SB-1. The use of a Form SB-1, which registers securities under the 1933 Act (versus the Regulation A exemption), may actually make it easier to qualify the offering under state securities laws.

Appendix 5 contains excerpts from a Regulation A offering circular prepared in the question-and-answer format and filed by Real Goods Trading Corporation with the Securities and Exchange Commission.

OUTLINE OF REGULATION A

A. *Overview*

1. This regulation grants an exemption from the registration provisions of the 1933 Act for public offerings of securities of no more than $5 million in a 12-month period, including no more than $1.5 million in non-issuer resales.

2. The nonfinancial portions of the Regulation A offering circular, which is included in the Regulation A offering statement, can be prepared in a question-and-answer format.

3. Except as provided by the test-the-waters provisions, no offers may be made until a Regulation A offering statement is filed with the SEC and no sales may be made until the offering statement has been qualified and an offering circular is delivered.

4. Pursuant to the test-the-waters provisions, an issuer may obtain indications of interest in a proposed offering prior to filing an offering statement; however, no solicitation or acceptance of money nor any commitment to purchase is permitted until

the offering statement is qualified. Copies of any written document must be submitted to the SEC.

5. The company and its controlling persons remain liable for material misstatements and omissions in the offering statement or the offering circular.

B. Issuer and Offering Requirements

1. The issuer:

   a. Must be organized in the United States or Canada

   b. Must neither be a reporting company nor an investment company

   c. Must not be a development stage company that either has no specific business plan or purpose, or has indicated that its business plan is to merge with an unidentified company or companies

   d. May not be issuing fractional undivided interests in oil or gas rights or similar interests in other mineral rights

   e. Must not be disqualified because of administrative or court orders as set forth in Rule 262

   Note: Rule 262 provides that if the issuer, any of its predecessors or any affiliated issuer, any of its directors, officers, general partners, or 10 percent equity owners, any promoter, any underwriter or partner, director, or officer of such underwriter are subject to certain specified civil, criminal, or administrative actions the exemption provided by Regulation A will not be available. The Rule provides that the SEC, upon a showing of good cause, may waive the disqualification provisions.

2. The aggregate amount offered and sold in reliance on the Regulation A exemption may not exceed $5 million in any 12-month period. Not more than

$1.5 million of such amount may be offered and sold by selling securityholders and no affiliate resales are permitted if the issuer has not had net income from continuing operations in at least one of its last two fiscal years.

Note: (1) In computing the aggregate amount offered, offers and sales made in the preceding 12 months not in reliance on Regulation A need not be included.

(2) If securities are offered for both cash and noncash consideration, the offering price should be based on the cash price. If the securities are not offered for cash, the offering price should be based on the value of consideration as established by bona fide sales of that consideration or, in the absence of sales, on the fair value as determined by an accepted standard.

3. Integration

a. There is a specific safe-harbor provision relating to integration that states that offers and sales made in reliance on Regulation A will not be integrated with any prior offers or sales. It further provides that there will be no integration with subsequent offers or sales that are (1) registered under the 1933 Act, (2) made in reliance on Rule 701 (stock option plans and certain other compensatory benefit plans) or Regulation S (foreign sales), (3) made pursuant to an employee benefit plan, or (4) made more than six months after the Regulation A offering is completed.

b. If the safe-harbor rule does not apply to particular offers or sales, such offers and sales still may not be integrated, depending upon the particular facts and circumstances. See Securities Act Release No. 4552 (November 6, 1962).

C. Offers Prior to and After Filing and Qualification of Offering Statement

1. Prior to Filing; Test-the-Waters Rule

   a. Prior to the filing of the offering statement, an issuer may publish or deliver a written document or make scripted radio or television broadcasts to determine whether there is any interest in the securities intended to be offered. A copy of this document should be submitted to the SEC's main office in Washington, DC (Attn: Office of Small Business Review).

   b. The written document or script of the broadcast must:

      (1) State that no money or other consideration is being solicited and, if sent in response, will not be accepted

      (2) State that no sales of the securities will be made or commitment to purchase accepted until delivery of an offering circular that includes complete information about the issuer and the offering

      (3) State that an indication of interest made by a prospective investor involves no obligation or commitment of any kind

      (4) Identify the chief executive officer of the issuer and identify briefly and in general its business and products

   c. No sales may be made until 20 days after the last publication or delivery of the document or radio or television broadcast.

   d. Any written document may include a coupon, returnable to the issuer, indicating interest in a potential offering.

   e. If an issuer has a bona fide change of intention and decides to register an offering after using the test-the-waters process, it must wait at least 30 days before filing a registration statement with the SEC.

2. After Filing and Before Qualification: After seven copies of the offering statement have been filed with the SEC's office in Washington, DC, the following activities are permissible:

   a. Oral offers may be made and copies of the preliminary offering circular may be delivered to prospective investors. The preliminary offering circular must be clearly marked as such, must contain substantially the same information as the final offering circular, and must indicate that no securities may be sold until a final offering circular is delivered.

   b. Advertisements indicating only (1) the name of the issuer, (2) the amount being offered and the offering price, (3) the general type of the issuer's business, and (4) the general character and location of its property may be used, if they state from whom an offering circular may be obtained.

3. After Qualification: After the offering statement has been qualified, oral offers and written offers, if accompanied or preceded by an offering circular, may be made if a preliminary or final offering circular is furnished to the purchaser at least 48 hours prior to the mailing of the confirmation and a final offering circular is delivered with the confirmation, unless it has previously been delivered.

D. *Information Required to Be Disclosed in Offering Circular*

1. The offering circular must include a balance sheet as of the end of the most recent fiscal year and statements of income, cash flows, and other stockholders'

equity for each of the two fiscal years preceding the date of the balance sheet.

2. For nonfinancial disclosure, the issuer may choose from three options:

   a. A question-and-answer format substantially similar to the SCOR document used by many states to register securities for small offerings may be used by a corporate issuer.

   b. The traditional Regulation A format, which is similar to a prospectus used in a registered offering, may be used by any issuer.

   c. Any issuer may choose to furnish the information required by Part I of Form SB-2.

3. The offering circular, which is a part of the offering statement, must include the narrative and financial information required by Form 1-A in a clear, concise, and understandable manner, and the cover page of every offering circular must include a legend indicating the SEC has not passed upon the merits or given its approval to any securities offered.

4. The offering circular must be signed by the issuer, its chief executive officer, chief financial officer, a majority of the members of its board of directors, and any selling securityholder.

5. Where the offering circular is distributed through electronic media, issues may satisfy legibility requirements applicable to printed documents by presenting all required information in a format readily communicated to investors.

E. Filing and Qualification of Offering Statement

An offering statement is qualified without SEC action 20 days after filing, unless a delaying notification is included providing that it must only be qualified by order of the SEC.

F. Sales

No sale of securities can be made until:

1. The Form 1-A offering statement has been qualified
2. A preliminary offering circular or final offering is furnished to the prospective purchaser at least 48 hours prior to the mailing of the confirmation of sale to that person
3. A final offering circular is delivered to the purchaser with the confirmation of sale, unless it has been delivered to that person at an earlier time

G. Sales Material and Subsequent Reports Regarding Sales and Use of Proceeds

1. Advertisements and other sales material may be used as indicated in Section C of this outline. Copies of such material should be filed with the office of the SEC where the offering statement was filed when the material is first published or delivered.
2. The issuer should report information concerning the amount of securities sold and the use of proceeds every six months after the offering statement has been qualified until substantially all of the proceeds have been applied or within 30 days after the completion of the offering, whichever is the latest event.

H. Substantial Good Faith Compliance Defense

1. Rule 260 provides that a failure to comply with a term, condition, or requirement of Regulation A

will not result in the loss of the exemption for any offer or sale to a particular individual, if the person relying on the exemption establishes:

a. The condition violated was not intended to protect the complaining individual

b. The failure to comply was insignificant to the offering as a whole (issuer requirements, aggregate offering limitations, and the requirements to file an offering statement and deliver an offering circular are always significant to the offering as a whole)

c. A good faith and reasonable attempt was made to comply with all of the requirements of Regulation A

2. Rule 260 preserves the SEC's right to pursue any failure in compliance, regardless of significance.

CHAPTER 9

SCOR: THE $1 MILLION DO-IT-YOURSELF REGISTERED OFFERING

Most states, officially or unofficially, permit the use of a simplified question-and-answer format to register securities under state securities laws when raising funds pursuant to SEC Rule 504, Regulation A, or so-called intrastate offerings.

This simplified form is the SCOR form (small corporate offering registration) or Form U-7 (also known as ULOR or uniform limited offering registration). It is also called Registration Form U-7.

The purpose of the SCOR form is to reduce the legal and accounting costs of preparing extensively documented reports. In general, the SCOR form has been praised as being user friendly. Many corporate executives have filed this form without incurring significant outside professional costs.

After the SCOR registration is effective, the company may generally solicit investors, whether or not they are accredited investors. Upon completion of the SCOR offering, a trading market can develop. This contrasts with the accredited investor offering in which most states that have adopted this exemption do not permit trading for at least a year.

The states, in conjunction with the American Bar Association's State Regulation of Securities Committee, developed the SCOR offering to facilitate raising capital by small businesses. The SCOR offering permits a company to raise $1,000,000 within approximately 12 months without federal review of the offering documents. It only requires a state or a regional review.

Theoretically, the small businessperson can respond to the SCOR question-and-answer format himself or herself, or with the advice of a general legal practitioner, and does not need the assistance of a securities law specialist. The SCOR form is then filed with the state or states in which the securities are to be sold.

This theory is somewhat questionable since the SCOR form is not exempt from the antifraud provisions of federal and state securities laws. As noted, these antifraud provisions can impose personal liability on the control persons of the company, including its directors and officers.

In addition, the SCOR form contains a number of sophisticated questions that may be beyond the knowledge of the company's officers or their general counsel. For example, question 45 of the form is as follows:

"Describe any other material factors, either adverse or favorable, that will or could affect the Company or its business (for example, discuss any defaults under major contracts, any breach of bylaw provisions, etc.) or which are necessary to make any other information in this Disclosure Document not misleading or incomplete."

The answer to this question requires a knowledge of what facts or circumstances the courts view as "material." Small business owners proceed at their own peril if they try to answer these questions without the assistance of a securities law specialist. It should also be noted that both federal and state securities laws provide for criminal sanctions for flagrant violations.

In light of these considerations, some companies are using sophisticated law firms to help prepare the SCOR form. The average cost of preparing and filing a SCOR form is $30,000.

It is true, however, that the exemption of the SCOR offering from federal registration by Rule 504 (discussed in the next section) helps minimize the costs of the offering. Also, the practice in this area has evolved into a system where state examiners play a large role in assisting companies with their SCOR document. State regional review of the SCOR document permits review and comment by only one state even though the offering is made in several states.

FEDERAL REGISTRATION EXEMPTION

Rule 504 under the 1933 Act provides an exemption from the registration provisions of federal law for certain offerings up to $1,000,000. The registration exemption, however, does not also exempt the offering from the antifraud and personal liability provisions of the law (as noted previously).

Rule 504 permits a qualified nonpublic company to raise up to $1 million, less the aggregate offering price of all securities sold by the company within 12 months before the start of and during the Rule 504 offering (subject to certain exceptions). Rule 504 does not require any specific disclosure to be made, and the offering circulars (prospectuses) are not subject to federal regulatory review.

More importantly, SEC Rule 504 does not prohibit a general solicitation of investors to market the offering if a SCOR registration is required or if the state permits a general solicitation of accredited investors (see Chapter 7). Thus, after a SCOR registration, marketing may

be accomplished by cold telephone calls and radio, television, and newspaper advertising without violating the
registration provisions of the 1933 Act. This contrasts
with the marketing of private placements that prohibit
general solicitations.

Of course, the company must satisfy the requirements
of state securities laws before the use of a general solicitation. However, if your state requires a SCOR registration,
the states generally prohibit any general solicitation *prior*
to the clearance of the SCOR form. This contrasts with the
Rule 504/accredited investor offering (see Chapter 7),
which permits general solicitation of accredited investors
without prior clearance from state regulators.

The business must file a Form D with the SEC not
later than 15 days after the first sale of securities. The
date of filing is the date on which the business mails the
notice by registered or certified mail to the SEC's principal office in Washington, DC, or the date the SEC otherwise receives it.

STATE SECURITIES LAWS

Although Rule 504 does not require any specific disclosure to investors, most state securities laws do.

Eligibility to Use SCOR

Registrations covered in the SCOR Policy Statement
dated April 28, 1996 must meet the following requirements. The issuer must:

- be a corporation or centrally managed limited liability company organized under the law of the
  United States or Canada, or any state, province or

territory or possession thereof, or the District of Columbia, and have its principal place of business in one of the foregoing;

- not be subject to the reporting requirements of Section 13 or 15(d) of the Securities Exchange Act of 1934;
- not be an investment company registered or required to be registered under the Investment Company Act of 1940;
- not be engaged in or propose to be engaged in petroleum exploration and production, mining, or other extractive industries;
- not be a development stage company that either has no specific business plan or purpose or has indicated that its business plan is to engage in merger or acquisition with an unidentified company or companies or other entity or person; and
- not be disqualified under other provisions of the Policy Statement.
- The offering price for common stock or common ownership interests (hereinafter, collectively referred to as common stock), the exercise price for options, warrants or rights to common stock, or the conversion price for securities convertible into common stock, must be greater or equal to US $1.00 per share or unit of interest. The issuer must agree with the Administrator that it will not split its common stock, or declare a stock dividend for two years after the effective date of the registration if such action has the effect of lowering the price below US $1.00.
- Commissions, fees or other remuneration for soliciting any prospective purchaser in connection with the offering in the state are only paid to persons who, if required to be registered or licensed, the

issuer believes, and has reason to believe, are appropriately registered or licensed in the state.

- Financial statements must be prepared in accordance with either US or Canadian generally accepted accounting principles. If appropriate, a reconciliation note should be provided. If the Company has not conducted significant operations, statements of receipts and disbursements shall be included in lieu of statements of income. Interim financial statements may be unaudited. All other financial statements must be audited by independent certified public accountants, provided, however, that if each of the following four conditions are met, such financial statements in lieu of being audited may be reviewed by independent certified public accountants in accordance with the Accounting and Review Service Standards promulgated by the American Institute of Certified Public Accountants or the Canadian equivalent:

  1. the Company shall not have previously sold securities through an offering involving the general solicitation of prospective investors by means of advertising, mass mailing, public meetings, "cold call" telephone solicitation, or any other method directed toward the public;

  2. the Company has not been previously required under federal, state, provincial or territorial securities laws to provide audited financial statements in connection with any sale of its securities;

  3. the aggregate amount of all previous sales of securities by the Company (exclusive of debt financing with banks and similar commercial lenders) shall not exceed US $1,000,000; and

  4. the amount of the present offering does not exceed US $1,000,000.

- The offering must be made in compliance with Rule 504 of Regulation D, Regulation A, or Rule 147 (intrastate offering) of the Securities Act of 1933. The issuer must comply with the General Instructions to SCOR in Part I of the NASAA SCOR Issuer's Manual.

Offers and Sales

The business cannot offer or sell securities pursuant to the SCOR offering until the state declares the registration effective. The business cannot make preeffective offers under the SCOR offering form. Thus, there is no testing the waters, as with Regulation A.

Escrow

If the proposed business of the company requires a minimum amount of proceeds to commence business, the SCOR form requires an escrow of all proceeds received from investors until the company raises the minimum amount. The escrow must be with a bank or a savings and loan association or other similar depository institution.

The Regulation A offering does not require an escrow. However, state securities officials could still require such an escrow under the Regulation A offering in order to permit offers and sales in a particular state.

Instructions and Form

Appendix 6 is Form U-7, which contains the SCOR form adopted in 1999. Form U-7 and a helpful Issuer's Manual can be downloaded from the Web site of the North American Securities Administrators Association (*www.NASAA.org*).

The Web site also contains other useful information. Note that the SCOR form and the Regulation A question-and-answer form are very similar. In fact, the Regulation A question-and-answer form was based in part on the SCOR form. Therefore, the Regulation A offering circular contained in Appendix 5 illustrates the method of answering similar SCOR questions.

CHAPTER 10

MERGERS WITH PUBLICLY HELD SHELL CORPORATIONS AND SPIN-OFFS

S hell mergers and spin-offs provide a company with the opportunity to create a public market place for its stock. A public market place facilitates raising additional capital and helps avoid the "illiquidity discount" applicable to the valuation of private companies.

A company does not automatically raise capital because its stock has become publicly traded by reason of a shell merger or spin-off. Therefore, companies that consider this nontraditional route should try to have investors lined up to invest in the company the moment its stock becomes publicly traded.

Dollar Time Group, Inc. (discount stores) and Prins Recycling Corp. (recycling) had private offerings under Rule 506/Section 4(2), which closed simultaneously with their shell mergers. This permitted these companies to negotiate better terms for the private offering than would otherwise have been possible.

Many major underwriters will decline to handle a traditional IPO that raises less than $20 million. This is partly due to the lack of institutional interest in these smaller IPOs. Another reason is that many major underwriters cannot make enough underwriting profit from these smaller IPOs to justify their effort and risk. At least one major underwriter has sought to solve this problem by doing private placement/shell mergers where less than $20 million in capital is required. The underwriter effort and risk in these private placement/shell mergers is sufficiently less than in a traditional IPO.

Typically, simultaneously with the shell merger or spin-off, a company registers the stock of the merged or spun-off company under Section 12 of the 1934 Act, and the merged or spun-off company becomes a reporting company (see Chapter 12).

SHELL MERGERS

There are a number of promoters who acquire or form publicly held shell corporations. These entities are called shells because they conduct no business whatsoever, but they do have a large number of shareholders. Some of these shells have significant capital, but many shells have no capital whatsoever. Some shells have tax loss carryovers from a prior business.

To become part of a shell, your corporation typically merges into a publicly held shell corporation. Prior to the merger you and the shell's promoter negotiate a percentage of the shell's stock that you would receive in the merger in exchange for the stock of your company, which you personally own. The percentage you receive depends upon whether the shell has capital or not, and the relative valuation of your company. If the shell has no capital, the shell stock you receive in the merger would typically equal 85 to 95 percent of the total outstanding stock.

In the Muriel Siebert Capital Markets, Inc./J. Michaels, Inc., merger, Muriel Siebert, the sole shareholder of the private company, received 97.5 percent of J. Michaels, Inc. stock, and the public shareholders of J. Michaels, Inc. received the remaining 2.5 percent.

The promoters of the shell typically have a relationship with broker-dealers who make a market in the shell stock after the merger and assist in raising additional capital. The promoters of the shell typically receive warrants and stock in the merged company. The promoter's stock ownership is included in the public stock ownership after the merger shown in Figure 10.1. If the shell has cash or other assets, the ownership by the public and promoters after the merger increases proportionately.

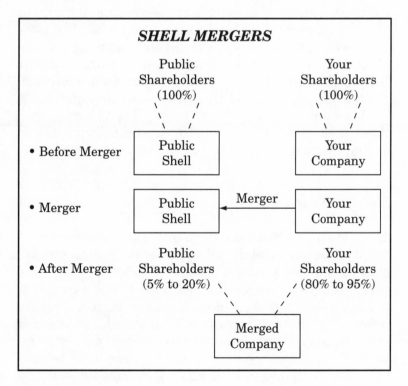

FIGURE 10.1

After the merger, your company should not suffer the same illiquidity discount that applies to a privately held company. Numerex Corp., currently traded on the NASDAQ National Market, is an example of a company that went public through a shell merger and then raised over $40 million in a traditional IPO.

Advantages

There are four major advantages of the shell merger. It is a less expensive method of going public, and if the shell has capital, you will know before the shell merger precisely how much equity you must give up for that capital. You may recall that in the traditional IPO, you do not have assurance of knowing how much capital you will actually receive until the effective date of the IPO, after you have already spent substantial sums. After the merger, the existence of a public trading market in your company's stock is very useful in attracting additional capital, since the market provides immediate liquidity for the investor. Finally, if the shell has a tax loss carryover, that carryover, subject to significant limitations, may be available to shelter the taxable income of your business.

Disadvantages

There are also major disadvantages of the shell merger. If the shell has no capital, you still have no assurance until after the merger as to how much capital you can raise and what valuation the market will give to your company. Some shells are promoted by less than the best quality broker-dealers, who typically maintain large spreads between the Bid and Asked prices for your stock (enlarging their profits or commissions). There is a certain stigma to shell mergers, which may prevent financing by some of the traditional capital sources; however, your company may not have qualified for financing by such traditional sources even if no shell merger ever occurred. As a final consideration, the shell may have undisclosed liabilities that your business will inherit.

Other Considerations

The depth of the public market after the shell merger is crucial to the success of any further capital raising efforts. If only one broker-dealer is making a market in the stock after the shell merger, investors will be rightfully leery of the market's liquidity. You should carefully investigate the background of the promoters of public shells prior to engaging in any shell merger. An ounce of prevention is worth a pound of cure.

As noted, the coupling of a private placement of securities (typically under Rule 506) with a shell merger is a useful device. The private placement permits the company to raise capital simultaneously with the shell merger. The shell merger creates a liquid market for the private placement securities. As a result, the investors typically can justify a higher valuation for the company since there is no need for an illiquidity discount.

SPIN-OFFS

There are two types of spin-offs: subsidiary spin-offs and spin-offs of unaffiliated company stock.

Subsidiary Spin-Offs

Spin-offs of subsidiaries or divisions of existing publicly held companies are a frequent occurrence. For example, the stock of GFC Financial Corp., a subsidiary of Dial Corp., was spun-off to the Dial stockholders. GFC Financial stock thereby became publicly held by the Dial stockholders and publicly traded. Also, the same market makers and broker-dealer network for Dial stock became available to GFC Financial and its new public stockholders. Quaker Oats spun off the stock of Fisher Price, the fourth largest toy company in the United States, to the shareholders of Quaker Oats.

These spin-offs are motivated by various considerations, such as:

- The desire to remove loss operations from the parent's financial statements
- The desire to permit investors in the parent to invest solely in one industry (a so-called pure stock play)
- The desire to create value for the parent's shareholders

The spin-off can be free of federal income taxes to the shareholders if certain requirements are satisfied.

Another form of spin-off involves the issuance of tracking stock. Tracking subsidiary stock is typically a special class of common stock issued by a parent corporation. It should provide a return on investment linked to the performance of a subsidiary. General Motors Class E and H shares are an example.

Spin-Offs of Unaffiliated Companies

An unaffiliated company can create a spin-off in two steps:

1. A small percentage of the stock of the company desiring to be spun-off is given to a publicly held sponsoring company without charge.
2. The sponsoring company declares a dividend in that stock payable to the shareholders of the sponsoring company.

The dividend makes the spun-off company a publicly traded company. Its public shareholders are the shareholders of the sponsoring company. With luck, the stock of the spun-off company will qualify for the NASDAQ Stock Market or the national stock exchanges. Ideally, market makers and other broker-dealers interested in the stock of the sponsoring company will also become interested in the stock of the spun-off company.

Spinning off the stock of an unaffiliated company is relatively rare. The primary reason is the sponsoring company's concern for its image and legal liability. Should the spun-off company fail, the sponsoring company may have unhappy shareholders. This may be true even though the shareholders of the sponsoring company did not pay a cent for the spun-off stock!

There are several SEC interpretations that indicate the sponsoring company may be a "statutory underwriter" of the spun-off company's stock. As a result, the sponsoring company may have legal liability for material misstatements or omissions made by the spun-off company.

To avoid the legal liability as a statutory underwriter, the sponsoring company should acquire the stock to be spun-off without a view to its distribution. Typically, a one- or two-year period between the date of acquisition of the stock by the sponsoring company and the date of the spin-off will avoid statutory underwriter liability.

The SEC's position on underwriter liability seriously undermines the willingness of civic-minded sponsoring companies to assist smaller, local start-up companies to become publicly held. It is hoped that, in the proper factual circumstances, the SEC will reconsider its position and permit these socially desirable spin-offs.

CHAPTER 11

TRADING ON THE NASDAQ STOCK MARKET AND NATIONAL SECURITIES EXCHANGES

I t is an important marketing tool for your IPO if you can state in your prospectus or offering circular that you intend to have the company's common stock listed for trading on a national securities exchange or on the NASDAQ Stock Market. The major places your company can trade its stock are:

- The New York Stock Exchange
- The NASDAQ Stock Market (NASDAQ)—the listing may be for either the NASDAQ National Market or the NASDAQ SmallCap Market
- The American Stock Exchange
- Other national and foreign stock exchanges

The NASDAQ Stock Market refers to the electronic inter-dealer quotation system operated by NASDAQ, Inc., a subsidiary of the National Association of Securities Dealers, Inc. (NASD). To qualify for the NASDAQ National Market (NM), a security must first qualify for inclusion in the NASDAQ Stock Market, then meet special requirements for designation as an NM security, which are discussed later.

If your company's stock does not qualify for any of the preceding, it will be quoted on either the NASDAQ Bulletin Board (Bulletin Board) or the so-called Pink Sheets. Both the Bulletin Board and the Pink Sheets are really only quotation media. In order to purchase or sell a Bulletin Board or Pink Sheet stock, a telephone call must be placed to the trading desk of the quoting broker or dealer. In contrast, a buy or sell order for a security quoted on the NASDAQ Stock Market can be placed automatically on the quotation system.

The Bulletin Board is an automated quotation service provided by NASDAQ for NASD members. Quotations only appear on the Bulletin Board when placed there by an NASD member. Recently adopted rules require Bulletin Board securities to be registered under Section 12 of the Securities Exchange Act of 1934 and, therefore, to be subject to the reporting requirements of that law.

The Pink Sheets, which obtain their name from the color of the paper on which they are distributed, are an inter-dealer quotation service provided by the National Quotation Bureau, Inc. Like the Bulletin Board, Pink Sheet quotations only appear when a broker or dealer inserts a "Bid" or "Asked" price in the Pink Sheets. The National Quotation Bureau, Inc. recently electronically automated the Pink Sheets, similar to the Bulletin Board, and continues the paper form of the Pink Sheets on a monthly basis. The Pink Sheets stocks are the least actively traded securities and are not required to be reporting companies.

Last sale prices are published for stock traded on the national stock exchanges, the NASDAQ Stock Market, and the Bulletin Board. However, only Bid and Asked prices are presently available for Pink Sheet stocks.

Both the NASDAQ Stock Market and the national securities exchanges charge listing fees and annual fees.

The New York Stock Exchange has the highest original listing fees, but not necessarily the highest annual fees. Although the New York Stock Exchange is still the most prestigious market, you must weigh the expense of original listing on that market against that prestige.

The listing and annual fees for the NASDAQ NM and the NASDAQ SmallCap Market appear at the end of this chapter.

INITIAL LISTING REQUIREMENTS

Tables 11.1 contain the listing criteria for the NASDAQ NM, the NASDAQ SmallCap Market, the New York Stock Exchange, and the American Stock Exchange. The table is current as of September 1999. All the exchanges and the NASDAQ continue to compete for listings from which they derive revenue. Accordingly, the listing standards are constantly being revised to reflect competitive conditions as well as changes in the market place.

OVER-THE-COUNTER MARKET VS. EXCHANGES

The over-the-counter (OTC) market encompasses all nonexchange traded securities. It is the second largest market in the world. The only larger market is the New York Stock Exchange. The OTC market has three distinct subgroups of securities:

- Those quoted on the NASDAQ Stock Market (either NM or NASDAQ SmallCap)
- Those quoted on the Bulletin Board
- Those quoted in the Pink Sheets

The OTC market is a dealer market. One or more dealers making markets in any   *(continued on page 168)*

TABLES 11.1
SUMMARY OF FINANCIAL REQUIREMENTS FOR INITIAL LISTING

The NASDAQ National Market

Requirements	Listing Standard 1	Listing Standard 2	Listing Standard 3
Net Tangible Assets[1]	$6 million	$18 million	N/A
Market Capitalization[2]	N/A	N/A	$75 million *or*
Total Assets	N/A	N/A	$75 million *and*
Total Revenue	N/A	N/A	$75 million
Pretax Income (in latest fiscal year or 2 of last 3 fiscal years)	$1 million	N/A	N/A
Public Float (shares)[3]	1.1 million	1.1 million	1.1 million
Operating History	N/A	2 years	N/A
Market Value of Public Float	$8 million	$18 million	$20 million
Minimum Bid Price	$5	$5	$5
Shareholders (round lot holders)[4]	400	400	400
Market Makers	3	3	4
Corporate Governance	Yes	Yes	Yes

1 Net tangible assets means total assets (excluding goodwill) minus total liabilities.

2 For initial or continued listing under standard 3, a company must satisfy one of the following to be in compliance: either the market capitalization requirement or the total assets *and* the total revenue requirements.

3 Public float is defined as shares that are not held directly or indirectly by any officer or director of the issuer or by any other person who is the beneficial owner of more than 10 percent of the total shares outstanding.

4 Round lot holders are considered holders of 100 shares or more.

NASDAQ SmallCap Market

Requirements	Listing Standard
Net Tangible Assets[1]	$4 million
	or
Market Capitalization	$50 million
	or
Net Income (in latest fiscal year or 2 of last 3 fiscal years)	$750,000
Public Float (shares)[2]	1 million
Market Value of Public Float	$5 million
Minimum Bid Price	$4
Market Makers	3
Shareholders (round lot holders)[3]	300
Operating History[4]	1 year
	or
Market Capitalization	$50 million
Corporate Governance	Yes

1 For initial or continued listing, a company must satisfy one of the following to be in compliance: the net tangible asset requirement (net tangible assets means total assets, excluding goodwill, minus total liabilities), the market capitalization requirement, or the net income requirement.

2 Public float is defined as shares that are not held directly or indirectly by any officer or director of the issuer or by any other person who is the beneficial owner of more than 10 percent of the total shares outstanding.

3 Round lot holders are considered holders of 100 shares or more.

4 If operating history is less than one year, initial listing requires market capitalization of at least $50 million.

New York Stock Exchange

U.S. Standards

Domestic listing requirements call for minimum distribution of a company's shares within the United States. Distribution of shares can be attained through U.S. public offerings, acquisitions made in the United States, or by other similar means. Note that there are alternatives to the round lot holder and pretax earnings standards.

MINIMUM QUANTITATIVE STANDARDS: DISTRIBUTION AND SIZE CRITERIA

Round Lot Holders (A) (number of holders of a unit of trading— generally 100 shares)	2,000
or	
Total Shareholders	2,200
Together with	
Average Monthly Trading Volume (for the most recent 6 months)	100,000
or	
Total Shareholders	500
Together with	
Average Monthly Trading Volume (for the most recent 12 months)	1,000,000
Public Shares (B)	1,000,000
Market Value of Public Shares (B, C):	
Public Companies	$100,000,000
IPOs, Spin-offs, Carve-outs	$60,000,000

MINIMUM QUANTITATIVE STANDARDS: FINANCIAL CRITERIA

Earnings

Aggregate Pretax Earnings (D) over the last 3 years of $6,500,000 achievable as:

Most Recent Year	$2,500,000
Each of 2 Preceding Years	$2,000,000

or

Most Recent Year $4,500,000
  (all 3 years must be profitable)

or

Operating Cash Flow

For companies with not less than $500 million in global market capitalization and $200 million in revenues in the last 12 months

Aggregate for the 3 Years Operating Cash Flow (E) $25,000,000
  (each year must report a positive amount)

or

Global Market Capitalization

Revenues for Last Fiscal Year	$250,000,000
Average Global Market Capitalization (F)	$1,000,000,000
REITs (less than 3 years operating history) (B)	
Stockholders' Equity	$60,000,000
Funds (less than 3 years operating history) (B)	
Net Assets	$60,000,000

(A) The number of beneficial holders of stock held in "street name" are considered in addition to the holders of record. The Exchange will make any necessary check of such holdings that are in the name of Exchange member organizations.

(B) In connection with initial public offerings, the NYSE will accept an undertaking from the company's underwriter to ensure that the offering will meet or exceed the NYSE's standards.

(C) If a company either has a significant concentration of stock or changing market forces have adversely impacted the public market value of a company that otherwise would qualify for an Exchange listing, such that its public market value is no more than 10 percent below the minimum, the Exchange will consider stockholders' equity of $60 million or $100 million, as applicable, as an alternate measure of size.

(D) Pretax income is adjusted for various items as defined in the NYSE Listed Company Manual.

(E) Represents net cash provided by operating activities excluding the changes in working capital or in operating assets and liabilities, as adjusted for various items as defined in the NYSE Listed Company Manual.

(F) Average global market capitalization for already existing public companies is represented by the most recent six months of trading history. For IPOs, spin-offs, and carve-outs, it is represented by the valuation of the company as represented by, in the case of a spin-off, the distribution ratio as priced, or, in the case of an IPO/carve-out, the as-priced offering in relation to the total company's capitalization.

New York Stock Exchange: Non-U.S. Standards

Non-U.S. corporations may elect to qualify for listing under either the alternate listing standards for non-U.S. corporations or under the NYSE's domestic listing criteria. However, an applicant company must meet all of the criteria within the standards under which it seeks to qualify for listing.

Alternate Listing Standards

The alternate listing standards are designed to enable major non-U.S. corporations to list their shares on the New York Stock Exchange. The principal criteria focus on worldwide rather than U.S. distribution of an overseas company's shares and apply where there is a broad, liquid market for a company's shares in its country of origin.

Round Lot Holders . . . . 5,000 worldwide
(number of holders
of a unit of trading—
generally 100 shares)

Public Shares (B). . . . . 2.5 million worldwide

Public Market Value (B, C). . . . . $100 million worldwide

MINIMUM QUANTITATIVE STANDARDS: FINANCIAL CRITERIA

Earnings

Pretax Income Aggregate . . . . $100 million
(for the last 3 years)

> *Together with*

Minimum in Each   . . . . $ 25 million
of the 2 Most Recent Years

> *or*

Operating Cash Flow

For companies with Market Capitalization* (*Worldwide) not less than $500 million and revenues (in most recent 12 months) of $200 million.

Aggregate Cash Flow . . . . $100 million
(for last 3 years) (E)

> *Together with*

Minimum in Each   . . . . $25 million
of the 2 Most Recent Years

> *or*

Global Market Capitalization

Market Capitalization.................. $1 billion*
                                                    (*worldwide)

and

Revenue (most recent fiscal year) .... $250 million

(A) The number of beneficial holders of stock held in "street name" will be considered in addition to the holders of record. The Exchange will make any necessary check of such holdings that are in the name of Exchange member organizations.

(B) In connection with initial public offerings, the NYSE will accept an undertaking from the company's underwriter to ensure that the offering will meet or exceed the NYSE's standards.

(C) If a company either has a significant concentration of stock or changing market forces have adversely impacted the public market value of a company that otherwise would qualify for an Exchange listing, such that its public market value is no more than 10 percent below the minimum, the Exchange will consider stockholders' equity of $60 million or $100 million, as applicable, as an alternate measure of size.

(E) Represents net cash provided by operating activities excluding the changes in working capital or in operating assets and liabilities, as adjusted for various items as defined in the NYSE Listed Company Manual.

American Stock Exchange: U.S. Companies

Regular Financial Guidelines:

Pretax Income . . . . $750,000 latest fiscal
year or 2 of most recent
3 years

Market Value of Public Float . . . . $ 3,000,000

Price . . . . $ 3.00

Operating History . . . . —

Stockholders' Equity $4,000,000

Alternate Financial Guidelines

Pretax Income . . . . —

Market Value of Public Float $15,000,000

Price . . . . $ 3.00

Operating History . . . . 3 years

Stockholders' Equity $4,000,000

Distribution Guidelines
(applicable to regular and alternate guidelines)

Alternative 1

Public Float 500,000

Public Stockholders 800

Average Daily Volume . . . . —

Alternative 2

Public Float 1,000,000

Public Stockholders 400

Average Daily Volume . . . . —

Alternative 3

Public Float 500,000

Public Stockholders 400

Average Daily Volume 2,000

American Stock Exchange: International Companies

Regular Financial Guidelines

Pretax Income $750,000 latest fiscal year or 2 of most recent 3 years
Market Value of Public Float $3,000,000
Price $3.00
Operating History . . . . —
Stockholders' Equity $4,000,000

Alternate Financial Guidelines

Pretax Income . . . . —
Market Value of Public Float $15,000,000
Price $3.00
Operating History . . . . 3 years
Stockholders' Equity $4,000,000

Distribution Guidelines
(applicable to regular and alternate guidelines)

Alternative 1

    Public Float 500,000
    Public Stockholders. 800
    Average Daily Volume. . . . . —

Alternative 2

    Public Float 1,000,000
    Public Stockholders. 400
    Average Daily Volume. . . . . —

Alternative 3

    Public Float 500,000
    Public Stockholders. 400
    Average Daily Volume. 2,000

Alternative 4

    Public Float 1,000,000
                                          Worldwide
    Public Stockholders. 800
                                          Worldwide
    Average Daily Volume. . . . . —

(continued from page 159)
particular OTC stock enter quotations on either the NAS-
DAQ Stock Market, the Bulletin Board, or the Pink Sheets.
There is no single specialist in the stock of OTC companies
maintaining a book on such stocks. Likewise, there is no
auction of any OTC stock conducted by any specialist.

The market-makers compete with each other as to
the price at which they are prepared to buy (the Bid) and
the price at which they are prepared to sell (the Ask) the
securities for which they act as market-maker. The market-makers' revenues are the differences between the Bid
and the Ask prices. The NASDAQ Stock Market claims
that, on average, each security listed has approximately
11 market makers.

The stock exchanges trade securities in a continuous,
two-sided auction market. In this market, each security
trade on an exchange occurs at one designated place on
the floor of that exchange called a "post." At each post
there are one or more exchange members who are registered with that exchange as specialists in one or more
securities. The larger exchanges allocate each equity security to a single specialist. They award these specialists, in
effect, a monopoly right to make a market in that security
on the exchange floor. The specialist, in return, under-
takes certain responsibility. If other markets simultaneously trade the security (NASDAQ or other exchanges),
the specialist must compete with these other markets.

With respect to the securities for which they specialize, specialists perform the dual functions of brokers and
dealers. In the capacity of a broker, the specialist holds
and executes buy and sell orders for others. Generally
these orders are forwarded to the specialist by exchange
members. The orders may be *market* orders (to buy or sell
a security at the best current market price), but they are
usually *limit* orders (orders to buy or sell a security at a
specific price) or *stop* orders.

The primary mechanism used by the specialist to
handle limit and stop orders is the specialist's "book." The

specialist is the only broker who has the "book." Limit and stop orders are entered into the book in the sequence in which the specialist receives them with the appropriate order. The specialist usually charges a commission for this activity.

The specialist's second function is to act as a dealer to the extent necessary to maintain fair and orderly markets. As a dealer, the specialist is responsible for purchasing and selling securities in a manner that contributes to the maintenance of a fair and orderly auction market in the specialist's assigned security or group of securities.

WHAT IS BEST?

There is significant controversy over the relative merits of a dealer market (the NASDAQ Stock Market) vs. an auction market (the stock exchanges). The best market provides reasonable price stability for your company's stock and avoids excessive dealer mark-ups.

Theoretically, a specialist market should provide better protection against wild price fluctuations and unreasonable mark-ups. However, the specialist system (as did the NASDAQ Stock Market) operated inconsistently during the 1987 stock market crash. Many of the specialists were inadequately capitalized and could not provide price stability in the face of the wave of sell orders that occurred in October 1987. Since that time, there has been some improvement in the specialist system.

If your company is stuck with a poor specialist on an exchange, you may try to change the specialist or, alternatively, qualify your company's securities on SmallCap NASDAQ or NM. However, if only a small number of dealers make a market in your company's stock on SmallCap NASDAQ or NM, you are more likely to get better results from an exchange listing.

If a large number of well-capitalized dealers make a market in your company's stock on the NASDAQ Stock

Market, these markets can, as a result of dealer competition, provide reasonable protection against wild price gyrations or unreasonable dealer mark-ups.

In general, exchange specialists have affirmative obligations to maintain a fair and orderly market in their stocks. OTC market makers have no affirmative obligations to continue to make markets and can withdraw at any time. However, a NASDAQ market-maker who without excuse withdraws its quotations may not again register as a market-maker in that security for 20 business days.

Stocks listed on the New York and American Stock Exchanges receive greater coverage in the media than do NASDAQ SmallCap securities. Typically, there is greater brokerage firm research in newly listed securities on the New York or American Stock Exchanges compared to NASDAQ SmallCap securities.

The New York Stock Exchange may provide IPOs with a more organized opening trading price than the NASDAQ Stock Market. The specialist system permits a single opening IPO market price, whereas the various brokers and dealers on the NASDAQ Stock Market could theoretically have differing opening market prices. The New York Stock Exchange continues to be the most prestigious market on which your company's securities can trade.

It is also clear that the majority of IPOs in the last ten years have been on the NASDAQ Stock Market, as shown in Table 11.2.

TICK RULE AND SHORT-SELLING

Exchange listed securities are subject to the "tick rule." This rule prohibits short-selling except on "plus ticks" or on "zero-plus ticks." A plus tick is a trade greater than the immediately preceding transaction and a zero-plus tick is a trade at a price greater than the last transaction at a different price.

TABLE 11.2
INITIAL PUBLIC OFFERINGS: 10-YEAR COMPARISON OF OFFERINGS ON NASDAQ, NYSE, AND AMEX[1]

	NASDAQ Offerings	Dollar Value of NASDAQ Offerings ($millions)	NYSE Offerings	Dollar Value of NYSE Offerings ($millions)	Amex Offerings	Dollar Value of Amex Offerings ($millions)	Total Offerings	Total Dollar Value of Offerings ($millions)[2]
1989	148	$2,159.29	26	$3,718.41	8	$237.44	182	$6,115.14
1990	134	$2,403.15	19	$2,074.17	5	$149.88	158	$4,627.19
1991	320	$7,730.16	49	$8,351.15	11	$268.98	380	$16,350.29
1992	442	$13,585.91	80	$15,661.62	6	$111.65	528	$29,359.19
1993	520	$16,069.65	97	$22,308.17	11	$146.85	628	$38,524.67
1994	444	$13,186.80	82	$18,163.61	13	$269.00	539	$31,619.40
1995	476	$16,733.92	72	$14,752.75	9	$238.08	557	$31,769.75
1996	680	$24,498.15	88	$11,947.60	18	$510.13	786	$36,955.87
1997	494	$19,371.03	87	$18,202.38	22	$799.18	603	$38,372.59
1998	273	$13,757.27	68	$35,848.15	21	$386.95	362	$49,992.37
Jan.1999	9	$568.01	2	$425.62	2	$20.05	13	$1,013.68
Feb. 1999	28	$3,333.43	6	$2,473.78	0	$0.00	34	$5,807.21
Mar. 1999	19	$1,518.18	4	$3,092.15	0	$0.00	23	$4,610.33
Apr. 1999	31	$2,262.84	4	$912.51	1	$22.00	36	$3,197.35
May 1999	51	$4,591.36	4	$6,685.71	1	$20.00	56	$11,297.08
Jun. 1999	31	$1,782.57	2	$772.40	1	$15.00	34	$2,569.97
Jul. 1999	61	$6,158.97	7	$6,986.82	1	$3.75	69	$13,149.55
YTD 1999	230	$20,215.36	29	$21,348.99	6	$80.80	265	$41,645.15

[1]Sources: Pre-1993: IDD Information Services, Inc.; 1994 through 1996: Securities Data Company; 1997: NASDAQ Issuer Services; 1998 through current: CommScan EquiDesk. All data exclude closed end funds and stock conversions. Pre-1997 data include firm-commitment underwritings only.

[2]Dollar Value of Offerings include overallotment (if applicable), and pre-1998 data exclude global shares offered.

For example, the exchange permits a short-sale at 20 as a plus tick if the prior trade were $19\frac{7}{8}$ and as a zero-plus tick if the two prior trades were $19\frac{7}{8}$ and 20, respectively. However, it would prohibit a short-sale at 20 if the prior tick were $20\frac{1}{8}$ or if the two prior ticks were $20\frac{1}{8}$ and 20, respectively.

There is currently no tick rule on the NASDAQ Stock Market. As a result, the stock exchanges argue that they have better protection against short-selling than the NASDAQ Stock Market. NASDAQ has adopted its own short-sale rule for NM securities but not for SmallCap NASDAQ Stock Market securities; the rule has been criticized because of its exemption of certain market making activities.

Extensive short-selling (bear raids) can have a disastrous effect on the price of your company's stock. The tick rule does not prevent short-selling per se. A persistent short-seller can easily accumulate a large short position despite the tick rule. Likewise, the tick rule does not prevent short-sellers from impeding a justified rise in the price of your company's stock. However, the tick rule does assist in preventing dramatic market price declines resulting from bear raids.

Fees

Table 11.3 shows the original listing fees and continuing annual fees for each of the major markets, assuming the company has 10 million outstanding shares.

Maintenance Criteria

Both NASDAQ and the stock exchanges have maintenance criteria your company must satisfy to continue trading your stock. Your company's common stock listing

TABLE 11.3

	NASDAQ National Market	NASDAQ SmallCap	NYSE U.S. Fees	AMEX U.S. Fees
Original Listing Fees	$70,625	$10,000	$102,100	$37,500
Annual Fees	$12,960	$4,000	$ 9,940	$11,000

is easier to retain than it was to initially qualify. For example, to have your stock continue to be designated as an NM security, your common stock, preferred stock, shares or certificates of beneficial interest of trusts, and limited partnership interests in foreign or domestic issues must meet the following quantitative maintenance standards for initial NM listing standard 1 or 2:

- Net Tangible Assets—$4 million
- Public Float Shares—750,000 shares
- Market Value of Public Float—$5 million
- Minimum Bid Price per Share—$1
- Shareholders (round lots)—400
- Market Makers—2

In addition, should an issuer file under any of the sections of the Bankruptcy Act or announce that its board of directors has authorized liquidation and is committed to proceed, the issuer's securities must not remain designated as an NM security unless the public interest and the protection of investors would be served by continued designation.

The maintenance requirements for NASDAQ Small-Cap include the following:

- Net Tangible Assets—$2 million

    or

- Market Capitalization—$35 million

or

- Net Income—$500,000 (in last fiscal year or 2 of last 3 fiscal years)
- Public Float (shares)—500,000
- Market Value of Public Float—$1 million
- Minimum Bid—$1
- Market Makers—2
- Shareholders (round lot holders)—300
- Corporate Governance

CORPORATE GOVERNANCE REQUIREMENTS

There are a number of corporate governance requirements applicable to companies listed on the NASDAQ Stock Market or on national securities exchanges. These corporate governance requirements can be found on the NASDAQ Stock Market Web site, *www.NASDAQ.com*. The most important governance requirements applicable to the NASDAQ Stock Market securities are:

- The board of directors must have an audit committee with a formal written charter meeting certain requirements and composed of at least 3 members, all of whom are independent directors[1], subject to

---

1 "Independent director" means a person other than an officer or employee of the company or its subsidiaries or any other individual having a relationship which, in the opinion of the company's board of directors, would interfere with the exercise of independent judgment in carrying out the responsibilities of a director. The following persons shall not be considered independent:

  (a)   a director who is employed by the corporation or any of its affiliates for the current year or any of the past three years;

  (b)   a director who accepts any compensation from the corporation or any of its affiliates in excess of $60,000 during the previous fiscal year, other than compensation for board service, benefits under a tax-qualified retirement plan, or non-discretionary compensation;

  (c)   a director who is a member of the immediate family of an individual who is, or has been in any of the past three years, employed by the

certain exceptions. All audit committee members must be able to read and understand fundamental financial statements and at least one audit committee member must have past employment experience in finance or accounting or other comparable experience and background.

- There must be annual shareholder meetings, with minimum quorum requirements and solicitation of proxies.

- The company must review all related party transactions and use the audit committee or a comparable body to review conflicts of interest.

In addition, shareholder approval for the issuance of securities is required when:

- The company establishes a stock option or purchase plan pursuant to which officers or directors may acquire stock that exceeds certain thresholds.

- The issuance will result in a change in control.

- The issuance is in connection with an acquisition in which a director, officer, or substantial shareholder of the company has a 5 percent or greater interest (or such persons collectively have a 10 percent or greater interest) and the present or potential issuance of common stock (or securities convertible

---

corporation or any of its affiliates as an executive officer. Immediate family includes a person's spouse, parents, children, siblings, mother-in-law, father-in-law, brother-in-law, sister-in-law, son-in-law, daughter-in-law, and anyone who resides in such person's home;

(d)   a director who is a partner in, or a controlling shareholder or an executive officer of, any for-profit business organization to which the corporation made, or from which the corporation received, payments (other than those arising solely from investments in the corporation's securities) that exceed 5 percent of the corporation's or business organization's consolidated gross revenues for that year, or $200,000, whichever is more, in any of the past three years;

(e)   a director who is employed as an executive of another entity where any of the company's executives serve on that entity's compensation committee.

into or exercisable for common stock) could result in an increase in common stock or voting power of 5 percent or more.

- Except in connection with a public offering for cash, the issuance or potential issuance of common stock (or securities convertible into or exercisable for common stock), in connection with an acquisition if the common stock has upon issuance 20 percent or more of the voting power or number of outstanding shares of common stock.

- Except in connection with a public offering, the sale or issuance of common stock (or securities convertible into or exercisable for common stock) at a price less than the greater of book or market value, which (together with certain insider sales) equals 20 percent or more of the common stock or voting power, or if the sale or issuance equals 20 percent or more of the common stock or voting power outstanding before the issuance for less than the greater of book or market value.

The company must be audited by an independent public accountant that is subject to peer review. Also, the NASDAQ Stock Market severely restricts creating two classes of stock after the IPO or other disenfranchising proposals.

Getting Your Stock in the Newspaper

If your stock is traded on the NASDAQ Stock Market or if the New York or American Stock Exchange lists it, its price will regularly appear in *The Wall Street Journal*. This assumes, of course, that there is trading in your stock on any particular day.

Newspapers other than *The Wall Street Journal* vary with regard to their practices of publishing stock quotations. In general, almost all newspapers that publish stock quotations include the New York Stock Exchange, American Stock Exchange, and NM. Many newspapers also publish stock quotations on NASDAQ SmallCap stocks and stocks of local interest.

If your stock does not qualify for listing on the NAS-DAQ Stock Market or a major national securities exchange, you may still be able to obtain newspaper coverage by listing your stock on a national stock exchange located in your local area such as the Boston Stock Exchange, Chicago Board Options Exchange, Inc., Cincinnati Stock Exchange, Chicago Stock Exchange, Pacific Stock Exchange, Inc., and the Philadelphia Stock Exchange, Inc.

THE NASDAQ NATIONAL MARKET FEE SCHEDULE

There is a separate annual fee structure for American Depository Receipts (ADRs) and a separate entry and annual fee structure for the NASDAQ SmallCap Market:

A. Entry and Annual Fees

1. There is a $5,000 one-time company initial listing fee that includes a nonrefundable $1,000 application fee.

2. The entry and annual fees are based on the company's total shares outstanding (TSO) for all classes of stock listed on the NASDAQ National Market, excluding convertible debentures. The NASDAQ calculates the entry and annual fees according to the following fee schedule. In the case of an initial public offering (IPO), NASDAQ applies the TSO reported in the company's final prospectus, or in the case of an annual fee, NASDAQ applies the TSO reported in the company's latest filing on record at year end.

Tier (based on total shares outstanding)	Entry Fee	Annual Fee
<1 million	$29,525	$10,710
1+ million to 2 million	33,750	10,960
2+ million to 3 million	43,750	11,210
3+ million to 4 million	48,750	11,460
4+ million to 5 million	55,000	11,710
5+ million to 6 million	58,725	11,960
6+ million to 7 million	61,875	12,210
7+ million to 8 million	64,375	12,460
8+ million to 9 million	67,875	12,710
9+ million to 10 million	70,625	12,960
10+ million to 11 million	73,875	17,255
11+ million to 12 million	76,625	17,505
12+ million to 13 million	79,875	17,755
13+ million to 14 million	82,000	18,005
14+ million to 15 million	83,500	18,255
15+ million to 16 million	85,500	18,505
16+ million to 20 million	90,000	18,755
20+ million to 25 million	90,000	22,795
25+ million to 50 million	90,000	26,625
50+ million to 75 million	90,000	32,625
75+ million to 100 million	90,000	43,125
100 million	90,000	50,000

THE NASDAQ SMALLCAP MARKET FEE STRUCTURE

There is a separate annual fee structure for American Depository Receipts (ADRs) and a separate entry and annual fee structure for the NASDAQ National Market.

Entry Fees

1. $5,000 one-time company listing fee
2. The variable fee schedule per each class of security is:
   a. All Equity Securities—The greater of $1,000 or $0.001 per share, not to exceed $5,000
   b. Convertible Debentures—The greater of $1,000 or $50 per million dollars fact amount of debentures, not to exceed $5,000
   c. Maximum entry fees to be paid per issuer cannot exceed $10,000 inclusive of $5,000 original company listing fee

Annual Fees

1. NASDAQ issuers are assessed a flat fee per issuer, listed as follows:
   a. $4,000 for the first class of securities
   b. $1,000 for each subsequent class of securities
   c. No maximum applies

CHAPTER 12

BEING PUBLIC

After the completion of your IPO, your company and its directors, officers, and principal stockholders are subject to certain duties under various provisions of the Securities Exchange Act of 1934 (The "1934 Act"), if *any* of the three following events occur:

1. If your company had, at any fiscal year end, assets exceeding $10 million and a class of equity securities held of record by 500 or more persons [Section 12(g)]

2. If a national securities exchange lists a class of your company's securities for trading [Section 12(b)]

3. If your company *voluntarily* registered a class of its equity securities under Section 12(g) of the 1934 Act (This registration might have occurred in order to qualify your stock for trading on the NASDAQ Stock Market or the Bulletin Board.)

Section 12 of the 1934 Act *requires* the registration of equity securities under that section (a) once an issuer has over 500 shareholders and over $10 million in assets or (b) upon the listing of the security for trading on a national securities exchange.

Registration under Section 12, whether required or voluntary, invokes other sections of the 1934 Act, including those dealing with filing reports with the SEC on Forms 10-K (yearly), 10-Q (quarterly), and 8-K (periodically) under Section 13 of the 1934 Act, the proxy and tender offer rules (Section 14 of the 1934 Act), and the short-swing profit rules (Section 16 of the 1934 Act).

Companies who register debt or equity securities under the 1933 Act and have more than 300 debtor equity securityholders are also required under Section 15(d) of the 1934 Act to file reports on Forms 10-K, 10-Q, and 8-K.

By 2000, there are expected to be 18,000 issuers filing reports with the SEC because of Section 12 and Section 15(d) of the 1934 Act. The forms for registering a class of equity securities under Section 12 depend upon whether your company registered its IPO under the 1933 Act.

The annual and quarterly report forms for small business issuers are called Form 10-KSB and Form 10-QSB, respectively. If your company is an SEC reporting company because it filed a 1933 Act Registration Statement for an IPO, a simple disclosure form is all it needs to submit.

In general, if your company acquired more than 500 shareholders through gradual accretion over a period of time without filing a 1933 Act Registration Statement, your company must file a rather extensive disclosure document (similar to a Form S-1 or Form SB-1 for a small business issuer) once it acquires more than $10 million in assets at the end of any fiscal year.

Many companies with over $10 million in assets attempt to avoid costs of registration under Section12(g) and subsequent reporting costs by attempting to limit their number of shareholders to a figure below 500. This is accomplished by buying back stock for the company's treasury, by placing charter or bylaw restrictions on transfers, and by taking other measures.

Occasionally, in the absence of restrictions, sophisticated shareholders attempt to secure bargaining leverage on companies by threatening to make family gifts sufficient to raise the number of shareholders to 500 or more, unless the company buys back the shareholder's stock at a premium. Companies that do not wish to be subject to this type of intimidation may wish to insert bylaw restrictions on these activities in their charter.

Some companies complete their IPOs and have fewer than 500 shareholders or less than $10 million in assets and never voluntarily register under Section 12(g) of the 1934 Act or have their securities registered in a national securities exchange. The preceding provisions and other provisions of the 1934 Act discussed in the remainder of this chapter (Forms 3, 4, and 5, the short-swing profit rules, and Schedules 13D and 13G) are, therefore, not applicable to such companies or their directors, officers, and principal shareholders. However, these companies and their directors, officers, and principal shareholders are still subject to the antifraud and antimanipulative provisions of the 1934 Act, such as Rules 10b-5 and Regulation M.

BRIEF SUMMARY

The following is a brief summary of the personal duties of directors, officers, and principal shareholders under the 1934 Act described in the remainder of this chapter, expressed in do's and don'ts.

Do

- File a Form 3 Report within 10 days after becoming a director, officer, or more than 10 percent stockholder of the company.
- File a Form 4 Report within 10 days after the end of any calendar month in which a change in your beneficial ownership of any equity security of the company has occurred.
- File a Form 5 Report within 45 days after the end of the company's fiscal year disclosing all transactions and holdings, if any, not previously disclosed during such year.
- File a Schedule 13D if during any 12-month period you acquire more than 2 percent of any class of equity securities registered under the 1934 Act and if, after such acquisition, you beneficially own more than 5 percent of such class and promptly file any required material amendments to Schedule 13D.
- File a Schedule 13G within 45 days after the end of any calendar year if you beneficially own more than 5 percent of any class of equity securities registered under the 1934 Act at year end and have been exempt from filing a Schedule 13D.

Don't

- Within a six-month period, make any purchase and sale, or sale and purchase, of any equity securities of the company if such transaction results in a short-swing profit.
- Make any short sales of the company's equity securities or sales against the box (as defined later in this chapter).

- Utilize material confidential information of the company for purposes of trading in the company's securities or engage in other manipulative or deceptive devices.

- Tip confidential information of the company to others, including securities analysts.

- Bid for or purchase any security of the company or any right thereto while you or the company are participating in a public distribution of such securities.

- Violate the provisions of the Foreign Corrupt Practices Act of 1977 or the duties of audit committee members.

- Participate or aid or abet in a violation of the 1934 Act by others or conspire to commit such violation.

- Sell restricted or control securities (as defined in Chapter 13) unless you comply with Rule 144 of the 1933 Act or another applicable exemption from the 1933 Act.

Always consult with the company's counsel or any personal attorney who specializes in securities law before engaging in any transaction in the securities of the company. Supply a copy of all reports filed with the SEC to the company's counsel.

FORM 3, FORM 4, AND FORM 5 REPORTS—SECTION 16(A) OF THE 1934 ACT

Section 16(a) of the 1934 Act requires a more than 10 percent beneficial owner of any class of equity securities registered under the 1934 Act, and all directors and officers of the issuer of such security, to file a Form 3 Report disclosing the amount of equity securities of such issuer of which they are beneficial owners. The Form 3 Report must be

filed on or before the effective date of the registration of
the company's securities under the 1934 Act or, if later,
within 10 days after such a person becomes a director, officer, or more than 10 percent beneficial owner. The term
"equity securities" includes not only common stock but
also (among other things) debt securities convertible into
common stock or having a right attached to subscribe for
common stock, warrants, and certain stock options.

There are no further reports that have to be filed
under Section 16(a) of the 1934 Act after filing the Form 3
Report unless a change in beneficial ownership of any
equity security of the company occurs during any calendar
month. If such a change occurs, the person must file a
Form 4 Report within 10 days after the end of each calendar month in which there has been such change in beneficial ownership unless the reporting of such change is
exempt. A change of beneficial ownership could occur not
only because of a sale or purchase of equity securities but
also as a result of a gift, a stock dividend, a stock split, the
receipt of certain stock options, the purchase or sale of put,
call, or convertible securities, or as a result of a change in
the nature of the ownership, such as a change from indirect ownership through a trust or corporation to direct
ownership. A Form 4 Report must be filed even though the
net result of all securities transactions during the calendar month results in no change at the end of the month.

A person must file a Form 5 Report within 45 days
after the end of the company's fiscal year disclosing all
exempt transactions during such year that were not previously disclosed. In this report the person must disclose (i)
all exempt transactions not previously reported during the
year and (ii) all holdings and transactions that should have
been reported during the most recent fiscal year (during
the two most recent fiscal years with respect to the first
Form 5 Report), but that were not. No Form 5 Report is
required, however, if all transactions and holdings otherwise required to be reported on the Form 5 were previously
reported. If no Form 5 is required to be filed with the SEC,

the director, officer, or over 10 percent beneficial holder should give the company a signed statement to such effect.

Reports on Form 3, Form 4, and Form 5 must be filed with the SEC and with each national securities exchange (if any) on which any class of equity securities of the company is listed and registered. Reports are not considered filed until they actually are received by the SEC or the exchange; however, a report transmitted by a delivery service that guaranteed delivery by the due date is deemed to be timely filed. Therefore, reports must be mailed for filing within sufficient time prior to their due dates so that they can be received by the SEC and the exchange within the required time period. An original or duplicate of each such report is also required to be sent simultaneously to the person designated by the company to receive such filings or to the company's corporate secretary if no person is designated.

Reports filed on Form 3, Form 4, and Form 5 are public information and the SEC publishes a monthly summary of such reports that is publicly distributed. The summary is scrutinized by certain individuals who are interested in instituting lawsuits against directors, officers, and more than 10 percent beneficial owners under Section 16(b) of the 1934 Act to recover short-swing profits. The company is required to disclose in its proxy statement and on Form 10-K annual reports the names of any person who failed to timely file a Form 3, Form 4, and Form 5 Report or who failed to disclose any holdings or transactions during the prior fiscal year. Finally, monetary fines for filing violations by a reporting person can be assessed by the SEC.

LIABILITY FOR SHORT-SWING PROFITS— SECTION 16(B) OF THE 1934 ACT

Section 16(b) permits the company (with certain exceptions) to recover any profit realized by a director, officer,

or more than 10 percent beneficial owner from any sale
and purchase, or purchase and sale, of any equity security
(whether or not registered under the 1934 Act) of the company within a period of less than six months' (short-swing)
profits. A short-swing profit is deemed to have been realized if, within a period of less than six months, there is
either (a) a purchase and subsequent sale of the equity
security at a higher price or (b) a sale and subsequent purchase of the equity security at a lower price. Liability for
short-swing profits may be imposed even though no equity
security of the company was registered under the 1934 Act
at the time of the initial purchase or sale, but was registered at the time of the corresponding sale or purchase,
and even though the purchaser or seller was not a director
or officer or more than 10 percent beneficial owner at both
the time of the purchase and the sale.

An action to recover short-swing profits may be instituted by the company or by the owner of any security of
the company if the company refuses to bring suit within
60 days after request or fails to prosecute the action dili-
gently. A securityholder bringing the suit need not have
been a securityholder at the time of the transaction in
question. Thus, it is possible for an individual who dis-
covers a short-swing profit from the published information to buy one share of stock and bring a suit in the name
of the company, even though the company refuses to bring
such a suit. The motivation for bringing this suit might
be the fact that the individual's attorney would be entitled, as an attorney's fee, to a portion of the profits that
the director, officer, or more than 10 percent beneficial
owner was required to pay back to the company.

The terms "sale" and "purchase," as interpreted by the
regulations of the SEC and the courts under Section 16,
have been applied to transactions that are not customarily
considered sales or purchases. For example, the receipt of
a stock option is considered a purchase for purposes of Section 16(b), unless the option is exempt by reason of being
granted pursuant to a plan approved by shareholders and

otherwise meeting the conditions set forth in Rule 16b-3. If the employee sells stock within six months before or after the date of the receipt of the non-exempt option, he may incur liability under Section 16(b).

Other situations that are not customarily thought of as sales and purchases but that nevertheless may constitute sales or purchases under Section 16(b), include certain mergers, the sale or purchase of stock convertible into common stock, debentures or warrants convertible into common stock, and the exercise for cash of certain stock appreciation rights. For example, a merger may (within certain exceptions) be deemed to involve the sale of the security being surrendered in the merger and the purchase of the security acquired in the merger. Thus, if the company is involved in a merger in which the company's shares are to be surrendered for shares of another issuer, the company's directors, officers, and more than 10 percent beneficial owners should avoid purchases of shares of the company within six months of the date of the merger, since such purchases may be matched with the sale of the company's shares deemed involved in the merger. Since the merger may also involve the purchase of the securities acquired in the merger, sales of such securities within six months before or after the merger could also create Section 16(b) liability.

Section 16(b) covers purchases or sales of equity securities that you "beneficially own." A person is considered the beneficial owner of any security if he or she, directly or indirectly, through any contract, arrangement, understanding, or otherwise, has or shares the opportunity, directly or indirectly, to profit from any transaction in such securities. As a result, you are deemed to beneficially own many securities that you do not legally own. For example, you generally are presumed to beneficially own securities legally owned by your spouse or minor children and certain relatives of yours or your spouse who share the same home. Thus, if you live with your mother-in-law, her purchases or sales may be matched with your own to impose Section 16(b) liability upon you. If you have the right to vest title in yourself to securities legally owned by another person, either immediately or at some future time, you may beneficially own such securities.

Liability under Section 16(b) cannot be avoided by establishing that the particular share certificates sold (or purchased) are not the same ones purchased (or sold) within the same six-month period. A purchase or sale may be deemed to have occurred on the trade date or the date a legally binding contract to purchase or sell is entered into and not necessarily on the date of closing or settlement.

Under present law, with certain exceptions, if there is a series of purchases and sales within a six-month period, the recoverable profit is computed by matching the highest sale price with the lowest purchase price of the same quantity; then the next highest sale price is matched with the next lowest purchase price, etc. As a result of this method of computing profits, a defendant suffered a judgment of approximately $300,000 even though he had an actual loss on his series of purchases and sales.

A purely objective standard is generally used under Section 16(b) to determine whether liability exists, that is, whether there is a sale and purchase or purchase and sale within a six-month period. It is irrelevant that the director, officer, or more than 10 percent beneficial owner acted in good faith or innocently or lacked any improper intent or used material nonpublic information. This objective standard has been tempered only in unusual situations that could not possibly allow for insider speculation and profiteering on nonpublic information.

SHORT SALES AND SALES AGAINST THE BOX— SECTION 16(C) OF THE 1934 ACT

Under Section 16(c) of the 1934 Act, a director, officer, or more than 10 percent beneficial owner is prohibited (with certain exceptions) from selling any equity security of the company that he or she does not own (short-sales) or, if he or she does own the equity security sold, from failing to make delivery against the sale within 20 days thereafter or to place it in the mails or other usual channels of transportation within five days after the sale (sales against the box). Persons violating this provision may, in addition to any civil liabilities, be subject to criminal penalties under Section 32(a) of the 1934 Act.

PERSONAL USE OF INSIDE INFORMATION— RULE 10B-5 UNDER THE 1934 ACT

Transactions in securities of the company by insiders may involve not only the provisions of Section 16 of the 1934 Act but also the antifraud and antimanipulative provisions of the 1933 and 1934 Acts as well. The most significant of these is Rule 10b-5 under the 1934 Act, the rule upon which the SEC based its complaint in the famous Texas Gulf Sulphur case.

Rule 10b-5 generally makes it unlawful for any person, directly or indirectly, by the use of any means or instrumentality of interstate commerce or of the mails or of any facilities of any national securities exchange, to employ any manipulative or deceptive device in connection with the purchase or sale of securities. Rule 10b-5 applies to both private as well as public purchases and sales of securities. A violation of Rule 10b-5 requires proof of "scienter," which means that the plaintiff must prove an intentional or at least a reckless act.

The most common example of the application of Rule 10b-5 is the use by an insider, for the purpose of trading in the company's securities, of information pertaining to the company that is not publicly available (herein called "confidential information") and that is material. The use of such material confidential information for trading purposes generally would be deemed manipulative or deceptive in connection with the purchase or sale of securities. Assuming the person with whom the insider dealt was not aware of this material confidential information, such person would have the right to rescind the purchase or sale or seek damages from the insider.

Rule 10b-5 differs from Section 16(b) in numerous ways, among which are the following:

- Unlike Section 16(b), it is not necessary under Rule 10b-5 to have both a purchase and a sale in order to render the insider liable. Thus, even though you made a purchase only or a sale only, if you utilized material confidential information you would be liable under Rule 10b-5 even though you had no liability under Section 16(b). Also, if you purchased in January and sold in September of the same year, you would avoid Section 16(b) liability, but if either the January purchase or the September sale involved the utilization of material confidential information, you would nevertheless be liable under Rule 10b-5.

- Rule 10b-5 generally extends to all persons having material confidential information, whereas Section 16(b) applies only to directors, officers, and more than 10 percent beneficial owners. Your secretary would be deemed an insider subject to Rule 10b-5 liability if he or she traded on or tipped material confidential information, even though he or she would have no liability under Section 16(b). The term "insider" when used in conjunction with Rule 10b-5 has been interpreted to include, with certain exceptions, all persons possessing material confidential information of the company, regardless of their position with or relation to the company.

- Rule 10b-5 applies to all securities of the company (whether debt or equity), whereas Section 16(b) applies only to equity securities of the company.

- It is generally a defense to Rule 10b-5 liability to show that you did not know or have reason to know of material confidential information of the company at the time of your trading. The fact that you did not possess or utilize material confidential information of the company in trading is generally no defense to Section 16(b) liability.

- It is generally a defense to Rule 10b-5 liability, but not to Section 16(b) liability, if you prove that the person with whom you dealt possessed the same material confidential information that you did.

In order to be liable under Rule 10b-5, it is necessary that you know or have reason to know that the confidential information is material and that it was obtained or used in breach of a fiduciary duty. What is material information and whether or not such information was obtained or used in violation of a fiduciary duty are of course difficult questions to determine. Courts have considered as material any information that could be considered important by the average prudent investor.

There are many occasions on which you have information that is not then available to the public. You may, for example, have access to the financial statements of the company that have not yet been publicly released. Making any purchase or sale of any company security during the period after such financial information is available to you, but before such statements are made generally available to the public, would create an inference that you had acted on the basis of this material confidential information.

There are periods of time in which prudence would dictate that you refrain from any trading in the company's securities, even though you do not possess any material confidential information or even though your possession of material confidential information is not your motivation for your trading. False appearances of your use of material confidential information can be as harmful to you and the company as its actual utilization. One of the most crucial times during which to avoid trading is right before the publication of financial information that may be deemed material to the average prudent investor. Likewise, trading should be avoided immediately prior to the public announcement of any material corporate development, such as the receipt or loss of a large contract, an acquisition or merger, a stock split or stock dividend, a public offering, an exchange or tender offer, a change in dividend rates or earnings, a call for redemption, a new product or discovery, etc. Your trading should not commence simultaneously with the public announcement; rather you should continue to refrain from trading until the trading market has had a chance to absorb the public announcement (usually 48 hours). As a general rule, trading should be avoided at any time that there is a pending material corporate development of which the trading market has not been informed.

Judicial decisions and SEC enforcement actions have extended the reach of Rule 10b-5 to situations where a person, albeit not an insider in the traditional sense, acquires or uses material confidential information unlawfully, in breach of a fiduciary duty to someone other than the person with whom the person traded. In addition, in 1984 the Insider Trading Sanctions Act of 1984 (ITSA) was signed by President Reagan. Under ITSA, the SEC may, among other things, bring an action seeking a penalty not to exceed three times the profit gained or the loss avoided by an unlawful purchase or sale against (1) any person who purchases or sells securities while in possession of material, nonpublic information in violation of the 1934 Act and the rules adopted thereunder, and (2) any person who, by communicating material, nonpublic information to such other person, aids and abets another in the purchase or sale of securities while in possession of material, nonpublic information.

One purpose of Rule 10b-5 is to ensure that neither party to a trade has an unfair advantage insofar as his or her knowledge of all material facts relating to the company.

It is possible that the company may have disclosed certain facts concerning a material corporate development but may not have disclosed them completely—the so-called half-truth problem. If an insider knowing the full story engages in trading, he will likewise be liable in the same manner as though the public did not have any information at all.

Rule 10b-5 and other rules and sections of the 1934 Act and 1933 Act also prohibit various types of manipulative or deceptive devices that do not depend on the utilization of material confidential information by insiders. For example, creating a false appearance of active trading in the company's stock by entering matching buy and sell orders, or engaging in a series of transactions to raise or depress the price of a security for the purpose of inducing the purchase or sale of security by others, would violate Rule 10b-5 as well as rules and sections of the 1934 Act and 1933 Act.

The violation of Rule 10b-5 can result in both civil and criminal liability. The civil liability may include a suit to recover any profits earned by the insider or, where appropriate, any profits lost by the person with whom he traded. The suit may be in the form of a direct suit by the person with whom the trade occurred or may be a suit by any stockholder (even though he was not on the other end of the trade) to recover for the company any profits realized by the insider. In addition, the SEC has brought civil injunctive proceedings against insiders trading on material confidential information. Finally, there is a possibility of criminal liability under the 1934 Act, although this has been reserved for very serious cases.

TIPPING OF MATERIAL CONFIDENTIAL INFORMATION—RULE 10B-5 UNDER THE 1934 ACT

Rule 10b-5 not only prohibits the utilization by insiders of confidential information for their own trading purposes, but also prohibits the tipping by the insider of such confidential information to others. The Texas Gulf Sulphur case established the principle that the insider who does the tipping is liable not only for his or her own profits but also for any profits realized by the tippee. In addition, it may be possible that the tipper would be held liable for the profits or losses of the entire class of buyers or sellers during the period between the time of the initial tip and the time that the tipped information is finally made public. If the tipper is a director, officer, or other employee of the company, the company may also be liable.

In any event, it is clear that you should avoid casual cocktail party conversations concerning the company except to the extent that your conversation relates only to publicly available information. As a director, officer, or principal stockholder, you will be constantly pressed for information concerning the company by friends, relatives, business associates, brokers, and analysts. It is important that you either refrain from giving any information or be very careful to stick to only publicly available information. In this connection, you should know that the SEC has brought actions against corporations and their officers for disclosing material confidential information to brokers or analysts prior to releasing such information to the public.

After your IPO, you will be constantly pressured by securities analysts for information. You may be required to report monthly by conference telephone calls to groups of analysts. Analysts will also individually telephone or visit you. It is a violation of Rule 106-5 for you to give any material information to an analyst that was not previously or simultaneously publicly disclosed.

SCHEDULES 13D AND 13G— SECTIONS 13(d) AND 13(g) OF THE 1934 ACT

Section 13(d) of the 1934 Act provides that any person who, after acquiring the beneficial ownership (directly or indirectly) of any equity security of a class registered under the 1934 Act, is a beneficial owner of more than 5 percent of such class must, within 10 days after such acquisition, file a Schedule 13D with the issuer of the security, with each exchange on which the security is traded and with the SEC.

There are various exemptions to this requirement. The most important exemption is that Schedule 13D does not have to be filed if the acquisition of the security, when taken together with all other acquisitions by the same person of securities of the same class during the preceding 12 months, does not exceed 2 percent of such class of securities. For example, if you own 3 percent of the common stock of the company registered under the 1934 Act and, within a 12-month period, increase your ownership of the common stock by more than 2 percent, you are required to file a Schedule 13D within 10 days after you have exceeded the 2 percent limit.

When two or more persons act as a group for the purpose of acquiring, holding, or disposing of securities of the company, such a group is considered a single person for Section 13(d) purposes. If you become part of such a group, the group is deemed to have acquired beneficial ownership of the securities of its members and, if the 5 percent threshold is met, the group will have to file a Schedule 13D within 10 days after its formation.

If any material change occurs in the facts set forth in the Schedule 13D you previously filed, an amendment to the Schedule must be promptly filed. A acquisition or disposition of beneficial ownership of securities in the amount equal to 1 percent or more of the class of securities is deemed material. Acquisitions or dispositions of less than 1 percent may be material, depending on the circumstances. Please note that a Schedule 13D must be filed even though the transaction in the securities was reported on a Form 4 or Form 5 Report.

As mentioned earlier, you can be the beneficial owner of securities that you do not legally own. For purposes of

Sections 13(d) and 13(g) of the 1934 Act, you beneficially own securities as to which you (directly or indirectly) have or share with others either (a) voting power (e.g., the power to direct the voting of the securities) or (b) investment power (e.g., the power to direct the disposition of the securities). In addition, if you have the right to acquire beneficial ownership of the security within the next 60 days (e.g., exercise of a stock option or warrant, conversion of a security, revocation or automatic termination of a trust or discretionary account), you beneficially own the security. Thus, if you own 4 percent of the common stock of the company and have stock options exercisable within the next 60 days for more than 1 percent of such stock, you must file a Schedule 13D within 10 days.

If you are not required to file a Schedule 13D because of an exemption and you are the beneficial owner of more than 5 percent of a class of securities registered under the 1934 Act at the end of the calendar year, then you may be required to file a Schedule 13G with the issuer of the security and with the SEC within 45 days of the end of such calendar year.

TRADING DURING DISTRIBUTION OF SECURITIES— REGULATION M UNDER THE 1934 ACT

Regulation M prohibits various persons, including the company, from certain types of trading activities, during the time a distribution of the company's securities is being made in which they participate. The term "distribution" is not defined in the 1934 Act but includes any registered or unregistered public sale of the securities of the company. A distribution may be deemed carried on when the company is issuing its securities in an acquisition or merger or pursuant to an earnout granted in a previous acquisition, or otherwise.

Regulation M prohibits participants in the distribution from bidding for or purchasing any security that is the subject of a distribution, or any security of the same class or series, or any right to purchase any such security (a warrant or call), or attempting to induce any person to purchase any such security or right, until the distribution has been completed (subject to certain exceptions). Under certain circumstances, Regulation M prohibitions may apply to directors, officers, and principal stockholders of a corporation engaged in a distribution of securities, whether or not such directors, officers, or principal stockholders are themselves engaged in the distribution. There is a great deal of uncertainty as to the date when a distribution begins and when it is deemed to have ended. In case of question, it is best to consult with counsel.

The purpose of Regulation M is to forestall any attempt to manipulate securities prices by means of bids or purchases during the course of a public distribution of such securities. The effect of bids for or purchases of securities being distributed may be to artificially inflate the price of the distributed securities above that price that would have prevailed in a free and open market.

FOREIGN CORRUPT PRACTICES ACT OF 1977— SECTIONS 10A, 13(B)(2), AND 30A OF THE 1934 ACT

The Foreign Corrupt Practices Act of 1977 amended the 1934 Act to impose certain accounting standards on public companies and to prohibit corrupt foreign payments by or on behalf of U.S. corporations (whether or not public), business entities, citizens, nationals, and residents.

Accounting Standards

Under the accounting standards, the company is required to:

A. Make and keep books, records, and accounts, which, in *reasonable detail*, accurately and fairly reflect the transactions and dispositions of the assets of the company

B.   Devise and maintain a system of internal account-
     ing controls sufficient to provide *reasonable assur-
     ance* that:

   (i)   Transactions are executed in accordance with
         management's general or specific authorization

   (ii) Transactions are recorded as necessary (a) to
         permit preparation of financial statements in
         conformity with generally accepted accounting
         principles or any other criteria applicable to
         such statements, and (b) to maintain accounta-
         bility for assets

   (iii) Access to assets is permitted only in accordance
         with management's general or specific authori-
         zation

   (iv) The recorded accountability for assets is com-
         pared with the existing assets at reasonable
         intervals and appropriate action is taken with
         respect to any differences

The words "reasonable detail" and "reasonable assurance" mean such level of detail and degree of assurance
as would satisfy prudent officials in the conduct of their
own affairs.

The 1934 Act's requirements with regard to the maintenance of books and records and a system of internal control were enacted largely in response to disclosures that
many U.S. corporations had established so-called off-the-
book accounts and slush funds. However, they are applicable to all public companies, whether or not they engage
in foreign business or employ slush funds.

It must be borne in mind that the accounting standards imposed by the 1934 Act are directed at the accuracy
of the company's books, records, and accounts, not just its
financial statements. Thus, even though the company has
not paid foreign bribes and even though its published

financial statements may be accurate in all respects, it could nonetheless be in violation of the 1934 Act if, for example, its books and records improperly characterized the nature of a perfectly legitimate item of expense.

Prudence would dictate that the company's accounting systems, including its system of internal controls, should be periodically reviewed with the company's auditors. This function may, of course, be delegated to the audit committee of the board of directors. However, neglect of this review function can have serious personal consequences for you as well as the company and could result in an SEC injunction or other sanction, a ban against your becoming a director or officer of a public company, or a potentially embarrassing SEC investigation and public report.

If you are a member of an audit committee, an SEC rule, generally effective for all shareholder votes occurring after December 15, 2000, imposes special duties upon you. These duties include preparing a report for inclusion in the company's proxy or information statement. The audit committee report, below which your name will appear, will state:

- Whether the audit committee has reviewed and discussed the audited financial statement with management
- Whether the audit committee has discussed with the independent auditor the matters required to be discussed by SAS 61, as modified or supplemented (which requires independent auditors to communicate certain matters relating to the conduct of the audit to the audit committee, including, among other things, accounting for significant unusual transactions, accounting policies in controversial or emerging areas, the process used in formulating sensitive accounting estimates and their reasonableness, and disagreements with management)
- Whether the audit committee has received the written disclosures and letter from the independent

accountants required by Independence Standards Board Standard No. 1, as modified or supplemented, and discussed the actual independence of the auditors

- Whether based on the above review and discussions of the audit committee, the audit committee *recommended* to the board of directors that the audited financial statements be included in the company's Form 10-K Report.

In addition, if an independent public accountant, in the course of an audit, detects an illegal act (whether or not material to the financial statements), the accountant must inform the appropriate level of management and, under certain circumstance in the absence of appropriate remedial action, may have a duty to report to the board of directors and the SEC.

Foreign Bribes

The Foreign Corrupt Practices Act of 1977 (as amended) also proscribes and criminalizes foreign corrupt payments. Generally speaking, the 1934 Act makes it illegal for any public company, as well as any officer, director, employee, agent, or stockholder acting on behalf of the company to pay, promise to pay, or authorize the payment of money or anything of value to:

- Any foreign official
- Any foreign political party or any official of such party
- Any candidate for foreign political office
- Any person whom the company knows or has reason to know will make a proscribed payment, or will promise to make or authorize payment of a proscribed payment

- For purposes of: (a) influencing any act or decision in his, her, or its official capacity; (b) inducing such person to do or omit to do any act in violation of a lawful duty to such person; or (c) securing any improper advantage; or (d) inducing such person to use his, her, or its influence with a foreign government or any instrumentality of such foreign government; in each case for the purpose of obtaining or retaining business for or with, or directing business to any person

The 1934 Act prohibits not only the payment of, but also the promise or authorization of, a corrupt foreign payment. Therefore, the law can be violated even if the payment is never in fact made. Since a corrupt payment requested by the foreign official (rather than offered to him or her) involves a decision to accede to the request, it is not a defense that the payment was requested. The statute contains several affirmative defenses to such payment including the lawfulness of the payment under foreign law. In addition, so-called grease payments (payments to ministerial or clerical employees of foreign governments or agencies, to speed them in the performance of or encourage them to in fact perform routine government action) are not prohibited by the 1934 Act. "Routine government action" is defined narrowly and would not include decisions to award new business.

It is clear that, if authorized, the making of a foreign corrupt payment by a foreign subsidiary of a U.S. company is prohibited by the 1934 Act. Also prohibited are payments to an agent (even one who is not himself subject to the 1934 Act) when it is known or should be known that he or she will be used to make corrupt payments.

If the company engages in foreign transactions, particularly those involving an agent, great care should be exercised to secure documentation to prove that the 1934 Act was not violated. It is prudent to secure an affidavit from any agents who are paid commissions attesting to their compliance with the 1934 Act. Obviously, such an affidavit is useless if company officials have reason to know that it is false.

Violations of the corrupt payment provisions of the 1934 Act are punishable by fines against corporations or business entities of up to $2 million and fines of up to $100,000 and imprisonment of up to five years, or both, for individuals who violate the 1934 Act. The 1934 Act further provides that fines imposed on an individual violator cannot be paid, directly or indirectly, by the company for whose benefit the bribe was paid or promised.

PARTICIPANTS, AIDERS AND ABETTORS, CONSPIRATORS, AND CONTROLLING PERSONS

The company has numerous duties under the 1934 Act. We have alluded to the company's obligation under Rule 10b-5 to immediately and fully disclose material corporate developments, at least in situations in which there is a duty to act. In addition, the company is obligated to file various reports with the SEC, including quarterly and annual reports and reports (Form 8-K) due within 15 days or more after certain events occur. If the company has a meeting of securityholders, the company must file proxy material with the SEC. The company must comply with the accounting and payment provisions of the Foreign Corrupt Practices Act of 1977. These are only a few examples.

You may be personally liable under the 1934 Act if the company violates any of its duties under the 1934 Act and you either directly or indirectly (using agents) participate in such violations or conspire to commit such violations, or if you are considered a person who controls the company (unless you acted in good faith and did not directly or indirectly induce the act constituting the violation). For example, if the company violates the 1934 Act by sending out a false or misleading press release or by filing with the SEC a false or misleading document, and you helped prepare that press release or other document, you could be liable as a participant and possibly as a conspirator. Likewise, if you participate in a violation of the 1934 Act by another person (such as a director, officer, or other employee of the company), or conspire with such a person to commit the violation, you could be liable for such other person's violation.

You may be liable as a participant in a violation of the 1934 Act even though you had no intent to deceive anyone, but were merely negligent in not discovering and remedying the violation. For example, a director may be liable for approving use of a management proxy statement that unknown to the director is false and misleading, if the director should by the exercise of due care have discovered the violation. A director cannot immunize himself or herself from liability by remaining ignorant of corporate affairs.

In 1994, the U.S. Supreme Court held that a private plaintiff could not maintain an aiding and abetting action under Rule 10b-5. The Private Securities Litigation Reform Act of 1995 reaffirmed the SEC's authority to maintain civil enforcement actions in court against aiders and abettors.

The SEC has taken the position that directors and officers of a public company may have a legal responsibility for the noncompliance by the company with the 1934 Act as well as other securities laws. On occasion, particularly where aider and abettor liability is not clear, the SEC publishes and publicly disseminates reports on the alleged derelictions of directors who were not sufficiently vigilant in their oversight of management. Where aider and abettor liability can be proved, possible criminal actions may be brought.

If you are personally liable as a participant, aider or abettor, or conspirator in the company's violation of the 1934 Act, you may be entitled to indemnification from the company, depending upon the nature of the violation and your participation in the violation.

The company should never send out a press or shareholders' release or file a document with the SEC unless it has been reviewed first by the company's counsel, since not only will the company be liable if a violation occurs, but also any participants, aiders and abettors, conspirators and, under certain circumstances, controlling persons.

CONCLUSION

As you can see, the applicable provisions of the 1934 Act (and, as you will find, Rule 144 of the 1933 Act discussed in Chapter 13) are extremely complicated. The worst thing that you can do is to try to be your own lawyer. The old saying that a person who represents himself has a fool for a client is particularly applicable in dealing with securities laws.

Your personal liability for violating the "do's and don'ts" of this chapter can range from an injunction entered against you by the SEC to criminal actions in appropriate cases. These private damage actions are becoming more frequent as the courts liberalize the requirements. For example, under the fraud-on-the-market theory, a shareholder may sue even if you can prove that the shareholder never read the company's disclosure document alleged to be false.

The utilization of one common sense rule should help to prevent you from violating the 1934 Act or Rule 144 of the 1933 Act: **Always consult with the company's counsel or any personal attorney who specializes in securities law prior to engaging in any transaction in the company's securities.** The consultation should be sufficiently in advance of the proposed transaction so that counsel has the time to properly advise you of the proposed transaction's consequences. The problems under the 1934 Act and 1933 Act are sufficiently complicated so that even the most expert counsel requires ample time to research and review the securities problems that you present. You should supply a copy of all reports filed with the SEC by you or your counsel to the company's counsel.

CHAPTER 13

RULE 144 OF THE 1933 ACT

T he 1933 Act prohibits (among other things) the use of any means or instruments of transportation or communication in interstate commerce or of the mails to make any offer of securities of a company unless you have filed a registration statement. It also prohibits any sale of securities unless a registration statement is effective. There are numerous securities and transaction exemptions from these prohibitions. The most common transactional exemptions are private placement transactions and transactions by or involving persons who are not issuers, underwriters, or dealers. A person who distributes control securities or restricted securities may be an underwriter under the law and subject to the registration provisions of the 1933 Act, unless that person complies with Rule 144 or some other applicable exemption from the registration provisions of the 1933 Act.

Control securities are securities of the company held by persons or groups controlling the company (a large stockholder or group of stockholders), controlled by the company (a subsidiary), or under common control with the company. For example, if a controlling stockholder of the company buys the company securities on the open market or otherwise acquires securities of the company (by private purchase, gift, or other ways), such securities are control securities.

The court may deem a person part of a "control group" of the company even though he or she does not personally own a significant amount of the company securities and even though the person does not in fact control the company. For example, the court might decide that a close relative of a controlling stockholder is part of a control group, especially if the relative is also a director of the company. Under such circumstances, the courts would consider all company securities held by the relative control securities. In some companies, the court may view all directors and officers as a group as constituting a control group.

Restricted securities are securities acquired in non-public offerings (generally private placements), directly or indirectly, from the company, from holders of control securities, or from other holders of restricted securities. For example, securities you acquire under a stock option plan, properly not registered under the 1933 Act because of the private placement exemption, are restricted securities.

Your security may be both a control security and a restricted security if, for example, you recently purchased the security from the company in a private placement and you are in a control relationship with the company. A control security ceases to be a control security when a person not in a control relationship with the company acquires it, but it may nevertheless continue to be a restricted security.

You cannot publicly sell control securities and restricted securities unless a current registration statement is in effect under the 1933 Act or Rule 144 or some other exemption from the registration provisions of the 1933 Act is available.

ONE-YEAR HOLDING PERIOD
FOR RESTRICTED SECURITIES

Rule 144 provides, among other things, if all conditions of the rule are met, that after one year has elapsed from the date you acquired restricted securities from the company or from a person or group in a control relationship with the company, you may sell limited amounts of restricted securities during successive three-month periods either in brokers' transactions or directly to market makers. Rule 144 likewise lets you sell limited amounts of control securities that are not also restricted securities during successive three-month periods in brokers' transactions or directly to market makers without compliance with the one-year holding period. The permission to sell is conditional: there must be adequate current public information available concerning the company and the seller must file a notice on Form 144 (subject to exceptions) concurrently with the sale.

The purpose of the one-year holding period for restricted securities is to prevent the holder of restricted securities from acting as a conduit for the distribution of securities by the company or by a person or group in a control relationship with the company. If you purchase the restricted securities from the company or such control person, the one-year period does not begin until you pay the full purchase price or other consideration to the company or control person. If you give a promissory note for all or a portion of the purchase price of the restricted securities, the SEC would not deem the issuance of that promissory note to be full payment of the purchase price, and accordingly, the one-year holding period would not commence unless the promissory note (a) provided for full recourse against the purchaser, (b) was secured by collateral (other than the restricted securities purchased) having a fair market value, which at all times until the note was paid, was at least equal to the unpaid balance of the note, and (c) was paid in full before sale under Rule 144. If you acquire outstanding restricted securities from someone who is not in a control relationship with the company, you only need to hold the restricted securities for the balance of the one-year period, that is, the law does not require you to satisfy a new one-year period.

Certain restricted securities are given retroactive holding periods under the so-called tacking provisions of Rule 144. For example, securities you acquire from the company as a stock dividend or pursuant to a stock split, reverse split, or recapitalization the law deems acquired at the same time as the restricted securities on which the dividend was paid or the restricted securities involved in the split or recapitalization. Likewise, securities you acquire upon conversion of convertible debentures or convertible preferred stock generally have holding periods retroactive to the date of the convertible debentures or preferred stock. Also, certain securities acquired by gifts, in certain partnership distributions, and pursuant to the earnout and market-floor provisions of agreements of sale can obtain retroactive holding periods. These are only a few examples.

Amount Salable Under Rule 144

Rule 144 allows you to sell a limited amount of securities every three months under its "leakage" provisions.

The amount of restricted and control securities you sell in any three-month period must not exceed the *greater* of (a) 1 percent of the class outstanding (as shown by the most recent report or statement published by the company), (b) the average weekly volume of trading in that securities reported on all national securities exchanges and/or reported through the automated quotation system of a registered securities association during the four calendar weeks preceding the filing of Form 144, or (c) the average weekly volume of trading reported through the consolidated reporting system during such four-week period. If, after filing a Form 144 covering a security traded on a national securities exchange, the average weekly trading volume of the security on all exchanges rises, you may file an amended Form 144 and sell the increased volume, provided you exclude your own trades from the new trading volume computations.

In computing the amount of restricted and control securities that you may sell under Rule 144 you must take into account the following:

1. If control securities (even though such securities are also restricted securities), all securities of the company, whether restricted, control, or otherwise, sold for your account during the preceding three-month period count against your Rule 144 sales limit. If you sell restricted securities (but not control securities), only other restricted securities of the same class sold for your account during the preceding three months count against your Rule 144 sales limit.

2. Sales made by your spouse, or any relative of you or your spouse who shares the same home, count as sales by you.

3. Sales made by any trust or estate in which you or any person referred to in paragraph 2 collectively own 10 percent or more of the total beneficial interest, or of which any such person serves as trustee, executor, or in any similar capacity, count as sales by you.

4. Sales by any corporation or other organization (except the company) in which you or any of the persons specified in paragraph 2 are the beneficial owners collectively of 10 percent or more of any class of equity securities, or 10 percent or more of the equity interest, count as sales by you.

5. Sales by any person from whom you received the restricted or control securities as a gift or as a partnership distribution within the last two years, count as sales by you.

6. Sales by any person to whom you gave a gift or made a partnership distribution of restricted or control securities within the last two years, count as sales by you.

7. Sales by other persons with whom you are acting in concert for the purpose of selling restricted or control securities, count as sales by you. In this connection, it would be wise to avoid any agreements with other holders of restricted or control securities as to the method of disposition of the securities unless you are prepared to have their sales count against your Rule 144 sales limit, and vice versa.

The preceding list is not intended to be exhaustive and other sales may in a given situation count against your Rule 144 sales limit.

ADEQUATE PUBLIC INFORMATION

The permission to sell restricted and control securities under Rule 144 is conditional upon there being adequate current information available to the public with regard to the company. Without discussing the various nuances of this requirement, it should be noted that you must represent to the SEC in your Form 144 that you do not know any material adverse information with regard to the current or prospective operation of the company that has not been publicly disclosed. If you have any reason to believe that any report the law requires your company to file under Section 13 of the 1934 Act has not been filed, the law prohibits you from engaging in Rule 144 sales.

MANNER OF SELLING

There are strict limitations on the manner of selling under Rule 144 with which you should be familiar. You must not solicit or arrange for the solicitation of orders to buy the restricted or control securities in anticipation of or in connection with your Rule 144 sale. Nor may you make any payment in connection with the offering or sale of these securities to any person other than the broker who executes your sell order.

Furthermore, with one exception, your securities must be sold in broker's transactions, as defined in Rule 144. This requires, among other things, that the broker do no more than execute your order as agent, receive no more than the usual customary broker's commissions, and neither solicit nor arrange for the solicitation of customers' orders to buy the securities in anticipation of or in connection with the transaction.

The exception to this rule is that you may bypass the broker and deal directly with so-called market-makers. Market-makers include any dealers, who, with respect to a particular security, hold themselves out (by entering quotations in an inter-dealer communication system or otherwise) as being willing to buy and sell such security for their own accounts on a regular or continuous basis.

FORM 144

Concurrently with any Rule 144 sale, you must file (subject to exceptions) a Form 144 with the SEC and, if any national securities exchange admits the security to trading, with the principal national securities exchange listing the security. The person filing a Form 144 must have a bona fide intention to sell the securities covered in that form within a reasonable time after the filing of the form.

EXEMPTION FOR RESTRICTED SECURITIES HELD TWO YEARS

There is an exception to compliance with certain of the provisions of Rule 144 for restricted securities that you beneficially own for two years. Restricted securities that are beneficially owned for at least two years by persons who are not and have not been for the previous three months controlling persons of the company, you may sell without restriction as to volume or the manner of sale without filing a Form 144 and whether or not there is adequate information about the company. For purposes of computing the two-year period, you may include the holding period of the donor of any restricted securities you receive as a gift and the holding period of any partnership from which you receive a partnership distribution.

CONTROL SECURITIES

There is no two-year rule for control securities. The leakage and other provisions of Rule 144 are applicable perpetually to control securities. To sell more control securities than the leakage provisions permit, the control securities must be either registered under the 1933 Act or sold in a private placement or another transaction exempt from the registration provisions of the 1933 Act.

CONCLUSION

Rule 144 is a complicated rule. You should not engage in a Rule 144 sale without consulting a securities lawyer. Many companies and stock transfer agents require a legal opinion before permitting a Rule 144 sale. Therefore, you should consult a securities lawyer in sufficient time before the proposed trade date for the Rule 144 sale so the lawyer can complete the necessary paperwork.

CHAPTER 14

THE STORY OF AN IPO

T he following story of the Microsoft 1986 IPO* provides you with a realistic picture of the traditional
IPO process, laced with all of its tensions and sus-
pense. The process starts with the business decision by
Microsoft to go public and ends with a sharp rise in the
after market trading price of its stock (which reflects the
tendency to underprice IPOs). In between are the selection of underwriters, the all-hands meetings, the due diligence and registration process, the hectic road shows, the
last minute haggling over underwriters' compensation,
and the finalization of the IPO offering price.]

Going public is one of capitalism's major sacraments, conferring instant superwealth on a few talented and lucky
entrepreneurs. Of the more than 1,500 companies that
have undergone this rite of passage in the past five years
[1981 through 1985], few have enjoyed a more frenzied
welcome from investors than Microsoft, the Seattle-based

maker of software for personal computers. Its shares, offered at $21 on March 13, zoomed to $35.50 on the over-the-counter market before settling back to a recent $31.25. Microsoft and its shareholders raised $61 million. The biggest winner was William H. Gates III, the company's co-founder and chairman. He got only $1.6 million for the shares he sold, but going public put a market value of $350 million on the 45% take he retains. A software prodigy who helped start Microsoft while still in his teens, Gates, at 30, is probably one of the 100 richest Americans.

Gates thinks other entrepreneurs might learn from Microsoft's experience in crafting what some analysts called "the deal of the year," so he invited *Fortune* along for a rare inside view of the arduous five-month process. Companies hardly ever allow such a close look at an offering because they fear that the Securities and Exchange Commission might charge them with touting their stock. Answers emerged to a host of fascinating questions, from how a company picks investment bankers to how the offering price is set. One surprising fact stands out from Microsoft's revelations: Instead of deferring to the priesthood of Wall Street underwriters, it took charge of the process from the start.

The wonder is that Microsoft waited so long. Founded in 1975, it is the oldest major producer of software for personal computers and, with $172.5 million in revenues over the last four quarters, the second largest after Lotus Development. Microsoft's biggest hits are the PC-DOS and MS-DOS operating systems, the basic software that runs millions of IBM personal computers and clones. The company has also struck it rich with myriad versions of computer languages and a slew of fast-selling applications programs such as spreadsheets and word-processing packages for IBM, Apple, and other personal computers.

Yet Microsoft stood pat when two of its arch competitors, Lotus and Ashton-Tate, floated stock worth a total of $74 million in 1983. Nor did it budge in 1984 and 1985, when three other microcomputer software companies managed to sell $54 million of stock. The reasons were simple. Unlike its competitors, Microsoft was not dominated by venture capital investors hungry to harvest some of their gains. The business gushed cash. With pretax profits running as high as 34% of revenues, Microsoft needed no outside money to expand. Most important, Gates values control of his time and his company more than personal wealth.

Money has never been paramount to this unmarried scion of a leading Seattle family, whose father is a partner in a top Seattle law firm and whose mother is a regent of the University of Washington and a director of Pacific Northwest Bell. Gates, a gawky, washed-out blond, confesses to being a "wonk," a bookish nerd, who focuses singlemindedly on the computer business though he masters all sorts of knowledge with astounding facility. Oddly, Gates is something of a ladies' man and a fiendishly fast driver who has racked up speeding tickets even in the sluggish Mercedes diesel he bought to restrain himself. Gates left Harvard after his sophomore year to sell personal computer makers on using a version of the Basic computer language that he had written with Paul Allen, the co-founder of Microsoft. Intensely competitive and often aloof and sarcastic, Gates threw himself into building a company dedicated to technical excellence. "All Bill's ego goes into Microsoft," says a friend. "It's his first-born child."

Gates feared that a public offering would distract him and his employees. "The whole process looked like a pain," he recalls, "and an ongoing pain once you're public. People get confused because the stock price doesn't reflect your financial performance. And to have a stock trader call up the chief executive and ask him questions is uneconomic—the ball bearings shouldn't be asking the driver about the grease."

But a public offering was just a question of time. To attract managers and virtuoso programmers, Gates had been selling them shares and granting stock options. By 1987, Microsoft estimated, over 500 people would own shares, enough to force the company to register with the SEC. Once registered, the stock in effect would have a public market, but one so narrow that trading would be difficult. Since it would have to register anyway, Microsoft might as well sell enough shares to enough investors to create a liquid market, and Gates had said that 1986 might be the year. "A projection of stock ownership showed we'd have to make a public offering at some point," says Jon A. Shirley, 48, Microsoft's pipe-smoking president and chief operating officer. "We decided to do it when we wanted to, not when we had to."

In April 1985 Gates, Shirley, and David F. Marquardt, 37, the sole venture capitalist in Microsoft (he and his firm had 6.2% of the stock), resolved to look into an offering. But Gates fretted. To forestall sticky questions from potential investors, he first wanted to launch two important products, one of them delayed over a year, and to sign a pending agreement with IBM for developing programs. He also wanted time to sound out key employees who owned stock or options and might leave once their holdings became salable on the public market. "I'm reserving the right to say no until October," Gates warned. "Don't be surprised if I call it off."

By the board meeting of October 28, held the day after a roller-skating party for Gates's 30th birthday, the chairman had done his soundings and felt more at ease, the board decided it was time to select underwriters and gave the task to Frank Gaudette, 50, the chief financial officer, who had come aboard a year before. Gaudette was just the man to shepherd Microsoft through Wall Street. He speaks in the pungent tones of New York City, where his late father was a mailman, and prides himself on street smarts. He had already helped manage offerings for three companies, all suppliers of computer software and services.

Aspiring underwriters, sniffing millions in fees, had been stroking Microsoft for years. They had enticed the company's officers to so-called technology conferences— bazaars where entrepreneurs, investors, and bankers look each other over. They had called regularly at Microsoft, trying to get close to Gates and Shirley. Gaudette had been sitting through an average of three sales pitches or get-acquainted dinners a month.

Gaudette proposed that since Microsoft was well established, it deserved to have a "class Wall Street name" as the lead underwriter. This investment firm would put together the syndicate of underwriters, which eventually was to number 114. It would also allocate the stock among underwriters and investors and pocket giant fees for its trouble. Gaudette suggested a "technology boutique" co-manager the offering to enhance Microsoft's appeal to investors who specialize in technology stocks.

Narrowing the field of boutiques was easy. Only four firms were widely known as specialists in financing technology companies: Alex. Brown & Sons of Baltimore, L.F. Rothschild Unterberg Towbin of New York, and two San Francisco outfits, Hambrecht & Quist and Robertson Colman & Stephens. Culling the list of Wall Street names took longer. Microsoft's managers concluded that some big firms, including Merrill Lynch and Shearson Lehman, had not done enough homework in high tech. The board pared the contenders to Goldman Sachs, Morgan Stanley, and Smith Barney. It also included Cable House & Ragen, a Seattle firm that could be a third co-manager if Gates and Shirley decided that pleasing local investors was worth the bother. "Get on the stick," Shirley told Gaudette. "Keep Bill and me out of it—we can't spend the time. Give us a recommendation in two or three weeks."

Early in November, Gaudette called the eight investment bankers who had survived the first cut. "I need half a day with you," he said. "Take your best shot, then wait for me to call back. I'll have a decision before Thanksgiving. But remember, it's my decision—don't try going around me to Bill or Jon." Gaudette made up a list of questions, ranging from the baldly general—"Why should your firm be on the front cover of a Microsoft prospectus?"—to the probingly particular, such as, "How would you distribute the stock, to whom, and why?"

After a whirlwind tour of New York, Baltimore and San Francisco, Gaudette made his recommendations to Gates and Shirley on November 21. Then he took off for a ten-day vacation in Hawaii, a belated celebration of his 50th birthday in the 50th state. No decision would be announced until his return. The investment bankers turned frantic. Theirs is a who-do-you-know business, and they mobilized their clients, many of them Microsoft customers or suppliers, to besiege Gates and Shirley.

Gaudette had methodically ranked the investment houses on a scale of 1 to 5 in 19 different categories. But he also stressed that any candidate could do the deal and that the chemistry between Microsoft and the firms would finally determine the winners. Among the major houses, Gaudette had been most impressed by Goldman Sachs, which tightly links its underwriting group with its stock traders and keeps close tabs on the identity of big institutional buyers. For those reasons, Gaudette thought Goldman would be especially good at maintaining an orderly market as Microsoft employees gradually cashed in their share.

On December 4, after conferring with Gates and Shirley, Gaudette phoned Eff W. Martin, 37, a vice president in Goldman's San Francisco office who had been calling on Microsoft for two years. "I like you guys," Gaudette said, "and Microsoft wants to give you dinner on December 11 in Seattle. Do you think you can find time to come?"

Dinner at the stuffy Rainer Club was awkward. The private room was large for the party of eight, and one wall was a sliding partition ideal for eavesdropping. Most of the party were meeting each other for the first time; however well they got along could make or break the deal. Microsoft's top dogs didn't make things easy. Gates, who had heard scare stories about investment bankers from friends like Mitchell Kapor, chairman of Lotus Development, was tired and prepared to be bored. Shirley was caustic, waiting to know exactly what Goldman imagined it could do for Microsoft.

For nearly an hour everyone stood in a semicircle as Martin and three colleagues explained their efforts to be tops in financing technology companies. An Oklahoman by birth and polite to a fault, Martin labored to kindle some rapport. But it was not until talk turned to pricing the company's stock that Gates folded his arms across his chest and started rocking to and from, a sure sign of interest. At the end of dinner, Martin, striving to conclude on a high note, gushed that Microsoft could have the "most visible initial public offering of 1986—or ever."

"Well, they didn't spill their food and they seemed like nice guys," Gates drawled to his colleagues afterward in the parking lot. "I guess we should go with them." He and Shirley drove back to Microsoft headquarters, discussing co-managing underwriters. Gaudette leaned toward Robertson Colman & Stephens. But Alex. Brown had been cultivating Microsoft longer than any other investment banking house. . . . Three days later the board quickly blessed the selection of Goldman Sachs and Alex. Brown.

The offering formally lumbered into gear on December 17 at an "all-hands meeting" at Microsoft. It was the first gathering of the principal players: the company with its auditors and attorneys as well as both managing underwriters and their attorney. Some confusion crept in at first. Heavy fog, a Seattle specialty, delayed the arrival of several key people until early afternoon. One of Microsoft's high priorities was making its prospectus "jury proof"—so carefully phrased that no stockholder

could hope to win a lawsuit by claiming he had been mis-
led. The company had insisted that the underwriters'
counsel be Sullivan & Cromwell, a hidebound Wall Street
firm. Gaudette was miffed to see that the law firm had
sent only an associate, not a partner.

The 27-point agenda covered every phase of the offering. Gates said the company was contemplating a $40-
million deal. Microsoft would raise $30 million by selling
two million shares at an assumed price of around $15.
Existing shareholders, bound by Gates's informal rule
that nobody should unload more than 10% of his holdings, would collect the other $10 million for 600,000 or so
shares. The underwriters, as is customary in initial public offerings, would be granted the option to sell more
shares. If they exercised an option for 300,000 additional
shares of stock held by the company, almost 12% of
Microsoft's stock would end up in public hands, enough to
create the liquid market the company wanted.

Gates had thought longest about the price. Guided by
Goldman, he felt the market would accord a higher price-
earnings multiple to Microsoft than to other personal
computer software companies like Lotus and Ashton-
Tate, which have narrower product lines. On the other
hand, he figured the market would give Microsoft a lower
multiple than companies that create software for main-
frame computers because they generally have longer
track records and more predictable revenues. A price of
roughly $15, more than ten times estimated earnings for
fiscal 1986, would put Microsoft's multiple right between
those of personal software companies and mainframers.

A host of questions came up at the all-hands meeting.
Both Shirley and Gates were concerned that going public
would interfere with Microsoft's ability to conduct business. Shirley wondered whether all three of Microsoft's
top officers would be needed for the "road show," meetings
at which company representatives would explain the
offering to stockbrokers and institutional investors. Gates

tried to escape the tour by saying, facetiously, "Hey, make the stock cheap enough and you won't need us to sell it!"

Microsoft's attorney, William H. Neukom, 44, a partner at Shidler McBroom Gates & Lucas—the Gates in the title being Bill's father, William H. Gates—raised another matter. The company would have to tone down its public utterances, he said, lest it appear to be "gun jumping," or touting the stock. Press releases could no longer refer to certain Microsoft programs as "industry standards," no matter how true the phrase. Neukom would review all the company's official statements, which came to include even a preface Gates was writing for a book on new computer technologies.

The most tedious part of taking the company public was writing a prospectus. It was a task rife with contradictions. By law Microsoft's stock could be sold on the basis of information in this document. If the SEC raised big objections to the preliminary version, Microsoft would have to circulate a heavily amended one, inviting rumors that the deal was fishy. However cheerful or gloomy the prospectus, many investors would fail to read it before buying. Then if the market price promptly fell, they would comb the text for the least hint of misrepresentation in order to sue. Still, the prospectus could not be too conservative. Like all such documents, it had to be a discreet sales tool, soft-pedaling weaknesses and stressing strengths, all the while concealing as much as possible from competitors.

Even before Microsoft had picked its underwriters, Robert A. Eshelman, 32, an attorney at Shidler McBroom, had started drafting the prospectus. That task took all of January. "As usual," says one of the investment bankers, "it was like the Bataan death march." Neukom, who had just left Shidler McBroom to join Microsoft, spent the first week of 1986 with Eshelman, sketching in ideas about the company's products and business. Two days a week for the next three weeks, many of the people who had been at the all-hands meeting reconvened at Microsoft's sleek headquarters in a Seattle suburb to edit the prospectus.

At the first sessions, on January 8 and 9, the underwriters brought along their security analysts to help conduct a "due diligence" examination, grilling the company's managers to uncover skeletons. Gaudette was mollified that Sullivan & Cromwell had now furnished a partner from its Los Angeles office, Charles F. Rechlin, 39. Gaudette had met him years before in New York but was bowled over by how much he had changed. Rechlin was 40 pounds lighter and sported shoulder-length hair and a fierce sunburn.

For ten hours Gates, Shirley, and other managers exhaustively described their parts of the business and fielded questions. Surprisingly, the Microsoft crew tended to be more conservative and pessimistic than the interrogators. Steven A. Ballmer, 30, a vice president sometimes described as Gates's alter ego, came up with so many scenarios for Microsoft's demise that one banker cracked: "I'd hate to hear you on a bad day."

By late January only one major item remained undecided—a price range for the stock. The bull market that began in September had kept roaring ahead, pushing up P/E multiples for other software companies. The underwriters suggested a price range of $17 to $20 a share. Gates insisted on, and got, $16 to $19. His argument was ultraconservative: $16 would guarantee that the underwriters would not have to go even lower to sell the shares, while a price of $20 would push Microsoft's market value above half-a-billion dollars, which he thought uncomfortably high. "That was unusual," says Christopher P. Forester, head of Goldman Sachs's high-technology finance group. "Few companies fight for a lower range than the underwriter recommends."

On February 1 a courier rushed the final proof of the prospectus to Los Angeles for Sullivan & Cromwell's approval and continued on to Washington, D.C., with 13 copies. Two days later Microsoft registered with the SEC, the underwriters sent out 38,000 copies of the prospectus, and the lawyers began waiting anxiously for comments from the regulators.

Gates coped with concerns of a different sort. Relatives, friends and acquaintances of Microsoft's managers—from Gates's doctor to a high school chum of Gaudette's—called begging to buy stock at the offering price. Except for about a dozen people, including Gates's grandmother and his former housekeeper, who wanted small lots for sentimental reasons, Gates turned most of them down. "I won't grant any of these goofy requests," he said. "I hate the whole thing. All I'm thinking and dreaming about is selling software, not stock."

Rehearsals for the road show dramatized how differently Gates and Gaudette approached the process of going public. Neukom, Microsoft's in-house attorney, had admonished Gates to say nothing to anybody that deviated from the prospectus or added new information. At Goldman Sachs's New York offices for a February 7 rehearsal, Gates wondered to himself, "With my mouth taped, what's the point of giving a speech?" Addressing about 30 investment bankers and salesmen, he assumed an uncharacteristic, robotic monotone while covering Microsoft's key strengths. He became annoyed when one critic commented, "It's a great first effort, but you can put more into it." Snapped Gates: "You mean I'm supposed to say boring things in an exciting way?"

Gaudette, however, was in his element. He praised and repraised the company's record, studding his talk with cliches and corny jokes. "When it comes to earnings," he exclaimed, showing a graph of quarterly change, "the pavement is bumpy, but the road goes only one way—up!" Describing Microsoft's $72 million in stockholders' equity and its lack of long-term debt, Gaudette teased Goldman Sachs with a competing investment house's slogan: "We made our money the old-fashioned way: We earned it!"

The road show previewed in Phoenix on February 18, and over the next ten days played eight cities, including engagements in London and Edinburgh. Halfway through, the pageant took on an almost festive air. Gates relaxed a bit, having been able to push his products as well as his stock at various ports of call. In London, Eff Martin of Goldman escorted the party to the Royal Observatory at Greenwich, found tickets for the smash musical Les Miserables, and arranged admittance to Annabel's, a popular club. Gates danced the night away with Ruthann Quindlen, a security analyst for Alex. Brown.

Festivity was appropriate. Every road show meeting attracted a full house, and many big institutional investors indicated they would take as much stock as they could get. By the end of February, the Dow Jones industrial average had passed 1700. In London, Martin told Gaudette that Goldman's marketing group considered the Microsoft issue very hot. The $16 to $19 price range would have to be raised, he said, and so would the number of shares to be sold.

The underwriters had wanted to come to market while euphoria from the road show ran high. But the SEC held the starting flag. On March 4 and 5 an SEC reviewer phoned in the commission's comments on the preliminary prospectus to Eshelman. The SEC had picked all sorts of nits, from how Microsoft accounted for returned merchandise to whether Gates had an employment contract (he does not). Its major concern appeared to be that the underwriters allocate shares widely enough to make the offering truly public and not just a bonanza for a handful of privileged investors. Eshelman was relieved. "It was a thorough review," he says, "but it was nothing to make my stomach drop."

On March 6 Microsoft's lawyers and auditors called the SEC to negotiate changes. Meanwhile, the company persuaded two stockholders to sell an additional 295,000 shares. The next day, as the lawyers pored over proofs of a revised prospectus at the San Francisco office of Bowne & Co., the financial printers, Gaudette zestfully battled to raise the price. Eff Martin of Goldman, who had flown up to Seattle that morning, had good news. The "book" on Microsoft—the list of buy orders from institutional investors—was among the best Goldman had ever seen. The underwriters expected the stock to trade at $25 a share, give or take a dollar, several weeks after opening. A sounding of big potential buyers showed that an offering price of $20 to $21 would get the deal done.

Gates asked Martin to leave while he conferred with Shirley and Gaudette. This was a different Gates from the one who two months before thought $20 too high. "These guys who happen to be in good with Goldman and get some stock will make an instant profit of $4," he said. "Why are we handing millions of the company's money to Goldman's favorite clients?" Gaudette stressed that unless Microsoft left some money on the table the institutional investors would stay away. The three decided on a range of $21 to $22 a share, and Gaudette put in a conference call to Goldman and Alex. Brown.

Eric Dobkin, 43, the partner in charge of common stock offerings at Goldman Sachs, felt queasy about Microsoft's counterproposal. For an hour he tussled with Gaudette, using every argument he could muster. Coming out $1 too high would drive off some high-quality investors. Just a few significant defections could lead other investors to think the offering was losing its luster. Dobkin raised the specter of Sun Microsystems, a maker of high-powered microcomputers for engineers that had gone public three days earlier in a deal co-managed by Alex. Brown. Because of overpricing and bad luck—competitors had recently announced new products—Sun's shares had dropped from $16 at the offering to $14.50 on the market. Dobkin warned that the market for software stocks was turning iffy.

Gaudette loved it. "They're in pain!" he crowed to Shirley. "They're used to dictating, but they're not running the show now and they can't stand it." Getting back on the phone, Gaudette crooned: "Eric, I don't mean to upset you, but I can't deny what's in my head. I keep thinking of all that pent-up demand from individual investors, which you haven't factored in. And I keep thinking we may never see you again, but you go back to the institutional investors all the time. They're your customers. I don't know whose interests you're trying to serve, but if you're playing both sides of the street, then we've just become adversaries."

As negotiations dragged on, Shirley became impatient. Eshelman, the securities lawyer from Shidler McBroom, was waiting in San Francisco to get a price range so he could send an amended prospectus off to the SEC. Finally Gaudette told Dobkin, "I've listened to your prayers. Now you're repeating yourself, and it's bullshit." The two compromised on a range of $20 to $22, with two provisos: Goldman would tell investors that the target price was $21 and nothing less, and Dobkin would report Monday on which investors had dropped out.

Monday's news was mixed. Six big investors in Boston were threatening to "uncircle"—to remove their names from Goldman Sachs's list. Chicago and Baltimore were fraying at the edges—T. Rowe Price, for instance, said it might drop out above $20—while the West Coast stood firm. The market had closed flat, worrying Goldman's salesmen. But their spirits revived the next day as the Dow surged 43 points. Gaudette, now confident that he and Dobkin could agree on a final offering price, flew with Neukom to San Francisco to pick up Martin, and the three boarded a red-eye flight for New York.

Sleepless but freshly showered and shaved, Gaudette reached Goldman Sachs's offices at 11 o'clock on Wednesday, March 12. Neukom walked over from Sullivan & Cromwell, where the other lawyers were preparing the last revision of the prospectus. After lunch the two Microsoft officers went to Dobkin's office and patched Shirley and Marquardt into a speakerphone.

The conferees had no trouble agreeing on a final price of $21. The market had risen another 14 points by noon. The reception for a $15 offering that morning by Oracle Systems, another software company, seemed a favorable omen: The stock had opened at $19.25. About half the potential dropouts, including T. Rowe Price, had decided to stay in.

The only remaining issue was the underwriting discount, or "spread"—the portion of the price that would go to the underwriters to cover salesmen's commissions, underwriting expenses, and management fees. Having agreed fairly easily over dollars, the two sides bogged down over pennies.

Microsoft had always had a low spread in mind, no more than 6.5% of the selling price. That was before negotiators at Sun Microsystems, where Marquardt is a director, wangled 6.13% on a $64 million offering. Gates wanted Microsoft to get at least as good a deal on its offering. But he had gone to Australia, where he was difficult to reach. In theory Gaudette lacked authority to go above 6.13%, or just under $1.29 a share.

Dobkin opened with an oration. He touched on what other Goldman clients had paid, noting that Sun's spread was off the bottom of the charts. He suggested that the managing underwriters deserved healthy compensation; after all, their marketing efforts had raised Microsoft's offering price 20%. Goldman's best offer, Dobkin said, was 6.5%, or $1.36 a share. But if pushed very hard and given no alternative, it might, just to keep things amicable, go as low as $1.34. Having given away $26,000—each penny of the spread was worth $31,000—Dobkin and his contingent left the room to let Microsoft's side confer.

When they returned, Gaudette declared that Bill Gates had given definite orders: no more than $1.28. Besides, he argued, Microsoft was a much easier deal to handle than Sun. As to the underwriters' marketing efforts, selling more shares at a higher price was its own reward since it automatically increased the money in their pockets.

At 3:30 the two sides were stalemated, Goldman Sachs now at $1.33 and Microsoft at $1.30. They were arguing over all of $93,000 in a total fee of more than $4 million, and pressure was building. The market was turning flat and would close in minutes. Members of the syndicate were clamoring to know whether the deal was done. Dobkin kept reiterating his arguments. "Eric, you're wasting my time," Gaudette sighed wearily, donning his coat. "I'm going to visit me sainted mother in Astoria. When you've got something to say, send a limo to pick me up." With that, the Goldman team left the room.

Dobkin returned alone and closed the door. "Sometimes these things go better with fewer people," he observed. Gaudette insisted he lacked authority to go higher. "All I can do is try to get another penny from Jon," he said. "But I'm calling him just one more time, so don't screw up." "Make the call,' Dobkin said.

Gaudette caught Shirley as he was leaving a Bellevue, Washington restaurant to buy a car for his daughter as a 16th birthday gift. The lowest spread they could get, Gaudette said, was $1.31. Though it was above Sun's spread, it was way below what any other personal computer software company had achieved. Shirley approved. Neukom beckoned Dobkin back into the room, and Gaudette uttered one phrase that betokened his assent to $1.31: "It's a go!" Dobkin hugged Gaudette. David Miller, a beefy ex-football player who was Goldman's syndicated manager for the offering, thundered down the stairs to his office bellowing to his assistant, "Doreen, we have a deal!"

Gaudette saved his cheers for the next morning. At 8 a.m. a courier had delivered Microsoft's "filing package" to the SEC—three copies of the final prospectus and a bundle of exhibits, including the underwriters' agreement to buy the shares, which had been signed only hours earlier. The commission declared at 9:15 that Microsoft's registration was effective. On the trading floor at Gold-man Sachs, Gaudette heard a trader say, "We're going to shoot the moon and open at 25!"

At 9:35 Microsoft's stock traded publicly on the over-the-counter market for the first time at $25.75. Within minutes Goldman Sachs and Alex. Brown exercised their option to take an extra 300,000 shares between them. Gaudette could hardly believe the tumult. Calling Shirley from the floor, he shouted into the phone, "It's wild! I've never seen anything like it—every last person here is trading Microsoft and nothing else."

The strength of retail demand caught everyone by sur-prise. By the end of the first day of trading, some 2.5 mil-lion shares had changed hands, and the price of Microsoft's stock stood at $27.75. The opportunity to take a quick profit was too great for many institutional investors to resist. Over the next few weeks they sold off roughly half their shares. An estimated one-third of the shares in Microsoft's offering has wound up in the hands of individuals.

In the wake of Microsoft's triumph, Gates still fears that being public will hurt the company. No longer able to offer stock at bargain prices, he finds it harder to lure tal-ented programmers and managers aboard. On the other hand, his greatly enriched executives have kept cool heads. Shirley, who cleared over $1 million on the shares he sold, has been the most lavish. He bought a 45-foot cabin cruiser, traded in two cars for fancier models, and may give in to his daughter's pleas for an exotic horse. Gates used part of the $1.6 million he got to pay off a $150,000 mortgage and may buy a $5,000 ski boat—if he finds time. One vice president who raked in more than $500,000 can think of nothing to buy except a $1,000 cus-tom-made bicycle frame; a programmer who received nearly $200,000 plans to use it to expand his working hours by hiring a housekeeper.

That's just the kind of attitude Gates prizes. Con-stantly urging people to ignore the price of Microsoft's stock, he warns that it may become highly volatile. A few weeks after the offering, strolling through the software development area, he noticed a chart of Microsoft's stock price posted on the door to a programmer's office. Gates was bothered. "Is this a distraction?" he asked.

[Note: The "distractions" that Bill Gates feared apparently did not affect the future growth and prosperity of his company. Since the 1986 IPO, Microsoft has grown to the point where today it is a dominant force in the software and computer industry.]

EXCERPTS FROM DRKOOP.COM, INC.'S PROSPECTUS DATED JUNE 8, 1999

PROSPECTUS
9,375,000 Shares

[LOGO OF DRKOOP APPEARS HERE]

Drkoop.com, Inc.

Common Stock

This is an initial public offering of 9,375,000 shares of common stock of Drkoop.com, Inc. Drkoop.com, Inc. is selling all of the shares of common stock offered under this prospectus.

There is currently no public market for the shares. Our common stock has been approved for listing on the Nasdaq National Market under the symbol "KOOP."

At our request, the underwriters will reserve at the initial public offering price up to $10 million of common stock for sale to each of Dell Computer Corporation and FHC Health Systems Investment Company, L.C., and up to $5 million of common stock for sale to Quintiles Transnational Corp., all of whom have expressed a non-binding interest in acquiring these shares. This would represent an aggregate of 2,777,777 shares of common stock at the initial public offering price.

Investing in our common stock involves a high degree of risk. See "Risk Factors" beginning on page 240 to read about risks that you should consider carefully before buying shares of our common stock.

Neither the Securities and Exchange Commission nor any other regulatory body has approved or disapproved these securities or passed upon the accuracy or adequacy of this prospectus. Any representation to the contrary is a criminal offense.

	Per Share	Total
Public offering price	$9.00	$84,375,000
Underwriting discounts and commissions	$0.63	$ 5,906,250
Proceeds, before expenses, to us	$8.37	$78,468,750

Drkoop.com, Inc. has granted the underwriters a 30-day option to purchase up to an additional 1,406,250 shares of common stock from us at the initial public offering price less the underwriting discount. The underwriters expect to deliver the shares on June 11, 1999.

Bear, Stearns & Co., Inc.
Hambrecht & Quist
Wit Capital Corporation
as e-Manager™

The date of this prospectus is June 8, 1999

Description of Artwork

Inside Front Cover Overleaf
Photograph of C. Everett Koop, M.D., with the following caption: "During my tenure as U.S. Surgeon General, I saw first-hand the powerful impact a well-informed public made on the nation's health. Now, the World Wide Web presents exciting new opportunities to empower consumers to become active, informed participants in managing their own healthcare. I firmly believe that this is the path to significantly improving the quality of healthcare for years to come."

Inside Front Cover
Pictures of the Drkoop.com logo and the logos of portals and other websites, traditional media and healthcare organization affiliates.

Underneath the Drkoop.com logo in the middle of the inside front cover is a caption that reads as follows: "We are an Internet-based consumer healthcare network that includes the interactive website, www.drkoop.com. Our network provides individuals with trusted healthcare content, services and tools to empower them to better manage their health. Our network affiliates include other Internet portals, websites, healthcare organizations and traditional sources of health and medical news."

The following caption is under the logos of the new media affiliates: "We distribute Drkoop.com content to affiliated portals and other websites that have established themselves as pathways for a broad variety of information. We intend to affiliate with selected websites that have the potential to drive traffic to our network and provide broad exposure to the Drkoop.com brand."

The following caption is under the logos of the traditional media affiliates: "Establishing affiliations with traditional media outlets allows us to deliver quality healthcare content to a targeted audience. Affiliates provide local, relevant information directly to a local audience. Through this unique means of distribution, Drkoop.com is building a leading network of health content and editorial-based, breaking health news on the Internet."

The following caption is under the logos of the healthcare industry affiliates: "Through our Community Partner Program, we enroll hospitals and health systems as local affiliates. This enables healthcare organizations to integrate the Drkoop.com brand and content into their on-line initiatives. Through this program, healthcare organizations can supply their patients with on-line health resources and interactive capabilities that allow patients to educate themselves and make informed decisions."

PROSPECTUS SUMMARY

This summary highlights certain information found in greater detail elsewhere in this prospectus. In addition to this summary, we urge you to read the entire prospectus carefully, especially the risks of investing in our common stock discussed under "Risk Factors," before you decide to buy our common stock.

Drkoop.com

Our Business

Our company operates Drkoop.com, an Internet-based consumer healthcare network consisting of a consumer-focused interactive website and affiliate relationships with Internet portals, certain other websites, healthcare organizations and traditional media outlets. Our website, www.drkoop.com, is a healthcare portal with the following components:

- dynamic healthcare content on a wide variety of subjects, including information on acute ailments, chronic illnesses, nutrition, fitness and wellness, and access to medical databases, publications, and real-time medical news;
- interactive communities consisting of over 130 hosted chat support groups and tools that permit users to personalize their on-line experience; and
- opportunities to purchase healthcare-related products and services on-line.

We launched our website in July 1998 and, according to commercial software that we utilize, by June 1, 1999 www.drkoop.com had attracted over 6 million unique users and enrolled over 280,000 registered users.

Our network affiliates provide easy access to the information and services we offer on www.drkoop.com to their respective customers. We believe that we will benefit from these affiliate relationships through:

- broader exposure of our brand;
- higher volumes of traffic being driven to www.drkoop.com; and
- a cost-effective method of acquiring and distributing local healthcare content.

Our Market Opportunity

Healthcare is the largest segment of the U.S. economy, representing the annual expenditure of roughly $1 trillion, and health and medical information is one of the fastest growing areas of interest on the Internet. According to Cyber Dialogue, an industry research firm, during the 12-month period ended July 1998, approximately 17 million adults in the United States searched on-line for health and medical information, and approximately 50% of these individuals made off-line purchases after seeking information on the Internet. Cyber Dialogue estimates that approximately 70% of the persons searching for health and medical information on-line believe the Internet empowers them by providing them with information before and after they go to a doctor's office. Cyber Dialogue also estimates that the number of adults in the United States searching for on-line health and medical information will grow to approximately 30 million in the year 2000, and they will spend approximately $150 billion for all types of health-related products and services off-line.

Our Business Model

Our company's founders, including former U.S. Surgeon General Dr. C. Everett Koop, created Drkoop.com to empower consumers to better manage their personal health with comprehensive, relevant and timely information. Our objective is to establish the Drkoop.com network as the most trusted and comprehensive source of consumer healthcare information and services on the Internet. Our business model is to earn advertising and subscription revenues from advertisers, merchants, manufacturers and healthcare organizations who desire to reach a highly targeted community of healthcare consumers on the Internet. We also earn revenues by facilitating e-commerce transactions, such as sales of prescription refills, vitamins and nutritional supplements, and insurance services offered by outside parties.

Our Strategy

Our business strategy incorporates the following key elements:

- establish the Drkoop.com brand so that consumers associate the trustworthiness and credibility of Dr. C. Everett Koop with our company;

- provide consumers with high quality healthcare content to attract users to www.drkoop.com and promote their loyalty to our website;
- syndicate content through affiliates to promote traffic growth;
- develop and expand on-line healthcare communities to allow users with similar health-related experiences to exchange information and gather news and knowledge in a secure, anonymous environment;
- provide consumers with unique features and tools, such as one that educates consumers on the interaction among various drugs and other substances;
- deploy a comprehensive personal medical record which will allow users to establish and maintain a lifelong record of their health and medical information in a secure portion of our database;
- provide an attractive website that can deliver advertising in a highly targeted manner, thereby commanding higher advertising rates; and
- facilitate e-commerce transactions offered by merchants, manufacturers and service providers to a highly targeted community of health-conscious consumers.

Recent Developments

On April 9, 1999 we entered into agreements with Infoseek Corporation and the Buena Vista Internet Group, a unit of The Walt Disney Company, under which we will be the exclusive provider of health and related content on three websites of the Go Network: Go.com Health Center, ESPN.com Training Room and the Family.com Health Channel. Under the Infoseek agreement, Drkoop.com will also be the premier health content provider for ABCnews.com. In addition, Drkoop.com will be the exclusive pharmacy and drugstore, health insurance and clinical trials partner in the Go.com Health Center. In the event Drkoop.com elects not to provide specific content, it may be obtained from a third party. We believe that these agreements will contribute substantially to our brand awareness and increase traffic on our website. The term of these agreements is for three years, although either party may elect to terminate the relationship after two years. We will pay Infoseek and Buena Vista approximately $57.9 million in total consideration.

Our principal executive offices are located at 8920 Business Park Drive, Suite 200, Austin, Texas 78759, and our telephone number is (512) 726-5110.

The Offering

Common stock offered . . . . . . 9,375,000 shares

Common stock outstanding
  after this offering . . . . 27,514,591 shares

Use of proceeds . . . . We intend to use the net proceeds of this offering to fund operating losses and for general corporate purposes, including expansion of our network, advertising, brand promotion, content development and working capital. We may also use a portion of the proceeds for strategic alliances and acquisitions and to repay debt. See "Use of Proceeds."

Nasdaq National
  Market symbol . . . . KOOP

The number of shares of common stock outstanding after this offering is based on shares outstanding on March 31, 1999. This calculation excludes:

- 10,492,530 shares of common stock issuable upon exercise of options outstanding under our Amended and Restated 1997 Stock Option Plan with a weighted average exercise

price of $0.53 per share (5,240,902 of these options were exercisable as of March 31, 1999; the balance are subject to future vesting requirements);
* 1,747,451 shares of common stock issuable upon exercise of options to be granted contemporaneously with this offering under our 1999 Equity Participation Plan with an exercise price equal to the public offering price listed on the cover of this prospectus;
* 33,482 shares of common stock issuable upon exercise of warrants with an exercise price of $4.78 per share; and
* 775,000 shares of common stock issuable upon exercise of warrants with an exercise price of $8.60 per share.

This calculation includes:

* 7,249,667 shares of common stock to be issued upon the conversion of all outstanding shares of convertible preferred stock;
* 439,187 shares of common stock issuable assuming conversion of all convertible notes outstanding at March 31, 1999 ($2.8 million aggregate principal amount plus accrued interest); and
* 1,345,185 shares of common stock to be issued upon the closing of this offering to satisfy in full a purchase option and related anti-dilution adjustment rights.

Please see "Management—Stock Option Plans" and "Description of Securities."

Conventions Which Apply to This Prospectus

Unless we indicate otherwise, all information in this prospectus reflects the following:

* a three-for-one stock split effected in March 1999;
* a five-for-two stock split effected in June 1999;
* no exercise by the underwriters of their overallotment option to purchase up to 1,406,250 additional shares of common stock;
* the conversion of all outstanding shares of our convertible preferred stock into 7,249,667 shares of our common stock upon the closing of this offering;
* the conversion of all convertible notes outstanding as of March 31, 1999 ($2.8 million aggregate principal amount plus accrued interest) into 439,187 shares of common stock upon the closing of this offering; and
* the issuance of 1,345,185 shares of common stock to satisfy in full a purchase option and related anti-dilution adjustment rights.

References in this prospectus to "Drkoop.com," "we," "our" and "us" refer to Drkoop.com, Inc., a Delaware corporation. References to the offering refer to the initial public offering of our common stock being made by this prospectus. Drkoop.com, Inc. was incorporated as a Texas corporation in July 1997 under the name Personal Medical Records, Inc., changed its name to Empower Health Corporation in April 1998 and reincorporated as Drkoop.com, Inc., a Delaware corporation, in March 1999. "Drkoop.com," "Dr. Koop's Community" and "Dr. Koop's Personal Medical Records" are trademarks of ours. Each trademark, trade name or service mark of any other company appearing in this prospectus belongs to its holder. . . .

RISK FACTORS

Any investment in our common stock involves a high degree of risk. You should consider carefully the following information about these risks, together with the other information contained in this prospectus, before you decide whether to buy our common stock. If any of the following risks actually occur, our business, results of operations and financial condition would likely suffer. In any such case, the market price of our common stock could decline, and you may lose all or part of the money you paid to buy our common stock.

Risks Related to Our Business

Our business is difficult to evaluate because we have an extremely limited operating history.

We were incorporated in July 1997 and launched our Internet operations in July 1998. Accordingly, we have an extremely limited operating history. An investor in our common stock must consider the risks, uncertainties, expenses and difficulties frequently encountered by companies in their early stages of development, particularly companies in new and rapidly evolving markets, including the Internet market. These risks and difficulties include our ability to:

- attract a larger audience of users to our Internet-based consumer healthcare network;
- increase awareness of our brand;
- strengthen user loyalty and increase the number of registered users;
- offer compelling on-line content, services and e-commerce opportunities;
- maintain our current, and develop new, affiliate relationships;
- attract a large number of advertisers who desire to reach our users;
- respond effectively to the offerings of competitive providers of healthcare information on the Internet;
- continue to develop and upgrade our technology; and
- attract, retain and motivate qualified personnel.

We also depend on the growing use of the Internet for advertising, commerce and communication, and on general economic conditions. We cannot assure you that our business strategy will be successful or that we will successfully address these risks or difficulties. If we fail to address adequately any of these risks or difficulties our business would likely suffer. Please see "Management's Discussion and Analysis of Financial Condition and Results of Operations" and our financial statements for detailed information on our extremely limited operating history.

Our business is changing rapidly, which could cause our quarterly operating results to vary and our stock price to fluctuate.

Our revenues and operating results may vary significantly from quarter to quarter due to a number of factors, not all of which are in our control. If we have a shortfall in revenue in relation to our expenses, or if our expenses precede increased revenues, then our business would be materially adversely affected. This would likely affect the market price of our common stock in a manner which may be unrelated to our long-term operating performance.

Important factors which could cause our results to fluctuate materially include:

- our ability to attract and retain users;
- our ability to attract and retain advertisers and sponsors and maintain advertiser and sponsor satisfaction;
- traffic levels on our Internet site;
- our ability to attract and retain customers and maintain customer satisfaction for our existing and future e-commerce offerings;
- new Internet sites, services or products introduced by us or our competitors;
- the level of Internet and other on-line services usage;
- our ability to upgrade and develop our systems and infrastructure and attract new personnel in a timely and effective manner;
- our ability to successfully integrate operations and technologies from any acquisitions, joint ventures, or other business combinations or investments; and
- technical difficulties or system downtime affecting the operation of our website.

Our revenues for the foreseeable future will remain dependent on user traffic levels, advertising and e-commerce activity on Drkoop.com and the level of affiliate subscriptions. Such future revenues are difficult to forecast. In addition, we plan to increase our sales and marketing operations, expand and develop content and upgrade and enhance our technology and infrastructure development in order to support our growth. Many of the expenses associated with these activities—for example, personnel costs and technology and infrastructure costs—are relatively fixed in the short-term. We may be unable to adjust spending quickly enough to offset any unexpected revenue shortfall, in which case our results of operations would suffer.

We have a history of losses and negative cash flow and anticipate continued losses.

Since our inception, we have incurred significant losses and negative cash flow, and as of March 31, 1999, had an accumulated deficit of approximately $23.9 million, which included $9.9 million for accretion to fair value of the mandatory redeemable Series B convertible preferred stock. We have not achieved profitability and expect to continue to incur operating losses for the foreseeable future as we fund operating and capital expenditures in areas such as expansion of our network, advertising, brand promotion, content development, sales and marketing, and operating infrastructure. Our business model assumes that consumers will be attracted to and use healthcare information and related content available on our Internet-based consumer healthcare network which will, in turn, allow us the opportunity to sell advertising designed to reach those consumers. Our business model also assumes that those consumers will access important healthcare needs through electronic commerce using our website and that local healthcare organizations will affiliate with us. This business model is not yet proven, and we cannot assure you that we will ever achieve or sustain profitability or that our operating losses will not increase in the future. We have received a report from our independent auditors for our fiscal year ended December 31, 1998 containing an explanatory paragraph that describes the uncertainty as to our ability to continue as a going concern due to our historical negative cash flow and because, as of the date they rendered their opinion, we did not have access to sufficient committed capital to meet our projected operating needs for at least the next twelve months. Upon completion of this offering, we will have available that capital. However, we cannot assure you that we will achieve profitable operations. Please see "Selected Financial Data" and "Management's Discussion and Analysis of Financial Condition and Results of Operations."

We must establish, maintain and strengthen our brand in order to attract users to our network and generate advertising, sponsorship and e-commerce revenue.

In order to expand our audience of users and increase our on-line traffic, we must establish, maintain and strengthen our brand. For us to be successful in establishing our brand, healthcare consumers must perceive us as a trusted source of healthcare information, and advertisers, merchants and manufacturers must perceive us as an effective marketing and sales channel for their products and services. We expect that we will need to increase substantially our marketing budget in our efforts to establish brand recognition and brand loyalty. Our business could be materially adversely affected if our marketing efforts are not productive or if we cannot strengthen our brand.

In addition, a key element of our strategy to establish, maintain and strengthen our brand is to encourage consumers to associate us with Dr. C. Everett Koop. We believe that consumers consider Dr. C. Everett Koop to be a trustworthy and credible leader in the healthcare field. We cannot assure you, however, that Dr. C. Everett Koop will maintain this reputation, any damage to which could materially adversely impact our business. In addition, if our relationship with Dr. C. Everett Koop terminates for any reason, we would need to change the name of our website and devote substantial resources towards building a new marketing and brand strategy.

Key elements of our marketing and brand building strategies are dependent on our relationship with Dr. C. Everett Koop.

A key element of our strategy is to associate our company with former U.S. Surgeon General C. Everett Koop, Chairman of the Board of our company and a person who we believe is viewed by consumers as a trustworthy and credible leader in the healthcare field. We are a party to an agreement, dated January 5, 1999, as amended, with Dr. C. Everett Koop which permits us to use his image, name and likeness in connection with healthcare-related services and products. Under this agreement, our use of Dr. C. Everett Koop's name, image or likeness is subject to his prior written approval of the resulting products, which may not be unreasonably withheld. As consideration for the Koop agreement, we are obligated to pay Dr. C. Everett Koop a royalty equal to 2% of our revenues derived from sales of our current products and up to 4% of our revenues derived from sales of new products during the term of the agreement, including any rebranding period. The Koop agreement is exclusive and for a term of five years, subject to automatic renewal for additional three-year terms unless it is terminated by either party within 120 days of the end of each term. If a voluntary termination is requested by Dr. C. Everett Koop and is not the result of a breach or default by us, we will have the right on a non-exclusive basis for three years following the end of the term to rebrand and sell approved products bearing the name, image or likeness of Dr. C. Everett Koop. If we default in our obligations and do not promptly cure the default, Dr. C. Everett Koop may terminate the Koop agreement, no rebranding period will apply and we would immediately lose all rights to use Dr. C. Everett Koop's name and likeness. Dr. C. Everett Koop may also terminate the Koop agreement upon a change in control of our company.

If our agreement with Dr. C. Everett Koop were terminated prior to the end of its current term or not renewed at the end of its current term, we would need to change the name of our website and devote substantial resources towards building a new marketing and brand strategy. Without our ability to use Dr. C. Everett Koop's name and likeness or Dr. C. Everett Koop's participation in our business, we may not be able to continue to attract a significant amount of user traffic and advertisers to our website. The potential also exists that if Dr. C. Everett Koop ends his affiliation with our company, we could suffer a significant loss of credibility and trust with healthcare consumers as a result. Any development that would cause Dr. C. Everett Koop to exercise his right to terminate his relationship with our company or which otherwise would cause us to lose the benefits of our affiliation with him would have a material adverse effect on our business, results of operation and financial condition. We do not maintain "key person" life insurance for Dr. C. Everett Koop or any of our personnel. Please see "Management—Agreements with Dr. C. Everett Koop."

We have committed significant financial and marketing resources to expand our network; if we are unable to earn revenues in excess of these commitments, our business will suffer.

In order to expand our network, we have entered into a number of strategic partnerships which involve the payment of significant funds for prominent or exclusive carriage of our healthcare information and services. These transactions are premised on the assumption that the traffic we obtain from these arrangements will permit us to earn revenues in excess of the payments made to partners. This assumption is not yet proven, and if we are unsuccessful in generating sufficient resources to offset these expenditures, we will likely be unable to operate our business. On April 9, 1999 we entered into agreements with Infoseek Corporation and the Buena Vista Internet Group, a unit of The Walt Disney Company, under which we will be the exclusive provider of health and related content on three websites of the Go Network. Under the Infoseek agreement, Drkoop.com will also be the premier health content provider for ABCnews.com. The term of these agreements is for three years for total consideration of approximately $57.9 million.

In order to attract and retain our audience of users, we must provide healthcare content, tools and other features which meet the changing demands of those users.

One of our fundamental business objectives is for Drkoop.com to be a trusted source for healthcare information and services. As with any form of consumer-oriented media, we have to provide editorial content, interactive tools and other features that consumers demand in order to continue to attract and retain our audience of users. We expect that competitive factors will create a continuing need for us to retain, improve and add to our editorial content, interactive tools and other features. We will not only have to expend significant funds and other resources to continue to improve our network, but we must also properly anticipate and respond to consumer preferences and demands. Competition for content will likely increase the fees charged by high quality content providers. The addition of new features will also require that we continue to improve the technology underlying our website. These requirements are significant, and we may fail to execute on them quickly and efficiently. If we fail to expand the breadth of our offerings quickly, or these offerings fail to achieve market acceptance, our business will suffer significantly.

Our business model relies on Internet advertising and sponsorship activities which may not be effective or profitable marketing media.

Our future is highly dependent on increased use of the Internet as an advertising medium. We expect to derive a substantial amount of our revenues from advertising and sponsorships. The Internet advertising market is new and rapidly evolving, and we cannot yet predict its effectiveness as compared to traditional media advertising. As a result, demand and market acceptance for Internet advertising solutions are uncertain. Most of our current or potential advertising customers have little or no experience advertising over the Internet and have allocated only a limited portion of their advertising budgets to Internet advertising. The adoption of Internet advertising, particularly by those entities that have historically relied upon traditional media for advertising, requires the acceptance of a new way of conducting business, exchanging information and advertising products and services. Such customers may find Internet advertising to be less effective for promoting their products and services relative to traditional advertising media. We cannot assure you that the market for Internet advertising will continue to emerge or become sustainable. If the market for Internet advertising fails to develop or develops more slowly than we expect, then our ability to generate advertising revenue would be materially adversely affected.

Various pricing models are used to sell advertising on the Internet. It is difficult to predict which, if any, will emerge as the industry standard, thereby making it difficult to project our future advertising rates and revenues. Our advertising revenues could be adversely affected if we are unable to adapt to new forms of Internet advertising. Moreover, "filter" software programs are available that limit or prevent advertising from being delivered to an Internet user's computer. Widespread adoption of this software could adversely affect the commercial viability of Internet advertising.

In order to execute our growth plan we must attract, retain and motivate highly skilled employees, and we face significant competition from other Internet and new media companies in doing so.

Our ability to execute our growth plan and be successful also depends on our continuing ability to attract, retain and motivate highly skilled employees. In addition to Dr. C. Everett Koop, Chairman of the Board, we depend on the continued services of key board members, our senior management and other personnel, particularly Donald W. Hackett, Chief Executive Officer. As we continue to grow, we will need to hire additional personnel in all operational areas. Competition for personnel throughout the Internet and related new-media industry is intense. We may be unable to retain our key employees or attract, assimilate or retain other highly qualified employees in the future. We have from time to time in the past experienced, and we expect to continue to experience in the future, difficulty in hiring and retaining highly skilled employees with appropriate qualifications. If we do not succeed in attracting new personnel or retaining and motivating our current personnel, our business will be adversely affected. Please see "Management" for detailed information on our key personnel.

In addition, as our market develops, seasonal and cyclical patterns may emerge. These patterns may affect our revenues. We cannot yet predict to what extent our operations will prove to be seasonal.

Due to the factors noted above and the other risks discussed in this section, you should not rely on quarter-to-quarter comparisons of our results of operations as indicators of future performance. It is possible that in some future periods our operating results may be below the expectations of public market analysts and investors. In this event, the price of our common stock may underperform or fall. Please see "Management's Discussion and Analysis of Financial Condition and Results of Operations."

We depend on third-party relationships, many of which are short-term or terminable, to generate advertising and provide us with content.

We depend, and will continue to depend, on a number of third-party relationships to increase traffic on Drkoop.com and thereby generate advertising and other revenues. Outside parties on which we depend include unrelated website operators that provide links to Drkoop.com, providers of healthcare content and the on-line property representation company which provides us with advertising sales services. Many of our arrangements with third-party Internet sites and other third-party service providers are not exclusive and are short-term or may be terminated at the convenience of either party. We cannot assure you that third parties regard our relationship with them as important to their own respective businesses and operations. They may reassess their commitment to us at any time in the future and may develop their own competitive services or products.

We intend to produce only a portion of the healthcare content that will be found on the Drkoop.com network. We will rely on third-party organizations that have the appropriate expertise, technical capability, name recognition, reputation for integrity, and willingness to syndicate product content for branding and distribution by others. As health-related content grows on the Internet, we believe that there will be increasing competition for the best product suppliers, which may result in a competitor acquiring a key supplier on an exclusive basis, or in significantly higher content prices. Such an outcome could make the Drkoop.com network less attractive or useful for an end user which could reduce our advertising and e-commerce revenues.

We cannot assure you that we will be able to maintain relationships with third parties that supply us with content, software or related products or services that are crucial to our success, or that such content, software, products or services will be able to sustain any third-party claims or rights against their use. Also, we cannot assure you that the content, software, products or services of those companies that provide access or links to our website will achieve market acceptance or commercial success. Accordingly, we cannot assure you that our existing relationships will result in sustained business partnerships, successful product or service offerings or the generation of significant revenues for us.

We have recently experienced and are currently experiencing rapid growth in our business, and our inability to manage this growth could harm our business.

We have experienced and are currently experiencing a period of significant growth. This growth has placed, and the future growth we anticipate in our operations will continue to place, a significant strain on our resources. As part of this growth, we will have to implement new operational and financial systems and procedures and controls, expand, train and manage our employee base, and maintain close coordination among our technical, accounting, finance, marketing, sales and editorial staffs. If we are unable to manage our growth effectively, our business, results of operations and financial condition could be adversely affected.

Several members of our senior management joined us in 1998 or early 1999, including Dennis J. Upah, Chief Operating Officer, and Susan M. Georgen-Saad, Chief Financial Officer. These individuals are currently becoming integrated with the other members of our management team. We cannot assure you that our management team will be able to work together effectively or successfully manage our growth. We believe that the successful integration of our management team is critical to our ability to effectively manage our operations and support our anticipated future growth.

Any future acquisitions we make of companies or technologies may result in disruptions to our business and/or the distraction of our management, due to difficulties in assimilating acquired personnel and operations.

We may acquire or make investments in complementary businesses, technologies, services or products if appropriate opportunities arise. From time to time we engage in discussions and negotiations with companies regarding our acquiring or investing in such companies' businesses, products, services or technologies, and we regularly engage in such discussions and negotiations in the ordinary course of our business. Some of those discussions also contemplate the other party making an investment in our company. To date we have entered into such relationships with Superior Consultant Holdings Corporation and HealthMagic, Inc. We cannot assure you that we will be able to identify future suitable acquisition or investment candidates, or if we do identify suitable candidates, that we will be able to make such acquisitions or investments on commercially acceptable terms or at all. If we acquire or invest in another company, we could have difficulty in assimilating that company's personnel, operations, technology and software. In addition, the key personnel of the acquired company may decide not to work for us. If we make other types of acquisitions, we could have difficulty in integrating the acquired products, services or technologies into our operations. These difficulties could disrupt our ongoing business, distract our management and employees, increase our expenses and adversely affect our results of operations. Furthermore, we may incur indebtedness or issue equity securities to pay for any future acquisitions. The issuance of equity securities would be dilutive to our existing stockholders. As of the date of this prospectus, we have no agreement to enter into any material investment or acquisition transaction.

If our ability to expand our network infrastructure is constrained in any way we could lose customers and suffer damage to our operating results.

Presently, a relatively limited number of consumers use our website. We must continue to expand and adapt our network infrastructure to accommodate additional users, increase transaction volumes and changing consumer and customer requirements. We may not be able to accurately project the rate or timing of increases, if any, in the use of our website or to expand and upgrade our systems and infrastructure to accommodate such increases. Our systems may not accommodate increased use while maintaining acceptable overall performance. Service lapses could cause our users to instead use the on-line services of our competitors.

Many of our service agreements, such as those with our Community Partners, contain performance standards. If we fail to meet these standards, our customers could terminate their agreements with us or require that we refund part or all of the license fees. The loss of any of our service agreements and/or associated revenue would directly and significantly impact our business. We may be unable to expand or adapt our network infrastructure to meet additional demand or our customers' changing needs on a timely basis, at a commercially reasonable cost, or at all.

We may have liability for information we provide on our website or which is accessed from our website.

Because users of our website access health content and services relating to a condition they may have or may distribute our content to others, third parties may sue us for defamation, negligence, copyright or trademark infringement, personal injury or other matters. We could also become liable if confidential information is disclosed inappropriately. These types of claims have been brought, sometimes successfully, against on-line services in the past. Others could also sue us for the content and services that are accessible from our website through links to other websites or through content and materials that may be posted by our users in chat rooms or bulletin boards. While our agreements, including those with content providers, in some cases provide that we will be indemnified against such liabilities, such indemnification, if available, may not be adequate. Our insurance may not adequately protect us against these types of claims. Further, our business is based on establishing the Drkoop.com network as a trustworthy and dependable provider of healthcare information and services. Allegations of impropriety, even if unfounded, could therefore have a material adverse effect on our reputation and our business.

Any failure or inability to protect our intellectual property rights could adversely affect our ability to establish our brand.

Our intellectual property is important to our business. We rely on a combination of copyright, trademark and trade secret laws, confidentiality procedures and contractual provisions to protect our intellectual property. Federal registrations are pending for the trademark "Drkoop.com," as well as other service and trademarks which incorporate the Dr. Koop name. Our right to use the Dr. Koop name is granted to us under an agreement with Dr. C. Everett Koop. If we lose our right to use the Dr. Koop name, we would be forced to change our corporate name and adopt a new domain name. These changes could confuse current and potential customers and would adversely impact our business. We also rely on a variety of technologies that are licensed from third parties, including our database and Internet server software, which is used in the Drkoop.com website to perform key functions. These third-party licenses may not be available to us on commercially reasonable terms in the future. For a more complete description of the risks we face relating to our intellectual property, please see "Business—Intellectual Property."

Year 2000 problems may disrupt our operations which could result in lost revenues and increased operating costs.

Because our business depends on computer software, we have begun to assess the Year 2000 readiness of our systems. We are also in the process of contacting certain third-party vendors, licensors and providers of hardware, software and services regarding their Year 2000 readiness. Following our Year 2000 assessment and after contacting these third parties, we will be able to make a final evaluation of our state of readiness, potential risks and costs, and to determine to what extent a contingency plan is necessary. Third-party software, hardware or services incorporated into our systems may need to be revised or replaced, which could be time consuming and expensive, potentially resulting in lost revenues and increased costs for us. For a preliminary evaluation of the potential impact of these Year 2000-related issues on us, please see "Management's Discussion and Analysis of Financial Condition and Results of Operations—Impact of the Year 2000."

We do not expect to pay dividends, and investors should not buy our common stock expecting to receive dividends.

We have never declared or paid any cash dividends on our capital stock. We presently intend to retain future earnings, if any, to finance the expansion of our business and do not expect to pay any cash dividends in the foreseeable future. Investors should not purchase our common stock with the expectation of receiving cash dividends.

We are subject to anti-takeover provisions in our charter and in our contracts that could delay or prevent an acquisition of our company, even if such an acquisition would be beneficial to our stockholders.

Certain provisions of our certificate of incorporation, our bylaws, Delaware law and contracts to which we are party could make it more difficult for a third party to acquire us, even if doing so might be beneficial to our stockholders. Please see "Management—Agreements with Dr. C. Everett Koop" and "Description of Securities."

Our business may face additional risks and uncertainties not presently known to us which could cause our business to suffer.

In addition to the risks specifically identified in this Risk Factors section or elsewhere in this prospectus, we may face additional risks and uncertainties not presently known to us or that we currently deem immaterial which ultimately impair our business, results of operations and financial condition.

Risks Related to Our Industry

Consumers and the healthcare industry must accept the Internet as a source of healthcare content and services for our business model to be successful.

To be successful, we must attract to our network a significant number of consumers as well as other participants in the healthcare industry. To date, consumers have generally looked to healthcare professionals as their principal source for health and wellness information. Our business model assumes that consumers will use healthcare information available on our network, that consumers will access important healthcare needs through electronic commerce using our website, and that local healthcare organizations will affiliate with us. This business model is not yet proven, and if we are unable to successfully implement our business model, our business will be materially adversely affected.

The Internet industry is highly competitive and changing rapidly, and we may not have the resources to compete adequately.

The number of Internet websites offering users healthcare content, products and services is vast and increasing at a rapid rate. These companies compete with us for users, advertisers, e-commerce transactions and other sources of on-line revenue. In addition, traditional media and healthcare providers compete for consumers' attention both through traditional means as well as through new Internet initiatives. We believe that competition for healthcare consumers will continue to increase as the Internet develops as a communication and commercial medium.

We compete directly for users, advertisers, e-commerce merchants, syndication partners and other affiliates with numerous Internet and non-Internet businesses, including:

- health-related on-line services or websites targeted at consumers, such as accesshealth.com, ahn.com, betterhealth.com, drweil.com, healthcentral.com, healthgate.com, intelihealth.com, mayohealth.org, mediconsult.com, onhealth.com, thriveonline.com and webmd.com;
- on-line and Internet portal companies, such as America Online, Inc.; Microsoft Network; Yahoo! Inc.; Excite, Inc.; Lycos Corporation and Infoseek Corporation;
- electronic merchants and conventional retailers that provide healthcare goods and services competitive to those available from links on our website;
- hospitals, HMOs, managed care organizations, insurance companies and other healthcare providers and payors which offer healthcare information through the Internet; and
- other consumer affinity groups, such as the American Association of Retired Persons, SeniorNet and ThirdAge Media, Inc. which offer healthcare-related content to specific demographic groups.

Many of these potential competitors are likely to enjoy substantial competitive advantages compared to our company, including:

- the ability to offer a wider array of on-line products and services;
- larger production and technical staffs;
- greater name recognition and larger marketing budgets and resources;
- larger customer and user bases; and
- substantially greater financial, technical and other resources.

To be competitive, we must respond promptly and effectively to the challenges of technological change, evolving standards and our competitors' innovations by continuing to enhance our products and services, as well as our sales and marketing channels. Increased competition could result in a loss of our market share or a reduction in our prices or margins. Competition is likely to increase significantly as new companies enter the market and current competitors expand their services. Please see "Business—Competition."

Since we operate an Internet-based network, our business is subject to government regulation relating to the Internet which could impair our operations.

Because of the increasing use of the Internet as a communication and commercial medium, the government has adopted and may adopt additional laws and regulations with respect to the Internet covering such areas as user privacy, pricing, content, taxation, copyright protection, distribution and characteristics and quality of production and services. For a description of risks associated with governmental regulation relating to the Internet, please see "Business—Governmental Regulation."

Since we operate a healthcare network over the Internet, our business is subject to government regulation specifically relating to medical devices, the practice of medicine and pharmacology, healthcare regulation, insurance and other matters unique to the healthcare area.

Laws and regulations have been or may be adopted with respect to the provision of healthcare-related·products and services on-line, covering areas such as:

- the regulation of medical devices;
- the practice of medicine and pharmacology and the sale of controlled products such as pharmaceuticals on-line;
- the regulation of government and third-party cost reimbursement; and
- the regulation of insurance sales.

FDA Regulation of Medical Devices. Some computer applications and software are considered medical devices and are subject to regulation by the United States Food and Drug Administration. We do not believe that our current applications or services will be regulated by the FDA; however, our applications and services may become subject to FDA regulation. Additionally, we may expand our application and service offerings into areas that subject us to FDA regulation. We have no experience in complying with FDA regulations. We believe that complying with FDA regulations would be time consuming, burdensome and expensive and could delay or prevent our introduction of new applications or services.

Regulation of the Practice of Medicine and Pharmacology. The practice of medicine and pharmacology requires licensing under applicable state law. We have endeavored to structure our website and affiliate relationships to avoid violation of state licensing requirements, but a state regulatory authority may at some point allege that some portion of our business violates these statutes. Any such allegation could result in a material adverse effect on our business. Further, any liability based on a determination that we engaged in the practice of medicine without a license may be excluded from coverage under the terms of our current general liability insurance policy.

Federal and State Healthcare Regulation. We earn a service fee when users on our website purchase prescription pharmacy products from certain of our e-commerce partners. The fee is not based on the value of the sales transaction. Federal and state "anti-kickback" laws prohibit granting or receiving referral fees in connection with sales of pharmacy products that are reimbursable under federal Medicare and Medicaid programs and other reimbursement programs. Although there is uncertainty regarding the applicability of these regulations to our e-commerce revenue strategy, we believe that the service fees we receive from our e-commerce partners are for the primary purpose of marketing and do not constitute payments that would violate federal or state "anti-kickback" laws. However, if our program were deemed to be inconsistent with federal or state law, we could face criminal or civil penalties. Further, we would be required either not to accept any transactions which are subject to reimbursement under federal or state healthcare programs or to restructure our compensation to comply with any applicable anti-kickback laws or regulations. In addition, similar laws in several states apply not only to government reimbursement but also to reimbursement by private insurers. If our activities were deemed to violate any of these laws or regulations, it could cause a material adverse affect on our business, results of operations and financial condition.

State Insurance Regulation. In addition, we market insurance on-line, offered by unrelated third parties, and receive referral fees from those providers in connection with this activity. The use of the Internet in the marketing of insurance products is a relatively new practice. It is not clear whether or to what extent state insurance licensing laws apply to our activities. If we were required to comply with such licensing laws, compliance could be costly or not possible. This could have a material adverse effect on our business. Please see "Business—Government Regulation."

There is no established market for the consumer healthcare e-commerce transactions we facilitate.

We plan to develop relationships with retailers, manufacturers and other providers to offer healthcare products and services through direct links from our website to their website. Such a strategy involves numerous risks and uncertainties. There is no established business model for the sale of healthcare products or services over the Internet. Accordingly, we have limited experience in the sale of products and services on-line and the development of relationships with retailers, manufacturers or other providers of such products and services, and we cannot predict the rate at which consumers will elect to engage in this form of commerce or the compensation that we will receive for enabling these transactions.

Consumers may sue us if any of the products or services that are sold through our website are defective, fail to perform properly or injure the user, even if such goods and services are provided by unrelated third parties. Some of our agreements with manufacturers, retailers and other providers contain provisions intended to limit our exposure to liability claims. These limitations may not however prevent all potential claims, and our insurance may not adequately protect us from these types of claims. Liability claims could require us to spend significant time and money in litigation or to pay significant damages. As a result, any such claims, whether or not successful, could seriously damage our reputation and our business.

Internet capacity constraints may impair the ability of consumers to access our website, which could hinder our ability to generate advertising revenue.

Our success will depend, in large part, upon a robust communications industry and infrastructure for providing Internet access and carrying Internet traffic. The Internet may not prove to be a viable commercial medium because of:

- inadequate development of the necessary infrastructure such as a reliable network backbone;
- timely development of complementary products such as high speed modems;
- delays in the development or adoption of new standards and protocols required to handle increased levels of Internet activity; or
- increased government regulation.

If the Internet continues to experience significant growth in the number of users and the level of use, then the Internet infrastructure may not be able to continue to support the demands placed on it.

Our business is dependent on the continuous, reliable and secure operation of our website and related tools and functions we provide.

We rely on the Internet and, accordingly, depend upon the continuous, reliable and secure operation of Internet servers and related hardware and software. Recently, several large Internet commerce companies have suffered highly publicized system failures which resulted in adverse reactions to their stock prices, significant negative publicity and, in certain instances, litigation. We have also suffered service outages from time to time, although to date none of these interruptions has materially adversely effected our business operations or financial condition. To the extent that our service is interrupted, our users will be inconvenienced, our commercial customers will suffer from a loss in advertising or transaction delivery and our reputation may be diminished. Some of these outcomes could directly result in a reduction in our stock price, significant negative publicity and litigation. Our computer and communications hardware are protected through physical and software safeguards. However, they are still vulnerable to fire, storm, flood, power loss, telecommunications failures, physical or software break-ins and similar events. We do not have full redundancy for all of our computer and telecommunications facilities and do not maintain a back-up data facility. Our business interruption insurance may be inadequate to protect us in the event of a catastrophe. We also depend upon third parties to provide potential users with web browsers and Internet and on-line services necessary for access to our website. In the past, our users have occasionally experienced difficulties with Internet and other on-line services due to system failures, including failures unrelated to our systems. Any sustained disruption in Internet access provided by third parties could adversely impact our business.

We retain confidential customer information in our database. Therefore, it is critical that our facilities and infrastructure remain secure and are perceived by consumers to be secure. Despite the implementation of security measures, our infrastructure may be vulnerable to physical break-ins, computer viruses, programming errors or similar disruptive problems. A material security breach could damage our reputation or result in liability to us.

Risks Related to This Offering

Investors will be relying on our management's judgment regarding the use of proceeds from this offering.

Our management will have broad discretion with respect to the use of the net proceeds from this offering, and investors will be relying on the judgment of our management regarding the application of these proceeds. Presently, anticipated uses include the funding of operating losses and for general corporate purposes, including expansion of our network, advertising, brand promotion, content development and working capital. We may also use a portion of the proceeds for strategic alliances and acquisitions and to repay debt. We have not yet determined the amount of net proceeds to be used specifically for each of the foregoing purposes. Please see "Use of Proceeds."

The liquidity of our common stock is uncertain since it has not been publicly traded.

There has not been a public market for our common stock. We cannot predict the extent to which investor interest in our company will lead to the development of an active, liquid trading market. Active trading markets generally result in lower price volatility and more efficient execution of buy and sell orders for investors. The initial public offering price for the shares will be determined by negotiations between us and the representatives of the underwriters and may not be indicative of prices that will prevail in the trading market. Please see "Underwriting."

Our need for additional financing is uncertain as is our ability to raise further financing if required.

We currently anticipate that our available cash resources combined with the net proceeds from this offering will be sufficient to meet our anticipated working capital and capital expenditure requirements for at least 12 months after the date of this prospectus. We may need to raise additional funds, however, to respond to business contingencies which may include the need to:

- fund more rapid expansion;
- fund additional marketing expenditures;
- develop new or enhance existing editorial content, features or services;
- enhance our operating infrastructure;
- respond to competitive pressures; or
- acquire complementary businesses or necessary technologies.

If additional funds are raised through the issuance of equity or convertible debt securities, the percentage ownership of our stockholders will be reduced, and these newly-issued securities may have rights, preferences or privileges senior to those of existing stockholders, including those acquiring shares in this offering. We cannot assure you that additional financing will be available on terms favorable to us, or at all. If adequate funds are not available or are not available on acceptable terms, our ability to fund our operations, take advantage of unanticipated opportunities, develop or enhance editorial content, features or services, or otherwise respond to competitive pressures would be significantly limited. Please see "Use of Proceeds" and "Management's Discussion and Analysis of Financial Condition and Results of Operations— Liquidity and Capital Resources."

Market prices of emerging Internet companies have been highly volatile, and the market for our stock may exhibit volatility as well.

The stock market has experienced significant price and trading volume fluctuations, and the market prices of technology companies, particularly Internet-related companies, have been extremely volatile. Recent initial public offerings by Internet companies have been accompanied by exceptional share price and trading volume changes in the first days and weeks after the securities were released for public trading. Investors may not be able to resell their shares at or above the initial public offering price. Please see "Underwriting." In the past, following periods of volatility in the market price of a public company's securities, securities class action litigation has often been instituted against that company.

Such litigation could result in substantial costs and a diversion of management's attention and resources.

We have negative net book value for accounting purposes, and new investors will suffer immediate and substantial dilution in the tangible net book value of their shares.

We expect the initial public offering price to be substantially higher than the net tangible book value per share of the common stock. The net tangible book value of a share of common stock purchased at the initial public offering price of $9.00 per share will be only $2.99. You may incur additional dilution if holders of stock options, whether currently outstanding or subsequently granted, exercise their options or if warrantholders exercise their warrants to purchase common stock. Please see "Dilution" for a summary of this dilution.

The large number of shares eligible for public sale after this offering could cause our stock price to decline.

The market price of our common stock could decline as a result of sales by our existing stockholders of a large number of shares of our common stock in the market after this offering or the perception that such sales could occur. These sales also might make it more difficult for us to sell equity securities in the future at a time and at a price that we deem appropriate. Please see "Shares Eligible for Future Sale" for a description of sales that may occur in the future.

Many corporate actions will be controlled by officers, directors and affiliated entities regardless of the opposition of other investors or the desire of other investors to pursue an alternative cause of action.

Our executive officers and directors and entities affiliated with them will, in the aggregate, beneficially own approximately 58% of our common stock following this offering. These stockholders will, if they act together, be able to exercise control over most matters requiring approval by our stockholders, including the election of directors and approval of significant corporate transactions. This concentration of ownership may also have the effect of delaying or preventing a change in control of our company, which could have a material adverse effect on our stock price. These actions may be taken even if they are opposed by the other investors, including those who purchase shares in this offering. Please see "Management" and "Principal Stockholders."

Forward-looking statements contained in this prospectus may not be realized.

This prospectus contains forward-looking statements that involve risks and uncertainties. Our actual results could differ materially from those anticipated in these forward-looking statements as a result of the risks faced by us described above and elsewhere in this prospectus. We undertake no obligation after the date of this prospectus to update publicly any forward-looking statements for any reason, even if new information becomes available or other events occur in the future.

USE OF PROCEEDS

The net proceeds to our company from the sale of the shares offered hereby (after deducting underwriting discounts and estimated offering expenses) are estimated to be approximately $77,113,750 ($88,884,062 if the underwriters' over-allotment option is exercised in full), at the initial public offering price of $9.00 per share.

We intend to use the net proceeds of this offering to fund operating losses and for general corporate purposes, including expansion of our network, advertising, brand promotion, content development and working capital. We may also use a portion of the proceeds for strategic alliances and acquisitions and to repay debt.

As of March 31, 1999, we had outstanding $2.8 million in principal amount of convertible notes and held binding commitments which would permit us to issue up to $3.5 million in additional convertible notes, all of which were issued prior to the completion of this offering. Upon the completion of this offering, up to $5.5 in million principal amount of such outstanding notes will be, at the option of each holder, convertible into common stock at a conversion price of $7.43 per share or redeemable for the principal amount plus accrued and unpaid interest at the rate of 7.0% per annum. For purposes of this prospectus, we have assumed that all outstanding notes are converted into common stock and thus do not require repayment in cash. To the extent any holder elects to receive cash, this will represent a use of the proceeds of this offering.

We have not yet determined the amount of net proceeds to be used specifically for each of the foregoing purposes. Accordingly, management will have significant flexibility in applying the net proceeds of this offering. Pending any such use, as described above, we intend to invest the net proceeds in high quality, interest-bearing instruments. See "Risk Factors—Any future acquisitions we make of companies or technologies may result in disruption to our business and/or the distraction of our management, due to difficulties in assimilating acquired personnel and operations." and "Investors will be relying on our management's judgment regarding the use of proceeds from this offering. . . ."

DILUTION

The pro forma net tangible book value of our company as of March 31, 1999 was $5,115,580, or $0.28 per share of common stock. Pro forma net tangible book value per share is equal to the amount of our company's total tangible assets (total assets less intangible assets) less total liabilities, divided by the pro forma number of shares of common stock outstanding as of March 31, 1999. Assuming the sale by us of the shares offered by this prospectus at the initial public offering price of $9.00 per share and after deducting underwriting discounts and the estimated offering expenses payable, the pro forma net tangible book value of our company as of March 31, 1999 would have been $82,229,330, or $2.99 per share of common stock. This represents an immediate increase in pro forma net tangible book value of $2.71 per share to existing stockholders and an immediate dilution in pro forma net tangible book value of $6.01 per share to new investors. That is, after this offering the excess of the tangible assets of Drkoop.com over its liabilities calculated on a per share basis will be less than the purchase price paid for those shares by investors in this offering. The following table illustrates this per share dilution:

Initial public offering price per share................	$9.00
Pro forma net tangible book value per share as of March 31, 1999 .... $0.28	
Pro forma increase in net tangible book value attributable to new investors................ 2.71	
Pro forma net tangible book value per share after this offering...............	2.99
Pro forma dilution per share to new investors.........	$6.01

The following table summarizes, on a pro forma basis as of March 31, 1999, the total number of shares of common stock purchased from us, the total consideration paid to us and the average price per share paid by existing stockholders and by new investors purchasing shares in this offering:

	Shares Purchased		Total Consideration		Average Price Per Share
	Number	Percent	Amount	Percent	
Existing stockholders	18,139,591	66%	$ 36,870,632	30%	$2.03
New investors	9,375,000	34	84,375,000	70	9.00
Total	27,514,591	100%	$121,245,632	100%	$4.41

The foregoing tables and calculations are based on shares outstanding on March 31, 1999 and exclude:

- 10,492,530 shares of common stock issuable upon exercise of options outstanding under our Amended and Restated 1997 Stock Option Plan with a weighted average exercise price of $0.53 per share (5,240,902 of these options were exercisable on March 31, 1999; the balance are subject to future vesting requirements);
- 1,747,451 shares of common stock issuable upon exercise of options to be granted contemporaneously with this offering under our 1999 Equity Participation Plan with an exercise price equal to the public offering price listed on the cover of this prospectus;
- 33,482 shares of common stock issuable upon exercise of warrants with an exercise price of $4.78 per share; and
- 775,000 shares of common stock issuable upon exercise of warrants with an exercise price of $8.60 per share.

The tables and calculations include:

- 7,249,667 shares of common stock to be issued upon the conversion of all outstanding shares of convertible preferred stock;
- 439,187 shares of common stock issuable upon conversion of all convertible notes outstanding at March 31, 1999 ($2.8 million aggregate principal amount plus accrued interest); and
- 1,345,185 shares of common stock to be issued upon the closing of this offering to satisfy in full a purchase option and related anti-dilution rights.

SELECTED FINANCIAL DATA

The following selected financial data should be read in conjunction with the financial statements and the notes to such statements and "Management's Discussion and Analysis of Financial Condition and Results of Operations" included elsewhere in this prospectus. The statement of operations data for the period from July 17, 1997 (inception) through December 31, 1997 and for the year ended December 31, 1998, and the balance sheet data at December 31, 1997 and 1998, are derived from our audited financial statements included elsewhere in this prospectus. Interim results for the periods ended March 31, 1998 and 1999 are derived from our unaudited financial statements which, in the opinion of management, reflect all adjustments necessary for a fair presentation of that data. Historical results are not indicative of the results to be expected in the future.

| | Period From Inception through December 31, 1997 | Year Ended December 31, 1998 | Three Months Ended | |
			March 31, 1998	March 31, 1999
	(in thousands, except per share data)			
STATEMENT OF OPERATIONS DATA:				
Revenues...............	$ —	$ 43	$ —	$ 404
Operating expenses:				
Production, content and product development	461	4,448	284	1,035
Sales and marketing ...	—	2,008	166	2,048
General and administrative	161	2,704	259	1,585
Total operating expenses ..	622	9,160	709	4,668
Loss from operations	(622)	(9,117)	(709)	(4,264)

			March 31, 1999		
Other income (expense), net	—	34	—	(31)	

Net loss	(622)	(9,083)	(709)	(4,295)
Accretion of redeemable securities to fair value . . .	(14,325)	—	(10,936)	
Dividend to preferred stockholders	—	—	—	(9,147)
Loss attributable to common stockholders	$ (622)	$(23,408)	$(709)	$(24,378)
Basic and diluted net loss per common share (1)	$ (.09)	$ (2.89)	$ (0.10)	$ (2.84)
Weighted average shares outstanding used in basic and diluted net loss per common share calculation (1)	6,750	8,100	7,030	8,569
Pro forma basic and diluted net loss per common shares (1) (2)		$ (.75)		$ (.26)
Weighted average shares used in computing pro forma basic and diluted net loss per common share calculation (1) (2)		12,111		16,347

	December 31, 1997	December 31, 1998	March 31, 1999		
			Actual	Pro Forma (2)	Pro Forma As Adjusted (2) (3)
		(in thousands, except per share data)			
BALANCE SHEET DATA:					
Cash and cash equivalents	$ 8	$ —	$ 2,021	$ 2,021	$79,135
Working capital (deficiency)	(649)	(2,905)	(3,038)	(286)	76,828
Total assets	43	380	11,717	11,717	88,831
Convertible notes payable to stockholder	—	451	2,741	—	—
Mandatorily redeemable convertible (Series B) preferred stock	—	18,406	29,342	—	—
Stockholders' equity (deficit)	(614)	(20,993)	(23,201)	8,893	86,007

(1) Please see the financial statements and the notes to such statements appearing elsewhere in this prospectus for the determination of shares used in computing basic and diluted and pro forma basic and diluted net loss per common share.

(2) Gives pro forma effect to all the following:

- the conversion of all outstanding shares of our convertible preferred stock into 7,249,667 shares of our common stock upon the closing of this offering;
- the conversion of all convertible notes outstanding as of March 31, 1999 ($2.8 million aggregate principal amount plus accrued interest) into 439,187 shares of common stock upon the closing of this offering; and
- the issuance of 1,345,185 shares of common stock to satisfy in full a purchase option and related anti-dilution adjustment rights.

(3) As adjusted to give effect to the sale of shares of common stock offered by us in this offering at the initial offering price of $9.00 per share, after deducting estimated underwriting discounts and commissions and estimated offering expenses payable by us.

MANAGEMENT'S DISCUSSION AND ANALYSIS
OF FINANCIAL CONDITION AND RESULTS OF OPERATIONS

The following discussion of the financial condition and results of operations of our company should be read in conjunction with the financial statements and the notes to those statements included elsewhere in this prospectus. This discussion contains forward-looking statements that involve risks and uncertainties. Please see "Risk Factors."

Overview

Our company operates Drkoop.com, an Internet-based consumer healthcare network. Our network consists of a consumer-focused interactive website which provides users with comprehensive healthcare information and services, as well as affiliate relationships with portals, other websites, healthcare organizations and traditional media outlets. Our website, www.drkoop.com, is a healthcare portal which integrates dynamic healthcare content on a wide variety of subjects, interactive communities and tools as well as opportunities to purchase healthcare-related products and services on-line.

Our company was founded in July 1997 as Personal Medical Records, Inc. From July to December 1997 our primary operating activities related to the development of software for Dr. Koop's Personal Medical Record SystemTM. A personal medical record is a software application designed for consumers to establish and maintain lifelong control of personal health and medical information and related expense records. We originally contemplated the PMR as a free-standing product. As we developed it, however, we concluded that the PMR was best suited as one component of an Internet-based network including healthcare information, interactive tools and other useful features. Accordingly, in early 1998 we changed our primary emphasis to the development of the software and hardware infrastructure for the Drkoop.com website, licensing and creating content, negotiating relationships with strategic partners, recruiting personnel and raising capital. We launched the Drkoop.com website in late July 1998. After the launch of the website and for the remainder of 1998, we focused on broadening the functionality of the website and attracting an audience to the Drkoop.com network. We presently expect to add a personal medical record feature to our website in the first half of 1999 as an element of our technology relationship with HealthMagic, Inc.

For 1998 and the quarter ended March 31, 1999, our revenues were derived primarily from recurring revenues from content subscriptions and software licensing through our Community Partner Program, and to a lesser extent from the sale of advertising. Content subscription and software licensing revenue accounted for $27,000 or 63% of revenues for the year ended December 31, 1998 and $216,000, or 53% of revenues for the quarter ended March 31, 1999.

In October 1998, we officially launched our first local affiliate subscription offering, the Dr. Koop Community Partner Program. Subscriptions to our Community Partner Program run from one to three years. Under this program, we develop co-branded Internet pages and software consisting of visual icons containing embedded links back to the Drkoop.com website for local healthcare organizations, such as hospitals and payor organizations. Advance billings and collections relating to future services are recorded as deferred revenue and recognized when revenue is earned. Sales of software licensed to CPP affiliates is recognized as revenue upon shipment of the software, provided that the portion of the contract allocated to the software license is based upon vendor specific objective evidence of fair value, and collectibility is probable. Content subscription revenue is recognized ratably over the term of the CPP contract, generally ranging from twelve to thirty-six months.

In November 1998, we sold our first advertising contract and in December began running advertising banners on the website. Advertising revenues are derived principally from short-term advertising contracts in which we typically guarantee a minimum number of user "impressions" to be delivered over a specified period of time for a fixed fee. Impressions are the times that an advertisement is viewed by users of our website. We recognize advertising revenues at the lesser of the ratio of impressions delivered over the total guaranteed impressions or the straight-line rate over the term of the contract, provided that no significant obligations remain and collection of the resulting receivable is probable. Our obligations typically include the guarantee of a minimum number of impressions, or times that an advertisement appears in pages viewed by the users of the Company's website. Historically we have utilized third party firms to sell and insert advertisements on Drkoop.com. Advertising rates, measured on a cost per thousand impressions basis, are dependent on whether the impressions are for general rotation throughout Drkoop.com or for targeted audiences and properties within specific areas of the website. Advertising revenue is recognized in the period in which the advertisement is displayed. Advertising revenue accounted for $15,000, or 35%, of revenues for the year ended December 31, 1998 and $188,000, or 47%, of revenues for the quarter ended March 31, 1999.

Sponsorship revenues are derived principally from contracts ranging from one to twelve months in which we commit to provide sponsors enhanced promotional opportunities that go beyond traditional banner advertising. Sponsorships are designed to support broad marketing objectives, including branding, awareness, product introductions, research and transactions, frequently on an exclusive basis. Sponsorship agreements typically include the delivery of a guaranteed minimum number of impressions and the design and development of customized pages on the website that enhance the promotional objectives of the sponsor. Costs associated with the creation of the customized pages are minimal and expensed as incurred. Sponsorship revenues are recognized at the lesser of the ratio of impressions delivered over the total guaranteed impressions or the straight line rate over the term of the contract, provided that no significant obligations remain and collection of the resulting receivable is probable. Company obligations typically include the guarantee of a minimum number of impressions.

In December 1998, we began to generate electronic commerce revenues through alliances with certain retailers of pharmaceuticals and related products and to provide insurance companies with the opportunity to sell products and services to our audience. We do not provide any of the goods or services offered. We receive compensation in the form of transaction fees or anchor tenant rental fees from third parties who have entered into preferred provider arrangements with us. Revenues from our share of the proceeds from the commerce partner's transactions are recognized by us upon notification from the commerce partner of sales attributable to users from the Drkoop.com website. E-commerce revenues were nominal for the year ended December 31, 1998 and the quarter ended March 31, 1999.

On January 29, 1999, we received $3.5 million in cash and acquired 10% of the outstanding stock of HealthMagic, Inc., a subsidiary of Adventist Health System Sunbelt Healthcare Corporation, in exchange for 2,615,677 shares of our Series C Convertible Preferred Stock, which will be converted into an equivalent number of shares of common stock upon the closing of this offering. We also established a technology relationship with HealthMagic, a supplier of applications to Internet companies, whereby we contributed to them our PMR product and received from them a license to use a broad range of Internet technologies, including a web-enabled personal medical record, personalization tools, and security and authentication features. HealthMagic will develop, implement and support

258   EXCERPTS FROM DRKOOP.COM, INC.'S PROSPECTUS

these technologies for us. Currently, we expect to deploy these features in the first half of 1999. We have capitalized the fair value of the licenses acquired based upon an analysis of the cost required to build the technology versus purchasing it from HealthMagic. In addition, on January 29, 1999 we entered into a master content subscription and software licensing agreement with Adventist for $500,000.

Contract research organizations offer comprehensive clinical trial services which are the basis for obtaining regulatory approval for drugs and medical devices. The identification and enrollment of qualified individuals into these studies is usually a time-consuming and expensive process. In December 1998 we implemented the Drkoop.com Clinical Research Center, a portion of our website designed to educate consumers about clinical trials, including how to find and enroll in an appropriate trial if the individual and their physician believe that it is a viable therapy option. We expect to receive transaction fee revenues for assisting contract research organizations in the identification and enrollment of qualified individuals into studies.

On March 10, 1999, we entered into a two year relationship with The @Home Network to be the anchor tenant partner within the Health Channel area of the @Home service. We will be the premier content provider appearing in the Health Channel. Under the terms of this agreement, we will have the ability to direct users to related commerce, community and interactive tool features appearing on the Drkoop.com website from within all health content appearing in the Health Channel. In addition, we will share in all advertising revenues generated by @Home in the Health Channel where our content dominates the related page. We will pay a carriage fee of $2.25 million to @Home in installments over the term of the agreement.

On April 9, 1999 we entered into agreements with Infoseek Corporation and the Buena Vista Internet Group, a unit of The Walt Disney Company, under which we will be the exclusive provider of health and related content on three websites of the Go Network: Go.com Health Center, ESPN.com Training Room and the Family.com Health Channel. Under the Infoseek agreement, Drkoop.com will also be the premier health content provider for ABCnews.com. In addition, Drkoop.com will be the exclusive pharmacy and drugstore, health insurance and clinical trials patron in the Go Health Center. In the event Drkoop.com elects not to provide specific content, it may be obtained from a third party. We believe that these agreements will contribute substantially to our brand awareness and increase traffic on our website. The term of these agreements is for three years, although either party may elect to terminate the relationship after two years. We will pay Infoseek and Buena Vista approximately $57.9 million in total consideration consisting of cash and warrants to purchase up to 775,000 shares of common stock for $8.60 per share assuming the agreements run for the full three years. The cash portion of this obligation is payable as approximately $16.2 million in the first year of the agreements, $18.2 million in the second year of the agreements and $21.3 million in the third year.

We recorded deferred stock compensation of $1.5 million and $3.1 million during the year ended December 31, 1998 and the quarter ended March 31, 1999, respectively, for the difference between the exercise price and the deemed fair value of certain stock options granted by us to our employees, of which $107,000 and $314,000 was recorded as compensation expense in 1998 and the quarter ended March 31, 1999. This accounting treatment will generate non-cash amortization expense of $2.0 million in 1999, $1.4 million in 2000, $748,000 in 2001, $311,000 in 2002 and $31,000 in 2003.

Since inception, we have incurred significant losses and negative cash flow, and as of March 31, 1999 we had an accumulated deficit of $23.9 million including $9.9 million for accretion to fair value of the mandatorily redeemable (Series B) convertible preferred stock. We have not achieved profitability and expect to continue to incur operating losses for the foreseeable future as we fund operating and capital expenditures in the areas of expansion of our network, advertising, brand promotion, content development, sales and marketing, and operating infrastructure. Our business model assumes that consumers will be attracted to and use healthcare information and related content available on our on-line network which will, in turn, allow us the opportunity to sell advertising designed to reach those consumers. Our business model also assumes that those users will access important healthcare needs through electronic commerce and that local healthcare participants will affiliate with us. This business model is not yet proven and we cannot assure you that we will ever achieve or sustain profitability or that our operating losses will not increase in the future. Please see "Risk Factors—Our business is difficult to evaluate because we have an extremely limited operating history" and "—We have a history of losses and negative cash flow and anticipate continued losses."

We have a very limited operating history on which to base an evaluation of our business and prospects. Our prospects must be considered in light of the risks, uncertainties, expenses and difficulties frequently encountered by companies in their early stages of development, particularly companies in new and rapidly evolving markets such as the Internet market. In view of the rapidly evolving nature of our business and our limited operating history, we believe that period-to-period comparisons of revenues and operating results are not necessarily meaningful and should not be relied upon as indications of future performance.

Results of Operations
Comparison of the three months ended March 31, 1999 to the three months ended March 31, 1998

Revenues. Our website, www.drkoop.com, was launched in July 1998. Revenues increased to $404,000 for the three months ended March 31, 1999 as compared to no revenues recorded for the three months ended March 31, 1998. Revenues for the quarter ended March 31, 1999 consisted of content subscription and software licenses of $216,000 or 53% of total revenues, including barter revenues of $32,000, and advertising and sponsorship revenue of $188,000 or 47% of total revenues including barter revenues of $20,000. The increase in content subscription and software license revenue was attributable to delivery of software licenses and content from six new contracts in the quarter ended March 31, 1999 under the Community Partner Program which ranged in value from $50,000 to $500,000 and had terms of one to three years. The increase in advertising and sponsorship revenues was attributable to an increase in the traffic to our website as well as an increase in the number of advertising arrangements entered into during late 1998 and the first quarter of 1999.

Production, content and product development. Production, content and product development expenses consist primarily of salaries and benefits, consulting fees and other costs related to content acquisition and licensing, software development, application development and website operations expense. Production, content and product development expenses increased by $751,000 or 265%, to $1.0 million for the quarter ended March 31, 1999, as compared to $284,000 for the quarter ended March 31, 1998. The primary reason for the increase was the addition of personnel which resulted in higher salaries, benefits, facilities and travel costs. We believe that additional significant investments in content development and operating infrastructure are required to remain competitive and therefore expect that production, content and product development expenses will continue to increase in absolute dollars for the foreseeable future.

Sales and marketing expenses. Sales and marketing expenses consist primarily of salaries and related costs, web-based advertising, commissions, general advertising and other related expenses. Sales and marketing expenses increased by $1.8 million to $2.0 million during the quarter ended March 31, 1999 as compared to $166,000 during the quarter ended March 31, 1998. The primary reasons for the increase were costs related to web-based advertising and promotion of the Drkoop.com website and a significant increase in the number of sales and marketing personnel resulting in higher salaries, benefits, facilities and travel costs. We expect that sales and marketing expenses will continue to grow in absolute dollars for the foreseeable future as we hire additional sales and marketing personnel and increase expenditures for advertising, brand promotion, public relations and other marketing activities.

General and administrative expenses. General and administrative expenses consist primarily of salaries and related costs for general corporate functions, including executive, finance, accounting, human resources, facilities and fees for professional services. General and administrative expenses increased by $1.3 million, or 512%, to $1.6 million for the quarter ended March 31, 1999 as compared to $259,000 for the quarter ended March 31, 1999. The primary reasons for the increase were the addition of personnel and the resultant increase in salaries, benefits, non cash compensation facilities and travel costs. We expect that we will incur additional general and administrative expenses as we continue to hire personnel and incur incremental costs related to the growth of the business and compliance with public company obligations, including directors' and officers' liability insurance, investor relations programs and fees for professional services. Accordingly, we anticipate that general and administrative expenses will continue to increase in absolute dollars in future periods, although at a slower rate than other major expense categories such as sales and marketing expense.

Interest income (expense). Interest expense was $31,000 for the quarter ended March 31, 1999 as compared to no expense for the quarter ended March 31, 1998. Interest expense relates to outstanding convertible notes.

Income Taxes. We have incurred net losses to date. As of March 31, 1999 we had a net operating loss carryforward of $13.5 million for financial reporting purposes. We have recorded a valuation reserve equal to the amount of the carryforward due to the uncertain realization of these tax benefits.

Comparison of the year ended December 31, 1998 to the period from July 17, 1997 (inception) through December 31, 1997

Revenues. For the year ended December 31, 1998, we recorded revenues of $43,000, with $27,000, or 63% of revenues, attributable to content subscription and software licenses and $16,000, or 37% of revenues, attributable to advertising; no revenues were recognized for the period from July 1997 (inception) to December 31, 1997.

Production, Content and Product Development Expense. Production, content and product development expenses consist primarily of salaries and benefits, consulting fees and other costs related to content acquisition and licensing, software development, application development and website operations expense. Production, content and product development expense increased by $4.0 million, or 866%, to $4.4 million for the year ended December 31, 1998 as compared to $461,000 for the period ended December 31, 1997. This increase was primarily attributable to increases in personnel and related costs to provide the infrastructure necessary to launch the Drkoop.com website in July 1998, as well as costs for product development work on the PMR. We believe that additional significant investments in content development and operating infrastructure are required to remain competitive and therefore expect that production, content and product development expense will continue to increase in absolute dollars for the foreseeable future.

Sales and Marketing Expense. Sales and marketing expenses consist primarily of salaries and related costs, web-based advertising, commissions, general advertising and other related expenses. We did not have any sales and marketing expense during the period ended December 31, 1997. During the year ended December 31, 1998, we incurred costs of $2.0 million as we built a direct sales organization comprised of 11 sales professionals. During 1998 we also implemented a variety of approaches to promote the Drkoop.com brand to attract new users, including advertising on the Internet, public relations campaigns and event marketing. We expect that sales and marketing expenses will continue to increase in absolute dollars for the foreseeable future as we hire additional sales and marketing personnel and increased expenditures for advertising, brand promotion, public relations and other marketing activities.

General and Administrative Expense. General and administrative expenses consist primarily of salaries and related costs for general corporate functions, including executive, finance, accounting, human resources, facilities and fees for professional services. General and administrative expenses increased by $2.5 million to $2.7 million for the year ended December 31, 1998 as compared to $161,000 for the period ended December 31, 1997. The increase in general and administrative expenses was primarily attributable to salaries and related expenses associated with hiring personnel and increased professional fees and facility-related expenses to support the growth of our operations. Administrative personnel headcount, including executive management, went from one person at December 31, 1997 to nine people at December 31, 1998. We expect that we will incur additional general and administrative expenses as we hire additional personnel and incur incremental costs related to the growth of the business and compliance with public company obligations, including directors and officers liability insurance, investor relations programs and fees for professional services. Accordingly, we anticipate that general and administrative expenses will continue to increase in absolute dollars in future periods, although at a slower rate than other major expense categories such as sales and marketing expense.

Interest and Other Income. Interest income includes interest income from the investment of cash and cash equivalents.

Income Taxes. We have incurred net losses to date. As of December 31, 1998, we had a net operating loss carryforward of $9.2 million for financial reporting purposes. We have recorded a valuation reserve equal to the amount of the carryforward due to the uncertain realization of these tax benefits.

Quarterly Results of Operations Data
The following table sets forth certain unaudited quarterly statement of operations data for the period from inception to December 31, 1997 and each of the five quarters ended March 31, 1999. In the opinion of management, this data has been prepared substantially on the same basis as the audited financial statements appearing elsewhere in this prospectus, including all necessary adjustments, consisting only of normal recurring adjustments necessary for a fair presentation of such data. The quarterly data should be read in conjunction with the financial statements and the notes to such statements appearing elsewhere in this prospectus. In view of the rapidly evolving nature of our business and our limited operating history, we believe that period-to-period comparisons of revenues and operating results are not necessarily meaningful and should not be relied upon as indications of future performance.

	Period From Inception to December 31, 1997	Year Ended December 31, 1998	Three Months Ended				
			March 31, 1998	June 30, 1998	September 30, 1998	December 31, 1998	March 31, 1999
				(in thousands)			
Revenues.......	$ —	$ —	$ —	$ —	$ —	$ 43	$ 404
Operating expenses							
Production, content and product development..	461	4,448	284	672	1,847	1,645	1,035
Sales and marketing....	—	2,008	166	181	646	1,015	2,048
General and administrative	161	2,704	259	562	870	1,013	1,585
Total operating expenses	622	9,160	709	1,415	3,363	3,673	4,668
Loss from operations....	(622)	(9,117)	(709)	(1,415)	(3,363)	(3,630)	(4,264)
Interest income (expense).....	—	33	—	14	13	6	(31)
Net loss........	$(622)	$(9,084)	$(709)	$(1,401)	$(3,350)	$(3,624)	$(4,295)

Revenues. Our initial revenues were recorded in the quarter ended December 31, 1998. Revenues to date have consisted of revenue attributable to content subscription, software licenses and advertising arrangements.

Production, content and product. Production, content and product expenses have fluctuated in the brief operating history of Drkoop.com. Production, content and product costs increased significantly in the third quarter of 1998 due primarily to development work on the personal medical record technology. Production, content and product expenses decreased in the quarters ended December 31, 1998 and March 31, 1999 as compared to the previous quarters due to the reduction in outsourced development on the personal medical record technology.

Sales and marketing. Sales and marketing expenses have increased every quarter. Sales and marketing expenses increased significantly in the third quarter of 1998 as compared to the prior quarter due to significant increases in advertising costs related to the launch of the Drkoop.com website and the hiring of additional marketing personnel to market the website and the initial hiring of sales personnel. The following quarterly increases in sales and marketing expenses resulted primarily from building our sales and marketing organization. The addition of sales and marketing personnel resulted in higher salaries, benefits and travel costs. We have also increased the amount expended on advertising each quarter.

General and administrative. General and administrative costs have increased every quarter as we have hired our executive team and built our administrative infrastructure.

As a result of our extremely limited operating history, we do not have historical financial data for a significant number of periods on which to base planned operating expenses. Quarterly revenues and operating results depend substantially on the advertising, sponsorship, subscription and e-commerce revenues received within the quarter, which are difficult to forecast accurately. Accordingly, the cancellation of a Community Partner Program subscription or the cancellation or deferral of a small number of advertising contracts or sponsorships could have a material adverse effect on our business, results of operations and financial condition. We may be unable to adjust spending in a timely manner to compensate for any unexpected revenue shortfall, and any significant shortfall in revenue in relation to our expectations would have an immediate adverse effect on our business, results of operation and financial condition. Due to the foregoing factors, it is possible that in some future periods our operating results may be below the expectations of public market analysts and investors. In this event, the price of our common stock may underperform or fall.

Seasonality

We believe that advertising sales in traditional media, such as television and radio, generally are lower in the first and third calendar quarters of each year. If our market makes the transition from an emerging to a more developed market, seasonal and cyclical patterns may develop in our industry and in the usage of our website. Seasonal and cyclical patterns in Internet advertising would affect our revenues. Those patterns may also develop on our website. Given the early stage of the development of the Internet and our company, however, we cannot predict to what extent, if at all, our operations will prove to be seasonal.

Liquidity and Capital Resources

Since inception, we have financed our operations primarily through private equity and debt financings. During the years ended December 31, 1997 and 1998, we received net proceeds from the sale of stock and issuance of convertible note payable to stockholder of $6,000 and $7.1 million, respectively. During the three months ended March 31, 1999 we received net proceeds of $5.8 million from the sale of stock and issuance of convertible notes payable.

Cash used in operating activities for the quarter ended March 31, 1998 of $502,000 was due primarily to net operating losses of $709,000 offset by increases in accounts payable and accrued expenses of $75,000 and $158,000, respectively. Cash used in operating activities for the quarter ended March 31, 1999 of $3.7 million resulted primarily from net operating losses of $4.3 million, a decrease in related party payable of $1.1 million and an increase in accounts receivable of $365,000, partly offset by an increase in accrued expenses of $807,000 and deferred revenue of $544,000. The increase in accounts receivable and deferred-revenue amounts are attributable primarily to Community Partner Program contracts. Net cash used in operating activities was $6.8 million for the year ended December 31, 1998 primarily attributable to net operating losses of $9.0 million offset by increases in accounts payable, accrued expenses and related party payable of $747,000, $458,000 and $872,000, respectively. Net cash provided by operating activities for the period from inception to December 31, 1997 of $44,000 was provided primarily through increases in accounts payable, accrued expenses and related party payable of $58,000, $62,000 and $537,000, respectively, offset by a net operating loss of $622,000.

Cash used in investing activities was $29,000 and $120,000 for the three months ended March 31, 1998 and March 31, 1999, respectively, and was $42,000 and $335,000 for the period from inception through December 31, 1997 and the year ended December 31, 1998. Net cash used in investing activities for these periods consisted primarily of capital expenditures for computer equipment.

Cash provided by financing activities was $519,000 and $5.8 million for the three months ended March 31, 1998 and March 31, 1999, respectively, and $6,000 and $7.1 million for the period from inception through December 31, 1997 and the year ended December 31, 1998, respectively. Cash provided by financing activities has been provided primarily from the sale of convertible preferred stock and issuance of convertible notes payable. Our financing activities to date are described in detail below.

From March 1, 1998 through April 6, 1998, we issued 619,102 shares of Series A 8% Convertible Preferred Stock to accredited investors for an aggregate purchase price of $743,000. These shares will be converted into 671,727 shares of common stock upon the closing of this offering.

On April 28, 1998, we issued 3,850,597 shares of Series B Non-voting Preferred Stock to Superior Consultant Holdings Corporation for a purchase price of $6.0 million. These shares will be converted into 3,962,265 shares of common stock upon the closing of this offering. In connection with this transaction we gave Superior the right to require us to repurchase their shares for the current fair market price during each of the 90-day periods following April 28, 2000 and April 28, 2001. Due to these terms, we are required under generally accepted accounting principles to accrete the Series B Non-voting Preferred Stock to its fair value for the periods reported. We incurred a charge for accretion to fair value for the redeemable stock of $14.3 million for the year ended December 31, 1998 which resulted in a fair value of $18.4 million as of December 31, 1998. We incurred a charge of $10.9 million for the quarter ended March 31, 1999 which resulted in a fair value of $29.3 million as of March 31, 1999. Upon the completion of an underwritten public offering of not less than $20.0 million, after which the common stock is listed on a national securities exchange or admitted for quotation on the Nasdaq National Market, the Series B Non-voting Preferred Stock is required to be converted into common stock. Upon conversion to common stock, the repurchase right held by Superior as holder of Series B Non-voting Preferred Stock terminates. In addition, Superior received the right to purchase an additional 3,850,597 shares of either Series B Non-voting Preferred Stock or common stock at a per share exercise price equal to 70% of the fair market value of the common stock on the date of exercise. The Superior purchase option will be terminated at the closing of this offering in consideration for the issuance of 1,210,665 shares of common stock, valued at $8.2 million, including shares to be issued as an anti-dilution adjustment. In addition, 134,520 shares, valued at $900,000, will be issued to satisfy an anti-dilution adjustment right held by the Series C preferred stockholder. These anti-dilution adjustments were specific to the Superior purchase option.

On December 24, 1998, we issued a convertible note payable to stockholder in the original principal amount of $800,000, $500,000 of which was received in 1998, bearing

interest at 6% per annum due December 24, 1999, along with five year warrants to purchase 33,482 shares of Series C Preferred Stock for an exercise price of $4.78 per share,
which will become the right to purchase 33,482 shares of common stock for $4.78 per share
upon the closing of this offering. Interest on the note is payable at maturity. At any time
prior to maturity any unpaid principal and interest may be converted into Series C Preferred Stock at a conversion price of $4.78 per share.

On January 29, 1999, we received $3.5 million in cash and acquired 10% of the out-
standing stock of HealthMagic, Inc., a subsidiary of Adventist Health System Sunbelt
Healthcare Corporation, in exchange for 2,615,677 shares of our Series C Convertible Preferred Stock, which will be converted into an equivalent number of shares of common stock
upon the closing of this offering. We recorded our 10% ownership in Healthmagic at $5.0 mil-
lion as investment in affiliate. We also established a technology relationship with Health-
Magic, a supplier of applications to Internet companies, whereby we contributed to them our
PMR product and received from them a license to use a broad range of Internet technologies,
including a web-enabled personal medical record, personalization tools, and security and
authentication features. HealthMagic will develop, implement and support these technologies for us. We did not attribute any value to the desktop-based PMR technology we contributed to HealthMagic as we believe the fair value was zero. We recorded the license
received from HealthMagic as an intangible asset in the total amount of $4.0 million.

On or prior to March 5, 1999, we entered into loan agreements pursuant to which the
investors are irrevocably obligated to loan to us the aggregate principal amount of up to
$5.5 million at an interest rate of 7% per annum. Upon the closing of this offering, the
principal amount borrowed under these agreements and all accrued interest will, solely at
the option of each investor, either be due and payable or convert into common stock at a
conversion price of $7.43 per share. We currently anticipate borrowing under these agree-
ments prior to the closing of this offering. As of March 31, 1999, we had borrowed $2.0 mil-
lion. We also have outstanding $800,000 in convertible notes issued in December 1998 and
January 1999 and which may be converted into common stock at a conversion price of
$4.78 per share.

We currently anticipate that our available cash resources combined with the net proceeds from this offering will be sufficient to meet our anticipated working capital and capital expenditure requirements for at least 12 months after the date of this prospectus.
These requirements are expected to include the funding of operating losses, working capital requirements and other general corporate purposes, including expansion of our network, advertising, brand promotion and content development. We may also elect to repay
debt and pursue one or more strategic alliances or acquisition transactions, although, as
of the date of this prospectus, we have no agreement to enter into any material investment
or acquisition transaction. We may need to raise additional funds, however, to respond to
business contingencies which may include the need to:

- fund more rapid expansion;
- fund additional marketing expenditures;
- develop new or enhance existing editorial content, features or services;
- enhance our operating infrastructure;
- respond to competitive pressures; or
- acquire complementary businesses or necessary technologies.

If additional funds are raised through the issuance of equity or convertible debt securities,
the percentage ownership of our stockholders will be reduced and these newly-issued securities may have rights, preferences or privileges senior to those of existing stockholders,
including those acquiring shares in this offering. We cannot assure you that additional
financing will be available on terms favorable to us, or at all. If adequate funds are not
available or are not available on acceptable terms, our ability to fund our operations, take
advantage of unanticipated opportunities, develop or enhance editorial content, features or
services, or otherwise respond to competitive pressures would be significantly limited. Our
business, results of operations and financial condition could be materially adversely
affected by any such limitation.

We have received a report from our independent auditors containing an explanatory paragraph that describes the uncertainty as to our ability to continue as a going concern due to our historical negative cash flow and because, as of the date they rendered their opinion, we did not have access to sufficient committed capital to meet our projected operating needs for at least the next twelve months. Upon completion of this offering, we will have available that capital. If capital requirements vary materially from those currently planned, we may require additional financing sooner than anticipated. If this offering is not successful and positive operating results are not achieved rapidly, we intend to reduce expenditures so as to minimize our requirements for additional financial resources, if such resources are not available on terms acceptable to us.

Impact of the Year 2000

Many currently installed computer systems and software products are coded to accept or recognize only two digit entries in the date code field. These systems may recognize a date using "00" as the year 1900 rather than the year 2000. As a result, computer systems and/or software used by many companies and governmental agencies may need to be upgraded to comply with such Year 2000 requirements or risk system failure or miscalculations causing disruptions of normal business activities.

State of Readiness

Costs. To date, we have not incurred any material costs in identifying or evaluating Year 2000 compliance issues. Most of our expenses have related to, and are expected to continue to relate to, the operating costs associated with time spent by employees in the evaluation process and Year 2000 compliance matters generally. We do not presently anticipate that such expenditures will be material.

Risks. We have made a preliminary assessment of the Year 2000 readiness of our operating and administrative systems and the third-party software, hardware and services used to host the Drkoop.com website. Our assessment plan consists of:

- contacting third-party vendors of material software, hardware and services that are both directly and indirectly related to the delivery of Drkoop.com services to our users;
- assessing and implementing repair or replacement of such components as required; and
- creating contingency plans in the event of Year 2000 failures.

We plan to perform a Year 2000 simulation on our systems, including the Drkoop.com website, during the second quarter of 1999 to test Year 2000 system readiness. Many of our vendors of material software, hardware and services have indicated that the products used by us are currently Year 2000 compliant. We are not currently aware of any internal Year 2000 compliance problems that could reasonably be expected to have a material adverse effect on our business, results of operations and financial condition, without taking into account the Company's efforts to avoid or fix such problems. However, there can be no assurance that we will not discover Year 2000 compliance problems in our computer infrastructure that will require substantial revisions or replacements. In addition, we cannot assure you that third-party software, hardware or services incorporated into our material systems or other systems upon which we are reliant will not need to be revised or replaced, which could be time consuming and expensive.

In addition, we cannot assure you that governmental agencies, utility companies, Internet access companies, third-party service providers and others outside of our control will be Year 2000 compliant. The failure by such entities to be Year 2000 compliant could result in a systemic failure beyond our control, such as a prolonged Internet, telecommunications or electrical failure, which could also prevent us from delivering Drkoop.com, decrease the use of the Internet or prevent users from accessing Drkoop.com, any of which would have a material adverse effect on our business, results of operations and financial condition.

Contingency Plan. As discussed above, we are engaged in an ongoing Year 2000 assessment and have developed preliminary contingency plans. The results of our analyses and the responses received from third-party vendors and service providers will be taken into account to revise our contingency plans as necessary. It is our goal to finalize our contingency plans by the end of the third quarter of 1999.

New Accounting Pronouncements

In June 1998, the FASB issued SFAS No. 133, "Accounting for Derivative Instruments and Hedging Activities." SFAS No. 133 establishes accounting and reporting standards for derivative instruments, including derivative instruments embedded in other contracts, and for hedging activities. SFAS No. 133 is effective for all fiscal quarters of fiscal years beginning after June 15, 1999. We currently do not engage or plan to engage in derivative instruments or hedging activities.

BUSINESS

Background

Our company operates Drkoop.com, an Internet-based consumer healthcare network. Our network consists of a consumer-focused interactive website which provides users with comprehensive healthcare information and services, as well as affiliate relationships with Internet portals, other websites, healthcare organizations and traditional media outlets. Our website, www.drkoop.com, is a healthcare portal which integrates dynamic healthcare content on a wide variety of subjects, interactive communities and tools, as well as opportunities to purchase healthcare-related products and services on-line. Our company's founders, including former U.S. Surgeon General Dr. C. Everett Koop, created Drkoop.com to empower consumers to better manage their personal health with comprehensive, relevant and timely information. Our objective is to establish the Drkoop.com network as the most trusted and comprehensive source of consumer healthcare information and services on the Internet.

We launched our website in July 1998. By June 1, 1999, www.drkoop.com had attracted over 6 million unique users and enrolled over 280,000 registered users, according to commercial software that we utilize. Our network is designed to provide consumers with a variety of healthcare content, including information on acute ailments, chronic illnesses, nutrition, fitness and wellness, and access to medical databases, publications, and real-time medical news. In addition, we offer eight interactive communities consisting of over 130 hosted chat support groups. Our support groups allow users to share experiences with others who face, or have faced, similar health conditions, leveraging the aggregate community to benefit each member. We also provide interactive tools that permit users to personalize their Drkoop.com experience and are developing additional features to expand the functionality of our website.

Currently, our affiliates consist of Internet portals and other websites, healthcare organizations and traditional media outlets. Each affiliate provides to its customers easy access to the information and services offered on Drkoop.com. Through these relationships, we believe that we will gain broad exposure of our brand, drive high volumes of traffic to the Drkoop.com website, and acquire and distribute relevant local content. We intend to expand our network by continuing to establish relationships with affiliates that have the ability to direct additional users to our website.

Our belief is that health-concerned consumers are highly motivated in their need to find accurate information and to act on it. Our strategy is to create a trusted brand that consumers will rely on for that information and for related e-commerce opportunities. Our business model is primarily to earn advertising, subscription and e-commerce transaction revenues from advertisers, merchants, manufacturers and healthcare organizations who desire to reach a highly targeted community of healthcare consumers on the Internet. For example, advertisers can target very specific audiences such as persons interested in a particular disease or individuals who desire to address a particular health condition. We also earn revenues by facilitating e-commerce transactions, such as sales of prescription refills, vitamins and nutritional supplements, and health insurance services, offered by outside parties.

Industry Overview

The Internet has become an important alternative to traditional media, enabling millions of consumers to seek information, communicate with one another and execute commercial transactions electronically. According to an industry research firm, the number of world-wide web users is expected to grow from approximately 100 million in 1998 to approximately 320 million by 2002. The Internet is distinct from traditional media in that it offers real-time access to dynamic and interactive content and instantaneous communication among users. These characteristics, combined with the fast growth of Internet users and usage, have created a powerful, rapidly expanding direct marketing and sales channel. Advertisers can target very specific demographic groups, measure the effectiveness of advertising campaigns and revise them in response to real-time feedback. Similarly, the Internet offers on-line merchants the ability to reach a vast audience and operate with lower costs and greater scale economies, while offering consumers greater selections, lower prices and heightened convenience, compared to conventional retailing. We believe that all participants in the healthcare industry will benefit from the Internet because of its unique attributes as an open, low-cost and flexible technology for the exchange of information and execution of electronic transactions.

Portals, such as AOL, Excite, the Go Network, Lycos, MSN and Yahoo!, have established themselves as leading pathways for a broad variety of information. Users are augmenting these portals with subject-specific vertical portals, which are becoming one of the fastest growing segments of the Internet. These vertical portals are using brand awareness driven by high quality topical content and significant market resources to establish themselves as destinations for highly concentrated groups of users.

In addition, on-line communities have emerged that allow users with similar interests to engage in interactive activities. Until recently, use of the Internet consisted mainly of users seeking one-way, static information on topics of interest to them. Technologies have recently been developed which allow users greater flexibility to create and personalize content, communicate with users having similar interests and engage in other interactive activities. We believe that on-line communities are particularly relevant to users interested in healthcare issues, since medical information is often complex and users value communication with peers who face, or have faced, the same health conditions, leveraging the aggregated community to benefit each member.

Healthcare is the largest segment of the U.S. economy, representing the annual expenditure of roughly $1 trillion, and health and medical information is one of the fastest growing areas of interest on the Internet. According to Cyber Dialogue, an industry research firm, during the 12-month period ended July 1998, approximately 17 million adults in the United States searched on-line for health and medical information, and approximately 50% of these individuals made off-line purchases after seeking information on the Internet. Cyber Dialogue estimates that approximately 70% of the persons searching for health and medical information on-line believe the Internet empowers them by providing them with information before and after they go to a doctor's office. Cyber Dialogue also estimates that the number of adults in the United States searching for on-line health and medical information will grow to approximately 30 million in the year 2000, and they will spend approximately $150 billion for all types of health-related products and services off-line. Accordingly, we believe that companies that establish a clear brand identity as a trusted source of on-line consumer healthcare information and services will have a significant opportunity to capitalize on multiple revenue sources, including direct-to-consumer advertising and e-commerce.

Business Strategy

Our objective is to establish the Drkoop.com network as the most trusted and comprehensive source of consumer healthcare information and services on the Internet. Our business strategy incorporates the following key elements:

Establish the Drkoop.com Brand. Our strategy is to create a strong brand with which consumers associate the trustworthiness and credibility of Dr. C. Everett Koop and which will enable us to implement his vision of empowering individuals to better manage their personal health. We also intend to enhance our brand through association with other notable leaders in the consumer healthcare field, such as ABC News Medical Correspondent Dr. Nancy Snyderman, a director of our company. Our company is currently engaged in a major campaign to increase awareness of the Drkoop.com brand among consumers, healthcare organizations, Internet portals and other websites. We intend to allocate significant resources to further develop and build brand recognition through on-line advertising, general advertising, strategic alliances and other marketing initiatives.

Provide Consumers with Healthcare Content of High Quality. We currently provide our users with high quality healthcare content, including information on acute ailments, chronic illnesses, nutrition, fitness and wellness, and access to medical databases, publications, and real-time medical news. This information is provided by established sources such as Dartmouth Medical School, Reuters, the National Institute of Health, Multum Interactive Services, Inc., and the American Cancer Society. We also offer a directory which compares and rates over 1,100 other health-oriented websites. Our strategy is to integrate dynamic healthcare information on a wide variety of subjects with relevant interactive communities and tools, and opportunities to purchase healthcare-related products and services on-line. We believe that the quality of our health information is a competitive advantage that will enable us to attract users to our website, promote user loyalty and increase page views per visit.

Syndicate Content Through Affiliates to Promote Traffic Growth. We have entered into relationships with portals and other websites which position Drkoop.com as their primary source for consumer healthcare content. In addition, we have entered into relationships with local hospitals, payor entities and local media outlets such as television stations. These relationships include the creation of co-branded websites and the distribution of branded healthcare information to affiliated entities. We intend to expand our network by continuing to establish relationships with affiliates that have the ability to direct additional users to our website.

Develop and Expand On-line Healthcare Communities. We currently offer our registered users free access to eight on-line communities consisting of over 130 hosted chat support groups. Our eight communities are organized by the following general health topics: Addiction & Recovery, Aging Healthy, General Health, Men's Health, Mental Health, Parenting & Children's Health, Physical Conditions and Women's Health. Our support groups cover topics including hepatitis C, child development, stress management and relaxation skills and anxiety disorders. Our communities and support groups allow users with similar health-related experiences to exchange information and gather news and knowledge in a secure, anonymous, on-line environment. Communities and support groups are hosted by selected moderators with experience both in the relevant topic and on-line forum moderating. We believe that our communities and support groups are an effective way to attract users to our website and strengthen their loyalty to the Drkoop.com network. In addition, by aggregating users interested in a particular health topic, we believe we can sell advertising in a highly targeted manner, thereby commanding higher advertising rates. Similarly, we offer merchants and others who engage in e-commerce the ability to market products and services to our community members.

Provide Consumers with Unique Features and Tools. Our website is designed to provide easy access to innovative features and tools. Currently, our most popular tool educates consumers on the interaction among various drugs and other substances. In addition, we recently acquired the right to deploy a comprehensive personal medical record which will allow users to establish and maintain a lifelong record of their health and medical information in a secure portion of our database. We intend to continue to add useful tools to enable our users to personalize their on-line experience. We believe that our tools and features will continue to encourage users to visit our website frequently and increase the likelihood of users selecting Drkoop.com as their preferred website for health-related issues.

Provide an Attractive Advertising Site. We believe our ability to target specific users, the interactive nature of our website and the demographic characteristics of our users will be attractive to pharmaceutical, healthcare and other companies that advertise on the Internet. By identifying users interested in a particular health-related topic or who desire to address a particular health condition, we believe we can deliver advertising in a highly targeted manner, thereby commanding higher advertising rates.

Enable High Value E-commerce Offerings. We enable e-commerce transactions offered by third parties. Our strategy involves permitting merchants, manufacturers and service providers access to a highly targeted community of health conscious consumers through our website and the health channels of our portal affiliates. We presently enable sales of prescription refills, vitamins and nutritional supplements and insurance services. Although we do not provide these products or services, we do provide links to the websites of third parties that provide these products or services. Some of these third parties have entered into preferred provider arrangements with us and pay us either a transaction fee for sales attributable to users from our website or an anchor tenant rental fee. Anchor tenant fees are annual fees paid by on-line merchants in exchange for a prominent link to their on-line stores. We believe that contextual merchandising of e-commerce transactions will attract users to our website and promote user loyalty.

The Drkoop.com Network
Our network consists of a consumer-focused interactive website which provides users with comprehensive healthcare information and services, as well as affiliate relationships with portals, other websites, local healthcare organizations and traditional media outlets. The website is a healthcare portal which integrates dynamic healthcare information on a wide variety of subjects, interactive communities and tools that enable our users to personalize their Drkoop.com experience and opportunities to purchase healthcare-related products and services on-line. Our affiliate relationships, we believe, allow us to gain broad exposure of our brand, drive high volumes of traffic to the Drkoop.com website, and acquire and distribute relevant content at the local level. Affiliates may use our content on television or radio, in print, radio or on-line, provided they credit Drkoop.com as the provider of the content and, where appropriate, pay a license fee. We believe that displaying logos and credits on every web page, program and publication where Drkoop.com content is displayed will help us build brand awareness and attract users to our website.

Website
Healthcare Information. Our goal is to provide consumer-focused information for the health-conscious public, individuals with a health condition, and individuals who have recovered from illness or injury, all at a level the average consumer can understand. We currently provide a variety of healthcare content, including information on acute ailments, chronic illnesses, mental health and behavioral issues, nutrition, fitness and wellness, and access to medical databases, other publications, and real-time medical news. To encourage interactivity, we provide links to relevant communities and other features from each content page. Examples of healthcare information that we currently provide include:

Information	*Sources*
• Physician-authored articles on common medical conditions	Dartmouth Medical School, Nancy Snyderman, M.D., Drkoop.com
• Updated health-related news and editorials on topics of current interest	Reuters
• General medical information and statistics	National Institute of Health, American Cancer Society

- Information regarding the interaction   Multum Interactive Services, Inc.
  among various drugs and other
  substances
- Directory of over 1,100 health-related   drkoop.com
  websites including ratings and reviews
- Information on pharmaceuticals and   Graedon Enterprises, Inc.
  over-the-counter drugs
- Clinical trials study information   Quintiles, Inc.

We expect that competitive factors will create a continuing need for us to improve and add to our healthcare content. Accordingly, we intend to seek additional sources of healthcare information and expand the breadth of our content offerings.

Interactive Communities. We currently offer eight interactive communities consisting of over 130 hosted chat support groups. These communities were developed to provide users with a mechanism to interact with others experiencing, or who have experienced, similar health conditions. We believe the communities and their support groups enable users to gain valuable insight, practical knowledge and support with regard to their health concerns which supplement their interaction with their physicians. Our eight communities are organized by the following general health topics: Addiction & Recovery, Aging Healthy, General Health, Men's Health, Mental Health, Parenting & Children's Health, Physical Conditions and Women's Health.

The Drkoop.com support groups differ from other Internet chat rooms and forums in that Drkoop.com selects hosts to be involved in each support group. Although most of our support groups are led by peer monitors, many of whom have faced similar health concerns, some are led by healthcare professionals with expertise in the specific area of health on which the support group is focused.

User demand has driven the expansion in the number of Drkoop.com support groups. Our support topics are typically proposed by a user. Accordingly, our support groups are dynamic and evolve as user interests change. We believe our support groups are distinct from other support rooms because Drkoop.com offers access to information and news relevant to the support topic on the corresponding web page. We believe that a user's participation in a focused chat will stimulate the user's interests in related support groups, contributing to more frequent usage and longer visits at our website. Examples of the interactive support groups that we currently offer include:

Addiction & Recovery
   Living with Sobriety

Aging Healthy
   Unique Exercise Ideas

General Health
   Angel Power
   Turning Back the Clock

Men's Health
   Beyond the Locker Room

Mental Health
   Anxiety Disorders
   Mood Disorders
   OCD Matters

Parenting & Children's Health
   Attachment Parenting
   Child Development
   Depression and Your Child
   Parenting an Only Child

Physical Conditions
   Beating the Pain
   Crohn's Colitis Support
   Joint Replacement Chat
   Hepatitis Central

Women's Health
   Balancing Work & Family
   Biological Clock Watchers
   Menopause Management

Tools. We currently provide interactive tools and other features that allow registered users to personalize their Drkoop.com experience and better manage the healthcare information available on our network. We believe our tools and features enable us to obtain and retain registered users. To enhance the experience of our current and future registered users, we intend to develop additional tools and features. Examples of tools that we have already developed or intend to develop include:

Existing Tools

Drug Checker. Our drug interaction tool, Drug Checker, allows users to quickly and easily search for information on a particular product and then check for interactions between it and other prescription and over-the-counter drugs. The tool enables the user to search for drugs by complete or partial name matching and returns a list of drugs for selection. Selection of more than one drug into the interaction list then permits the user to test for interaction among the selected drugs. The tool also provides drug-food interaction data when available. Drug Checker uses the Multum database which we have modified with an easy to use interface.

Health Search. This tool allows users to search the entire Drkoop.com website and related healthcare websites for specific health and medical information. We also provide easy access to Medline, a large database of medical information provided by the National Library of Medicine and CancerLit, the National Cancer Institute's bibliographic database.

Health Site Reviews. We have created a directory of third party health-related websites using an industry standard rating scheme from the Healthcare Information Technology Institute. Our rating methodology produces an overall website score based on several criteria including credibility, accuracy, disclosure, links, design and interactivity. This tool enables a user to search for the highest rated healthcare websites categorized by various healthcare conditions.

Health Risk Assessments. Our first health risk assessment tool, Tobacco Risk Profiler, enables users to understand their reliance on tobacco and assess a variety of treatment methods. This tool is integrated with content and interactive community features to provide an educational and supportive experience for users suffering from nicotine addiction. We expect to introduce a variety of health risk assessments allowing users a quick and easy way to assess their health and find corrective measures they can take to reduce any health-related risks.

Health Polls. Our health polls provide users with opportunities to answer a variety of health related questions on-line. We can obtain valuable information from our users as to their interests and demographics. The survey information is then used to make the related community more aware of current healthcare issues.

Preventionnaire. This interactive questionnaire, residing in our Prevention Center, is designed to help consumers identify their healthcare needs. After answering a series of questions tailored to the user's sex and age, the tool advises the user to consult with his or her physician on a variety of preventive tests or immunizations to maintain good health.

Future Tools

Listed below are some of the tools that we are presently developing. Deployment of these tools will involve our successful acquisition and integration of the required content and related technology. We cannot assure you that these tools will be successfully deployed on a timely basis, or at all, or that users will find these features attractive.

Dr. Koop's Personal Medical Record. We intend to offer a personal medical record which will allow users to establish and maintain a lifelong record of personal health and medical information in a secure portion of our database. We presently expect to add a personal medical record feature to our website in the first half of 1999 as an element of our technology relationship with HealthMagic.

My Health@drkoop.com. This product is intended to allow consumers to receive email newsletters with news and information tailored to their specific needs. We presently expect to add this tool to our website in the first half of 1999.

Recipe Database. This feature is intended to provide a customized, searchable database of recipes meeting specific dietary requirements of the user, such as low-fat, low-salt diets. We presently expect to add this tool to our website in the second half of 1999.

Personal Health Shopper. This tool is intended to enable consumers to enter their preferences for shopping and allow us to customize information and new product offerings for the users. We presently expect to add this tool to our website in the second half of 1999.

Physician Databases. We intend to provide to consumers access to physician databases permitting them to find doctors in their local area. In February 1999, we entered into a content agreement with Physicians' Online which will allow us to implement a physician database on our website. We are currently in the process of deploying this tool.

Insurance Assessment. This interactive questionnaire is designed to enable consumers to better understand their health insurance needs and assist them in making a purchase decision. We presently expect to add this tool to our website in the first half of 1999.

Affiliates

Portals and Other Websites. The distribution of Drkoop.com content to affiliated portals and other websites is designed to rapidly increase brand awareness through co-promotion and direct links with the affiliate's server. We intend to affiliate with selected websites that have the potential to drive traffic to our website and provide broad exposure to the Drkoop.com brand. Currently, portals are the leading aggregators of traffic on the Internet. Users are augmenting these portals with subject-specific vertical portals, which are becoming one of the fastest growing segments of the Internet. These vertical portals are using brand awareness driven by quality topical content and significant market resources to establish themselves as destinations for highly concentrated groups of users. Examples of relationships that we have already established include:

The Go Network. Drkoop.com has entered into agreements with Infoseek Corporation and the Buena Vista Internet Group, a unit of The Walt Disney Company, under which Drkoop.com will be the exclusive provider of health related content on three websites of the Go Network: Go.com Health Center on Infoseek, ESPN.com Training Room and the Family.com Health Channel. Under the Infoseek agreement, Drkoop.com will also be the premier health content provider for ABCnews.com. In addition, Drkoop.com will be the exclusive pharmacy and drugstore, health insurance and clinical trials partner in the Go.com Health Center. Under these agreements, users on the Go Network will be able to access various health information, services, interactive tools and commerce opportunities through a co-branded location (http://go.drkoop.com) served by Drkoop.com. In the event Drkoop.com elects not to provide specific content, it may be obtained from a third party. We believe that these agreements will contribute substantially to our brand awareness and increase traffic on our website.

The term of both agreements is for three years, except that each of the parties may elect to terminate the relationship after two years. We will pay Infoseek and the Buena Vista Internet Group approximately $57.9 million in total consideration consisting of cash and warrants to purchase 775,000 shares of common stock at an exercise price of

$8.60 per share over the full three year term. None of the warrants are exercisable prior to one year after issuance.

Salon Internet, Inc. Salon Internet, Inc. and Drkoop.com expect to launch a health and wellness site called Salon Health in the first half of 1999. Salon Health will create a unique blend of editorial content and integrated health information for its users. Drkoop.com will be the exclusive provider of health information for Salon Health. This initiative is expected to introduce a complete storefront offering of drugstore related products. Our agreement with Salon has a three-year term. The parties will share in revenues generated through the storefront and in advertising revenue. We will pay Salon a fee for running a minimum number of Drkoop.com banner advertisements on the Salon site.

WellSt.com. Drkoop.com has been selected as the provider of traditional health and medical information for WellSt.com, a division of Element Media, Inc., an alternative health company. The WellSt.com agreement has a three-year term under which we will be the exclusive provider of traditional healthcare content to WellSt.com, except that WellSt.com may use other sources to the extent that we decline to develop any specific content. WellSt.com will be the preferred provider of alternative medicine and health information on Drkoop.com. The parties have agreed to undertake joint marketing activities of mutual benefit and will share in revenues generated through the use of the other party's content. We believe this strategic partnership will allow Drkoop.com to reach a unique audience that is interested in alternative medicine and health information.

Physicians' Online. Drkoop.com will provide content and services to Physicians' Online, one of the largest Internet communities of doctors. Drkoop.com and Physicians' Online will also undertake joint marketing and sales of the personal medical record software and services to hospitals and other managed health facilities and will share in the revenue generated from these activities. Physicians' Online provides doctors with access to medical databases, clinical symposia, medical news and other medical resources, and has a membership in excess of 170,000 doctors. Our agreement with Physicians' Online has a one-year term during which each party will promote the other party's website and share in various revenue sources.

iSyndicate. iSyndicate, a service that connects small sites in search of content with content providers, has selected Drkoop.com as a provider of health information to its 13,000 affiliate sites. Under this agreement, iSyndicate affiliates can choose to provide headlines, teasers or full-text content to their users. The iSyndicate agreement has a one-year term under which iSyndicate will market the Drkoop.com content under the several different marketing models. We pay a fee for each user who links to Drkoop.com from a headline or teaser on an affiliate site, and we receive a fee when an affiliate elects to license the full-text Drkoop.com content to be hosted and displayed on the affiliate's site.

SeniorNet. SeniorNet.org, the world's largest trainer of older adults about computer technology and the Internet, has selected Drkoop.com to be the exclusive provider of health information and services to users of the SeniorNet On-Line Community. Through this strategic partnership, Drkoop.com will provide our healthcare content and our products and services that will empower SeniorNet users to better manage their health. SeniorNet operates over 140 SeniorNet Learning Centers across the United States, providing access to over 100,000 older adults, while educating them on how to use the SeniorNet website and the Internet. In addition to the content partnership, Drkoop.com plans to release a co-branded version of the Dr. Koop's Personal Medical Record for members of the SeniorNet On-Line Community. The Drkoop.com health content and PMR will become part of the Learning Center curriculum, which is used to educate more than 45,000 older adults each year. We will pay SeniorNet a fee for this exclusive relationship.

Yahoo! Drkoop.com has entered into a relationship with Yahoo! to syndicate Dr. Nancy Snyderman's Daily Health offering for use in Yahoo! Health, with a launch expected in the second quarter of 1999. Under this agreement, Dr. Snyderman will appear daily on Yahoo! in a Drkoop.com branded environment where users of Yahoo! Health are able to read Dr. Snyderman's responses to user-submitted questions. Users who wish to ask Dr. Snyderman a question through an email interface will be transferred to the "Ask Dr. Nancy Snyderman" area of the Drkoop.com website. New answers and archives will be posted daily on Yahoo! Health. This is a non-paid relationship between the two companies.

@Home Network. Drkoop.com entered into a two year relationship with The @Home Network to be the anchor tenant partner within the Health Channel area of the @Home service. Drkoop.com will be the premier content provider appearing in the Health Channel. Under the terms of this agreement, Drkoop.com will have the ability to direct users to related commerce, community and interactive tool features appearing on the Drkoop.com website from within all health content appearing in the Health Channel. In addition, Drkoop.com will share in all advertising revenues generated by @Home in the Health Channel where Drkoop.com content dominates the related page. Drkoop.com will pay a carriage fee of $2.25 million to @Home for the right to be the premier content provider in the @Home Health Channel.

Healthcare Organizations. Drkoop.com enrolls healthcare organizations as local affiliates through our Community Partner Program. This program allows local organizations such as hospitals, health systems and other healthcare organizations to integrate the Drkoop.com brand and content into their on-line initiatives. Under this program, we develop co-branded Internet pages linked to Drkoop.com for local healthcare organizations. The Community Partner Program enables healthcare organizations to supply their patients with on-line health resources and interactive capabilities integrated with specific information about their facilities. This program provides consumers with the ability to educate themselves, make an informed decision, and take action through a healthcare organization's local website, strengthening the relationship between the consumer and the organization. Those consumers are introduced to the Drkoop.com brand through our association with their local provider or payor. Examples of local healthcare organizations that have enrolled in our Community Partner Program include:

Adventist Health System. Adventist Health System currently operates 31 hospitals in nine states and has more than 4,900 licensed beds. Adventist Health System also operates 27 extended-care facilities with more than 3,000 long-term care beds. Florida Hospital, part of Adventist Health System, serves the 2.6 million residents of the Orlando area.

Highmark. Highmark, created in 1996 by the consolidation of Blue Cross of Western Pennsylvania and Pennsylvania Blue Shield, is one of the ten largest health insurers in the United States. Highmark offers managed care programs, health plans, traditional health insurance coverage, life and casualty insurance, and dental and vision programs to approximately 18 million people.

MemorialCare. MemorialCare is a comprehensive healthcare system servicing the over 14 million residents of Los Angeles and Orange Counties in California. MemorialCare offers Southern Californians four major medical centers and a children's hospital, as well as a number of subsidiary facilities.

Tallahassee Memorial HealthCare. Tallahassee Memorial HealthCare provides Floridians with a comprehensive system of patient and healthcare services coordinated under certain specialty centers. These specialty centers include Tallahassee Memorial Hospital, the eighth largest hospital in Florida, and eleven satellite facilities in five counties. Founded more than fifty years ago, Tallahassee Memorial HealthCare currently services a population of over 500,000 individuals.

Scott and White Hospital and Clinic. Scott and White is one of the largest multi-specialty hospital and clinic groups in the United States. Their more than 515 physicians and scientists service the 1.8 million residents of Central Texas as well as patients from throughout the United States and many foreign countries.

Baptist Health Systems. Baptist Health Systems is South Florida's largest not-for-profit health care organization with 7,400 employees. The health system includes Baptist Hospital, Baptist Children's Hospital, Miami Cardiac & Vascular Institute, Homestead Hospital, Mariners Hospital in Tavernler and a full spectrum of outpatient diagnostic and treatment facilities. Baptist Health Systems serves the 3.5 million residents of the Miami area.

Promina Health Systems. Promina Health Systems is a local, not-for-profit organization created by local doctors and hospitals who have come together to protect and improve community-based health care for the 4.3 million residents of metro Atlanta.

Contracts we enter into under our Community Partner Program typically specify performance standards that require us to:

- provide up to 10 customized website pages;
- maintain operation of our website for at least 95% of the time; and/or
- provide monthly traffic reports to our community partners.

Traditional Media. We also intend to establish additional affiliate relationships with traditional media outlets. There are many areas of overlap with television and print that allow for collaboration in the delivery of quality healthcare content to an audience. Late breaking news, daily syndicated articles and other timely relevant content can be distributed as an information feed in multiple formats. For example, network television affiliates carry local, relevant information directly to local audiences. Similarly, by distributing content at the affiliate level, Drkoop.com can be the leading syndicate of Internet-ready health content and editorial-based, breaking health news. The content that resides on our website can also be distributed through newspapers, trade journals, periodicals, and a variety of other print media. By aligning Drkoop.com and our notable leaders in the healthcare field, Dr. C. Everett Koop and Dr. Nancy Snyderman, with high profile publications, we have the opportunity to build brand awareness of Drkoop.com. Links from traditional media websites to our website create additional channels for generating traffic to the Drkoop.com website. Examples of traditional media programs include:

Health Resource Marketing. Drkoop.com has an agreement with Health Resource Publishing, a division of Catalina Marketing, Inc., to place advertisements for the Drkoop.com site on up to 50% of the HRP newsletters distributed through chain drugstores. HRP estimates that it will distribute up to 20 million newsletters monthly during 1999. Additionally, personalized healthcare content from the Drkoop. com site will be included in the HRP newsletters thus reaching a highly targeted health conscious population with branded content and promotion.

Granite Broadcasting. We have entered into an agreement with Granite Broadcasting Corporation, a publicly-traded owner of ten ABC, CBS, NBC and WB television stations in markets such as San Francisco, Detroit and Buffalo. A program was initiated in September 1998 with KEYE, Granite's CBS affiliate in Austin, Texas, in which Drkoop.com provides the station with Internet health content, and the station provides both local promotion of Drkoop.com and daily prompting of the station's viewers to Drkoop.com following relevant health stories on the station's local newscasts.

ABC Affiliates. Drkoop.com's multi-year agreement with Infoseek for the Go Network Internet properties provides that the websites of all ABC affiliates who participate in the network's Local Net Internet service, currently 115 stations, will be linked to Drkoop.com. ABC will also provide details to all of its affiliates regarding how they can participate as a full Drkoop.com affiliate in their local news coverage and promotion. ABC affiliates receive first right of negotiation for participation in this program.

Revenue Opportunities

Our operating strategy is presently comprised of three primary means of generating revenue:

- advertising;
- content syndication; and
- electronic commerce.

Advertising

The healthcare industry spends billions of dollars every year to market products and services to consumers. Jupiter Communications projects that the on-line health advertising segment will grow from $12.3 million in 1998 to $265 million in 2002. We believe that health portals and other vertically focused websites are uniquely positioned to attract a significant share of these advertising expenditures. By identifying users interested in a particular health-related topic or who desire to address a particular health condition, we believe we can sell advertising in a highly targeted manner, thereby commanding higher advertising rates.

Merchants can purchase advertising on our website in two ways. Banner advertising is generally sold based on the number of impressions received by the advertisement and its position on the website. This type of advertising frequently encourages the user to move to other web pages which describe the advertiser's product and solicit a direct response from the user. Sponsorships are contracts that typically grant advertisers rights to promote their products on a specific portion of the website. Sponsorships are designed to support broad marketing objectives, including brand awareness, product introductions, research and transactions, generally on an exclusive basis. Accordingly, sponsorships are sold based on their duration, the portion of the website sponsored and the number of impressions delivered. Some of our advertisers and sponsors include:

- Pfizer, a pharmaceutical company, which advertises Zithromax, a children's antibiotic, in our Ear, Nose and Throat and Children's Health sections;
- Biogen, a pharmaceutical manufacturer, which advertises Avonex, a Multiple Sclerosis medication, in our Multiple Sclerosis disease section;
- Schering-Plough, a pharmaceutical company, which has sponsored our allergy health topic with Claritin. The integrated sponsorship includes logo links, keywords, and banner impressions; and
- SmithKline Beecham, a pharmaceutical company, which has sponsored the Drkoop.com smoking cessation center with Nicorette/Nicoderm.

One form of direct response advertising involves pre-screening and identifying potential participants in clinical trials. In 1997, approximately $19 billion was spent by the private sector on human health research and development in the United States alone, according to the Pharmaceutical Manufacturers Association. A significant portion of these costs are incurred in the later stages of clinical development, where large numbers of subjects are enrolled into studies designed to provide the bulk of the safety and efficacy data needed to obtain a product license from the FDA. The identification and enrollment of qualified individuals into these studies is usually a time-consuming and expensive process.

In December 1998 we implemented the Drkoop.com Clinical Research Center, a portion of our website designed to help educate consumers about clinical trials: what they are; what to expect; and how to find and enroll in an appropriate trial if the individual and their physician believe that this is a viable therapy option. When this feature is fully developed, consumers will be able to search a database of clinical trials by geography and by disease. We believe that on-line pre-screening will reduce the number of inappropriate contacts and result in only qualified people being referred to the clinical trial sponsors. Drkoop.com will derive a per respondent advertising fee for this recruitment service.

Content Syndication

We license our content and certain interactive tools through a broad variety of affiliated websites. The majority of the licensed content is provided by third-parties and is not produced by us. The primary source of content syndication revenue is our Community Partner Program. Under the Community Partner Program, we develop co-branded Internet pages and software consisting of visual icons containing links back to the Drkoop.com website for local healthcare organizations, such as hospitals and payor organizations. Licensing fees are typically determined based on the channel for which the content will be used. Content syndication agreements generally stipulate that all content provided by Drkoop.com must retain a legend indicating "Provided by Drkoop.com" and is subject to an acceptable use policy that defines how and where the content may be used. Editorial content and/or content control generally remain the exclusive right of the Drkoop.com network. We believe that by allowing other high-traffic websites and portals to offer our content we will gain broad exposure of our brand and drive high volumes of traffic to the Drkoop.com website, thereby allowing us to generate more advertising and e-commerce revenues. While we expect to also generate significant revenues from certain of our syndication programs, this revenue source is expected to become a smaller proportion of our overall revenues as our audience continues to grow.

E-Commerce

We provide users with the ability to access e-commerce opportunities provided by outside parties in numerous locations throughout the Drkoop.com website. For example, users can access prescription refill services through pages relevant to a particular condition. We also plan to offer the Drkoop.com Health Store, a section of the website which aggregates all of the e-commerce opportunities found throughout the site into one comprehensive storefront that users can navigate to find the specific products or services offered by outside parties. E-commerce interfaces on Drkoop.com, whether in the Drkoop.com Health Store or in other locations within the website's general content, are being designed to be informative and easy to use.

We currently offer two primary categories of products and services which users can purchase from third parties through our website:

On-line Pharmacy Products. According to industry statistics, the retail prescription drug market in 1997 accounted for approximately $89.1 billion in sales generated by 2.6 billion prescriptions. Over-the-counter medications and the other health and beauty aids accounted for $26.8 billion and $26.9 billion in retail sales, respectively, in 1997. Due to the convenience, privacy, cost-savings and selection that can be offered to consumers via the Internet, we believe that the on-line pharmacy will become a major factor in retail pharmacy sales and will capture a significant portion of these sales in the near future. Moreover, direct deliveries of prescription drugs to the home via mail accounts for a significant proportion of all prescription drug sales. We expect that this distribution channel will expand to include other products traditionally associated with retail pharmacy stores.

Our personal drugstore provides links to 23 traditional and on-line pharmacies where users can order prescription refills and other pharmacy products over the Internet. We are also offering e-commerce anchor tenant positions to online and traditional pharmacies on a category-exclusive basis to allow consumers to link to their online stores. We receive an annual rental fee for these anchor tenant positions. Our first contract is with Vitamin Shoppe, an online vitamin and supplement company, and we are in advanced discussions with several other parties regarding similar arrangements. We also intend to offer anchor tenant positions for the online pharmacy on the Go! Health Network.

Insurance. The individual health insurance market is estimated to be an $85 billion per year industry, according to AM Best. In the past decade, the AMA estimates that the number of Americans without health insurance increased from 32 million to 43.4 million. Our website provides access to an insurance center consisting of comparisons of different insurance plans designed to assist users in determining their individual health coverage needs and coverage options. This service is designed to provide useful, consumer-oriented information and to enable the purchase of insurance coverage through various links with qualified insurers.

Our current insurance partners include:

- Quotesmith.com, an on-line insurance website where users can obtain instant quotes from 375 leading insurance companies. We have implemented a co-branded version of their instant quote system.
- American Health Value, a user-friendly Medical Savings Account (MSA) administrator offering consumers access to their MSA funds with a Visa card. We link to their website through our Personal Insurance Center.
- HealthCore Medical Solutions, a health and consumer benefits marketing company, which offers its members discounts on eye care, dental and pharmacy benefits. We link to their website through our Personal Insurance Center.
- eHealthInsurance.com, an online retail health insurance provider. We link to their website through our Personal Insurance Center.

Sales

As of March 31, 1999, we had a direct sales organization consisting of 11 sales professionals with an average of 14 years of sales experience, and had also contracted with WinStar Interactive, an on-line property representation company. We have seven geographically-based sales representatives with extensive healthcare backgrounds calling on large integrated health systems and payors in major metropolitan areas selling Drkoop.com's Community Partner Program. We also have two sales representatives with pharmaceutical backgrounds who call directly on pharmaceutical companies. In addition, one of our sales representative with an insurance background calls on payors for enrollment in our insurance commerce initiative. Further, members of management and the sales force call on portals and other websites to establish affiliate relationships. We also use WinStar to call on the interactive agencies and media buyers for both sponsorship and banner advertising. As of March 31, 1999, approximately 60 percent of the advertising commitments received by us had been secured by our direct sales force, with the balance secured by WinStar.

For the year ending December 31, 1998, sales to individual customers constituting 10% or more of revenue included Memorial Care Hospital (63%), PCS Health Systems (23%), and Medtronic (12%).

Marketing and Public Relations

We employ a variety of methods to promote the Drkoop.com brand to attract user traffic and affiliate relationships. Our public relations staff oversees a comprehensive pubic relations program targeting consumer, trade and healthcare media. In addition, we also conduct media outreach programs consisting of public service announcements and other promotional activities targeting radio, broadcast, and print media on a national and local basis.

Advertising. Media purchasing is a significant component to the brand awareness and customer acquisition strategy for Drkoop.com. We believe that click-through banner advertising has been the accepted means to drive traffic across the Internet for several years. We believe that we must continue to promote Drkoop.com to the mass Internet audience through banner advertising in order to attract first time users. Depending on the source, we can use a banner advertisement to direct a user to our homepage or to a place in the website that contains topical information of interest to them. We also intend to pursue general advertising through conventional media.

Public awareness campaigns are a significant part of the user generation plans for Drkoop.com. By strategically aligning Drkoop.com with health-related initiatives and charity organizations, we believe we will be able to reach a large audience to help raise awareness for specific causes or organizations. By creating opportunities for users to participate in awareness campaigns, we believe we can raise money for organizations and charities, and at the same time drive new registered users to Drkoop.com.

Public Relations. As a well recognized, trusted spokesperson on America's health, we believe that Dr. C. Everett Koop is in a unique position to raise consumer awareness of health-related issues and our company. Since the launch of our website, Dr. C. Everett Koop has participated in several industry events that have dramatically raised our visibility in the Internet healthcare market. We expect Dr. C. Everett Koop to continue to raise awareness of our company's mission to empower consumers with information and services to better manage their personal healthcare and our initiatives to serve them, by participating in public relations and public service activities.

Technology

A component of our strategy is to apply existing technologies in novel ways to deliver content and provide services to our users. The various features of the Drkoop.com network are implemented using a combination of commercially available and proprietary software components. We favor licensing and integrating "best of breed" commercially available technology from industry leaders. We reserve internal development of software for those components that are either unavailable on the market or that have major strategic advantages when developed internally. We believe that this component style approach is more manageable, reliable, and scaleable than single-source solutions. In addition, the emphasis on commercial components speeds development time, which is an advantage when competing in a rapidly evolving market. Consistent with our preference for off-the-shelf software components, we rely primarily on industry-standard Microsoft operating systems, development, and infrastructure components including NT, Internet Information Server, Microsoft Site Server, Visual Interdev, and others. We have also created a content management and development system and specialized applications, one example of which is the drug interaction application built upon the Multum commercial database.

In January 1999, we entered into a strategic technology relationship with Health-Magic, Inc. which includes a long-term fully paid license to use a broad range of Internet technologies, such as a web-based personal medical record, personalization tools, and security and authentication features. Under this arrangement, HealthMagic will develop, implement, and support these technologies for us, thereby permitting internal resources to address other needs. Our relationship with HealthMagic, we believe, will allow us to improve the functionality of our website with lower risk and at less cost than if we developed this technology ourselves. We expect that as we deploy the HealthMagic applications we will become dependent on that company for our personal medical record feature and for personalization tools currently in development.

Operating Infrastructure

The Drkoop.com website is based on a technical operating infrastructure, the Drkoop.com web platform, which is designed to be highly scaleable and reliable. The Drkoop.com web platform consists of several subsystems, including a scaleable web cluster used to service user requests for web pages. The web cluster is controlled by a hardware cluster manager which continuously monitors the performance and availability of the individual servers within the web cluster. In the event of an individual server failure or when a server requires maintenance, the hardware cluster manager automatically distributes incoming requests to other available servers without disrupting the user's experience.

The Drkoop.com web platform consists of readily available, off-the-shelf, computer systems, including dual Intel Pentium servers in a fully redundant configuration. The Drkoop.com web platform was designed using a proprietary architecture deploying primarily Microsoft technology running the Windows/NT Operating System. Other Microsoft web enabling technologies used in the Drkoop.com web platform include:

- Microsoft Membership and Personalization Server—software that captures user data and enables the Drkoop.com experience to be customized for each user;
- Microsoft SQL Server—database software used to store user data and content; and
- Microsoft Internet Information Server—software which enables pages to be displayed to the user.

Our data center is maintained offsite by a third party and provides us with multiple backbone connections to the Internet and a fault-tolerant network design. In addition, electricity for running the Drkoop.com web platform is protected by uninterruptible power systems including back-up diesel generators. We have an operations and disaster recovery plan, and Drkoop.com is backed up nightly to an off-site storage facility. We do not maintain a back-up data center.

Competition

A large number of Internet companies compete for users, advertisers, e-commerce transactions and other sources of on-line revenue. The number of Internet websites offering users healthcare content, products and services is vast and increasing at a rapid rate. In addition, traditional media and healthcare providers compete for consumers' attention both through traditional means as well as through new Internet initiatives. We believe that competition for healthcare consumers will continue to increase as the Internet grows as a communication and commercial medium.

We compete directly for users, advertisers, e-commerce merchants, syndication partners and other affiliates with numerous Internet and non-Internet businesses, including:

- health-related on-line services or websites targeted at consumers such as accesshealth.com, ahn.com, betterhealth.com, drweil.com, healthcentral.com, health gate.com, intelihealth.com, mayohealth.org; mediconsult.com, onhealth.com, thrive online.com and webmd.com;
- on-line and Internet portal companies, such as America Online, Inc.; Microsoft Network; Yahoo! Inc.; Excite, Inc.; Lycos Corporation and Infoseek Corporation;
- electronic merchants and conventional retailers such as CVS, Rite Aid Corporation, Walgreens, Advanced Paradigm, Express Scripts, Inc. and Merck-Medco, that provide healthcare goods and services competitive to those available from links on our website;
- hospitals, HMOs, managed care organizations and other healthcare providers and payors such as Columbia/HCA Healthcare Corporation, Kaiser Permanente and VHA, Inc., which offer healthcare information through the Internet; and
- other consumer affinity groups, such as the American Association of Retired Persons, SeniorNet and ThirdAge Media, Inc., which offer healthcare-related content to special demographic groups.

We believe that competition in our industry is based primarily on:

- the quality and market acceptance of healthcare content;
- brand recognition; and
- the quality and market acceptance of new enhancements to current content, features and tools.

Although our competitive position in our market as compared to our competitors is difficult to characterize due principally to the variety of current and potential competitors and the emerging nature of the market, we believe that we presently compete favorably with respect to these factors. However, we believe that our markets are still evolving, and we cannot assure you that we will compete successfully in the future. Additionally, many of our competitors are likely to enjoy substantial competitive advantages compared to our company, including:

- the ability to offer a wider array of on-line products and services;
- larger production and technical staffs;
- greater name recognition and larger marketing budgets and resources;
- larger customer and user bases; and
- substantially greater financial, technical and other resources.

To be competitive, we must respond promptly and effectively to the challenges of technological change, evolving standards and our competitors' innovations by continuing to enhance our products and services, as well as our sales and marketing channels. Increased competition could result in a loss of our market share or a reduction in our prices or margins, any of which could adversely affect our business. Competition is likely to increase significantly as new companies enter the market and current competitors expand their services.

Intellectual Property

Our intellectual property is important to our business. We rely on a combination of copyright, trademark and trade secret laws, confidentiality procedures and contractual provisions to protect our intellectual property. We intend to file for federal trademark registrations for the mark "Drkoop.com," as well as other service and trademarks which incorporate the Dr. Koop name. Our right to use the Dr. Koop name is granted to us under an agreement with Dr. C. Everett Koop. If we lose our right to use the Dr. Koop name, we would be forced to change our corporate name and adopt a new domain name. These changes could confuse current and potential customers and would adversely impact our business. See "Management—Agreements with Dr. C. Everett Koop."

Our efforts to protect our intellectual property may not be adequate. Our competitors may independently develop similar technology or duplicate our products or services. Unauthorized parties may infringe upon or misappropriate our products, services or proprietary information. In addition, the laws of some foreign countries do not protect proprietary rights as well as the laws of the United States, and the global nature of the Internet makes it difficult to control the ultimate destination of our products and services. In the future, litigation may be necessary to enforce our intellectual property rights or to determine the validity and scope of the proprietary rights of others. Any such litigation could be time-consuming and costly.

We could be subject to intellectual property infringement claims as the number of our competitors grows and the content and functionality of our website overlaps with competitive offerings. Defending against these claims, even if not meritorious, could be expensive and divert our attention from operating our company. If we become liable to third parties for infringing their intellectual property rights, we could be required to pay a substantial damage award and forced to develop noninfringing technology, obtain a license or cease using the applications that contain the infringing technology or content. We may be unable to develop noninfringing technology or content or obtain a license on commercially reasonable terms, or at all.

We also rely on a variety of technologies that are licensed from third parties, including our database and Internet server software, which are used in the Drkoop.com website to perform key functions. These third-party licenses may not be available to us on commercially reasonable terms in the future. The loss of or inability to maintain any of these licenses could delay the introduction of software enhancements, interactive tools and other features until equivalent technology could be licensed or developed. Any such delay could materially adversely affect our ability to attract and retain users.

Government Regulation

General

There is an increasing number of laws and regulations pertaining to the Internet. In addition, a number of legislative and regulatory proposals are under consideration by federal, state, local and foreign governments and agencies. Laws or regulations may be adopted with respect to the Internet relating to liability for information retrieved from or transmitted over the Internet, on-line content regulation, user privacy, taxation and quality of products and services. Moreover, it may take years to determine whether and how existing laws such as those governing issues such as intellectual property ownership and infringement, privacy, libel, copyright, trade mark, trade secret, obscenity, personal privacy, taxation, regulation of professional services, regulation of medical devices and the regulation of the sale of other specified goods and services apply to the Internet and Internet advertising. The requirement that we comply with any new legislation or regulation, or any unanticipated application or interpretation of existing laws, may decrease the growth in the use of the Internet, which could in turn decrease the demand for our service, increase our cost of doing business or otherwise have a material adverse effect on our business, results of operations and financial condition.

On-line Content Regulations. Several federal and state statutes prohibit the transmission of indecent, obscene or offensive content over the Internet to certain persons. In addition, pending legislation seeks to ban Internet gambling and federal and state officials have taken action against businesses that operate Internet gambling activities. The enforcement of these statutes and initiatives, and any future enforcement activities, statutes and initiatives, may result in limitations on the type of content and advertisements available on Drkoop.com. Legislation regulating on-line content could slow the growth in use of the Internet generally and decrease the acceptance of the Internet as an advertising and e-commerce medium, which could have a material adverse effect on our ability to generate revenues.

Privacy Concerns
The Federal Trade Commission is considering adopting regulations regarding the collection and use of personal identifying information obtained from individuals when accessing websites, with particular emphasis on access by minors. Such regulations may include requirements that companies establish certain procedures to, among other things:

- give adequate notice to consumers regarding information collection and disclosure practices;
- provide consumers with the ability to have personal identifying information deleted from a company's database;
- provide consumers with access to their personal information and with the ability to rectify inaccurate information;
- clearly identify affiliations or a lack thereof with third parties that may collect information or sponsor activities on a company's website; and
- obtain express parental consent prior to collecting and using personal identifying information obtained from children under 13 years of age.

Such regulation may also include enforcement and redress provisions. While we have implemented programs designed to enhance the protection of the privacy of our users, including children, there can be no assurance that such programs will conform with any regulations adopted by the FTC. Moreover, even in the absence of such regulations, the FTC has begun investigations into the privacy practices of companies that collect information on the Internet. One such investigation has resulted in a consent decree pursuant to which an Internet company agreed to establish programs to implement the principles noted above. We may become subject to such an investigation, or the FTC's regulatory and enforcement efforts may adversely affect the ability to collect demographic and personal information from users, which could have an adverse effect on the our ability to provide highly targeted opportunities for advertisers and e-commerce marketers. Any such developments could have a material adverse effect on the our business, results of operations and financial condition.

It is also possible that "cookies" may become subject to laws limiting or prohibiting their use. The term "cookies" refers to information keyed to a specific server, file pathway or directory location that is stored on a user's hard drive, possibly without the user's knowledge and which is used to track demographic information and to target advertising. Certain currently available Internet browsers allow users to modify their browser settings to remove cookies at any time or prevent cookies from being stored on their hard drives. In addition, a number of Internet commentators, advocates and governmental bodies in the United States and other countries have urged the passage of laws limiting or abolishing the use of cookies. Limitations on or elimination of the use of cookies could limit the effectiveness of the our targeting of advertisements, which could have a material adverse effect on our ability to generate advertising revenue.

The European Union has adopted a directive that imposes restrictions on the collection and use of personal data. Under this EU directive, EU citizens are guaranteed certain rights, including the right of access to their data, the right to know where the data originated, the right to have inaccurate data rectified, the right to recourse in the event of unlawful processing and the right to withhold permission to use their data for direct marketing. The EU directive could, among other things, affect U.S. companies that collect information over the Internet from individuals in EU member countries, and may impose restrictions that are more stringent than current Internet privacy standard in the United States. In particular, companies with offices located in EU countries will not be allowed to send personal information to countries that do not maintain adequate standards of privacy. The EU directive does not, however, define what standards of privacy are adequate. As a result, there can be no assurance that the EU directive will not adversely affect the activities of entities such as our company that engage in data collection from users in EU member countries.

Planned features of our website include the retention of personal information about our users which we obtain with their consent. We have a stringent privacy policy covering this information. However, if third persons were able to penetrate our network security and gain access to, or otherwise misappropriate, our users' personal information, we could be subject to liability. Such liability could include claims for misuses of personal information, such as for unauthorized marketing purposes or unauthorized use of credit cards. These claims could result in litigation, our involvement in which, regardless of the outcome, could require us to expend significant financial resources. Moreover, to the extent any of the data constitute or are deemed to constitute patient health records, a breach of privacy could violate federal law.

Data Protection. Legislative proposals have been made by the federal government that would afford broader protection to owners of databases of information, such as stock quotes and sports scores. Such protection already exists in the EU. If enacted, this legislation could result in an increase in the price of services that provide data to websites. In addition, such legislation could create potential liability for unauthorized use of such data.

Internet Taxation. A number of legislative proposals have been made at the federal, state and local level, and by foreign governments, that would impose additional taxes on the sale of goods and services over the Internet and certain states have taken measures to tax Internet-related activities. Although Congress recently placed a three-year moratorium on state and local taxes on Internet access or on discriminatory taxes on electronic commerce, existing state or local laws were expressly excepted from this moratorium. Further, once this moratorium is lifted, some type of federal and/or state taxes may be imposed upon Internet commerce. Such legislation or other attempts at regulating commerce over the Internet may substantially impair the growth of commerce on the Internet and, as a result, adversely affect our opportunity to derive financial benefit from such activities.

Domain Names. Domain names are the user's Internet "address." Domain names have been the subject of significant trademark litigation in the United States. There can be no assurance that third parties will not bring claims for infringement against us or Dr. C. Everett Koop for the use of this trademark. Moreover, because domain names derive value from the individual's ability to remember such names, there can be no assurance that our domain names will not lose their value if, for example, users begin to rely on mechanisms other than domain names to access on-line resources.

The current system for registering, allocating and managing domain names has been the subject of litigation and of proposed regulatory reform. There can be no assurance that our domain names will not lose their value, or that we will not have to obtain entirely new domain names in addition to or in lieu of its current domain names, if such litigation or reform efforts result in a restructuring in the current system.

FDA Regulation of Medical Devices

Some computer applications and software are considered medical devices and are subject to regulation by the United States Food and Drug Administration. We do not believe that our current applications or services will be regulated by the FDA; however, our applications and services may become subject to FDA regulation. Additionally, we may expand our application and service offerings into areas that subject us to FDA regulation. We have no experience in complying with FDA regulations. We believe that complying with FDA regulations would be time consuming, burdensome and expensive and could delay or prevent our introduction of new applications or services.

Regulation of the Practice of Medicine and Pharmacology

The practice of medicine requires licensing under applicable state law. We have endeavored to structure our website and affiliate relationships to avoid violation of state licensing requirements. For example, we have included notices where we have deemed appropriate advising our users that the data provided on the Drkoop.com network is not a substitute for consultation with their personal physician. Similar guidelines have been adopted governing the activities of moderators in our interactive communities, many of whom are not licensed physicians. However, the application of this area of the law to Internet services such as Drkoop.com is novel and, accordingly, a state regulatory authority may at some point allege that some portion of our business violates these statutes.

Similarly, we provide information about drugs and other prescription medications on our website and enable e-commerce transactions with third parties who sell these products. We have included within our website disclaimers and other notices that we have deemed appropriate to advise users that the information provided is not intended to be a substitute for consultation with a licensed pharmacist. For example, use of our drug interaction database requires that the user affirmatively click on a dialog box on the website page to indicate acceptance of the notices before being given access to the database. However, as with the practice of medicine, the application of this area to Internet services such as Drkoop.com is novel and, accordingly, a state regulatory authority may at some point allege that some portion of our business violates state or federal law governing the dispensing of pharmacy products. Any application of the regulation of the practice of medicine or pharmacology to us could result in a material adverse affect on our business, results of operations and financial condition. Further, any liability based on a determination that we engaged in the practice of medicine without a license may be excluded from coverage under the terms of our current general liability insurance policy.

Federal and State Healthcare Regulation

We earn a service fee when users on our website purchase prescription pharmacy products from certain of our e-commerce partners. The fee is not based on the value of the sales transaction. Federal and state "anti-kickback" laws govern certain financial arrangements among healthcare service providers and others who may be in a position to refer or recommend patients to such providers. These laws prohibit, among other things, certain direct and indirect payments that are intended to induce the referral of patients to, the arranging for services by, or the recommending of, a particular provider of health care items or services. The federal healthcare program's anti-kickback law has been broadly interpreted to apply to contractual relationships between healthcare providers and sources of patient referrals. Such laws apply to the sales of pharmacy products that are reimburseable under federal Medicare and Medicaid programs and other reimbursement programs. Violation of these laws can result in civil and criminal penalties.

As the primary purpose of marketing is to generate business by referring or recommending, the Office of Inspector General of the United States Department of Health and Human Services has recognized that "many marketing and advertising activities may involve at least technical violations of the federal anti-kickback statute." Because of the breadth of the federal anti-kickback statute, Congress required DHHS to promulgate regulatory safe harbors to protect activities which do not harm federal healthcare programs. Some of our electronic commerce activities do not qualify for safe harbor protection under the federal anti-kickback statute because the aggregate compensation received by us for these services is not fixed in advance and takes into consideration the volume of business generated, because we receive a fixed service fee per completed prescription drug product transaction. Failure to meet a safe harbor, however, does not mean that the arrangement violates the statute. Instead, an analysis of the factual elements must be made. Alternatively, the OIG is authorized to issue advisory opinions regarding the interpretation and applicability of the federal anti-kickback statute, including whether an activity or proposed activity constitutes grounds for the imposition of civil or criminal sanctions. We have not sought such an opinion and are aware of no opinion that has been issued related to Internet sales activities. If our program was deemed to be inconsistent with the federal anti-kickback statute, we could face civil and criminal penalties. Further, we would be required either not to accept any transactions which are subject to reimbursement under federal or state healthcare programs or restructure our compensation structure to comply with the statute and any applicable regulations. Presently, federal and state programs provide only limited cost reimbursement for prescription drugs, although there have been proposals made from time to time to expand the benefits of these programs. In addition, similar laws in several states apply not only to government reimbursement but also to reimbursement by private insurers. Although there is uncertainty regarding the applicability of these "anti-kickback" laws, we believe that the service fees we receive from our e-commerce partners are for the primary purpose of marketing and do not constitute payments that would violate present federal or state law. If, however, our activities were deemed to violate any of these laws, it could cause a material adverse affect on our business, results of operations and financial condition.

State Insurance Regulation

We market insurance on-line and receive transaction fees in connection with this activity. All of the insurance products are offered by unrelated third-party providers who we believe to be appropriately licensed under applicable law. The use of the Internet in the marketing of insurance products is a relatively new practice. It is not clear whether or to what extent state insurance licensing laws apply to our activities. If we were required to comply with such licensing laws, compliance could be costly or not possible and could have a material adverse effect on our business.

Jurisdiction

Due to the global reach of the Internet, it is possible that, although our transmissions over the Internet originate primarily in the State of Texas, the governments of other states and foreign countries might attempt to regulate Internet activity and our transmissions or take action against us for violations of their laws. There can be no assurance that violations of such laws will not be alleged or charged by state or foreign governments and that such laws will not be modified, or new laws enacted, in the future. Any of the foregoing could have a material adverse effect on our business, results of operations and financial condition.

Human Resources

As of March 31, 1999, we had 73 full-time employees. None of our employees are represented by a union. We believe that our relationship with our employees is good.

Facilities

We currently lease approximately 11,000 square feet of office space in Austin, Texas, under a lease expiring on October 31, 2000. We believe that our facilities are adequate for our current operations and that additional leased space can be obtained if needed.

Legal Proceedings

On April 12, 1999, a civil complaint was filed as Agrawal v. Drkoop.com, Inc., Donald W. Hackett and John F. Zaccaro in the District Court of Travis County, Texas, 126 Judicial District, Case No. 99-04294. In the lawsuit, plaintiff attempts to allege causes of action including fraud, constructive fraud, promissory estoppel, negligent misrepresentation, breach of contract, conversion, stock fraud, defamation and misrepresentation. Plaintiff claims, among other things, that misrepresentations were made to him regarding his involvement in the early stages of development of Drkoop.com and we breached a consulting agreement entered into between him and our company in September 1998. Plaintiff seeks recovery of actual damages which he alleges to be $4 million, punitive damages alleged to be in excess of $5 million, attorneys fees and costs and a temporary and permanent injunction prohibiting Drkoop.com from offering stock for sale to the public unless and until we recognize plaintiff's alleged right to options to acquire 232,500 shares of our common stock which he claims are owed to him under the consulting agreement. In the event an injunction is granted, we will not complete this offering in a timely manner, if at all. We believe that the claims made by plaintiff are without merit and intend to defend this lawsuit vigorously. We filed a counterclaim against the plaintiff on April 27, 1999 in which we allege causes of action including breach of contract, fraudulent inducement, breach of fiduciary duty and professional malpractice.

FIRM-COMMITMENT IPO UNDERWRITINGS FILED WITH THE SEC, WHICH WERE PUBLICLY OFFERED DURING 1999, LISTED BY NAME OF LEAD MANAGING UNDERWRITER

Lead Underwriter	Issuer	Offer Date	Offering Amount (in Millions of Dollars)	Business
Allen & Co., Inc.	Women First Healthcare, Inc.	06/28/99	49.500	Pharmaceutical Preparations
Anderson & Strudwick, Inc.	Hersha Hospitality Trust	01/21/99	12.000	Hotels & Motels
Ashtin Kelly & Co.	Suncoast Bancorp, Inc.	06/30/99	7.000	National Commercial Banks
	Marine Bancshares, Inc.	02/05/99	11.500	National Commercial Banks
B.T. Alex. Brown	Private Business, Inc.	05/26/99	34.800	Bank Services and Products
	NetObjects, Inc.	05/07/99	72.000	Software and Solutions for Web Sites
	FlyCast Communications Corp.	05/04/99	75.000	Web-Based Advertising Solutions
	Proxicom, Inc.	04/19/99	58.500	Internet Solutions for Companies
	iTurf, Inc.	04/09/99	92.400	Internet Community Services
	Autobytel.com, Inc.	03/26/99	103.500	Vehicle Purchasing Internet Site
	OneMain.com, Inc.	03/25/99	187.000	Internet Service
	Pinnacle Holdings, Inc.	02/19/99	280.000	Wireless Communications Tower Spaces
	Smith Gardner & Associates, Inc.	01/29/99	52.920	Software Solutions for Non-store Marketing
	MarketWatch.com, Inc.	01/15/99	46.750	Internet Based Business News
Banc of America Securities, L.L.C.	eCollege.com	12/14/99	55.000	Services-Educational Services
	Metalink, Ltd.	12/01/99	48.000	Semiconductors & Related Devices
	Metron Technology, B.V.	11/18/99	48.750	Special Industry Machinery, NEC
	PC-Tel, Inc.	10/18/99	78.200	Services-Computer Programming, Data Processing, Etc.
	Streamline.com, Inc.	06/17/99	45.000	Services-Business Services, NEC
BancBoston Robertson Stephens	NetSolve, Inc.	09/29/99	48.100	Services-Computer Integrated Systems Design
	Keynote Systems, Inc.	09/24/99	56.000	Services-Business Services, NEC

Lead Underwriter	Issuer	Offer Date	Offering Amount (in Millions of Dollars)	Business
	eGain Communications Corp.	09/23/99	60.000	Services-Prepackaged Software
	MyPoints.com, Inc.	08/19/99	40.000	Services-Computer Programming, Data Processing, Etc.
	Quest Software, Inc.	08/12/99	61.600	Services-Prepackaged Software
	Cobalt Group, Inc.	08/05/99	49.500	Services-Computer Processing & Data Preparation
	Accrue Software, Inc.	07/30/99	39.000	Services-Prepackaged Software
	Packeteer, Inc.	07/28/99	60.000	Services-Computer Integrated Systems Design
	Primus Knowledge Solutions, Inc.	07/01/99	45.650	Services-Prepackaged Software
	Persistence Software, Inc.	06/25/99	33.000	Services-Prepackaged Software
	Stamps.com, Inc.	06/25/99	55.000	Retail-Catalog & Mail Order Houses
	Globespan, Inc./DE	06/23/99	48.750	Semiconductors & Related Devices
	Ramp Networks, Inc.	06/22/99	44.000	Internet Access Solutions
	Student Advantage, Inc.	06/18/99	48.000	Services-Membership Organizations
	Alloy Online, Inc.	05/14/99	55.500	Retail-Misc. General Merchandise Stores
	MapQuest.com, Inc.	05/04/99	69.000	Services-Computer Processing & Data Preparation
	Mpath Interactive, Inc./CA	04/29/99	70.200	Services-Advertising
	Net Perceptions, Inc.	04/23/99	51.100	Services-Prepackaged Software
	Value America, Inc./VA	04/08/99	126.500	Retail-Retail Stores, NEC
	Critical Path, Inc.	03/29/99	108.000	Services-Business Services, NEC
	Multex.com, Inc.	03/17/99	42.000	Services-Computer Processing & Data Preparation
	FlashNet Communications, Inc.	03/16/99	51.000	Consumer Internet Access
	Bottomline Technologies, Inc./DE	02/12/99	44.200	Services-Prepackaged Software

Lead Underwriter	Issuer	Offer Date	Offering Amount (in Millions of Dollars)	Business
Barron Chase Securities, Inc.	Modem Media. Poppe Tyson, Inc.	02/04/99	41.600	Services-Business Services, NEC
	Eagle Supply Group, Inc.	03/12/99	12.813	Acquirer of Roofing Supply Wholesalers
	Qiao Xing Universal Telephone, Inc.	02/16/99	8.800	Telephone & Telegraph Apparatus
Bear Stearns & Co., Inc.	MotherNature.com, Inc.	12/10/99	53.300	Retail-Convenience Stores
	ASD Systems, Inc	11/10/99	40.000	Services-Business Services, NEC
	SonicWALL, Inc.	11/10/99	56.000	Services-Business Services, NEC
	Pac-West Telecomm, Inc.	11/03/99	91.000	Radio Broadcasting Stations
	Data Return Corp.	10/27/99	81.250	Services-Business Services, NEC
	Viador, Inc.	10/26/99	36.000	Services-Prepackaged Software
	World Wrestling Federation Entertainment, Inc.	10/18/99	170.000	Services-Amusement & Recreation Services
	TriZetto Group, Inc.	10/07/99	37.800	Services-Computer Processing & Data Preparation
	XM Satellite Radio Holdings, Inc.	10/04/99	120.000	Communication Services, NEC
	FTD.com, Inc.	09/28/99	36.000	Services-Business Services, NEC
	Webstakes.com, Inc.	09/23/99	50.050	Services-Business Services, NEC
	Splitrock Services, Inc.	08/02/99	90.000	Services-Computer Integrated Systems Design
	Digex, Inc./DE	07/29/99	170.000	Telephone Communications (No Radio Telephone)
	Divicore, Inc.	07/15/99	60.000	Services-Prepackaged Software
	Ravisent Technologies, Inc.	07/15/99	60.000	Video/Audio Streaming Software
	Digital Island, Inc.	06/29/99	60.000	Telephone Communications (No Radio Telephone)
	US SEARCH.com, Inc.	06/25/99	54.000	Services-Business Services, NEC
	Drkoop.com, Inc.	06/08/99	84.375	Services-Misc Health & Allied Services, NEC

Lead Underwriter	Issuer	Offer Date	Offering Amount (in Millions of Dollars)	Business
	Wit Capital Group, Inc.	06/04/99	68.400	Security Brokers, Dealers & Flotation Companies
	CAIS Internet, Inc.	05/20/99	114.000	Services-Computer Processing & Data Preparation
	AppliedTheory Corp.	04/30/99	72.000	Services-Computer Integrated Systems Design
	Statia Terminals Group, N.V.	04/23/99	152.000	Water Transportation
	MiningCo.com, Inc.	03/24/99	75.000	Internet News, Information and Entertainment Service
	Prodigy Communications Corp.	02/10/99	150.000	Services-Computer Programming, Data Processing, Etc.
	Vialog Corp.	02/05/99	38.943	Telephone Communications (No Radio Telephone)
	Covad Communications Group, Inc.	01/21/99	140.400	Telephone & Telegraph Apparatus
Bluestone Capital Partners, L.P.	Litronic, Inc.	06/09/99	40.700	Internet Data Security Services
C.E. Unterberg, Towbin	TrueTime, Inc.	12/16/99	15.000	Radio & TV Broadcasting & Communications Equipment
Cardinal Capital Management, Inc.	EDGAR Online, Inc.	05/26/99	34.200	Business and Financial Information
	U.S. Laboratories, Inc.	02/23/99	6.000	Services-Testing Laboratories
CIBC World Markets	GRIC Communications, Inc.	12/15/99	64.400	Services-Business Services, NEC
	PNV, Inc.	11/23/99	63.750	Communication Services, NEC
	Altigen Communications, Inc.	10/04/99	32.500	Telephone & Telegraph Apparatus
	NETsilicon, Inc.	09/15/99	36.750	Semiconductor Manufacturer
	N2H2, Inc.	07/29/99	65.000	Provider of Internet Content Filtering Services
	MCM Capital Group, Inc.	07/09/99	22.500	Consumer Receivables Collection
	Financial Institutions, Inc.	06/24/99	18.667	National Commercial Banks
	AudioCodes, Ltd.	05/28/99	49.000	Wireless Communications Equipment

Lead Underwriter	Issuer	Offer Date	Offering Amount (in Millions of Dollars)	Business
Credit Suisse First Boston	Egreetings Network	12/16/99	60.000	Digital Greetings
	Caliper Technologies, Inc.	12/14/99	72.000	Laboratory Analytical Instruments
	El Sitio, Inc.	12/09/99	131.200	Services-Prepackaged Software
	VA Linux Systems, Inc.	12/09/99	132.000	Electronic Computers
	FogDog Sports, Inc.	12/08/99	66.000	Retail-Miscellaneous Shopping Good Stores
	Knot, Inc.	12/01/99	35.000	Periodicals: Publishing or Publishing and Printing
	Digital Impact, Inc./DE	11/22/99	67.500	Services-Business Services, NEC
	Symyx Technologies, Inc.	11/18/99	77.532	Services-Commercial Physical & Biological Research
	Retek, Inc.	11/17/99	82.500	Services-Prepackaged Software
	Virata Corp.	11/16/99	70.000	Semiconductors & Related Devices
	Wireless Facilities, Inc.	11/04/99	60.000	Services-Miscellaneous Business Services
	City Telecom HK, Ltd.	11/03/99	83.111	Telephone Communications (No Radio Telephone)
	InterTrust Technologies Corp.	10/26/99	117.000	Services-Computer Programming Services
	BSQUARE Corp./WA	10/19/99	60.000	Services-Business Services, NEC
	Netcentives, Inc.	10/13/99	72.000	Services-Business Services, NEC
	Interwoven, Inc.	10/07/99	53.550	Services-Prepackaged Software
	QXL.com, P.L.C.	10/07/99	84.111	Services-Business Services, NEC
	Silicon Image, Inc.	10/05/99	46.800	Electronic Components & Accessories
	TiVo, Inc.	09/29/99	88.000	Cable & Other Pay Television Services
	Spinnaker Exploration Co.	09/28/99	116.000	Crude Petroleum & Natural Gas
	Manulife Financial Corp.	09/24/99	544.550	Insurance
	E.piphany, Inc.	09/21/99	66.400	Services-Business Services, NEC

Lead Underwriter	Issuer	Offer Date	Offering Amount (in Millions of Dollars)	Business
	Vitria Technology, Inc.	09/16/99	48.000	Services-Prepackaged Software
	Mortgage.com, Inc.	08/11/99	56.500	Mortgage Bankers & Loan Correspondents
	Tumbleweed Communications Corp.	08/05/99	48.000	Communication Services, NEC
	Fairchild Semiconductor International, Inc.	08/03/99	370.000	Semiconductors & Related Devices
	NetIQ Corp.	07/29/99	39.000	Services-Prepackaged Software
	American National Can Group, Inc.	07/28/99	510.000	Metal Fabrication
	Liberate Technologies	07/27/99	100.000	Services-Prepackaged Software
	Freeserve, P.L.C.	07/26/99	362.250	Services-Computer Programming, Data Processing, Etc.
	Tanning Technology Corp.	07/22/99	60.000	Services-Computer Integrated Systems Design
	MP3.com, Inc.	07/20/99	345.723	Phonograph Records & Prerecorded Audio Tapes & Disks
	Gadzoox Networks, Inc.	07/19/99	73.500	Electronic Components & Accessories
	Audible, Inc.	07/15/99	36.000	Services-Business Services, NEC
	Efficient Networks, Inc.	07/14/99	60.000	Communication Services, NEC
	Clarent Corp./CA	07/01/99	60.000	Services-Prepackaged Software
	Commerce One, Inc.	07/01/99	69.300	Services-Computer Integrated Systems Design
	Software.com, Inc.	06/23/99	90.000	Services-Computer Integrated Systems Design
	TD Waterhouse Group, Inc.	06/23/99	1008.000	Security & Commodity Brokers, Dealers, Exchanges & Services
	AppNet, Inc./DE	06/17/99	72.000	Services-Business Services, NEC

Lead Underwriter	Issuer	Offer Date	Offering Amount (in Millions of Dollars)	Business
	Phone.com, Inc.	06/10/99	64.000	Internet Software for Wireless Phones
	Capital Environmental Resource, Inc.	06/02/99	35.846	Refuse Systems
	CareerBuilder, Inc.	05/11/99	58.500	Services-Personal Services
	Latitude Communications, Inc.	05/06/99	36.000	Wholesale-Computer & Peripheral Equipment & Software
	Radio One, Inc.	05/05/99	156.000	Radio Broadcasting Stations
	Silknet Software, Inc.	05/05/99	45.000	Services-Prepackaged Software
	Informatica Corp.	04/28/99	44.000	Services-Prepackaged Software
	Razorfish, Inc.	04/26/99	48.000	Services-Computer Integrated Systems Design
	USInternetworking, Inc.	04/08/99	126.000	Services-Computer Programming Services
	Ducati Motor Holding, S.P.A.	03/24/99	285.663	Motorcycles
	Autoweb.com, Inc.	03/22/99	70.000	Services-Automotive Repair, Services & Parking
	Intraware, Inc.	02/25/99	64.000	Communication Services, NEC
	Onyx Software Corp./WA	02/11/99	40.300	Services-Prepackaged Software
	Korn/Ferry International	02/10/99	164.500	Services-Employment Agencies
	Entercom Communications Corp.	01/28/99	306.619	Radio Broadcasting Stations
	Allaire Corp.	01/22/99	50.000	Services-Prepackaged Software
Cruttenden Roth, Inc.	Plastic Surgery Co.	12/10/99	11.200	Services-Management Services
	Netgateway, Inc.	11/18/99	23.100	Services-Computer Integrated Systems Design
	Perfumania.com, Inc.	09/29/99	24.500	Retail-Drug Stores and Proprietary Stores
	Duraswitch Industries, Inc.	08/26/99	10.000	Electronic Components, NEC
	Troy Group, Inc.	07/22/99	17.500	Computer & Office Equipment

Lead Underwriter	Issuer	Offer Date	Offering Amount (in Millions of Dollars)	Business
	QuePasa.com, Inc.	06/24/99	48.000	Services-Advertising
	AremisSoft Corp./DE	04/22/99	16.500	Services-Prepackaged Software
	Claimsnet.com, Inc.	04/06/99	20.000	E-commerce for Healthcare Transactions
D.A. Davidson & Co.	Jore Corp.	09/23/99	40.000	Cutlery, Handtools & General Hardware
	Direct Focus, Inc.	05/04/99	20.500	Developer and Marketer of Premium Priced, Branded Consumer Products
Dain Rauscher Wessels	ShopNow.com, Inc.	09/29/99	87.000	Services-Computer Processing & Data Preparation
	Watchguard Technologies, Inc.	07/30/99	45.500	Services-Prepackaged Software
	Aironet Wireless Communication, Inc.	07/29/99	66.000	High Speed, Standards-Based Wireless Local Area Networking Solutions
	WebTrends Corp.	02/19/99	45.500	Services-Prepackaged Software
Deutsche Banc Alex. Brown	DSL.net, Inc.	10/06/99	53.906	Telephone Communications (No Radio Telephone)
	ACME Communications, Inc.	09/29/99	115.000	Television Broadcasting Stations
	Foundry Networks, Inc.	09/27/99	125.000	Computer Communications Equipment
	FreeShop.com, Inc.	09/27/99	38.400	Services-Business Services, NEC
	Bluestone Software, Inc.	09/23/99	60.000	Services-Prepackaged Software
	Trintech Group, P.L.C.	09/23/99	66.990	Services-Prepackaged Software
	Broadbase Software, Inc.	09/22/99	56.000	Services-Business Services, NEC
	YesMail.com, Inc.	09/22/99	37.400	Services-Advertising Agencies
	Luminant Worldwide Corp.	09/16/99	83.970	Services-Computer Programming, Data Processing, Etc.
	U.S. Aggregates, Inc.	08/13/99	75.000	Mining, Quarrying of Nonmetallic Minerals (No Fuels)
	Netscout Systems, Inc.	08/12/99	33.000	Network and Application Performance Management

Lead Underwriter	Issuer	Offer Date	Offering Amount (in Millions of Dollars)	Business
	HotJobs.com, Ltd.	08/10/99	24.000	Services-Business Services, NEC
	Salem Communications Corp./DE	07/01/99	189.000	Radio Broadcasting Stations
	United Therapeutics Corp.	06/17/99	54.000	Pharmaceutical Preparations
	Ditech Corp.	06/09/99	33.000	Telephone & Telegraph Apparatus
	Skechers USA, Inc.	06/09/99	77.000	Wholesale-Apparel, Piece Goods & Notions
Deutsche Bank, A.G.	Golden Telecom, Inc.	10/01/99	55.800	Radio Telephone Communications
Dirks & Co., Inc.	TownPagesNet.com, P.L.C.	04/30/99	22.000	Services-Computer Integrated Systems Design
	Log On America, Inc.	04/22/99	22.000	Services-Computer Processing & Data Preparation
	Digital Lava, Inc.	02/18/99	18.120	Video Publishing Software
Donaldson, Lufkin & Jenrette	Xpedior, Inc.	12/15/99	162.165	Services-Business Services, NEC
	MedicaLogic, Inc.	12/09/99	100.300	Services-Computer Processing & Data Preparation
	GetThere.com, Inc.	11/22/99	80.000	Services-Business Services, NEC
	Official Payments Corp.	11/22/99	75.000	Provider of Electronic Payment Options to Government Entities
	SciQuest.com, Inc.	11/19/99	120.000	Services-Business Services, NEC
	Rainmaker Systems, Inc.	11/17/99	40.000	Services-Business Services, NEC
	Quintus Corp.	11/16/99	81.000	Services-Prepackaged Software
	Data Critical Corp.	11/09/99	35.000	Electronic Components & Accessories
	Be Free, Inc.	11/03/99	67.200	Services-Computer Processing & Data Preparation
	JNI Corp.	10/26/99	93.100	Semiconductors & Related Devices
	E-Stamp Corp.	10/08/99	119.000	Services-Business Services, NEC
	Jupiter Communications, Inc.	10/08/99	65.625	Services-Business Services, NEC

Lead Underwriter	Issuer	Offer Date	Offering Amount (in Millions of Dollars)	Business
	AirGate PCS, Inc.	09/27/99	113.900	Telephone Communications (No Radio Telephone)
	Medscape, Inc.	09/27/99	53.664	Services-Business Services, NEC
	NovaMed Eyecare, Inc.	08/18/99	32.000	Services-Management Services
	Wink Communications, Inc.	08/18/99	76.000	Radio & TV Broadcasting & Communications Equipment
	IXnet, Inc.	08/12/99	97.500	Telephone Communications (No Radio Telephone)
	Braun Consulting, Inc.	08/10/99	28.000	Services-Miscellaneous Business Services
	Netia Holdings, S.A.	07/29/99	121.000	Telephone Communications (No Radio Telephone)
	JFAX.com, Inc.	07/23/99	80.750	Telegraph & Other Message Communications
	Insight Communications Co., Inc.	07/20/99	563.500	Cable & Other Pay Television Services
	Voyager.net, Inc.	07/20/99	135.000	Services-Computer Processing & Data Preparation
	Paradyne Networks, Inc.	07/16/99	102.000	Electronic Components & Accessories
	GoTo.com, Inc.	06/18/99	90.000	Services-Business Services, NEC
	Network Access Solutions Corp.	06/04/99	78.047	Telephone Communications (No Radio Telephone)
	Zany Brainy, Inc.	06/03/99	61.000	Retail-Hobby, Toy & Game Shops
	DLJdirect, Inc.	05/25/99	320.000	Online Brokerage
	David's Bridal, Inc.	05/21/99	104.000	Retail-Women's Clothing Stores
	Nextera Enterprises, Inc.	05/18/99	115.000	Services-Management Consulting Services
	NextCard, Inc.	05/14/99	120.000	Personal Credit Institutions
	Media Metrix, Inc.	05/07/99	51.000	Services-Business Services, NEC
	Sagent Technology, Inc.	04/14/99	45.000	Services-Prepackaged Software
	Boyds Collection, Inc.	03/05/99	288.000	Wholesale-Miscellaneous Nondurable Goods
	Neon Systems, Inc.	03/05/99	40.500	Services-Prepackaged Software

Lead Underwriter	Issuer	Offer Date	Offering Amount (in Millions of Dollars)	Business
EBI Securities Corp.	Invitrogen Corp.	02/26/99	52.500	Biological Products (No Diagnostic Substances)
Everen Securities, Inc.	Netivation.com, Inc.	06/22/99	25.000	Services-Prepackaged Software
	Sun Community Bancorp, Ltd.	07/02/99	26.400	State Commercial Banks
	PrivateBancorp, Inc.	06/30/99	16.200	State Commercial Banks
Fahnestock & Co., Inc.	Web Street, Inc.	11/17/99	41.250	Services-Business Services, NEC
Ferris, Baker Watts, Inc.	Musicmaker.com, Inc.	07/07/99	117.600	Retail-Catalog & Mail Order Houses
First Union Capital Markets Corp.	HeadHunter.net, Inc.	08/19/99	30.000	Services-Advertising
	MIIX Group, Inc.	07/30/99	40.500	Insurance Carriers, NEC
Friedman, Billings, Ramsey & Co Inc.	NetCreations, Inc.	11/12/99	42.900	Services-Business Services, NEC
	American Home Mortgage Holdings, Inc.	10/01/99	14.962	Mortgage Bankers & Loan Correspondents
	Oswego County Bancorp, Inc.	05/14/99	5.405	Savings Institution, Not Federally Chartered
	Atlantic Preferred Capital Corp.	01/27/99	12.600	Real Estate
Gerard, Klauer, Mattison & Co.	NetRadio Corp.	10/14/99	35.200	Radio Broadcasting Stations
	WorldGate Communications, Inc.	04/15/99	105.000	Cable & Other Pay Television Services
Gilford Securities, Inc.	Perficient, Inc.	07/29/99	8.000	Services-Computer Programming Services
	ID Systems, Inc.	06/30/99	14.000	Communications Equipment, NEC
Goldman Sachs International	Jazztel, P.L.C.	12/08/99	176.652	High-Speed Telecommunications
Goldman, Sachs & Co.	Maxygen, Inc.	12/15/99	96.000	Services-Commercial Physical & Biological Research
	Tritel, Inc.	12/13/99	237.352	Radio Telephone Communications
	Freemarkets, Inc.	12/09/99	172.800	Services-Business Services, NEC
	AGENCY.com, Ltd.	12/08/99	153.400	Services-Business Services, NEC
	Classic Communications, Inc.	12/07/99	206.250	Cable & Other Pay Television Services

Lead Underwriter	Issuer	Offer Date	Offering Amount (in Millions of Dollars)	Business
	Alaska Communications Systems Group, Inc.	11/17/99	140.000	Local Telephone, Wireless, Long Distance, Data and Internet Services
	Terra Networks, S.A.	11/15/99	334.310	Services-Computer Programming, Data Processing, Etc.
	Expedia, Inc.	11/09/99	72.800	Transportation Services
	Charter Communications, Inc./MO	11/08/99	3230.000	Cable & Other Pay Television Services
	Cobalt Networks, Inc.	11/04/99	110.000	Electronic Components & Accessories
	WebVan Group, Inc.	11/04/99	375.000	Services-Business Services, NEC
	Allied Riser Communications Corp.	10/28/99	283.500	Telephone Communications (No Radio Telephone)
	Plug Power, Inc.	10/28/99	90.000	Electrical Industrial Apparatus
	Calico Commerce, Inc.	10/06/99	56.000	Services-Business Services, NEC
	Neuberger Berman, Inc.	10/06/99	232.000	Investment Advice
	PlanetRX.com, Inc.	10/06/99	96.000	Retail-Miscellaneous Shopping Good Stores
	Ashford.com, Inc.	09/23/99	81.250	Retail-Hobby, Toy & Game Shops
	NetZero, Inc.	09/23/99	160.000	Services-Computer Programming, Data Processing, Etc.
	Kana Communications, Inc.	09/21/99	49.500	Services-Business Services, NEC
	LookSmart, Ltd.	08/19/99	92.400	Costume Jewelry & Novelties
	Active Software, Inc.	08/12/99	38.500	Services-Computer Integrated Systems Design
	Red Hat, Inc.	08/11/99	84.000	Services-Computer Programming, Data Processing, Etc.
	Internet Initiative Japan Co.	08/03/99	164.680	Information Retrieval Services

Lead Underwriter	Issuer	Offer Date	Offering Amount (in Millions of Dollars)	Business
	1-800-Flowers.com, Inc.	08/02/99	126.000	Retail-Retail Stores, NEC
	Allscripts Inc./IL	07/23/99	112.000	Wholesale-Drugs Proprietaries & Druggists' Sundries
	InsWeb Corp.	07/22/99	85.000	Services-Business Services, NEC
	Engage Technologies, Inc.	07/20/99	90.000	Services-Business Services, NEC
	Convergent Communications, Inc./CO	07/19/99	126.000	Telephone Communications (No Radio Telephone)
	TIBCO Software, Inc.	07/13/99	109.500	Services-Computer Integrated Systems Design
	Network Plus Corp.	06/29/99	128.000	Telephone Communications (No Radio Telephone)
	Seminis, Inc.	06/29/99	206.250	Agriculture Production - Crops
	E-LOAN, Inc.	06/28/99	49.000	Mortgage Bankers & Loan Correspondents
	Juniper Networks, Inc.	06/24/99	163.200	Computer Communications Equipment
	Viant Corp.	06/17/99	48.000	Services-Miscellaneous Business Services
	BackWeb Technologies, Ltd.	06/07/99	66.000	Services-Prepackaged Software
	Inet Technologies, Inc.	05/26/99	92.000	Telephone & Telegraph Apparatus
	barnesandnoble.com, Inc.	05/25/99	450.000	Retail-Computer & Prerecorded Tape Stores
	StarMedia Network, Inc.	05/25/99	105.000	Services-Computer Processing & Data Preparation
	TC Pipelines, L.P.	05/24/99	235.750	Natural Gas Transmission
	Tenfold Corp./UT	05/20/99	79.900	Services-Computer Programming Services
	eToys, Inc.	05/19/99	166.400	Retail-Hobby, Toy & Game Shops
	TheStreet.com	05/10/99	104.500	Services-Computer Processing & Data Preparation
	Northpoint Communications Group, Inc.	05/05/99	360.000	Telephone Communications (No Radio Telephone)
	Portal Software, Inc.	05/05/99	56.000	Services-Computer Programming Services

Lead Underwriter	Issuer	Offer Date	Offering Amount (in Millions of Dollars)	Business
	Goldman Sachs Group, Inc.	05/03/99	3657.000	Investment Banking
	StanCorp Financial Group, Inc.	04/15/99	330.600	Services-Hospitals
	ZDNet (Ziff-Davis, Inc.)	03/30/99	190.000	Computing & Technology Information
	iVillage, Inc.	03/18/99	87.600	Services-Computer Integrated Systems Design
	pcOrder.com, Inc.	02/25/99	46.200	Retail-Computer & Computer Software Stores
	United Pan-Europe Communications, N.V.	02/12/99	1311.200	Cable & Other Pay Television Services
Gruntal & Co., Inc.	Fashionmall.com, Inc.	05/21/99	39.000	Retail-Miscellaneous Shopping Good Stores
Gunn Allen Financial, Inc.	Intelli-Check, Inc.	11/18/99	7.500	Services-Prepackaged Software
Hambrecht & Quist, Inc.	PFSweb, Inc.	12/02/99	52.700	Services-Business Services, NEC
	SmarterKids.com, Inc.	11/23/99	63.000	Services-Business Services, NEC
	Management Network Group, Inc.	11/22/99	78.455	Services-Management Consulting Services
	LifeMinders.com, Inc.	11/19/99	58.800	Services-Business Services, NEC
	Immersion Corp.	11/12/99	51.000	Computer Peripheral Equipment, NEC
	ECTel, Inc.	10/26/99	42.000	Telecommunications Monitoring Equipment and Software
	Garden.com, Inc.	09/15/99	49.200	Services-Computer Programming Services
	Mission Critical Software, Inc.	08/04/99	60.000	Services-Prepackaged Software
	Quotesmith.com, Inc.	08/03/99	52.000	Services-Computer Processing & Data Preparation
	Net2Phone, Inc.	07/30/99	81.000	Telephone Communications (No Radio Telephone)
	Art Technology Group, Inc.	07/20/99	60.000	Services-Prepackaged Software
	National Information Consortium	07/15/99	156.000	Services-Business Services, NEC

Lead Underwriter	Issuer	Offer Date	Offering Amount (in Millions of Dollars)	Business
	Point of Sale, Ltd.	07/10/99	19.250	Prepackaged Software
	nFront, Inc.	06/29/99	39.000	Services-Business Services, NEC
	ESPS, Inc.	06/16/99	26.250	Services-Prepackaged Software
	F5 Networks, Inc.	06/04/99	30.000	Services-Computer Integrated Systems Design
	SalesLogix Corp.	05/27/99	29.925	Services-Prepackaged Software
	Newgen Results Corp.	05/21/99	48.425	Services-Business Services, NEC
	@plan, Inc.	05/20/99	35.000	Services-Advertising
	AdForce, Inc.	05/07/99	67.500	Outsourced Internet Ad Management
	Launch Media, Inc.	04/23/99	74.800	Communication Services, NEC
	Accredo Health, Inc.	04/15/99	48.000	Services-Misc. Health & Allied Services, NEC
	Catapult Communications Corp.	02/11/99	33.525	Services-Prepackaged Software
	SERENA Software, Inc.	02/11/99	78.000	Services-Prepackaged Software
Howe Barnes Investments, Inc.	Team Financial, Inc./KS	06/22/99	11.250	National Commercial Banks
ING Barings Furman Selz, L.L.C.	Intelligent Life Corp.	05/13/99	45.500	Services-Business Services, NEC
	Albany Molecular Research, Inc.	02/04/99	50.000	Medicinal Chemicals & Botanical Products
Institutional Equity Corp.	StreaMedia Communications, Inc.	12/21/99	10.200	Communication Services, NEC
Interstate Johnson Lane Corp.	Community Capital Bancshares, Inc.	03/11/99	10.000	National Bank Holding Company
Invemed Associates	InterWorld Corp.	08/10/99	45.000	Services-Prepackaged Software
J.C. Bradford & Co.	Trex Co., Inc.	04/08/99	41.030	Non-wood Decking Products
J.P. Morgan & Co.	Interactive Pictures Corp.	08/05/99	75.600	Services-Prepackaged Software
	Biopure Corp.	07/30/99	42.000	Biological Products (No Diagnostic Substances)
	Hoover's, Inc.	07/21/99	45.500	Services-Business Services, NEC

Lead Underwriter	Issuer	Offer Date	Offering Amount (in Millions of Dollars)	Business
	Genentech, Inc.	07/19/99	1940.000	Biotechnology
	Online Resources and Communications Corp.	06/04/99	43.400	E-Commerce Solutions
	CONSOL Energy, Inc.	04/29/99	361.600	Coal Mining
	Valley Media, Inc.	03/26/99	56.000	Music and Video Products
	RoweCom, Inc.	03/08/99	49.600	E-Commerce Solutions
J.P. Morgan Securities, Ltd.	ebookers.com, P.L.C.	11/11/99	61.200	Web-Based Travel Products and Services
Jefferies & Co., Inc.	ZipLink, Inc.	05/26/99	49.000	Services-Business Services, NEC
Joseph Stevens & Co., L.P.	BiznessOnline.com, Inc.	05/12/99	29.000	Services-Computer Integrated Systems Design
Josephthal & Co.	American National Financial, Inc.	02/12/99	10.500	Title Insurance Services
Kashner Davidson Securities Corp.	Able Energy, Inc.	06/22/99	7.000	Retail-Retail Stores, NEC
	Outlook Sports Technology, Inc.	03/18/99	2.320	Designer and Marketer of Premium Quality Golf Equipment, Apparel and Accessories
Keefe Bruyette & Woods, Inc.	Eldorado Bancshares, Inc.	04/06/99	19.099	National Commercial Banks
	Jacksonville Bancorp, Inc./FL	02/09/99	15.000	State Commercial Banks
Ladenburg Thalmann & Co., Inc.	topjobs.net, P.L.C.	04/27/99	39.600	Services-Employment Agencies
Legg, Mason, Wood, Walker, Inc.	Greater Atlantic Financial Corp.	06/25/99	19.000	Savings Institution, Not Federally Chartered
Lehman Brothers	Tularik, Inc.	12/09/99	97.300	Services-Commercial Physical & Biological Research
	HealthCentral.com, Inc.	12/07/99	82.500	Services-Computer Integrated Systems Design
	Harris Interactive, Inc.	12/06/99	81.200	Services-Management Consulting Services
	Deltathree.com, Inc.	11/22/99	90.000	Services-Business Services, NEC
	Mediaplex, Inc.	11/19/99	72.000	Online Marketing Services

Lead Underwriter	Issuer	Offer Date	Offering Amount (in Millions of Dollars)	Business
	Korea Thurnet Co., Ltd.	11/16/99	181.800	Services-Computer Programming, Data Processing, Etc.
	CVC, Inc.	11/12/99	35.000	Semiconductors & Related Devices
	Somera Communications, Inc.	11/11/99	102.000	Wholesale-Electronic Parts & Equipment, NEC
	Baltimore Technologies, P.L.C.	10/27/99	121.450	Services-Prepackaged Software
	Spanish Broadcasting Systems, Inc.	10/27/99	435.748	Radio Broadcasting Stations
	Jacada, Ltd.	10/14/99	49.500	Web-Enabling Software for Businesses
	ITXC Corp.	09/27/99	75.000	Telephone Communications (No Radio Telephone)
	Alteon WebSystems, Inc.	09/23/99	76.000	Electronic Components, NEC
	U.S. Interactive, Inc./PA	08/09/99	28.650	Services-Management Consulting Services
	Internet Gold-Golden Lines, Ltd.	08/05/99	54.000	Information Retrieval Services
	VersaTel Telecom International, N.V.	07/23/99	223.316	Telephone Communications (No Radio Telephone)
	Talk City, Inc.	07/19/99	60.000	Services-Business Services, NEC
	China.com Corp.	07/12/99	84.940	Internet Portal, Content and Services
	Liquid Audio, Inc.	07/08/99	63.000	Services-Computer Integrated Systems Design
	SBA Communications Corp.	06/16/99	90.000	Construction Special Trade Contractors
	High Speed Access Corp.	06/04/99	169.000	Services-Computer Programming, Data Processing, Etc.
	WESCO International, Inc.	05/11/99	175.050	Wholesale-Electrical Apparatus & Equipment, Wiring Supplies
	Maker Communications, Inc.	05/10/99	43.550	Semiconductors & Related Devices

Lead Underwriter	Issuer	Offer Date	Offering Amount (in Millions of Dollars)	Business
	Heidrick & Struggles International, Inc.	04/27/99	58.800	Services-Personal Services
	Delta Galil Industries, Ltd.	03/25/99	22.500	Textiles
	Antenna TV, S.A.	03/03/99	115.500	Television Broadcasting Stations
	VerticalNet, Inc.	02/10/99	56.000	Services-Advertising
	Pacific Internet, Ltd.	02/05/99	51.000	Information Retrieval Services
	Tut Systems, Inc.	01/28/99	45.000	Telephone & Telegraph Apparatus
McDonald Investments, Inc.	Tower Financial Corp.	01/26/99	22.000	State Commercial Banks
Merrill Lynch & Co.	Infonet Services Corp.	12/15/99	1076.928	Services-Business Services, NEC
	Optio Software, Inc.	12/14/99	50.000	Wholesale-Computer & Peripheral Equipment & Software
	OpenTV Corp.	11/23/99	150.000	Services-Computer Programming Services
	Finisar Corp.	11/11/99	154.850	Semiconductors & Related Devices
	Edison Schools, Inc.	11/10/99	122.400	Services-Educational Services
	Next Level Communications, Inc.	11/09/99	170.000	Telephone Communications (No Radio Telephone)
	Aether Systems, Inc.	10/20/99	96.000	Services-Computer Integrated Systems Design
	ZapMe! Corp.	10/19/99	99.000	Services-Computer Programming, Data Processing, Etc.
	Satyam Infoway, Ltd.	10/18/99	75.150	Services-Computer Programming, Data Processing, Etc.
	EPCOS, A.G.	10/14/99	1419.600	Electronic Components Developer
	Blackrock Inc./NY	10/01/99	126.000	Services-Facilities Support Management Services
	ICICI, Ltd.	09/22/99	273.913	Finance Services
	Interactive Intelligence, Inc.	09/22/99	34.710	Services-Prepackaged Software

Lead Underwriter	Issuer	Offer Date	Offering Amount (in Millions of Dollars)	Business
	Netro Corp.	08/18/99	40.000	Radio & TV Broadcasting & Communications Equipment
	Internet Capital Group, Inc.	08/04/99	178.800	Services-Business Services, NEC
	Pivotal Corp.	08/04/99	42.000	Services-Business Services, NEC
	Quokka Sports, Inc.	07/27/99	60.000	Services-Miscellaneous Amusement & Recreation
	Scientific Learning Corp.	07/21/99	36.800	Services-Educational Services
	Provantage Health Services, Inc.	07/14/99	100.800	Services-Specialty Outpatient Facilities, NEC
	Interliant, Inc.	07/07/99	70.000	Services-Business Services, NEC
	Showcase Corp./MN	06/29/99	27.000	Services-Computer Integrated Systems Design
	CyberSource, Inc.	06/23/99	44.000	Services-Computer Processing & Data Preparation
	CareInsite, Inc.	06/15/99	101.700	Services-Computer Processing & Data Preparation
	Azurix Corp.	06/09/99	695.400	Water Supply
	Pantry, Inc.	06/08/99	81.250	Retail-Convenience Stores
	iXL Enterprises, Inc.	06/02/99	72.000	Services-Computer Integrated Systems Design
	Tuesday Morning Corp./DE	04/21/99	99.000	Retail-Variety Stores
	MIH, Ltd.	04/13/99	163.350	Cable & Other Pay Television Services
	Rhythms NetConnections, Inc.	04/06/99	196.875	Telephone Communications (No Radio Telephone)
	PLX Technology, Inc.	04/05/99	29.700	Semiconductors & Related Devices
	Pepsi Bottling Group, Inc.	03/30/99	2300.000	Beverages
	American Axle & Manufacturing Holdings, Inc.	01/28/99	119.000	Motor Vehicle Parts & Accessories
Merrill Lynch Far East, Ltd.	i-Cable Communications, Ltd.	11/18/99	218.700	Cable & Other Pay Television Services
Merrill Lynch International, Ltd.	ENEL Societa per Azioni	11/01/99	16281.720	Electric Services

Lead Underwriter	Issuer	Offer Date	Offering Amount (in Millions of Dollars)	Business
	National Bank of Greece, S.A.	10/16/99	75.700	Commercial Banks, NEC
	Bord Telecom Eireann P.L.C.	07/07/99	1382.475	Telephone Communications (No Radio Telephone)
Millenium Financial Group, Inc.	GenesisIntermedia.com, Inc.	06/14/99	17.000	Services-Miscellaneous Business Services
Morgan Stanley Dean Witter	McAfee.com Corp.	12/01/99	75.000	Services-Business Services, NEC
	NDS Group, P.L.C.	11/22/99	180.000	Services-Prepackaged Software
	CacheFlow, Inc.	11/18/99	120.000	Services-Computer Integrated Systems Design
	Agilent Technologies, Inc.	11/17/99	2160.000	Instruments for Measuring & Testing of Electricity & Electric Signals
	Metasolv Software, inc.	11/17/99	95.000	Services-Computer Programming Services
	United Parcel Service, Inc.	11/09/99	5470.000	Trucking & Courier Services (No Air)
	KPNQwest, B.V.	11/08/99	915.640	Telephone Communications (No Radio Telephone)
	Tickets.com, Inc.	11/03/99	83.750	Services-Amusement & Recreation Services
	Akamai Technologies, Inc.	10/28/99	234.000	Services-Business Services, NEC
	Triton PCS Holdings, Inc.	10/27/99	180.000	Radio Telephone Communications
	Partner Communications Co., Ltd.	10/26/99	525.000	Radio Telephone Communications
	Sycamore Networks, Inc.	10/21/99	284.050	Telephone & Telegraph Apparatus
	Martha Stewart Living Omnimedia, Ltd.	10/18/99	129.600	Periodicals: Publishing or Publishing and Printing
	Women.com Networks, Inc.	10/14/99	37.500	Miscellaneous Publishing
	Illuminet Holdings, Inc.	10/07/99	74.100	Telephone Communications (No Radio Telephone)
	Ultrapar Participacoes	10/06/99	201.150	Petroleum Gas Distributor
	Breakaway Solutions, Inc.	10/05/99	42.000	Services-Business Services, NEC

Lead Underwriter	Issuer	Offer Date	Offering Amount (in Millions of Dollars)	Business
	Digital Insight Corp.	09/30/99	52.500	Services-Business Services, NEC
	Internap Network Services Corp./WA	09/29/99	190.000	Services-Business Services, NEC
	Agile Software Corp.	08/19/99	63.000	Services-Prepackaged Software
	Silverstream Software, Inc.	08/17/99	48.000	Services-Computer Integrated Systems Design
	Homestore.com, Inc.	08/04/99	140.000	Real Estate Agents & Managers (for Others)
	Lennox International, Inc.	07/28/99	159.375	Air Cond. & Warm Air Heating Equip. & Comm. & Indl. Refrig. Equip.
	Drugstore.com, Inc.	07/27/99	90.000	Retail-Drug Stores and Proprietary Stores
	Chemdex Corp.	07/26/99	112.500	Wholesale-Chemicals & Allied Products
	Yankee Candle Co., Inc.	07/01/99	225.000	Miscellaneous Manufacturing Industries
	Ask Jeeves, Inc.	06/30/99	42.000	Services-Business Services, NEC
	Ariba, Inc.	06/22/99	115.000	Services-Prepackaged Software
	Brocade Communications Systems, Inc.	05/24/99	61.750	Services-Prepackaged Software
	Redback Networks, inc.	05/17/99	57.500	Services-Business Services, NEC
	Scient Corp.	05/13/99	60.000	Services-Computer Programming, Data Processing, Etc.
	Copper Mountain Networks, Inc.	05/12/99	84.000	Telephone & Telegraph Apparatus
	Time Warner Telecom, Inc.	05/11/99	252.000	Telephone Communications (No Radio Telephone)
	Destia Communications, Inc.	05/05/99	65.000	Telecommunications Provider
	Marimba, Inc.	04/29/99	80.000	Services-Prepackaged Software
	Extreme Networks, Inc.	04/08/99	119.000	Computer Communications Equipment
	Priceline.com, Inc.	03/29/99	160.000	Services-Computer Integrated Systems Design

Lead Underwriter	Issuer	Offer Date	Offering Amount (in Millions of Dollars)	Business
	Vignette Corp.	02/18/99	76.000	Services-Prepackaged Software
	Healtheon Corp.	02/10/99	40.000	Services-Computer Processing & Data Preparation
	Del Monte Foods Co.	02/04/99	300.000	Canned, Fruits, Veg. & Preserves, Jams & Jellies
	Delphi Automotive Systems Corp.	02/04/99	1700.000	Motor Vehicle Parts & Accessories
	Perot Systems Corp.	02/01/99	104.000	Services-Educational Services
	NVIDIA Corp./CA	01/21/99	42.000	Semiconductors & Related Devices
NationsBanc Montgomery Securities, Inc.	MKS Instruments, Inc.	03/29/99	91.000	Industrial Instruments for Measurement, Display and Control
	InfoSys Technologies, Ltd.	03/11/99	61.200	Services-Computer Programming Services
	Packaged Ice, Inc.	01/29/99	91.375	Miscellaneous Food Preparations & Kindred Products
Needham & Co., Inc.	Collectors Universe, Inc.	11/05/99	24.000	Services-Business Services, NEC
	Datalink Corp.	08/06/99	19.500	Services-Computer Integrated Systems Design
Neidiger, Tucker, Bruner, Inc.	Cavion Technologies, Inc.	10/29/99	7.800	Services-Business Services, NEC
Network 1 Financial Securities	International Smart Sourcing, Inc.	04/23/99	5.750	Plastics Products, NEC
Nomura Securities International	Trend Micro, Inc.	07/07/99	42.350	Anti-virus Software Solutions
Nutmeg Securities, Ltd.	Hi-Q Wason, Inc.	09/21/99	6.300	Wholesale-Groceries & Related Products
PaineWebber, Inc.	NetRatings, Inc.	12/08/99	68.000	Services-Business Services, NEC
	CompuCredit Corp.	04/22/99	60.000	Personal Credit Institutions
Paulson Investment Co., Inc.	AdStar.com, Inc.	10/06/99	15.500	Services-Business Services, NEC
	Careside, Inc.	06/16/99	15.000	Surgical & Medical Instruments & Apparatus
	Dag Media, Inc.	05/12/99	8.125	Miscellaneous Publishing

Lead Underwriter	Issuer	Offer Date	Offering Amount (in Millions of Dollars)	Business
Piper Jaffray, Inc.	MicroFinancial, Inc.	02/05/99	60.000	Miscellaneous Business Credit Institution
Prime Charter, Ltd.	Educational Video Conferencing, Inc.	02/23/99	14.400	Services-Educational Services
Prudential Securities, Inc.	Loislaw.com, Inc.	09/29/99	55.720	Services-Computer Programming, Data Processing, Etc.
	PurchasePro.com, Inc.	09/13/99	48.000	Services-Business Services, NEC
	Bamboo.com, Inc.	08/25/99	28.000	Services-Business Services, NEC
	Lionbridge Technologies, Inc./DE	08/20/99	35.000	Services-Business Services, NEC
	BigStar Entertainment, Inc./NY	08/02/99	25.000	Retail-Computer & Prerecorded Tape Stores
	VaxGen, Inc.	06/29/99	40.300	Pharmaceutical Preparations
Raymond James & Associates, Inc.	Insurance Management Solutions Group, Inc.	02/11/99	36.850	Fire, Marine & Casualty Insurance
Redstone Securities Corp.	Rampart Capital Corp.	09/21/99	7.600	Finance Services
Robertson Stephens & Co.	C-bridge Internet Solutions, Inc.	12/17/99	64.000	Services-Business Services, NEC
	OnDisplay, Inc.	12/17/99	98.000	Services-Business Services, NEC
	eBenx, Inc.	12/10/99	100.000	Services-Business Services, NEC
	INTEREP National Radio Sales, Inc.	12/09/99	65.000	Radio Broadcasting Stations
	Preview Systems, Inc.	12/08/99	79.800	Services-Business Services, NEC
	Digimarc Corp.	12/02/99	80.000	Wholesale-Paper and Paper Products
	iManage, Inc.	11/17/99	39.600	Services-Prepackaged Software
	Rudolph Technologies, Inc.	11/12/99	76.800	Industrial Instruments for Measurement, Display and Control
	Sage, Inc./CA	11/11/99	36.000	Electronic Components, NEC

Lead Underwriter	Issuer	Offer Date	Offering Amount (in Millions of Dollars)	Business
	iBasis, Inc.	11/10/99	108.800	Services-Business Services, NEC
	Predictive Systems, Inc.	10/27/99	72.000	Services-Computer Programming Services
	MCK Communications, Inc.	10/22/99	54.400	Telephone & Telegraph Apparatus
	NaviSite, Inc.	10/22/99	77.000	Services-Business Services, NEC
	Charlotte Russe Holding, Inc.	10/20/99	31.900	Retail-Women's Clothing Stores
	iGO Corp.	10/14/99	60.000	Retail-Catalog & Mail Order Houses
	QuickLogic Corp.	10/14/99	66.670	Semiconductors & Related Devices
	ReSourcePhoenix.com	10/14/99	32.000	Services-Computer Programming Services
	SmartDisk Corp.	10/06/99	39.000	Computer Peripheral Equipment, NEC
	Daleen Technologies, Inc.	10/01/99	49.200	Services-Prepackaged Software
	Vixel Corp.	10/01/99	77.400	Services-Computer Programming Services
Robinson Humphrey Co., Inc.	Netzee, Inc.	11/09/99	62.274	Services-Business Services, NEC
Ryan Beck & Co.	National Medical Health Card Systems, Inc.	07/28/99	15.000	Services-Misc. Health & Allied Services, NEC
S.G. Cowen	Crossroads Systems, Inc.	10/19/99	67.500	Computer Peripheral Equipment, NEC
	Cybergold, Inc.	09/22/99	45.000	Services-Advertising Agencies
S.G. Securities	Thomson Multimedia	11/02/99	476.607	Household Audio & Video Equipment
Salomon Smith Barney	AirNet Communications Corp.	12/06/99	77.000	Radio & TV Broadcasting & Communications Equipment
	TeleCorp PCS, Inc.	11/22/99	184.000	Radio & TV Broadcasting & Communications Equipment
	Chartered Semiconductor Manufacturing, Ltd.	10/29/99	450.000	Semiconductors & Related Devices

Lead Underwriter	Issuer	Offer Date	Offering Amount (in Millions of Dollars)	Business
	Radio Unica Communications Corp.	10/18/99	109.440	Radio Broadcasting Stations
	Williams Communications Group, Inc.	10/01/99	680.800	Telephone Communications (No Radio Telephone)
	Radware, Ltd.	09/29/99	63.000	Electronic Computers
	LaBranche & Co., Inc.	08/19/99	147.000	Security Brokers, Dealers & Flotation Companies
	Alliance Resource Partners, L.P.	08/16/99	147.250	Bituminous Coal & Surface Mining
	Blockbuster, Inc. (Viacom International)	08/10/99	465.000	Services-Video Tape Rental
	Creo Products, Inc.	07/28/99	75.000	Printing Trades Machinery & Equipment
	Focal Communications Corp.	7/28/99	129.350	Radio Telephone Communications
	Mail.com, Inc.	06/17/99	47.950	Services-Advertising
	Juno Online Services, Inc.	05/25/99	84.500	Services-Computer Programming, Data Processing, Etc.
	Argosy Education Group, Inc.	03/08/99	28.000	Services-Educational Services
	Corporate Executive Board Co.	02/22/99	155.557	Services-Management Consulting Services
	Corinthian Colleges, Inc.	02/04/99	48.600	Services-Educational Services
	MEDE America, Inc.	02/01/99	60.000	Services-Computer Processing & Data Preparation
Schneider Securities, Inc.	Pentastar Communications, Inc.	10/26/99	12.500	Telephone Communications (No Radio Telephone)
	Leisure Time Casinos & Resorts, Inc.	09/15/99	8.400	Services-Miscellaneous Amusement & Recreation
	Multi-Link Telecommunications, Inc.	05/14/99	7.200	Services-Business Services, NEC
Scott & Stringfellow	US Concrete, Inc.	05/25/99	30.400	Concrete Products, Except Block & Brick

Lead Underwriter	Issuer	Offer Date	Offering Amount (in Millions of Dollars)	Business
SoundView Technology Group, Inc.	Telemate.net Software, Inc.	09/29/99	49.000	Services-Business Services, NEC
Spencer Edwards, Inc.	Pacific Softworks, Inc.	07/29/99	4.988	Services-Computer Programming Services
Strasbourger Pearson Tulcin Wolff, Inc.	IT Staffing, Ltd.	06/02/99	5.500	Services-Computer Programming, Data Processing, Etc.
The Seidler Companies	Peace Arch Entertainment Group	07/29/99	6.000	Television Programming
Thomas Weisel Partners, L.L.C.	Z-Tel Technologies, Inc.	12/15/99	102.000	Telegraph & Other Message Communications
	Exactis.com, Inc.	11/19/99	53.200	Telegraph & Other Message Communications
	Cysive, Inc.	10/15/99	56.950	Services-Computer Programming Services
	VitaminShoppe.com, Inc.	10/08/99	50.000	Retail-Catalog & Mail Order Houses
	Rubio's Restaurant, Inc.	05/21/99	33.075	Retail-Eating Places
Tucker Anthony Cleary Gull	Gaiam, Inc.	10/28/99	8.525	Services-Business Services, NEC
U.S. Bancorp Piper Jaffray, Inc.	HomeServices.com, Inc.	10/07/99	48.750	Real Estate Agents & Managers (for Others)
	Interspeed, Inc.	09/24/99	42.000	Telephone & Telegraph Apparatus
	Continuus Software Corp./CA	07/29/99	20.189	Services-Computer Programming Services
	Biomarin Pharmaceutical, Inc.	07/23/99	58.500	Pharmaceutical Preparations
	Commtouch Software, Ltd.	07/13/99	48.000	Communication Services, NEC
	Internet.com Corp.	06/24/99	47.600	Services-Business Services, NEC
	Buca, Inc./MN	04/21/99	36.910	Retail-Eating Places
Van Kasper	Keith Companies, Inc.	07/12/99	13.500	Engineering/Construction Consulting
Volpe Brown Whelan & Co.	ImageX.com, Inc.	08/26/99	21.000	Commercial Printing
	Be, Inc.	07/20/99	36.000	Services-Computer Integrated Systems Design
	Comps.com, Inc.	05/05/99	67.500	Services-Computer Processing & Data Preparation

Lead Underwriter	Issuer	Offer Date	Offering Amount (in Millions of Dollars)	Business
W.R. Hambrecht & Co.	Andover.net, Inc.	12/08/99	72.000	Services-Business Services, NEC
	Salon Internet, Inc.	06/22/99	26.250	Services-Computer Integrated Systems Design
	Ravenswood Winery, Inc.	04/08/99	10.500	Beverages
Warburg Dillon Read, L.L.C.	eSpeed, Inc.	12/10/99	198.000	Security & Commodity Brokers, Dealers, Exchanges & Services
	HealthExtras, Inc.	12/09/99	60.500	Services-Health Services
Westport Resources Investment Services, Inc.	Implant Sciences Corp.	06/23/99	7.500	Surgical & Medical Instruments & Apparatus
	Immtech International, Inc.	04/26/99	10.000	Services-Testing Laboratories
Whale Securities Corp.	E-Cruiter.com, Inc.	12/07/99	14.700	Services-Business Services, NEC
	Internet Financial Services, Inc.	04/20/99	14.000	Finance Services
William Blair & Co.	Prism Financial Corp.	05/25/99	35.000	Mortgage Bankers & Loan Correspondents
	OneSource Information Services, Inc.	05/19/99	43.632	Services-Computer Processing & Data Preparation
	Cheap Tickets, Inc.	03/19/99	52.500	Transportation ServicesWR Hambrecht & Co.
	Ravenswood Winery, Inc.	04/08/99	10.500	Beverages

Partial data for Appendix 2 supplied by Global Securities Information, www.gsionline.com.

Underwriting Discount and Certain Expenses of Firm-Commitment IPOs Filed with the SEC, Which Were Publicly Offered During 1999, Listed by Name of Lead Managing Underwriter

Lead Underwriter	Issuer	Offer Date	Offering Amount (in Millions of Dollars)	Price per Share (in Dollars)	Underwriter Discount per Share (in Dollars)	Accounting Fees (in Dollars)	Legal Fees (in Dollars)	Printing Fees (in Dollars)
Ace Diversified Capital, Inc.	Cyber Merchants Exchange, Inc.	05/14/99	20.000	8.000	0.560	25,000	40,000	20,000
Allen & Co., Inc.	Women First Healthcare, Inc.	06/28/99	49.500	11.000	0.770	360,000	365,000	275,000
Allen C. Ewing & Co.	First Capital Bank Holding Corp.	04/12/99	10.000	10.000	0.500	3,500	35,000	5,000
Ashtin Kelly & Co.	Suncoast Bancorp, Inc.	06/30/99	7.000	10.000	0.620	26,000	75,000	40,000
	Marine Bancshares, Inc.	02/05/99	11.500	10.000	0.280	35,500	120,000	40,000
Banc of America Securities, L.L.C.	eCollege.com	12/14/99	55.000	11.000	0.770	250,000	300,000	250,000
	MetaLink, Ltd.	12/01/99	48.000	12.000	0.840	80,000	400,000	200,000
	Metron Technology, N.V.	11/18/99	48.750	13.000	0.910	150,000	265,000	100,000
	PC-Tel, Inc.	10/18/99	78.200	17.000	1.190	300,000	790,000	150,000
	Streamline.com, Inc.	06/17/99	45.000	10.000	0.700	400,000	400,000	120,000
Banc Stock Financial Services, Inc.	First Capital Bancshares, Inc./SC	03/30/99	7.200	10.000	0.700	5,000	30,000	15,000
BancBoston Robertson Stephens	NetSolve, Inc.	09/29/99	48.100	13.000	0.910	185,000	250,000	125,000
	Keynote Systems, Inc.	09/24/99	56.000	14.000	0.980	250,000	250,000	125,000
	eGain Communications Corp.	09/23/99	60.000	12.000	0.840	400,000	275,000	150,000
	MyPoints.com, Inc.	08/19/99	40.000	8.000	0.560	250,000	300,000	200,000
	Quest Software, Inc.	08/12/99	61.600	14.000	0.980	175,000	350,000	160,000
	Cobalt Group, Inc.	08/05/99	49.500	11.000	0.770	200,000	300,000	100,000
	Accrue Software, Inc.	07/30/99	39.000	10.000	0.700	200,000	225,000	150,000
	Packeteer, Inc.	07/28/99	60.000	15.000	1.050	350,000	400,000	175,000

Lead Underwriter	Issuer	Offer Date	Offering Amount (in Millions of Dollars)	Price per Share (in Dollars)	Underwriter Discount per Share (in Dollars)	Accounting Fees (in Dollars)	Legal Fees (in Dollars)	Printing Fees (in Dollars)
	Primus Knowledge Solutions, Inc.	07/01/99	45.650	11.000	0.770	250,000	500,000	175,000
	Persistence Software, Inc.	06/25/99	33.000	11.000	0.770	250,000	350,000	135,000
	Stamps.com, Inc.	06/25/99	55.000	11.000	0.770	150,000	250,000	100,000
	Globespan, Inc./DE	06/23/99	48.750	15.000	1.050	450,000	750,000	300,000
	Ramp Networks, Inc.	06/22/99	44.000	11.000	0.770	200,000	300,000	160,000
	Student Advantage, Inc.	06/18/99	48.000	8.000	0.560	315,000	350,000	175,000
	Alloy Online, Inc.	05/14/99	55.500	15.000	1.050	300,000	700,000	250,000
	MapQuest.com, Inc.	05/04/99	69.000	15.000	1.050	550,000	450,000	150,000
	Mpath Interactive, Inc./CA	04/29/99	70.200	18.000	1.260	207,000	300,000	225,000
	Net Perceptions, Inc.	04/23/99	51.100	14.000	0.980	225,000	350,000	150,000
	Value America, Inc./VA	04/08/99	126.500	23.000	1.610	950,000	775,000	275,000
	Critical Path, Inc.	03/29/99	108.000	24.000	1.680	200,000	250,000	200,000
	Multex.com, Inc.	03/17/99	42.000	14.000	0.980	175,000	350,000	175,000
	FlashNet Communications, Inc.	03/16/99	51.000	17.000	1.190	250,000	550,000	300,000
	Bottomline Technologies, Inc./DE	02/12/99	44.200	13.000	0.910	350,000	450,000	198,500
	Modem Media Poppe Tyson, Inc.	02/04/99	41.600	16.000	1.120	1,314,000	450,000	450,000
Barron Chase Securities, Inc.	Eagle Supply Group, Inc.	03/12/99	12.813	5.000	0.450	275,000	300,000	130,000
	Qiao Xing Universal Telephone, Inc.	02/16/99	8.800	5.500	0.495	223,000	146,000	110,000

Lead Underwriter	Issuer	Offer Date	Offering Amount (in Millions of Dollars)	Price per Share (in Dollars)	Underwriter Discount per Share (in Dollars)	Accounting Fees (in Dollars)	Legal Fees (in Dollars)	Printing Fees (in Dollars)
Bear Stearns & Co., Inc.	MotherNature.com, Inc.	12/10/99	53.300	13.000	0.910	150,000	350,000	125,000
	ASD Systems, Inc.	11/10/99	40.000	8.000	0.560	250,000	350,000	350,000
	SonicWALL, Inc.	11/10/99	56.000	14.000	0.980	250,000	380,000	335,000
	Pac-West Telecomm, Inc.	11/03/99	91.000	10.000	0.300	300,000	450,000	250,000
	Data Return Corp.	10/27/99	81.250	13.000	0.910	200,000	200,000	300,000
	Viador, Inc.	10/26/99	36.000	9.000	0.630	400,000	400,000	130,000
	World Wrestling Federation Entertainment, Inc.	10/18/99	170.000	17.000	1.190	500,000	500,000	430,000
	Trizetto Group, Inc.	10/07/99	37.800	9.000	0.630	500,000	200,000	175,000
	XM Satellite Radio Holdings, Inc.	10/04/99	120.000	12.000	0.810	200,000	500,000	200,000
	FTD.com, Inc.	09/28/99	36.000	8.000	0.560	500,000	500,000	200,000
	Webstakes.com, Inc.	09/23/99	50.050	14.000	0.980	275,000	500,000	250,000
	Splitrock Services, Inc.	08/02/99	90.000	10.000	0.675	150,000	450,000	280,000
	Digex, Inc./DE	07/29/99	170.000	17.000	1.190	850,000	350,000	425,000
	Divicore, Inc.	07/15/99	60.000	12.000	0.840	350,000	625,000	200,000
	Ravisent Technologies, Inc.	07/15/99	60.000	12.000	0.840	$350,000	625,000	200,000
	Digital Island, Inc.	06/29/99	60.000	10.000	0.700	175,000	350,000	200,000
	US SEARCH.com, Inc.	06/25/99	54.000	9.000	0.630	250,000	375,000	150,000
	Drkoop.com, Inc.	06/08/99	84.375	9.000	0.630	195,000	600,000	350,000
	WIT Capital Group, Inc.	06/04/99	68.400	9.000	0.630	300,000	650,000	350,000
	CAIS Internet, Inc.	05/20/99	114.000	19.000	1.330	500,000	550,000	850,000

Lead Underwriter	Issuer	Offer Date	Offering Amount (in Millions of Dollars)	Price per Share (in Dollars)	Underwriter Discount per Share (in Dollars)	Accounting Fees (in Dollars)	Legal Fees (in Dollars)	Printing Fees (in Dollars)
	AppliedTheory Corp.	04/30/99	72.000	16.000	1.120	300,000	320,000	350,000
	Statia Terminals Group, N.V.	04/23/99	152.000	20.000	1.300	450,000	1,900,000	350,000
	MiningCo.com, Inc.	03/24/99	75.000	25.000	1.750	400,000	425,000	250,000
	Prodigy Communications Corp.	02/10/99	150.000	15.000	1.010	625,000	350,000	250,000
	Vialog Corp.	02/05/99	38.943	8.000	0.560	250,000	400,000	300,000
	Covad Communications Group, Inc.	01/21/99	140.400	18.000	1.120	200,000	250,000	200,000
Berthel Fisher & Co.	Lehigh Acres First National Bancshares, Inc.	09/14/99	10.000	10.000	0.800	2,000	40,000	20,000
BlueStone Capital Partners, L.P.	Litronic, Inc.	06/09/99	40.700	11.000	0.770	675,000	835,000	225,000
B.T. Alex. Brown	Private Business, Inc.	05/26/99	34.800	8.000	0.560	125,000	300,000	125,000
	NetObjects, Inc.	05/07/99	72.000	12.000	0.840	450,000	400,000	150,000
	Flycast Communications Corp.	05/04/99	75.000	25.000	1.750	200,000	325,000	200,000
	Proxicom, Inc.	04/19/99	58.500	13.000	0.091	350,000	500,000	350,000
	iTURF, Inc.	04/09/99	92.400	22.000	1.540	300,000	300,000	150,000
	Autobytel.com, Inc.	03/26/99	103.500	23.000	1.610	500,000	685,000	410,000
	OneMain.com, Inc.	03/25/99	187.000	22.000	1.485	6,000,000	2,000,000	1,200,000
	Pinnacle Holdings, Inc.	02/19/99	369.000	14.000	0.840	350,000	450,000	300,000
	Smith Gardner & Associates, Inc.	01/29/99	52.920	12.000	0.840	250,000	250,000	150,000

Lead Underwriter	Issuer	Offer Date	Offering Amount (in Millions of Dollars)	Price per Share (in Dollars)	Underwriter Discount per Share (in Dollars)	Accounting Fees (in Dollars)	Legal Fees (in Dollars)	Printing Fees (in Dollars)
	MarketWatch.com, Inc.	01/15/99	46.750	17.000	1.190	450,000	450,000	300,000
C.E. Unterberg, Towbin	TrueTime, Inc.	12/16/99	15.000	5.000	0.350	85,000	125,000	100,000
	EDGAR Online, Inc.	05/26/99	34.200	9.500	0.670	250,000	400,000	250,000
	Optibase, Ltd.	04/07/99	30.450	7.000	0.490	0	0	0
Canaccord Capital Corp.	Panoramic Care Systems, Inc.	06/24/99	1.100	1.000	0.075	3,000	50,000	5,000
Capital Growth Management, Inc.	HealthTronics, Inc./GA	05/20/99	6.000	6.000	0.600	90,000	60,000	10,000
Capital Resources, Inc.	Steelton Bancorp, Inc.	05/14/99	4.428	10.000	0.700	30,000	55,000	35,000
	First Bancorp of Indiana, Inc.	02/11/99	21.850	10.000	0.340	70,000	160,000	95,000
Cardinal Capital Management, Inc.	U.S. Laboratories, Inc.	02/23/99	6.000	6.000	0.600	110,000	125,000	65,000
Charles Webb & Co.	MFS Financial, Inc.	11/10/99	59.513	10.000	0.250	100,000	225,000	220,000
	Security Financial Bancorp, Inc.	11/10/99	21.275	10.000	0.340	70,000	120,000	90,000
	Evertrust Financial Group, Inc.	08/12/99	74.750	10.000	0.370	75,000	225,000	180,000
	Jade Financial Corp.	08/12/99	16.675	8.000	0.290	75,000	180,000	75,000
	Alaska Pacific Bancshares, Inc.	05/14/99	8.050	10.000	0.630	60,000	125,000	0
CIBC World Markets	Capitol Federal Financial	02/11/99	500.000	10.000	0.150	450,000	950,000	125,000
	GRIC Communications, Inc.	12/15/99	64.400	14.000	0.980	700,000	550,000	250,000
	PNV, Inc.	11/23/99	63.750	17.000	1.190	175,000	450,000	250,000
	Altigen Communications, Inc.	10/04/99	32.500	10.000	0.700	320,000	350,000	20,000

Lead Underwriter	Issuer	Offer Date	Offering Amount (in Millions of Dollars)	Price per Share (in Dollars)	Underwriter Discount per Share (in Dollars)	Accounting Fees (in Dollars)	Legal Fees (in Dollars)	Printing Fees (in Dollars)
	NETsilicon, Inc.	09/15/99	36.750	7.000	0.490	150,000	250,000	400,000
	N2H2, Inc.	07/29/99	65.000	13.000	0.910	150,000	275,000	80,000
	MCM Capital Group, Inc.	07/09/99	22.500	10.000	0.700	130,000	300,000	200,000
	Financial Institutions, Inc.	06/24/99	18.667	14.000	0.980	175,000	155,000	55,000
	AudioCodes, Ltd.	05/28/99	49.000	14.000	0.980	0	0	0
CNL Securities, Inc.	CNL Hospitality Properties, Inc.	04/23/99	165.000	10.000	0.750	100,000	250,000	200,000
Coast Partners Securities, Inc.	Coastal Community Group, Inc.	08/25/99	10.000	10.000	0.950	7,120	70,000	14,150
Credit Suisse First Boston	Egreetings Network	12/16/99	60.000	10.000	0.700	350,000	650,000	200,000
	Caliper Technologies Corp.	12/14/99	72.000	16.000	1.120	250,000	400,000	150,000
	El Sitio, Inc.	12/09/99	131.200	16.000	1.120	300,000	1,220,000	500,000
	VA Linux Systems, Inc.	12/09/99	132.000	30.000	2.100	550,000	500,000	200,000
	FogDog Sports, Inc.	12/08/99	66.000	11.000	0.770	350,000	650,000	275,000
	Knot, Inc.	12/01/99	35.000	10.000	0.700	250,000	350,000	250,000
	Digital Impact, Inc./DE	11/22/99	67.500	15.000	1.050	325,000	500,000	250,000
	Symyx Technologies, Inc.	11/18/99	77.532	14.000	0.980	250,000	300,000	200,000
	Retek, Inc.	11/17/99	82.500	15.000	1.050	650,000	750,000	225,000
	Virata Corp.	11/16/99	70.000	14.000	0.980	350,000	500,000	250,000
	Wireless Facilities, Inc.	11/04/99	60.000	15.000	1.050	275,000	400,000	150,000
	City Telecom (HK), Ltd.	11/03/99	83.111	14.454	0.901	0	0	0
	InterTrust Technologies Corp.	10/26/99	117.000	18.000	1.260	250,000	450,000	150,000

Lead Underwriter	Issuer	Offer Date	Offering Amount (in Millions of Dollars)	Price per Share (in Dollars)	Underwriter Discount per Share (in Dollars)	Accounting Fees (in Dollars)	Legal Fees (in Dollars)	Printing Fees (in Dollars)
	BSQUARE Corp./WA	10/19/99	60.000	15.000	1.050	100,000	350,000	200,000
	Netcentives, Inc.	10/13/99	72.000	12.000	0.840	500,000	375,000	150,000
	Interwoven, Inc.	10/07/99	53.550	17.000	1.190	225,000	425,000	250,000
	QXL.com, P.L.C.	10/07/99	90.418	16.150	1.130	900,000	850,000	700,000
	Silicon Image, Inc.	10/05/99	46.800	12.000	0.840	250,000	450,000	250,000
	TiVo, Inc.	09/29/99	88.000	16.000	1.120	300,000	450,000	225,000
	Spinnaker Exploration Co.	09/28/99	116.000	14.500	0.910	400,000	250,000	115,000
	E.piphany, Inc.	09/21/99	66.400	16.000	1.120	200,000	400,000	150,000
	Vitria Technology, Inc.	09/16/99	48.000	16.000	1.120	250,000	400,000	150,000
	Mortgage.com, Inc.	08/11/99	56.500	8.000	0.560	375,000	425,000	200,000
	Tumbleweed Communications Corp.	08/05/99	48.000	12.000	0.840	300,000	450,000	220,000
	Fairchild Semiconductor International, Inc.	08/03/99	370.000	18.500	1.110	450,000	950,000	1,000,000
	NetIQ Corp.	07/29/99	39.000	13.000	0.910	400,000	400,000	200,000
	American National Can Group, Inc.	07/28/99	510.000	17.000	0.850	2,500,000	1,000,000	250,000
	Liberate Technologies	07/27/99	100.000	16.000	1.120	330,000	500,000	300,000
	Freeserve, P.L.C.	07/26/99	362.250	23.670	1.065	0	0	0
	Tanning Technology Corp.	07/22/99	60.000	15.000	1.050	200,000	750,000	200,000
	MP3.com, Inc.	07/20/99	345.723	28.000	1.960	450,000	375,000	450,000
	Gadzoox Networks, Inc.	07/19/99	73.500	21.000	1.470	200,000	450,000	140,000

Lead Underwriter	Issuer	Offer Date	Offering Amount (in Millions of Dollars)	Price per Share (in Dollars)	Underwriter Discount per Share (in Dollars)	Accounting Fees (in Dollars)	Legal Fees (in Dollars)	Printing Fees (in Dollars)
	Audible, Inc.	07/15/99	36.000	9.000	0.630	250,000	275,000	250,000
	Efficient Networks, Inc.	07/14/99	60.000	15.000	1.050	175,000	300,000	250,000
	Clarent Corp./CA	07/01/99	60.000	15.000	1.050	250,000	500,000	200,000
	Commerce One, Inc.	07/01/99	69.300	21.000	1.470	325,000	375,000	150,000
	Software.com, Inc.	06/23/99	90.000	15.000	1.050	400,000	300,000	200,000
	TD Waterhouse Group, Inc.	06/23/99	1008.000	24.000	1.140	1,800,000	1,700,000	1,000,000
	AppNet, Inc./DE	06/17/99	72.000	12.000	0.840	1,000,000	850,000	600,000
	Phone.com, Inc.	06/10/99	64.000	16.000	1.120	350,000	375,000	200,000
	Unwired Planet, Inc.	06/10/99	64.000	16.000	1.120	350,000	375,000	200,000
	Capital Environmental Resource, Inc.	06/02/99	35.846	11.000	0.770	580,000	465,000	234,000
	CareerBuilder, Inc.	05/11/99	58.500	13.000	0.910	150,000	300,000	225,000
	Latitude Communications, Inc.	05/06/99	36.000	12.000	0.840	275,000	350,000	200,000
	Radio One, Inc.	05/05/99	156.000	24.000	1.620	503,000	921,000	495,000
	Silknet Software, Inc.	05/05/99	45.000	15.000	1.050	220,000	280,000	175,000
	Informatica Corp.	04/28/99	44.000	16.000	1.120	225,000	225,000	160,000
	Razorfish, Inc.	04/26/99	48.000	16.000	1.120	800,000	550,000	350,000
	USinternetworking, Inc.	04/08/99	126.000	21.000	1.470	100,000	250,000	300,000
	Ducati Motor Holding, S.P.A.	03/24/99	285.663	31.670	2.009	0	0	0
	Autoweb.com, Inc.	03/22/99	70.000	14.000	0.980	200,000	395,000	175,000
	Intraware, Inc.	02/25/99	64.000	16.000	1.120	175,000	350,000	250,000

Lead Underwriter	Issuer	Offer Date	Offering Amount (in Millions of Dollars)	Price per Share (in Dollars)	Underwriter Discount per Share (in Dollars)	Accounting Fees (in Dollars)	Legal Fees (in Dollars)	Printing Fees (in Dollars)
	Onyx Software Corp./WA	02/11/99	40.300	13.000	0.910	175,000	200,000	150,00
	Korn Ferry International	02/10/99	164.500	14.000	0.875	1,300,000	1,600,000	850,000
	Entercom Communications Corp.	01/28/99	306.619	22.500	1.350	1,350,000	525,000	550,000
Cruttenden Roth, Inc.	Allaire Corp.	01/22/99	50.000	20.000	1.400	280,000	375,000	125,000
	Plastic Surgery Co.	12/10/99	11.200	8.000	0.640	450,000	700,000	370,000
	Netgateway, Inc.	11/18/99	23.100	7.000	0.490	100,000	225,000	75,000
	Perfumania.com, Inc.	09/29/99	24.500	7.000	0.490	200,000	300,000	130,000
	Duraswitch Industries, Inc.	08/26/99	10.000	5.000	0.400	160,000	250,000	250,000
	Troy Group, Inc.	07/22/99	17.500	7.000	0.630	300,000	250,000	200,000
	QuePasa.com, Inc.	06/24/99	48.000	12.000	1.080	125,000	575,000	150,000
	AremisSoft Corp./DE	04/22/99	16.500	5.000	0.400	250,000	400,000	350,000
	Claimsnet.com, Inc.	04/06/99	20.000	8.000	0.660	35,000	200,000	60,000
D.A. Davidson & Co.	Jore Corp.	09/23/99	40.000	10.000	0.700	300,000	225,000	100,000
	Direct Focus, Inc.	05/04/99	20.500	20.500	1.435	120,000	150,000	115,000
Dain Rauscher Wessels	ShopNow.com, Inc.	09/29/99	87.000	12.000	0.840	200,000	450,000	165,000
	Watchguard Technologies, Inc.	07/30/99	45.500	13.000	0.910	350,000	500,000	200,000
	Aironet Wireless Communication, Inc.	07/29/99	66.000	11.000	0.770	644,525	611,212	470,952
David Lerner Associates	WebTrends Corp.	02/19/99	45.500	13.000	0.910	135,000	250,000	120,000
	Apple Suites, Inc.	08/03/99	300.000	9.000	0.900	100,000	350,000	300,000

Lead Underwriter	Issuer	Offer Date	Offering Amount (in Millions of Dollars)	Price per Share (in Dollars)	Underwriter Discount per Share (in Dollars)	Accounting Fees (in Dollars)	Legal Fees (in Dollars)	Printing Fees (in Dollars)
Deutsche Banc Alex. Brown	DSL.net, Inc.	10/06/99	53.906	7.500	0.525	350,000	350,000	175,000
	ACME Communications, Inc.	09/29/99	115.000	23.000	1.610	150,000	500,000	175,000
	Foundry Networks, Inc.	09/27/99	125.000	25.000	1.750	250,000	450,000	100,000
	FreeShop.com, Inc.	09/27/99	38.400	12.000	0.840	200,000	250,000	170,000
	Bluestone Software, Inc.	09/23/99	60.000	15.000	1.050	125,000	300,000	350,000
	Trintech Group, P.L.C.	09/23/99	66.990	11.550	0.810	199,500	833,823	250,000
	Broadbase Software, Inc.	09/22/99	56.000	14.000	0.980	275,000	425,000	250,000
	YesMail.com, Inc.	09/22/99	37.400	11.000	0.770	300,000	400,000	170,000
	Luminant Worldwide Corp.	09/16/99	83.970	18.000	1.260	3,000,000	2,000,000	350,000
	U.S. Aggregates, Inc.	08/13/99	75.000	15.000	1.050	400,000	450,000	475,000
	Netscout Systems, Inc.	08/12/99	33.000	15.000	0.770	225,000	300,000	120,000
	HotJobs.com, Ltd.	08/10/99	24.000	8.000	0.560	500,000	285,000	300,000
	Salem Communications Corp./DE	07/01/99	189.000	22.500	1.430	200,000	600,000	230,000
	United Therapeutics Corp.	06/17/99	54.000	12.000	0.840	225,000	400,000	200,000
	Ditech Corp.	06/09/99	33.000	11.000	0.770	230,000	300,000	175,000
	Skechers USA, Inc.	06/09/99	77.000	11.000	0.770	225,000	300,000	225,000
Deutsche Bank, A.G.	Golden Telecom, Inc.	10/01/99	55.800	12.000	0.780	600,000	730,000	1,600,000
DG Bank	POET Holdings, Inc.	11/12/99	51.548	13.050	0.653	300,000	400,000	150,000
Dirks & Co., Inc.	TownPagesNet.com, P.L.C	04/30/99	22.000	10.000	0.850	275,000	475,000	220,000
	Log On America, Inc.	04/22/99	22.000	10.000	0.825	50,000	125,000	75,000
	Digital Lava, Inc.	02/18/99	18.120	15.100	1.262	250,000	350,000	100,000

Lead Underwriter	Issuer	Offer Date	Offering Amount (in Millions of Dollars)	Price per Share (in Dollars)	Underwriter Discount per Share (in Dollars)	Accounting Fees (in Dollars)	Legal Fees (in Dollars)	Printing Fees (in Dollars)
Donaldson, Lufkin & Jenrette	Xpedior, Inc.	12/15/99	162.165	19.000	1.330	1,200,000	400,000	400,000
	MedicaLogic, Inc.	12/09/99	100.300	17.000	1.190	350,000	250,000	350,000
	GetThere.com	11/22/99	80.000	16.000	1.120	600,000	700,000	600,000
	Official Payments Corp.	11/22/99	75.000	15.000	1.050	450,000	850,000	450,000
	SciQuest.com, Inc.	11/19/99	120.000	16.000	1.120	270,000	430,000	125,000
	Rainmaker Systems, Inc.	11/17/99	40.000	8.000	0.560	425,000	460,000	200,000
	Quintus Corp.	11/16/99	81.000	18.000	1.260	475,000	500,000	250,000
	Data Critical Corp.	11/09/99	35.000	10.000	0.700	200,000	300,000	200,000
	Be Free, Inc.	11/03/99	67.200	12.000	0.840	300,000	350,000	150,000
	JNI Corp.	10/26/99	93.100	19.000	1.330	500,000	300,000	150,000
	E-Stamp Corp.	10/08/99	119.000	17.000	1.190	200,000	350,000	200,000
	Jupiter Communications, Inc.	10/08/99	65.625	21.000	1.470	300,000	350,000	250,000
	Airgate PCS, Inc.	09/27/99	113.900	17.000	1.190	250,000	350,000	350,000
	Medscape, Inc.	09/27/99	53.664	8.000	0.560	425,000	650,000	600,000
	NovaMed Eyecare, Inc.	08/18/99	32.000	8.000	0.560	175,000	1,200,000	225,000
	Wink Communications, Inc.	08/18/99	76.000	16.000	1.120	100,000	250,000	240,000
	IXnet, Inc.	08/12/99	97.500	15.000	1.013	650,000	900,000	200,000
	Braun Consulting, Inc.	08/10/99	28.000	7.000	0.490	350,000	350,000	275,000
	Netia Holdings, S.A.	07/29/99	121.000	22.000	1.155	170,000	400,000	650,000
	JFAX.COM, Inc.	07/23/99	80.750	9.500	0.665	300,000	425,000	200,000
	Insight Communications Co., Inc.	07/20/99	563.500	24.500	1.445	900,000	700,000	600,000

Lead Underwriter	Issuer	Offer Date	Offering Amount (in Millions of Dollars)	Price per Share (in Dollars)	Underwriter Discount per Share (in Dollars)	Accounting Fees (in Dollars)	Legal Fees (in Dollars)	Printing Fees (in Dollars)
	Voyager Net, Inc.	07/20/99	135.000	15.000	1.050	585,000	500,000	250,000
	Paradyne Networks, Inc.	07/16/99	102.000	17.000	1.190	250,000	425,000	200,000
	GoTo.com, Inc.	06/18/99	90.000	15.000	1.050	200,000	450,000	250,000
	Network Access Solutions Corp.	06/04/99	78.047	12.000	0.840	150,000	300,000	300,000
	Zany Brainy, Inc.	06/03/99	61.000	10.000	0.700	300,000	325,000	175,000
	David's Bridal, Inc.	05/21/99	104.000	13.000	0.880	475,000	425,000	150,000
	Nextera Enterprises, Inc.	05/18/99	115.000	10.000	0.675	500,000	850,000	400,000
	NextCard, Inc.	05/14/99	120.000	20.000	1.400	250,000	550,000	240,000
	Media Metrix, Inc.	05/07/99	51.000	17.000	1.190	130,000	350,000	150,000
	Sagent Technology, Inc.	04/14/99	45.000	9.000	0.630	150,000	325,000	0
	Boyds Collection, Ltd.	03/05/99	288.000	18.000	16.920	750,000	500,000	415,000
	Neon Systems, Inc.	03/05/99	40.500	15.000	1.050	150,000	150,000	100,000
	Invitrogen Corp.	02/26/99	52.500	15.000	1.050	150,000	250,000	125,000
EBI Securities Corp.	Netivation.com, Inc.	06/22/99	25.000	10.000	0.750	200,000	300,000	125,000
Everen Securities, Inc.	Sun Community Bancorp, Ltd.	07/02/99	26.400	16.000	1.120	65,000	150,000	150,000
Fahnestock & Co., Inc.	PrivateBancorp, Inc.	06/30/99	16.200	18.000	1.260	80,000	350,000	120,000
Ferris, Baker Watts, Inc.	Web Street, Inc.	11/17/99	41.250	11.000	0.770	320,000	450,000	200,000
First American Investment Banking Corp.	Musicmaker.com, Inc.	07/07/99	117.600	14.000	0.980	250,000	400,000	350,000
	Pelican Financial, Inc.	11/10/99	6.720	7.000	1.110	100,000	145,000	75,000

Lead Underwriter	Issuer	Offer Date	Offering Amount (in Millions of Dollars)	Price per Share (in Dollars)	Underwriter Discount per Share (in Dollars)	Accounting Fees (in Dollars)	Legal Fees (in Dollars)	Printing Fees (in Dollars)
First Financial United Investments, Ltd.	United Mortgage Trust	06/04/99	50.000	20.000	2.100	5,000	75,000	16,000
First Level Capital, Inc.	Nolbo, Inc.	08/13/99	1.800	6.000	0.600	20,000	60,000	70,000
First Union Capital Markets Corp.	Headhunter.NET, Inc.	08/19/99	30.000	10.000	0.700	150,000	275,000	250,000
	MIIX Group, Inc.	07/30/99	40.500	13.500	0.945	290,000	350,000	176,000
Friedman, Billings, Ramsey & Co., Inc.	NetCreations, Inc.	11/12/99	42.900	13.000	0.910	350,000	600,000	400,000
	American Home Mortgage Holdings, Inc.	10/01/99	14.962	6.000	0.420	350,000	275,000	150,000
	Oswego County Bancorp, Inc.	05/14/99	5.405	10.000	1.310	170,000	225,000	60,000
	Atlantic Preferred Capital Corp.	01/27/99	12.600	10.000	0.400	40,000	300,000	0
Gerard, Klauer, Mattison & Co.	NetRadio Corp.	10/14/99	35.200	11.000	0.770	225,000	545,000	235,000
	WorldGate Communications, Inc.	04/15/99	105.000	21.000	1.470	150,000	250,000	175,000
Gilford Securities, Inc.	Perficient, Inc.	07/29/99	8.000	8.000	0.800	100,000	225,000	85,000
	I.D. Systems, Inc.	06/30/99	14.000	7.000	0.560	100,000	225,000	53,000
Global Financial Group	Proformance Research Organization, Inc.	02/16/99	5.000	5.000	0.500	25,000	50,000	13,000
GMA Partners	United Americas Bankshares, Inc.	07/06/99	12.000	10.000	0.330	5,000	62,000	8,000
Goldman Sachs International	Jazztel, P.L.C.	12/08/99	176.652	17.447	0.960	425,000	850,000	500,000
Goldman, Sachs & Co.	Maxygen, Inc.	12/15/99	96.000	16.000	1.120	300,000	300,000	180,000

Lead Underwriter	Issuer	Offer Date	Offering Amount (in Millions of Dollars)	Price per Share (in Dollars)	Underwriter Discount per Share (in Dollars)	Accounting Fees (in Dollars)	Legal Fees (in Dollars)	Printing Fees (in Dollars)
	Tritel, Inc.	12/13/99	237.352	18.000	1.260	250,000	750,000	250,000
	Freemarkets, Inc.	12/09/99	172.800	48.000	3.360	550,000	800,000	350,000
	AGENCY.COM, Ltd.	12/08/99	153.400	26.000	1.820	1,500,000	500,000	300,000
	Classic Communications, Inc.	12/07/99	206.250	25.000	1.710	350,000	875,000	950,000
	Alaska Communications Systems Group, Inc.	11/17/99	140.000	14.000	0.910	300,000	1,500,000	300,000
	Terra Networks, S.A.	11/15/99	334.310	13.410	0.402	1,500,000	1,500,000	730,000
	Expedia, Inc.	11/09/99	72.800	14.000	0.980	900,000	400,000	300,000
	Charter Communications, Inc./MO	11/08/99	3230.000	19.000	0.760	8,000,000	9,999,999	8,750,000
	Cobalt Networks, Inc.	11/04/99	110.000	22.000	1.540	250,000	350,000	275,000
	Webvan Group, Inc.	11/04/99	375.000	15.000	0.900	350,000	750,000	600,000
	Allied Riser Communications Corp.	10/28/99	283.500	18.000	1.080	400,000	1,000,000	250,000
	Plug Power, Inc.	10/28/99	90.000	15.000	1.050	180,000	310,000	130,000
	Calico Commerce, Inc.	10/06/99	56.000	14.000	0.980	500,000	650,000	475,000
	Neuberger Berman, Inc.	10/06/99	232.000	32.000	2.080	200,000	1,000,000	350,000
	PlanetRx.com	10/06/99	96.000	16.000	1.120	240,000	400,000	350,000
	Ashford.com, Inc.	09/23/99	81.250	13.000	0.910	200,000	350,000	185,000
	NetZero, Inc.	09/23/99	160.000	16.000	1.120	350,000	400,000	250,000
	Kana Communications, Inc.	09/21/99	49.500	15.000	1.050	400,000	600,000	225,000
	LookSmart, Ltd.	08/19/99	92.400	12.000	0.840	300,000	400,000	250,000
	Active Software, Inc.	08/12/99	38.500	11.000	0.770	300,000	400,000	225,000

Lead Underwriter	Issuer	Offer Date	Offering Amount (in Millions of Dollars)	Price per Share (in Dollars)	Underwriter Discount per Share (in Dollars)	Accounting Fees (in Dollars)	Legal Fees (in Dollars)	Printing Fees (in Dollars)
	Red Hat, Inc.	08/11/99	84.000	14.000	0.980	250,000	500,000	125,000
	Internet Initiative Japan, Inc.	08/03/99	164.680	23.000	1.550	0	0	0
	1-800-Flowers.com, Inc.	08/02/99	126.000	21.000	1.470	300,000	500,000	350,000
	Allscripts Inc./IL	07/23/99	112.000	16.000	1.120	250,000	575,000	100,000
	InsWeb Corp.	07/22/99	85.000	17.000	1.190	279,000	300,000	230,000
	Engage Technologies, Inc.	07/20/99	90.000	15.000	1.050	250,000	400,000	200,000
	Convergent Communications, Inc./CO	07/19/99	126.000	15.000	1.050	150,000	400,000	250,000
	TIBCO Software, Inc.	07/13/99	109.500	15.000	1.050	1,000,000	500,000	300,000
	Network Plus Corp.	06/29/99	128.000	16.000	1.120	150,000	350,000	300,000
	Seminis, Inc.	06/29/99	206.250	15.000	0.870	450,000	1,200,000	650,000
	E-LOAN, Inc.	06/28/99	49.000	14.000	0.980	550,000	700,000	500,000
	Juniper Networks, Inc.	06/24/99	163.200	34.000	2.380	250,000	450,000	200,000
	Viant Corp.	06/17/99	48.000	16.000	1.120	225,000	295,000	125,000
	BackWeb Technologies, Ltd.	06/07/99	66.000	12.000	0.840	300,000	500,000	150,000
	Inet Technologies, Inc.	05/26/99	92.000	16.000	1.120	375,000	575,000	200,000
	barnesandnoble.com, Inc.	05/25/99	450.000	18.000	1.080	325,000	475,000	325,000
	StarMedia Network, Inc.	05/25/99	105.000	15.000	1.050	400,000	500,000	250,000
	TC Pipelines, L.P.	05/24/99	235.750	20.500	1.300	200,000	1,300,000	1,000,000
	Tenfold Corp./UT	05/20/99	79.900	17.000	1.190	375,000	350,000	128,000
	eToys, Inc.	05/19/99	166.400	20.000	1.350	320,000	400,000	500,000
	TheStreet.com	05/10/99	104.500	19.000	1.330	250,000	850,000	700,000

Lead Underwriter	Issuer	Offer Date	Offering Amount (in Millions of Dollars)	Price per Share (in Dollars)	Underwriter Discount per Share (in Dollars)	Accounting Fees (in Dollars)	Legal Fees (in Dollars)	Printing Fees (in Dollars)
	NorthPoint Communications Group, Inc.	05/05/99	360.000	24.000	1.680	350,000	400,000	250,000
	Portal Software, Inc.	05/05/99	56.000	14.000	0.980	350,000	500,000	200,000
	Goldman Sachs Group, Inc.	05/03/99	3657.000	53.000	2.250	1,600,000	900,000	3,610,000
	StanCorp Financial Group, Inc.	04/15/99	330.600	23.750	1.420	150,000	650,000	400,000
	Hugoton Royalty Trust	04/08/99	142.500	9.500	0.665	155,000	385,000	325,000
	ZDNet (Ziff-Davis, Inc.)	03/30/99	190.000	19.000	1.330	1,000,000	1,500,000	1,325,000
	iVillage, Inc.	03/18/99	87.600	24.000	1.680	425,000	600,000	650,000
	pcOrder.com, Inc.	02/25/99	46.200	21.000	1.470	475,000	375,000	200,000
	United Pan-Europe Communications, N.V.	02/12/99	1311.200	32.780	1.639	0	0	0
Gruntal & Co., Inc.	Fashionmall.com, Inc.	05/21/99	39.000	13.000	0.910	100,000	150,000	70,000
Gunn Allen Financial, Inc.	Intelli-Check, Inc.	11/18/99	7.500	7.500	0.675	100,000	150,000	75,000
Hambrecht & Quist, Inc.	PFSweb, Inc.	12/02/99	52.700	17.000	1.190	1,400,000	700,000	260,000
	SmarterKids.com, Inc.	11/23/99	63.000	14.000	0.980	350,000	350,000	150,000
	Management Network Group, Inc.	11/22/99	78.455	17.000	1.190	250,000	350,000	250,000
	LifeMinders.com, Inc.	11/19/99	58.800	14.000	0.980	350,000	300,000	400,000
	Immersion Corp.	11/12/99	51.000	12.000	0.840	320,000	400,000	150,000
	Garden.com, Inc.	09/15/99	49.200	12.000	0.840	350,000	500,000	185,000

Lead Underwriter	Issuer	Offer Date	Offering Amount (in Millions of Dollars)	Price per Share (in Dollars)	Underwriter Discount per Share (in Dollars)	Accounting Fees (in Dollars)	Legal Fees (in Dollars)	Printing Fees (in Dollars)
	Mission Critical Software, Inc.	08/04/99	60.000	16.000	1.120	179,000	350,000	175,000
	Quotesmith.com, Inc.	08/03/99	52.000	11.000	0.770	300,000	300,000	200,000
	Net2Phone, Inc.	07/30/99	81.000	15.000	1.050	300,000	900,000	400,000
	Art Technology Group, Inc.	07/20/99	60.000	12.000	0.840	175,000	350,000	125,000
	National Information Consortium	07/15/99	156.000	12.000	0.840	300,000	400,000	150,000
	nFront, Inc.	06/29/99	39.000	10.000	0.700	225,000	400,000	150,000
	ESPS, Inc.	06/16/99	26.250	7.500	0.525	450,000	400,000	175,000
	F5 Networks, Inc.	06/04/99	30.000	10.000	0.700	200,000	350,000	120,000
	SalesLogix Corp.	05/27/99	29.925	9.000	0.630	200,000	200,000	150,000
	Newgen Results Corp.	05/21/99	48.425	13.000	0.910	175,000	175,000	175,000
	@plan, Inc.	05/20/99	35.000	14.000	0.980	150,000	225,000	150,000
	Adforce, Inc.	05/07/99	67.500	15.000	1.050	225,000	450,000	150,000
	Launch Media, Inc.	04/23/99	74.800	22.000	1.540	225,000	250,000	175,000
	Accredo Health, Inc.	04/15/99	48.000	16.000	1.120	450,000	370,000	0
	Catapult Communications Corp.	02/11/99	33.525	10.000	0.700	245,000	300,000	230,000
Howe Barnes Investments, Inc.	SERENA Software, Inc.	02/11/99	78.000	13.000	0.910	250,000	250,000	175,000
	Team Financial, Inc./KS	06/22/99	11.250	11.250	0.788	80,000	125,000	80,000
ING Barings Furman Selz, L.L.C.	Intelligent Life Corp.	05/13/99	45.500	13.000	0.910	310,000	250,000	83,000

Lead Underwriter	Issuer	Offer Date	Offering Amount (in Millions of Dollars)	Price per Share (in Dollars)	Underwriter Discount per Share (in Dollars)	Accounting Fees (in Dollars)	Legal Fees (in Dollars)	Printing Fees (in Dollars)
Institutional Equity Corp.	Albany Molecular Research, Inc.	02/04/99	50.000	20.000	1.400	200,000	450,000	150,000
	Streamedia Communications, Inc.	12/21/99	10.200	8.500	0.850	40,000	120,000	40,000
Interstate Johnson Lane Corp.	Community Capital Bancshares, Inc.	03/11/99	10.000	10.000	0.640	6,000	115,000	55,000
Invemed Associates	InterWorld Corp.	08/10/99	45.000	15.000	1.050	300,000	300,000	200,000
J.C. Bradford & Co.	Trex Co., Inc.	04/08/99	41.030	10.000	0.700	250,000	300,000	250,000
J.P. Morgan & Co.	Interactive Pictures Corp.	08/05/99	75.600	18.000	1.260	150,000	250,000	120,000
	Biopure Corp.	07/30/99	42.000	12.000	0.840	175,000	450,000	315,000
	Hoover's, Inc.	07/21/99	45.500	14.000	0.980	150,000	300,000	150,000
	Genentech	07/19/99	1940.000	97.000	2.425	850,000	650,000	250,000
	Online Resources & Communications Corp.	06/04/99	43.400	14.000	0.980	300,000	250,000	225,000
	CONSOL Energy, Inc.	04/29/99	361.600	16.000	0.800	550,000	625,000	300,000
	Valley Media, Inc.	03/26/99	56.000	16.000	1.120	600,000	600,000	5,000
	RoweCom, Inc.	03/08/99	49.600	16.000	1.120	300,000	320,000	150,000
J.P. Morgan Securities, Ltd.	ebookers.com, P.L.C.	11/11/99	61.200	18.000	1.260	700,000	1,000,000	200,000
Jefferies & Co., Inc.	ZipLink, Inc.	05/26/99	49.000	14.000	0.980	150,000	425,000	160,000
Joseph Charles & Associates, Inc.	Thermoview Industries, Inc.	12/02/99	6.903	5.500	0.520	1,125,000	475,000	750,000

Lead Underwriter	Issuer	Offer Date	Offering Amount (in Millions of Dollars)	Price per Share (in Dollars)	Underwriter Discount per Share (in Dollars)	Accounting Fees (in Dollars)	Legal Fees (in Dollars)	Printing Fees (in Dollars)
Joseph Stevens & Co., L.P.	BiznessOnline.com	05/12/99	29.000	10.000	0.700	350,000	450,000	100,000
Josephthal & Co.	American National Financial, Inc.	02/12/99	10.500	6.000	0.450	175,000	268,000	135,000
Kashner Davidson Securities Corp.	Able Energy, Inc.	06/22/99	7.000	7.000	0.700	25,000	100,000	55,000
	Outlook Sports Technology, Inc.	03/18/99	2.320	5.800	0.493	100,000	100,000	125,000
Keefe, Bruyette & Woods, Inc.	Eldorado Bancshares, Inc.	04/06/99	19.099	10.000	0.700	100,000	450,000	200,000
	Jacksonville Bancorp, Inc./FL	02/09/99	15.000	10.000	0.000	2,000	30,000	8,000
Ladenburg, Thalmann & Co., Inc.	topjobs.net, P.L.C.	04/27/99	39.600	12.000	0.840	0	0	0
Lasalle Street Securities, Inc.	LCM Internet Growth Fund, Inc.	10/26/99	25.000	10.000	0.550	1,000	55,000	6,000
Legg, Mason, Wood, Walker, Inc.	Greater Atlantic Financial Corp.	06/25/99	19.000	9.500	0.665	75,000	200,000	105,000
Lehman Brothers	Tularik, Inc.	12/09/99	97.300	14.000	0.980	150,000	425,000	150,000
	HealthCentral.com	12/07/99	82.500	11.000	0.770	400,000	550,000	400,000
	Harris Interactive, Inc.	12/06/99	81.200	14.000	0.980	200,000	250,000	150,000
	Deltathree.com, Inc.	11/22/99	90.000	15.000	1.050	375,000	650,000	250,000
	Mediaplex, Inc.	11/19/99	72.000	12.000	0.840	275,000	350,000	250,000
	Korea Thurnet Co., Ltd.	11/16/99	181.800	18.000	1.260	220,000	1,150,000	150,000
	CVC, Inc.	11/12/99	35.000	10.000	0.700	265,000	300,000	150,000
	Somera Communications, Inc.	11/11/99	102.000	12.000	0.840	425,000	400,000	200,000

Lead Underwriter	Issuer	Offer Date	Offering Amount (in Millions of Dollars)	Price per Share (in Dollars)	Underwriter Discount per Share (in Dollars)	Accounting Fees (in Dollars)	Legal Fees (in Dollars)	Printing Fees (in Dollars)
	Baltimore Technologies, P.L.C.	10/27/99	121.450	24.788	1.301	1,600,000	1,200,000	350,000
	Spanish Broadcasting Systems, Inc.	10/27/99	435.748	20.000	1.250	325,000	450,000	75,000
	ITXC Corp.	09/27/99	75.000	12.000	0.840	275,000	400,000	275,000
	Alteon WebSystems, Inc.	09/23/99	76.000	19.000	1.330	200,000	400,000	175,000
	U.S. Interactive, Inc./PA	08/09/99	28.650	10.000	0.700	350,000	500,000	200,000
	Internet Gold-Golden Lines, Ltd.	08/05/99	54.000	12.000	0.840	0	0	0
	VersaTel Telecom International, N.V.	07/23/99	223.316	10.510	0.630	250,000	500,000	900,000
	Talk City, Inc.	07/19/99	60.000	12.000	0.840	275,000	500,000	125,000
	China.com Corp.	07/12/99	84.940	20.000	1.400	0	0	0
	Liquid Audio, Inc.	07/08/99	63.000	15.000	1.050	150,000	300,000	150,000
	SBA Communications Corp.	06/16/99	90.000	9.000	0.630	200,000	400,000	200,000
	High Speed Access Corp.	06/04/99	169.000	13.000	0.875	250,000	600,000	350,000
	WESCO International, Inc.	05/11/99	175.050	18.000	1.120	300,000	400,000	135,000
	Maker Communications, Inc.	05/10/99	43.550	13.000	0.910	200,000	200,000	200,000
	Heidrick & Struggles International, Inc.	04/27/99	58.800	14.000	0.980	1,325,000	1,000,000	500,000
	Delta Galil Industries, Ltd.	03/25/99	22.500	9.000	0.585	300,000	400,000	100,000
	Antenna TV, S.A.	03/03/99	115.500	15.000	0.638	600,000	700,000	350,000
	VerticalNet, Inc.	02/10/99	56.000	16.000	1.120	350,000	400,000	300,000

Lead Underwriter	Issuer	Offer Date	Offering Amount (in Millions of Dollars)	Price per Share (in Dollars)	Underwriter Discount per Share (in Dollars)	Accounting Fees (in Dollars)	Legal Fees (in Dollars)	Printing Fees (in Dollars)
	Pacific Internet, Ltd.	02/05/99	51.000	17.000	1.110	170,000	300,000	200,000
	Tut Systems, Inc.	01/28/99	45.000	18.000	1.260	261,000	375,000	364,000
Loeb Partners Corp.	Evercel, Inc.	02/22/99	8.334	6.000	0.225	125,000	375,000	100,000
McDonald Investments, Inc.	Tower Financial Corp.	01/26/99	22.000	10.000	0.625	25,000	125,000	50,000
Merrill Lynch & Co.	Infonet Services Corp.	12/15/99	1076.928	21.000	1.000	1,400,000	600,000	350,000
	Optio Software, Inc.	12/14/99	50.000	10.000	0.700	300,000	300,000	178,000
	OpenTV Corp.	11/23/99	150.000	20.000	1.400	375,000	1,000,000	300,000
	Finisar Corp.	11/11/99	154.850	19.000	1.330	240,000	300,000	150,000
	Edison Schools, Inc.	11/10/99	122.400	18.000	1.260	400,000	600,000	400,000
	Next Level Communications, Inc.	11/10/99	170.000	20.000	1.400	500,000	1,600,000	400,000
	Aether Systems, Inc.	10/20/99	96.000	16.000	1.120	400,000	500,000	250,000
	ZapMe! Corp.	10/19/99	99.000	11.000	0.770	250,000	250,000	150,000
	Satyam Infoway, Ltd.	10/18/99	75.150	18.000	1.260	120,000	500,000	200,000
	Blackrock, Inc./NY	10/01/99	126.000	14.000	0.945	750,000	1,100,000	375,000
	ICICI, Ltd.	09/22/99	273.913	9.800	0.392	0	0	0
	Interactive Intelligence, Inc.	09/22/99	34.710	13.000	0.910	125,000	100,000	225,000
	Muniholdings Michigan Insured Fund II, Inc.	09/14/99	51.000	15.000	0.000	0	35,000	35,000
	Netro Corp.	08/18/99	40.000	8.000	0.560	250,000	300,000	250,000
	Internet Capital Group, Inc.	08/04/99	178.800	12.000	0.840	500,000	450,000	200,000
	Pivotal Corp.	08/04/99	42.000	12.000	0.840	160,000	490,000	160,000

Lead Underwriter	Issuer	Offer Date	Offering Amount (in Millions of Dollars)	Price per Share (in Dollars)	Underwriter Discount per Share (in Dollars)	Accounting Fees (in Dollars)	Legal Fees (in Dollars)	Printing Fees (in Dollars)
	Quokka Sports, Inc.	07/27/99	60.000	12.000	0.840	250,000	350,000	325,000
	Scientific Learning Corp.	07/21/99	36.800	16.000	1.120	200,000	400,000	150,000
	Muniholdings Florida Insured Fund V	07/20/99	52.500	15.000	0.000	0	35,000	35,000
	Provantage Health Services, Inc.	07/14/99	100.800	18.000	1.260	290,000	250,000	225,000
	Interliant, Inc.	07/07/99	70.000	10.000	0.700	300,000	550,000	500,000
	Showcase Corp./MN	06/29/99	27.000	9.000	0.630	150,000	175,000	150,000
	CyberSource Corp.	06/23/99	44.000	11.000	0.770	200,000	200,000	150,000
	CareInsite, Inc.	06/15/99	101.700	18.000	1.260	300,000	400,000	100,000
	Azurix Corp.	06/09/99	695.400	19.000	1.140	1,600,000	950,000	0
	Pantry, Inc.	06/08/99	81.250	13.000	0.910	280,000	350,000	200,000
	iXL Enterprises, Inc.	06/02/99	72.000	12.000	0.840	1,200,000	1,500,000	740,897
	Muniholdings Insured Fund III, Inc.	05/25/99	102.000	15.000	0.000	0	25,000	35,000
	Tuesday Morning Corp./DE	04/21/99	99.000	15.000	1.050	200,000	220,000	150,000
	MIH, Ltd.	04/13/99	163.350	18.000	1.260	1,550,000	1,500,000	0
	Rhythms NetConnections, Inc.	04/06/99	196.875	21.000	1.391	200,000	600,000	500,000
	PLX Technology, Inc.	04/05/99	29.700	9.000	0.630	150,000	200,000	85,000
	Pepsi Bottling Group, Inc.	03/30/99	2300.000	23.000	0.918	3,250,000	700,000	885,000
	Muniholdings Insured Fund II, Inc.	02/23/99	144.000	15.000	0.000	7,000	40,000	35,000

Lead Underwriter	Issuer	Offer Date	Offering Amount (in Millions of Dollars)	Price per Share (in Dollars)	Underwriter Discount per Share (in Dollars)	Accounting Fees (in Dollars)	Legal Fees (in Dollars)	Printing Fees (in Dollars)
	Muniholdings Pennsylvania Insured Fund	02/23/99	28.125	15.000	0.000	7,000	40,000	35,000
	Gabelli Asset Management, Inc.	02/10/99	105.000	17.500	1.225	750,000	400,000	375,000
	American Axle & Manufacturing Holdings, Inc.	01/28/99	119.000	17.000	1.190	500,000	500,000	535,000
	Muniholdings California Insured Fund IV, Inc.	01/26/99	129.000	15.000	0.000	7,000	55,000	35,000
	Muniholdings Florida Insured Fund IV	01/26/99	121.500	15.000	0.000	7,000	55,000	35,000
	Muniholdings Michigan Insured Fund, Inc.	01/26/99	60.375	15.000	0.000	7,000	55,000	35,000
	Muniholdings New Jersey Insured Fund III, Inc.	01/26/99	70.500	15.000	0.000	7,000	55,000	35,000
	Muniholdings New York Insured Fund III, Inc.	01/26/99	75.000	15.000	0.000	7,000	55,000	35,000
Merrill Lynch Far East, Ltd.	i-Cable Communications, Ltd.	11/18/99	218.700	27.000	1.350	0	0	0
Merrill Lynch International, Ltd.	ENEL Societa per Azioni	11/01/99	16281.720	45.227	0.769	1,000,000	1,800,000	1,300,000
	National Bank of Greece, S.A.	10/16/99	75.700	15.140	0.416	0	0	0
	Bord Telecom Eireann, P.L.C.	07/07/99	1382.475	15.990	0.320	0	0	0
Millenium Financial Group, Inc.	GenesisIntermedia.com, Inc.	06/14/99	17.000	8.500	0.680	150,000	225,000	175,000

Lead Underwriter	Issuer	Offer Date	Offering Amount (in Millions of Dollars)	Price per Share (in Dollars)	Underwriter Discount per Share (in Dollars)	Accounting Fees (in Dollars)	Legal Fees (in Dollars)	Printing Fees (in Dollars)
Morgan Stanley Dean Witter	McAfee.com Corp.	12/01/99	75.000	12.000	0.840	300,000	400,000	150,000
	NDS Group, P.L.C.	11/22/99	180.000	20.000	1.200	320,000	650,000	588,000
	CacheFlow, Inc.	11/18/99	120.000	24.000	1.680	400,000	400,000	300,000
	Agilent Technologies, Inc.	11/17/99	2160.000	30.000	1.275	3,000,000	2,500,000	500,000
	Metasolv Software, Inc.	11/17/99	95.000	19.000	1.330	325,000	430,000	320,000
	United Parcel Service, Inc.	11/09/99	5470.000	50.000	1.750	500,000	2,000,000	2,000,000
	KPNQwest, B.V.	11/08/99	915.640	20.810	0.730	0	0	0
	Tickets.com, Inc.	11/03/99	83.750	12.500	0.875	250,000	500,000	350,000
	Akamai Technologies, Inc.	10/28/99	234.000	26.000	1.820	350,000	450,000	150,000
	Triton PCS Holdings, Inc.	10/27/99	180.000	18.000	1.260	150,000	990,000	200,000
	Partner Communications Co., Ltd.	10/26/99	525.000	13.500	0.570	1,000,000	1,100,000	500,000
	Sycamore Networks, Inc.	10/21/99	284.050	38.000	2.660	300,000	300,000	150,000
	Martha Stewart Living Omnimedia, Inc.	10/18/99	129.600	18.000	1.260	500,000	1,000,000	150,000
	Women.com Networks, Inc.	10/14/99	37.500	10.000	0.700	325,000	500,000	200,000
	Illuminet Holdings, Inc.	10/07/99	74.100	19.000	1.330	200,000	250,000	150,000
	Breakaway Solutions, Inc.	10/05/99	42.000	14.000	0.980	500,000	400,000	150,000
	Digital Insight Corp.	09/30/99	52.500	15.000	1.050	250,000	350,000	250,000
	Internap Network Services Corp./WA	09/29/99	190.000	20.000	1.400	250,000	425,000	200,000
	Agile Software Corp.	08/19/99	63.000	21.000	1.470	225,000	400,000	150,000
	Silverstream Software, Inc.	08/17/99	48.000	16.000	1.120	300,000	300,000	175,000

Lead Underwriter	Issuer	Offer Date	Offering Amount (in Millions of Dollars)	Price per Share (in Dollars)	Underwriter Discount per Share (in Dollars)	Accounting Fees (in Dollars)	Legal Fees (in Dollars)	Printing Fees (in Dollars)
	Homestore.com, Inc.	08/04/99	140.000	20.000	1.400	750,000	500,000	500,000
	Lennox International, Inc.	07/28/99	159.375	18.750	1.265	225,000	400,000	200,000
	Drugstore.com, Inc.	07/27/99	90.000	18.000	1.260	200,000	350,000	300,000
	Chemdex Corp.	07/26/99	112.500	15.000	1.050	250,000	350,000	225,000
	Yankee Candle Co., Inc.	07/01/99	225.000	18.000	1.170	1,300,000	1,000,000	750,000
	Ask Jeeves, Inc.	06/30/99	42.000	14.000	0.980	350,000	400,000	200,000
	Ariba, Inc.	06/22/99	115.000	23.000	1.610	450,000	450,000	350,000
	Brocade Communications Systems, Inc.	05/24/99	61.750	19.000	1.330	250,000	300,000	175,000
	Redback Networks, Inc.	05/17/99	57.500	23.000	1.610	250,000	400,000	150,000
	Scient Corp.	05/13/99	60.000	20.000	1.400	300,000	700,000	165,000
	Copper Mountain Networks, Inc.	05/12/99	84.000	21.000	1.470	125,000	250,000	125,000
	Time Warner Telecom, Inc.	05/11/99	252.000	14.000	0.910	200,000	950,000	500,000
	Destia Communications, Inc.	05/05/99	65.000	10.000	0.700	100,000	500,000	300,000
	Marimba, Inc.	04/29/99	80.000	20.000	1.400	200,000	350,000	250,000
	Extreme Networks, Inc.	04/08/99	119.000	17.000	1.190	300,000	425,000	200,000
	Priceline.com, Inc.	03/29/99	160.000	16.000	1.120	575,000	850,000	700,000
	Vignette Corp.	02/18/99	76.000	19.000	1.330	250,000	400,000	200,000
	Healtheon Corp.	02/10/99	40.000	8.000	0.560	0	0	300,000
	Del Monte Foods Co.	02/04/99	300.000	15.000	0.900	600,000	650,000	625,000
	Delphi Automotive Systems Corp.	02/04/99	1700.000	17.000	0.789	2,000,000	1,650,000	3,020,000

Lead Underwriter	Issuer	Offer Date	Offering Amount (in Millions of Dollars)	Price per Share (in Dollars)	Underwriter Discount per Share (in Dollars)	Accounting Fees (in Dollars)	Legal Fees (in Dollars)	Printing Fees (in Dollars)
	Perot Systems Corp.	02/01/99	104.000	16.000	1.120	550,000	550,000	250,000
	NVIDIA Corp./CA	01/21/99	42.000	12.000	0.840	175,000	400,000	150,000
NationsBanc Montgomery Securities, Inc.	MKS Instruments, Inc.	03/29/99	91.000	14.000	0.980	150,000	150,000	120,000
	InfoSys Technologies, Ltd.	03/11/99	61.200	34.000	1.680	250,000	650,000	300,000
	Packaged Ice, Inc.	01/29/99	91.375	8.500	0.595	240,000	325,000	275,000
Needham & Co., Inc.	Collectors Universe, Inc.	11/05/99	24.000	6.000	0.420	225,000	155,000	200,000
	Datalink Corp.	08/06/99	19.500	7.500	0.525	180,000	150,000	45,000
Neidiger, Tucker, Bruner, Inc.	Cavion Technologies, Inc.	10/29/99	7.800	6.500	0.650	92,000	240,000	80,000
Network 1 Financial Securities	International Smart Sourcing, Inc.	04/23/99	5.750	4.500	0.450	200,000	270,000	150,000
Nomura Securities	Toyota Motor Corp.	09/28/99	455.925	60.790	2.110	3,300,000	1,000,000	500,000
Nutmeg Securities, Ltd.	Hi-Q Wason, Inc.	09/21/99	6.300	7.000	0.700	70,000	85,000	30,000
PaineWebber, Inc.	NetRatings, Inc.	12/08/99	68.000	17.000	1.190	275,000	425,000	150,000
	CompuCredit Corp.	04/22/99	60.000	12.000	0.810	150,000	350,000	225,000
	Eaton Vance California Municipal Income Trust	01/26/99	91.500	15.000	0.000	5,000	25,000	120,000
	Eaton Vance Florida Municipal Income Trust	01/26/99	54.750	15.000	0.000	25,000	25,000	120,000
	Eaton Vance Massachusetts Municipal Income Trust	01/26/99	33.000	15.000	0.000	5,000	25,000	120,000
	Eaton Vance Michigan Municipal Income Trust	01/26/99	27.000	15.000	0.000	5,000	25,000	120,000

Lead Underwriter	Issuer	Offer Date	Offering Amount (in Millions of Dollars)	Price per Share (in Dollars)	Underwriter Discount per Share (in Dollars)	Accounting Fees (in Dollars)	Legal Fees (in Dollars)	Printing Fees (in Dollars)
	Eaton Vance Municipal Income Trust	01/26/99	210.000	15.000	0.000	5,000	50,000	265,000
	Eaton Vance New Jersey Municipal Income Trust	01/26/99	58.500	15.000	0.000	5,000	25,000	120,000
	Eaton Vance New York Municipal Income Trust	01/26/99	69.750	15.000	0.000	5,000	25,000	120,000
	Eaton Vance Ohio Municipal Income Trust	01/26/99	36.000	15.000	0.000	5,000	25,000	120,000
	Eaton Vance Pennsylvania Municipal Income Trust	01/26/99	34.500	15.000	0.000	5,000	25,000	120,000
Paulson Investment Co., Inc.	AdStar.com, Inc.	10/06/99	15.500	15.500	1.066	145,500	250,000	50,000
	Careside, Inc.	06/16/99	15.000	7.500	0.460	200,000	500,000	300,000
	Dag Media, Inc.	05/12/99	8.125	6.500	0.585	180,000	175,000	75,000
Peacock, Hislop, Staley & Given, Inc.	First Coastal Bancshares	02/26/99	7.950	26.500	0.325	50,000	180,000	40,000
Piper Jaffray, Inc.	Microfinancial, Inc.	02/05/99	60.000	15.000	1.050	314,000	371,241	215,000
Prime Charter, Ltd.	Educational Video Conferencing, Inc.	02/23/99	14.400	12.000	0.840	125,000	500,000	75,000
Prudential Securities, Inc.	Loislaw.com, Inc.	09/29/99	55.720	14.000	0.980	200,000	250,000	245,000
	PurchasePro.com, Inc.	09/13/99	48.000	12.000	0.840	250,000	600,000	300,000
	bamboo.com, Inc.	08/25/99	28.000	7.000	0.490	300,000	350,000	400,000
	Lionbridge Technologies, Inc./DE	08/20/99	35.000	10.000	0.700	300,000	300,000	150,000

Lead Underwriter	Issuer	Offer Date	Offering Amount (in Millions of Dollars)	Price per Share (in Dollars)	Underwriter Discount per Share (in Dollars)	Accounting Fees (in Dollars)	Legal Fees (in Dollars)	Printing Fees (in Dollars)
	BigStar Entertainment, Inc./NY	08/02/99	25.000	10.000	0.700	115,000	375,000	340,000
	VaxGen, Inc.	06/29/99	40.300	13.000	0.910	100,000	300,000	200,000
Raymond James & Associates, Inc.	Insurance Management Solutions Group, Inc.	02/11/99	36.850	11.000	0.770	400,000	200,000	250,000
Redstone Securities Corp.	Rampart Capital Corp.	09/21/99	7.600	19.000	1.850	40,000	80,000	40,000
Robertson Stephens & Co.	C-bridge Internet Solutions, Inc.	12/17/99	64.000	16.000	1.120	200,000	400,000	125,000
	OnDisplay, Inc.	12/17/99	98.000	28.000	1.960	250,000	300,000	250,000
	eBenx, Inc.	12/10/99	100.000	20.000	1.400	125,000	275,000	125,000
	INTEREP National Radio Sales, Inc.	12/09/99	65.000	12.000	0.840	250,000	350,000	275,000
	Preview Systems, Inc.	12/08/99	79.800	21.000	1.470	200,000	400,000	225,000
	Digimarc Corp.	12/02/99	80.000	20.000	1.400	250,000	500,000	225,000
	iManage, Inc.	11/17/99	39.600	11.000	0.770	350,000	350,000	250,000
	Rudolph Technologies, Inc.	11/12/99	76.800	16.000	1.120	0	0	0
	Sage, Inc./CA	11/11/99	36.000	12.000	0.840	230,000	300,000	330,000
	iBasis, Inc.	11/10/99	108.800	16.000	1.120	400,000	450,000	175,000
	Predictive Systems, Inc.	10/27/99	72.000	18.000	1.260	150,000	500,000	250,000
	MCK Communications, Inc.	10/22/99	54.400	16.000	1.120	250,000	400,000	100,000
	NaviSite, Inc.	10/22/99	77.000	14.000	0.980	450,000	750,000	185,000
	Charlotte Russe Holding, Inc.	10/20/99	31.900	11.000	0.770	350,000	300,000	225,000
	iGo Corp.	10/14/99	60.000	12.000	0.840	325,000	450,000	275,000

Lead Underwriter	Issuer	Offer Date	Offering Amount (in Millions of Dollars)	Price per Share (in Dollars)	Underwriter Discount per Share (in Dollars)	Accounting Fees (in Dollars)	Legal Fees (in Dollars)	Printing Fees (in Dollars)
	QuickLogic Corp.	10/14/99	66.670	10.000	0.700	275,000	375,000	200,000
	ReSourcePhoenix.com	10/14/99	32.000	8.000	0.560	325,000	350,000	250,000
	SmartDisk Corp.	10/06/99	39.000	13.000	0.910	500,000	400,000	100,000
	Daleen Technologies, Inc.	10/01/99	49.200	12.000	0.840	250,000	300,000	200,000
	Vixel Corp.	10/01/99	77.400	18.000	1.260	350,000	500,000	150,000
Robinson Humphrey Co., Inc.	Netzee, Inc.	11/09/99	62.274	14.000	0.980	950,000	400,000	350,000
Rockcrest Securities, L.L.C.	bright-technologies.com, Inc.	08/13/99	9.450	5.250	0.525	50,000	100,000	75,000
Ryan Beck & Co.	National Medical Health Card Systems, Inc.	07/28/99	15.000	7.500	0.675	450,000	250,000	125,000
	Hudson City Bancorp, Inc.	05/14/99	716.163	10.000	0.160	185,000	1,000,000	1,300,000
	Village Financial Corp.	02/03/99	12.000	10.000	0.630	30,000	100,000	10,000
S.G. Cowen	Crossroads Systems, Inc.	10/19/99	67.500	18.000	1.260	280,000	350,000	225,000
	Cybergold, Inc.	09/22/99	45.000	9.000	0.630	200,000	350,000	200,000
S.G. Securities	Thomson Multimedia	11/02/99	476.607	22.588	0.542	0	0	0
Salomon Smith Barney	AirNet Communications Corp.	12/06/99	77.000	14.000	0.980	400,000	400,000	150,000
	TeleCorp PCS, Inc.	11/22/99	184.000	20.000	1.350	250,000	550,000	250,000
	DECS Trust VI	11/12/99	394.375	39.438	0.000	10,000	10,000	10,000
	Chartered Semiconductor Manufacturing, Ltd.	10/29/99	450.000	20.000	0.900	380,000	1,000,000	250,000
	Radio Unica Communications Corp.	10/18/99	109.440	16.000	1.120	300,000	300,000	600,000

Lead Underwriter	Issuer	Offer Date	Offering Amount (in Millions of Dollars)	Price per Share (in Dollars)	Underwriter Discount per Share (in Dollars)	Accounting Fees (in Dollars)	Legal Fees (in Dollars)	Printing Fees (in Dollars)
	Williams Communications Group, Inc.	10/01/99	680.800	23.000	1.320	1,800,000	1,800,000	1,700,000
	RADWARE, Ltd.	09/29/99	63.000	18.000	1.260	250,000	500,000	250,000
	Blackrock Pennsylvania Strategic Municipal Trust	08/24/99	26.250	15.000	0.675	25,000	115,000	68,500
	Blackrock Strategic Municipal Trust	08/24/99	100.500	15.000	0.675	25,000	150,000	111,000
	LaBranche & Co., Inc.	08/19/99	147.000	14.000	0.980	300,000	600,000	200,000
	Alliance Resource Partners, L.P.	08/16/99	147.250	19.000	1.210	475,000	1,350,000	450,000
	Blockbuster, Inc. (Viacom International)	08/10/99	465.000	15.000	0.713	1,500,000	2,000,000	1,200,000
	DECS Trust V	08/06/99	95.625	19.125	0.000	0	0	0
	Creo Products, Inc.	07/28/99	75.000	15.000	1.050	125,000	350,000	150,000
	Focal Communications Corp.	07/28/99	129.350	13.000	0.910	75,000	350,000	250,000
	Mail.com, Inc.	06/17/99	47.950	7.000	0.490	300,000	400,000	275,000
	Juno Online Services, Inc.	05/25/99	84.500	13.000	0.910	175,000	350,000	250,000
	Nuveen Dividend Advantage Municipal Fund	05/25/99	514.500	15.000	0.675	7,500	68,000	245,000
	Argosy Education Group, Inc.	03/08/99	28.000	14.000	0.980	335,000	365,000	100,000
	Corporate Executive Board Co.	02/22/99	155.557	19.000	1.330	450,000	900,000	350,000
	DECS Trust IV	02/10/99	162.500	13.000	0.000	10,000	10,000	75,000

Lead Underwriter	Issuer	Offer Date	Offering Amount (in Millions of Dollars)	Price per Share (in Dollars)	Underwriter Discount per Share (in Dollars)	Accounting Fees (in Dollars)	Legal Fees (in Dollars)	Printing Fees (in Dollars)
	Corinthian Colleges, Inc.	02/04/99	48.600	18.000	1.260	750,000	700,000	300,000
	MEDE America Corp.	02/01/99	60.000	13.000	0.910	800,000	500,000	300,000
Sandler O'Neill & Partners, L.P.	American Financial Holding Corp., Inc.	10/12/99	361.675	10.000	0.200	350,000	925,000	700,000
	Rome Bancorp, Inc.	08/12/99	14.864	7.000	0.420	100,000	350,000	80,000
	NCRIC Group, Inc.	05/10/99	12.880	7.000	0.580	175,000	250,000	37,000
	First Federal Bankshares, Inc.	02/12/99	35.650	10.000	0.400	75,000	270,000	370,000
	FloridaFirst Bancorp	02/12/99	23.512	10.000	0.440	125,000	240,000	125,000
	Mercer Insurance Group, Inc.	01/26/99	33.925	10.000	0.730	150,000	350,000	350,000
	Woronoco Bancorp, Inc.	01/13/99	48.300	10.000	0.290	80,000	225,000	350,000
Schneider Securities, Inc.	Pentastar Communications, Inc.	10/26/99	12.500	10.000	0.750	200,000	300,000	120,000
	Leisure Time Casinos & Resorts, Inc.	09/15/99	8.400	12.000	0.960	250,000	250,000	200,000
	MultiLink Telecommunications, Inc.	05/14/99	7.200	6.000	0.600	50,000	80,000	80,000
Scott & Stringfellow	U.S. Concrete, Inc.	05/25/99	30.400	8.000	0.560	2,380,000	850,000	250,000
SoundView Technology Group, Inc.	Telemate.net Software, Inc.	09/29/99	49.000	14.000	0.980	350,000	150,000	150,000
Spencer Edwards, Inc.	Pacific Softworks, Inc.	07/29/99	4.988	5.250	0.525	40,000	65,000	35,000
Strasbourger, Pearson, Tulcin, Wolff, Inc.	IT Staffing, Ltd.	06/02/99	5.500	5.000	0.500	70,000	150,000	75,000
Thomas Weisel Partners, L.L.C.	Z-Tel Technologies, Inc.	12/15/99	102.000	17.000	1.190	450,000	400,000	300,000

Lead Underwriter	Issuer	Offer Date	Offering Amount (in Millions of Dollars)	Price per Share (in Dollars)	Underwriter Discount per Share (in Dollars)	Accounting Fees (in Dollars)	Legal Fees (in Dollars)	Printing Fees (in Dollars)
	Exactis.com, Inc.	11/19/99	53.200	14.000	0.980	100,000	300,000	175,000
	Cysive, Inc.	10/15/99	56.950	17.000	1.190	100,000	200,000	250,000
	VitaminShoppe.com, Inc.	10/08/99	50.000	11.000	0.770	225,000	500,000	300,000
	Rubio's Restaurants, Inc.	05/21/99	33.075	10.500	0.740	200,000	250,000	150,000
Trident Securities	First Deposit Bancshares, Inc.	05/14/99	14.490	10.000	10.000	50,000	160,000	110,000
	FPB Financial Corp.	05/14/99	3.910	10.000	0.800	37,000	82,500	55,000
	Indian Village Bancorp, Inc.	05/14/99	5.865	10.000	0.650	65,000	95,000	70,000
	First Community Financial Corp./NC	05/07/99	31.050	15.000	0.490	75,000	155,000	100,000
	1ST State Bancorp, Inc.	02/11/99	47.610	16.000	0.430	125,000	160,000	150,000
	PFSB Bancorp, Inc.	02/11/99	7.475	10.000	0.720	70,000	160,000	75,000
Tucker Anthony Cleary Gull	Gaiam, Inc.	10/28/99	8.525	5.000	0.500	200,000	320,000	160,000
	HomeServices.com, Inc.	10/07/99	48.750	15.000	1.050	1,245,000	900,000	475,000
U.S. Bancorp Piper Jaffray, Inc.	Interspeed, Inc.	09/24/99	42.000	12.000	0.840	325,000	350,000	125,000
	Continuus Software Corp./CA	07/29/99	20.189	8.000	0.560	175,000	300,000	125,000
	BioMarin Pharmaceutical, Inc.	07/23/99	58.500	13.000	0.910	105,000	525,000	365,000
	Commtouch Software, Ltd.	07/13/99	48.000	16.000	1.120	400,000	900,000	300,000
	Internet.com Corp.	06/24/99	47.600	14.000	0.980	200,000	600,000	275,000
	Buca, Inc./MN	04/21/99	36.910	12.000	0.840	225,000	225,000	210,000

Lead Underwriter	Issuer	Offer Date	Offering Amount (in Millions of Dollars)	Price per Share (in Dollars)	Underwriter Discount per Share (in Dollars)	Accounting Fees (in Dollars)	Legal Fees (in Dollars)	Printing Fees (in Dollars)
Volpe Brown Whelan & Co.	ImageX.com, Inc.	08/26/99	21.000	7.000	0.490	300,000	500,000	150,000
	Be, Inc.	07/20/99	36.000	6.000	0.420	300,000	350,000	150,000
	COMPS.COM, Inc.	05/05/99	67.500	15.000	1.050	200,000	250,000	120,000
W.R. Hambrecht & Co.	Andover.net, Inc.	12/08/99	72.000	18.000	1.170	200,000	300,000	100,000
	Salon Internet, Inc.	06/22/99	26.250	10.500	0.525	300,000	400,000	250,000
	Ravenswood Winery, Inc.	04/08/99	10.500	10.500	0.420	25,000	85,000	60,000
Warburg Dillon Read, L.L.C.	eSpeed, Inc.	12/10/99	198.000	22.000	1.430	400,000	1,500,000	225,000
	HealthExtras, Inc.	12/09/99	60.500	11.000	0.770	125,000	400,000	115,000
Wedbush Morgan Securities	Keith Companies, Inc.	07/12/99	13.500	9.000	0.630	480,000	274,000	200,000
Wells Investment Securities, Inc.	Wells Real Estate Fund XII, L.P.	03/22/99	70.000	10.000	0.000	25,000	250,000	300,000
Westminster Securities Corp.	ForeignTV.com, Inc.	04/13/99	10.200	6.000	0.480	10,000	120,000	50,000
Westport Resources Investment Services, Inc.	Implant Sciences Corp.	06/23/99	7.500	7.500	0.750	272,140	250,000	100,000
	Immtech International, Inc.	04/26/99	10.000	10.000	0.990	125,000	280,000	70,000
Whale Securities Corp.	E-Cruiter.com, Inc.	12/07/99	14.700	6.000	0.530	95,000	255,000	125,000
	Internet Financial Services, Inc.	04/20/99	14.000	7.000	0.650	180,000	130,000	130,000
William Blair & Co.	Prism Financial Corp.	05/25/99	35.000	14.000	0.980	185,000	300,000	180,000
	OneSource Information Services, Inc.	05/19/99	43.632	12.000	0.840	275,000	270,000	125,000
	Cheap Tickets, Inc.	03/19/99	52.500	15.000	1.050	100,000	300,000	150,000

Partial data for Appendix 3 supplied by Global Securities Information, www.gsionline.com.

APPENDIX 4

TIMETABLE FOR TRADITIONAL IPO

TIMETABLE FOR AN INITIAL PUBLIC OFFERING

The following is a typical timetable for an IPO, which usually involves at least a four-month period:

Participants

Company:	CO
Underwriter:	U
Underwriters' Counsel:	UC
Company Counsel:	CC
Accountants:	A

Summary of Key Dates

Organizational Meeting	January 7
Filing with SEC	Week of February 24
Receive SEC Comments	Week of March 23
Commence Marketing	Week of March 30
Offering	Week of April 13
Closing	Week of April 20

Date	Description of Action	Responsibility
January 7	Organizational Meeting	All Hands
	1. Obtain name, address and phone number of all hands.	
	2. Discuss financial to be used in registration statement.	
	3. Assignment of responsibilities.	
	4. Selection of financial printer and bank note company.	

5. Statements by officers and directors before, during, and after registration period.

6. Discuss Board meetings, including dates, preparation of resolutions authority given to special or executive committees and power of attorney for interim amendment and price amendment.

7. Discuss Blue Sky considerations.

8. Discuss pre-filing press release.

9. Outline of prospectus.

10. Distribute underwriter's due diligence outline and document request.

11. Distribute internal Company projections.

12. Distribute last three years' financial statements.

13. Any other necessary action with respect to the offering:

   • Selection of directors

   • Status of audit

January 7–10	Company ceases further distribution of publicity relating to Company without prior clearance from CC and UC.	UC, CC
	Begin preparation of underwriting agreement and agreement among underwriters.	
Week of January 27	Begin review of corporate minute bookand other relevant documents to becompleted prior to filing.	UC, CC
	Prepare and distribute officer's and director's questionnaires to be returned prior to effective date.	CO, CC
	Contact printer, transfer agent and engraver.	CC
	Draft of Company financial distributed to working group.	CO, A

Week of February 3	Draft of S-1 and underwriting contracts distributed to working group.	CC, UC
	Drafting session/site visits.	All Hands
	U receive draft of financial on acquisitions.	CO, A
	Due diligence with accountants on Company financial and acquisition financial.	U, UC
Week of February 10	Due diligence.	U, UC
	Next draft of registration statement, underwriting contracts distributed to working group.	CO, CC
	Drafting session with focus on acquisition disclosure.	All Hands
	Due diligence on Company.	U, UC
Week of February 17	Third draft of registration statement distributed to working group.	CO, CC
	Third drafting session.	All Hands
Week of February 24	Prepare and circulate draft news release relating to initial filing.	CO, CC
	Print registration statement and related documents in form ready for filing andarrange for signing where necessary.	CO
	Registration statement (together with exhibits, certified check for filing fee, powers of attorney, certified resolutions) filed with Securities and Exchange Commission ("SEC") in Washington, D.C.	CC
	Requisite copies of registration statement, preliminary prospectus, and underwriting agreement, together with filing fee, to be mailed to National Association of Securities Dealers, Inc. ("NASD").	UC

1934 Act Registration Statement on Form 8-A filed with SEC acceleration requested to coincide with effectiveness of S-1.

Issue press release regarding filing.	CO, U
Begin Blue Sky qualification.	UC
Ascertain review status with SEC.	CC
Begin preparation of road show presentation and schedule.	CO, U

Week of March 23 and March 30

Receive SEC comments (assume 30-day review at SEC).	All Hands
File amendment #1 to S-1 and Acceleration Request. Prepare and clear press release relating to actual offering.	CO, U, CC
Underwriters' questionnaires returned.	U
Produce, execute, and deliver letter to SEC notifying of clearance by NASD of underwriting arrangements.	UC
SEC declares offering effective.	
Underwriters commence distribution to prospective syndicate underwriters of an invitation accompanied by:	U

1. Preliminary prospectus.
2. Proof of underwriting booklet.
3. Blue Sky memorandum.
4. Underwriters' questionnaire.
5. Underwriters' power of attorney.

Information meetings in various cities ("road show")	CO, U

Week of April 13	New Board of Special or Executive Committee designated by Board of Directors approves terms of offering, filing of price amendment and other necessary action.	CO
	Prepare prospectus.	All Hands
	CO and U agree on terms and other matters.	CO, U
	Sign up underwriters by power of attorney starting at 9:00 a.m. (EST).	U
	Issue press release with final terms of the offerings.	CO, U
	Advise Blue Sky commissions where required.	UC
	File prospectus.	CC
	File final documents with NASD.	UC
	Tombstone achievement is published.	U
Week of April 20	Closing	All Hands

Preparation of Documents	Initial Responsibility
1. Registration Statement	
a. Cover page, stabilization language, underwriting section, back page	U
b. Selected financial data	CO, A
c. Capitalization	CO, A
d. Reminder of prospectus, including summary page	CO, CC
e. Part II of Registration Statement	
• Item 14 Other expenses of Issuance and Distribution	CO, CC
• Item 15 Indemnification of Directors and Officers	CO, CC
• Item 16 Exhibits	CO, CC
• Item 17 Undertakings	CO, CC
2. Agreement among underwriters	U, UC
3. Underwriting agreement	U, UC
4. Underwriters' questionnaires	U, UC
5. Powers of attorney (for underwriters)	U, UC
6. Officers' and directors' questionnaires	CO, CC
7. Opinion of counsel for the Company	CC
8. Opinion of counsel for the Underwriters	UC
9. Accountant's comfort letter	A
10. Resolutions of Board of Directors special or executive committees	CO, CC
11. Press release—Initial filing	CC, U
• Offering	CC, U
12. Blue Sky memorandum	UC
13. Tombstone advertisement	U
14. Transmittal letters to SEC	CO, CC

EXCERPTS FROM REGULATION A OFFERING CIRCULAR OF REAL GOODS TRADING CORPORATION DATED JUNE 21, 1993

OFFERING CIRCULAR
June 21, 1993

REAL GOODS TRADING CORPORATION

(Exact name of Company as set forth in Charter)

Type of securities offered: Common Stock
Maximum number of securities offered: 600,000
Minimum number of securities offered: Not applicable
Price per share: $6.00
Total proceeds: If maximum sold: $3,600,000
                         If minimum sold: Not applicable
(For use of proceeds and offering expenses, see Question Nos. 9 and 10)

Is a commissioned selling agent selling the securities in this offering? [x] Yes [ ] No. A portion of the offering may be sold by selling agents.

If yes, what percent is commission of price to public? 6% of selling price of shares sold by selling agent to selling agents' customers; 3% of selling price of shares sold by selling agents to the Company's customers. The Company believes that it will sell a significant portion of the shares without commission.

Is there other compensation to selling agent(s)? [x] yes [ ] No
If one of the selling agents has sold at least $200,000 of securities, then that selling agent will be entitled to provide ongoing investor relations services for compensation related to the results of that agent's services and that selling agent will be reimbursed for certain due diligence costs.
(See question No. 22.)

Is there a finder's fee or similar payment to any person? [ ] Yes [x] No (See Question No. 22)

Is there an escrow of proceeds until minimum is obtained? [x] Yes [ ] No (See Question No. 26). Escrow applies only to residents of Mississippi and Texas.

Is this offering limited to members of a special group, such as employees of the Company or individuals? [ ] Yes [x] No (See Question No. 25)

Is transfer of the securities restricted? [ ] Yes [x] No (See Question No. 25)
INVESTMENT IN SMALL BUSINESS INVOLVES A HIGH DEGREE OF RISK, AND INVESTORS SHOULD NOT INVEST ANY FUNDS IN THIS OFFERING UNLESS THEY CAN AFFORD TO LOSE THEIR INVESTMENT IN ITS ENTIRETY. SEE QUESTION NO. 2 FOR THE RISK FACTORS THAT MANAGEMENT BELIEVES PRESENT THE MOST SUBSTANTIAL RISKS TO AN INVESTOR IN THIS OFFERING.

IN MAKING AN INVESTMENT DECISION INVESTORS MUST RELY ON THEIR OWN EXAMINATION OF THE PERSON OR ENTITY CREATING THE SECURITIES AND THE TERMS OF THE OFFERING, INCLUDING THE MERITS AND RISKS INVOLVED. THESE SECURITIES HAVE NOT BEEN RECOMMENDED BY ANY FEDERAL OR STATE SECURITIES COMMISSION OR REGULATORY AUTHORITY. FURTHERMORE, THE AUTHORITIES HAVE NOT PASSED UPON THE ACCURACY OR THE ADEQUACY OF THIS DOCUMENT. ANY REPRESENTATION TO THE CONTRARY IS A CRIMINAL OFFENSE.

THE U.S. SECURITIES AND EXCHANGE COMMISSION DOES NOT PASS UPON THE MERITS OF ANY SECURITIES OFFERED OR THE TERMS OF THE OFFERING. NOR DOES IS PASS UPON THE ACCURACY OR COMPLETENESS OF ANY OFFERING CIRCULAR OR SELLING LITERATURE THESE SECURITIES ARE OFFERED UNDER AN EXEMPTION FROM REGISTRATION; HOWEVER, THE COMMISSION HAS NOT MADE AN INDEPENDENT DETERMINATION THAT THESE SECURITIES ARE EXEMPT FROM REGISTRATION.

This Company:

[ ]	Has never conducted operations.
[ ]	Is in the development stage.
[x]	Is currently conducting operations.
[x]	Has shown a profit in the last fiscal year.
[ ]	Other (specify):
	(Check at least one, as appropriate)

SEE QUESTION NO. 2 FOR THE RISK FACTORS THAT MANAGEMENT BELIEVES PRESENT THE MOST SUBSTANTIAL RISKS TO AN INVESTOR IN THIS OFFERING.

This offering has been registered for offer and sale in the following states:

State	State file no.	Effective Date	State	State file no.	Effective Date
Alaska	93-01193	2/26/93	Montana	N.A.	4/8/93
Arizona	S-32568	6/14/93	Nebraska	246	2/24/93
California	5055173	2/25/93	Nevada	R93-29	*
Colorado	Exempt	2/26/93	New Hampshire	N.A.	4/1/99
Connecticut	SQ-22786	3/26/93	New Jersey	SR-7258	4/14/93
Delaware	N.A.	3/26/93	New Mexico	P930182	1/28/93
Dist. Columbia	Exempt	2/26/93	New York	S-25 81 45	2/26/93
Georgia	SEN930402128	2/5/93	North Carolina	799	*
Hawaii	N.A.	6/3/93	North Dakota	397	3/4/93
Idaho	43060	2/26/93	Ohio	81829	2/26/93
Illinois	9325199	3/19/93	Oklahoma	IA 354-93	*
Indiana	93004RQ	4/12/93	Oregon	93-00-11	3/1/93
Iowa	I-29155	3/29/93	Pennsylvania	92-12-14C	6/15/93
Kansas	93-S-1123	3/17/93	Rhode Island	N.A.	2/26/93
Kentucky	29062	5/24/93	South Carolina	RE6073	3/29/93
Louisiana	N.A.	3/26/93	South Dakota	N.A.	4/1/93
Maine	93-30-32	*	Texas	A 4179	4/13/93
Maryland	SR920675	3/18/93	Utah	2-6933/A17548-06	4/5/93
Massachusetts	930122-C	3/23/93	Vermont	1/22/93-01	*
Michigan	153236	*	Virginia	N.A.	*
Minnesota	R36415	*	Washington	C-35554	2/26/93
Mississippi	FI-93-02-002	4/30/93	West Virginia	N.A.	4/12/93
Missouri	N.A.	*			

N.A. Number not available

*State has not provided an effective date as of the date of this Offering Circular

TABLE OF CONTENTS

The Company 4
Risk Factors 4
Business and Properties 7
Offering Price Factors 22
Use of Proceeds 24
Capitalization. 29
Description of Securities 30
Plan of Distribution 31
Dividends, Distribution, and Redemptions 32
Officers and Key Personnel of the Company 33
Directors of the Company 35
Principal Shareowners. 37
Management Relationships, Transactions, and Remuneration 38
Litigation 39
Federal Tax Aspects. 39
Miscellaneous Factors 40
Management's Discussion and Analysis of Certain Relevant Factors 53

THIS OFFERING CIRCULAR CONTAINS ALL OF THE REPRESENTATIONS BY THE COMPANY CONCERNING THIS OFFERING, AND NO PERSON SHALL MAKE DIF-FERENT OR BROADER STATEMENTS THAN THOSE CONTAINED HEREIN. INVESTORS ARE CAUTIONED NOT TO RELY UPON ANY INFORMATION NOT EXPRESSLY SET FORTH IN THIS OFFERING CIRCULAR.

This Offering Circular, together with Financial Statements and other Attachments, con-sists of a total of 53 pages.

THE COMPANY

1. *Exact corporate name*: Real Goods Trading Corporation

State and date of incorporation: California, 18 June 1990. Successor to proprietorship founded in 1986.

Street address of principal office: 966 Mazzoni St., Ukiah, CA 95482

Company Telephone Number: (707)458-9292 *Fiscal year*: 1 April–31 March. Unless otherwise indicated, references to years are to the Company's fiscal year.

Person(s) to contact at Company with respect to offering: John Schaeffer, President

RISK FACTORS

2. List in the order of importance the factors which the Company considers to be the most substantial risks to an investor in this offering in view of all facts and circumstances or which otherwise make the offering one of high risk or speculative (i.e., those factors which constitute the greatest threat that the investment will be lost in whole or in part, or not provide an adequate return).

(1) Dependence on Chief Executive Officer

The Company's business is dependent, to a large extend, upon the services of John Schaeffer, founder, Chairman of the Board, President and Chief Executive Officer. The Company's operations could be adversely affected if, for any reason, Mr. Schaeffer ceases to be active in the Company's management. The Company has reduced this risk by retaining an experienced management team and insuring the life of Mr. Schaeffer for $1 Million. There can be no assurance, however, that the Company's efforts will be successful. John Schaeffer is 43 years old. For a description of the Company's management team, see questions 29-32.

(2) Competition

The mail order catalog business in the energy-efficiency and alternative energy fields is highly competitive. The Company competes primarily with other alternative mail order catalogs and secondarily with retail stores on the basis of price, breadth of product offerings, and information. Additionally, as alternative energy has become more accepted, some public utility companies are planning to enter the alternative energy production field. Wider public acceptance of alternative energy may draw additional competitors into the field. Several of the Company's competitors and potential competitors have financial resources superior to those of the Company. As these competitors enter the field, the Company's market share may fail to increase or may decrease despite the efforts of the Company to focus upon products unavailable elsewhere and to provide superior service. See 3(c) for further details on competition.

(3) Recent Sales Results

Catalog vendors such as the Company can control their growth to a greater extent than many other businesses by the rate at which they "prospect"—i.e., mail to rented lists. As the recent economic slowdown became clearer, the Company chose to reduce its prospecting, thus reducing the rate of sales growth from the substantial rate of prior years to a rate of 26% in fiscal 1992-93. While management believes that the Company can grow by prospecting, sales per catalog mailed to rented lists are generally materially lower than sales per catalog mailed to the Company's two-year buyer list. Thus, the cost of obtaining new customers may be greater than the cost of retaining current customers, and the productivity of new customers may be less than that of current customers.

(4) Weakening of Gasoline and Oil Prices

The Company believes that its sales are adversely affected by periods of decreased energy prices. The Company's products are less competitive in terms of price when energy prices are lower. Although the Company's sales have grown each year, during periods of high and low energy prices alike, any future declines in energy prices are likely to have an adverse effect upon sales.

(5) Reliance on Outside Supplies

It has been the Company's policy not to manufacture or assemble any of the products it sells. Management believes this policy provides the most flexibility to meet customer needs, while reducing the Company's risk and its need for capital investment. However, because of this policy, the Company may experience delays in production and delivery which are beyond its control and which may result in canceled orders, reduced sales, and other events which may negatively affect income.

(6) Limit on Dividends

The Company currently has a line of credit for $400,000 with National Bank of The Redwoods. The business loan agreement pertaining to the line of credit prevents the Company from paying any dividends without the written consent of the bank. The Company has no present intention to pay dividends.

(7) Shareowner's Lack of Ability to Direct Corporate Actions

If all the shares being offered are sold, the Company's founders will still own 75.6% of the total shares outstanding. As a result, new shareowners will lack the ability to affect corporate actions.

(8) Increases in the Cost of Mailing and Paper

The Company spends significant amounts of money on paper for the production of catalogs and on mailing the catalogs and packages to its customers. Although the Company is satisfied with the current paper prices, there is no assurance that paper prices will not increase in the future. The United States Postal Service, which handles approximately 20% of the Company's orders, has increased rates in the past and the Company believes that similar increases are likely for shipments handled by United Parcel Service, Federal Express, and the other carriers utilized by the Company. Higher costs of mailing, shipping, and paper would increase the Company's cost of doing business and, to the extent such increases cannot be passed on to customers in the form of higher product or handling and shipping costs, could adversely affect its earnings.

(9) Potential State Sales Tax Liability

Various states have increasingly taken the position that mail order companies are responsible for collecting sales or use tax with respect to sales made to residents in their states even if the only contact with such states is the mailing of catalogs and products into such states. In 1992 the U.S. Supreme Court ruled that it is up to the U.S. Congress to decide whether sales tax may be charged to out of state customers by mail order companies. A subcommittee of the Ways and Means Committee of the House of Representatives is conducting hearings on legislation to require mail order retailers to collect sales or use tax from out-of-state purchasers. Although the Company cannot predict the likelihood of passage of legislation or its final form, if such legislation is passed it could have an adverse effect upon the Company by increasing the Company's costs of doing business and by increasing the cost of its products to its customers.

(10) Reliance on Foreign Suppliers

In recent years, approximately 15% of the Company's inventory was manufactured by foreign sources. As a result, the Company is subject to the risks of doing business abroad, including adverse fluctuations in currency exchange rates (particularly those of the U.S. dollar against certain Asian currencies), changes in import duties or quotas and transportation, labor disputes and strikes. Although the Company has not experienced a material disruption of its operations to date, there is no assurance that this trend will continue. The occurrence of any one or more of the foregoing could adversely impact the Company's operations and earnings.

(11) Limited Trading Market

Since completion of its initial public offering in February 1992, a limited, order matching service has been provided in the company's shares by Mutual Securities, Inc./Cowles, Sabol & Co., Inc., a broker-dealer registered with the SEC and under certain state securities laws ("the broker"). The broker uses its best efforts to execute orders to buy and sell the Company's shares upon request. This arrangement is, however, subject to the availability of persons known to the broker to be interested in selling or buying, and agreement upon a price for any transactions. During the year ended March 31, 1993, approximately 34,000 shares were traded in this manner through the broker. The broker does not maintain an inventory of the Company's stock or otherwise function as a "market maker" in the stock. California residents may not be solicited to buy or to sell the stock, which decreases the effectiveness of this order matching procedure. There is no contract or other agreement between the broker and the Company, and the broker may choose to cease this function at any time.

Upon completion of this offering, the Company believes the additional registered securities broker-dealers will execute orders to buy and sell the Company's shares and that they may function as "market makers," maintaining an inventory and soliciting orders to buy and sell the shares. If substantially all the shares being offered are sold, the Company believes it will meet the standards for having trading information about its shares quoted on the NASDAQ basic listing/"Small-Cap issues" market, and it will apply for that status.

The Company's common stock has been accepted for trading on the Pacific Stock Exchange, through its proposal "SCOR" listing program pending approval of that program by the Securities and Exchange Commission. There can be no assurance of that approval. Upon approval from the Securities and Exchange Commission and upon the Company's registration under the Securities Exchange Act of 1934 and provided the Company continues to meet the applicable Pacific Stock Exchange requirements, the Company believes that its common stock will be listed on the Pacific Stock Exchange.

There is no assurance that any broker-dealers, including the broker, will maintain a market at any time or that the Company's trading information will be included in the NASDAQ system. There may be no organized trading market for the Company's common stock. Even if there is a trading market established, the ability of a shareowner to sell his or her shares will depend on the existence of persons interested in buying shares. There can be no assurance that people will be interested in buying the Company's stock.

(12) Dilution

Investors in the Company's shares being offered will pay a price per share considerably in excess of the cash originally invested by the founders, John and Nancy Schaeffer. In 1986, the Schaeffers began the business with $3,000 of capital. At March 31, 1993, the Company's "net tangible book value" (tangible assets of the Company, less its liabilities) was $1,154,600, equivalent to $0.41 per share outstanding at that date. After giving effect to the offering, assuming the sale of 600,000 shares at $6 per share, the net tangible book value will be $1.24 per share. This is a dilution in net tangible book value to investors who buy shares in this offering of $4.76 per share. (See Item 7 of this Offering Circular for a description of the offering price factors and the consideration for shares issued to the founders.)

(13) Erosion of Revenues per Catalog over Time

While the Company is currently experiencing a rate 50% over the mail order industry average for revenues per catalog mailed, there can be no assurances that this high rate will continue. As the Company expands its mailing plan, it is likely that the revenues per catalog sent will decrease.

(14) Limited Retail Store Experience

The Company's marketing plan calls for the opening of three retail stores. The Company has limited experience with retail stores. There can be no assurance that the first store will be successful or, if it is successful, that other retail stores will be successful.

(15) New Construction

If a substantial number of the shares offered hereby are sold, the Company intends to use a substantial portion of the proceeds to construct a headquarters/warehouse/demonstration site. The Company does not have significant experience with projects of this magnitude and there can be no assurance that the Company will not experience material adverse effects such as cost overruns and delays.

Note: In addition to the above risks, businesses are often subject to risks not foreseen or fully appreciated by management. In reviewing this Offering Circular potential investors should keep in mind other possible risks that could be important.

BUSINESS AND PROPERTIES

3. *With respect to the business of the Company and its properties:*

   (a) *Describe in detail what business the Company does and proposes to do, including what products or goods are or will be produced or services that are or will be rendered.*

The Company's business is the sale of products and equipment that facilitate "independent living." This market consists of two primary segments—alternative energy and conservation. These products are principally marketed through the Company's catalogs and its Alternative Energy Sourcebook. Adjacent to its headquarters, the Company also has a showroom from which it makes retail sales.

Alternative Energy Market

Approximately 51% of the Company's business is generated from the alternative energy market. The Company believes it is the largest and oldest mail order supplier of alternative energy and energy-sensible products in the world. Through its catalogs (2,547,750 mailed in fiscal 1992-93) and its Alternative Energy Sourcebook™ (discussed later), it offers power systems for remote homes using alternative sources of energy including photovoltaic (solar-electric), hydro-electric, and wind-electric, as well as emerging alternative technologies like hydrogen fuel cells, and a new generation of photovoltaic cells. The Company endeavors to provide a full array of appliance systems components and technical service, for every aspect of living away from power lines. These products include battery storage systems, power conversion devices, charge controllers, meters, gasoline generators, low voltage water pumping systems, solar and propane gas water heaters, refrigerators, solar cooling devices, composting toilets, and a wide variety of low-voltage household appliances.

The traditional market for these power systems has been remote homes in excess of one quarter mile from the power companies' lines in the USA and, to a substantially lesser extent, in remote villages in third world countries. Foreign sales account for approximately 2% of the Company's business. The Company has customers in over 100 countries. The Company also provides solar-electric systems for governmental agencies (approximately 2% of its business) including the United States Interior Department, the Bureau of Land Management, the U.S. Forest Service, and occasionally the military.

Conservation Market

In the past several years, the Company's mail order catalog has also been successful at marketing energy saving and conservation products to urban and suburban dwellers. This "conservation market" represents approximately 49% of the Company's business. These products include a full spectrum of energy-efficient lighting including outdoor and solar lighting; water saving devices including low flow showerheads, low-flush toilets, and faucet aerators; recycled paper products including toilet paper, paper towels, and facial tissue; and products used in recycling such as canvas and string bags, recycling bins, and paper recycling devices. To this same clientele, the Company markets non-toxic household products, water and air purification devices, magnetic radiation meters, and a large selection of solar toys, gifts, T-shirts and books.

The Company puts a great emphasis on education and produces and sells a wide variety of educational materials. Recognizing that the alternative energy field is relatively new and that misinformation is common, the Company publishes and periodically revises its Alternative Energy Sourcebook, a 500+ page textbook, that also includes nearly all of the products that the Company sells.

The AE Sourcebook is currently distributed by Ten Speed Press in Berkeley, California, which sells the book in 44 English speaking countries. The United States retail price is $16. The Company sells approximately 65,000 Sourcebooks annually. The Company also markets many books on specific aspects of alternative energy and conservation within its quarterly catalogs.

Retail Locations

The Company operates a showroom for its products at its headquarters in Ukiah. The showroom has become increasingly popular over the last year as, with little advertising, it has become known to mail order buyers and local shoppers alike. In-store customer traffic increased from an average of 10 sales per day in early 1990 to over 30 sales per day currently. In calendar 1990, showroom sales of $235,000 accounted for 5% of the Company's revenues. In fiscal 1993, showroom sales more than doubled to $608,448. Because of the showroom's success and many inquiries regarding retail representation, the Company is evaluating options for retail expansion. The company has tested consumer response to its merchandise premise with an educational kiosk located in two locations of a prominent "green" retailer, Terra Verde Trading Company of New York and Santa Monica. Considerable research will be devoted to this area as the Company seeks the best way to make its merchandise more available to consumers. The Company has entered into a letter of intent to acquire a retail location in Wisconsin.

The subject of retail expansion strategies has occupied significant management resources in the past year. In studying in great detail the geographic distribution of mail order sales, the San Francisco Bay Area has emerged as a prime market for opening a retail outlet. The Company will not open a store until other components of its strategy are in place and the results from retail tests, such as the one being conducted with Terra Verde, are fully understood. Background research is expected to be complete in mid calendar 1993. Additional expansion activities currently under consideration include:

– Establishing a destination retail location in conjunction with a new facility at a yet-to-be-determined site in Mendocino County, California, near the present Company headquarters.

– Opening three prototype retail locations that can serve as models for either future expansion or franchising.

(b) *Describe how these products or services are to be produced or rendered and how and when the Company intends to carry out its activities. If the Company plans to offer a new product(s), state the present stage of development, including whether or not a working prototype(s) is in existence. Indicate if completion of development of the product would require a material amount of the resources of the Company, and the estimated amount. If the Company is or is expected to be dependent upon one or a limited number of suppliers for essential raw materials, energy or other items, describe. Describe any major existing supply contracts.*

The Company currently purchases from a vendor base of more than 200 suppliers. The Company's largest single product area is photovoltaic products. While there are many suppliers of photovoltaic modules, the Company has chosen to limit the majority of its purchases to the two with whom it has developed long term relationships. Because some of the products in the alternative energy field are new, the number of suppliers for these products is limited and the Company is dependent upon these manufacturers to perform according to their promises. The Company generally does not need to enter into long-term contracts with its suppliers as the merchandise is most often readily available. The Company currently has six-month, non-binding, open purchase orders with Carrizo Solar in Albuquerque, NM to purchase a large quantity of recycled photovoltaic modules and twelve-month, non-binding, open purchase orders with Solar Electric Specialties of Willits, California for purchase of Siemens photovoltaic modules. The Company has a 90-day return arrangement with its vendors for any of its products that are returned from customers in original condition. The Company has historically experienced product returns of 5-6% which management believes is not substantial in the industry.

The Company sources new products for its periodic catalogs through a variety of methods including attending specialized trade shows domestically and internationally, studying market trends, and evaluating the products of the many vendors that solicit the Company. The Company believes it is unique in gathering many new products and new product development ideas from its customers. It offers its customers a $25 reward form coming up with new products that it later includes in its catalogs and a $500 reward for product development ideas that the Company can have manufactured to later include in its product offerings on a proprietary basis.

The Company has pursued several co-development efforts with other companies. A product called the Solar SunShed has been offered for sale beginning in the fall of 1992. This effort took an existing garden shed engineered and marketed by the Gardeners' Supply Company of South Burlington, VT and solarized it with components sourced by Real Goods. The first units were shipped in September, 1992. The rationale of this project is to create an affordable (less than $2500) independently-powered structure that can be purchased by a person interested in energy independence, but who is not ready or willing to commit to living in a remote home location. It is expected that the market niche for this product will take several years to fully develop. The Company believes that the "Solar SunShed" will begin to bring the two markets of conservation and alternative energy together and enhance its overall product lines to both markets. There can be no assurance that the "Solar SunShed" will be successful.

A second co-development project has taken place in the information field with Chelsea Green Publishing Company of Port Mills, VT. In this project a reference book on small wind systems has been customized to Real Goods specifications. Written by an acknowledged expert in the field (Paul Gipe), the book fills a conspicuous gap in the energy marketplace. The Company has sold more than a thousand copies of the best available wind generation reference, which contains information that is in some cases twenty years out of date. Not only will this Real Goods Guide to Small Wind Systems update the body of knowledge and give the Company a new product to sell, but it should also convince more people of the viability of small wind systems, thereby stimulating the need for equipment that the Company sells as well.

Both co-development projects have led to cross-marketing opportunities. In both instances the Company has been able to share consumerships with its co-venture partner, a technique that provides an extremely efficient and low-cost source of new inquiries and buyers.

(c) *Describe the industry in which the Company is selling or expects to sell its products or services and, where applicable, any recognized trends within the industry. Describe that part of the industry and the geographic area in which the business competes or will compete. Indicate whether competition is or is expected to be by price, service, or other basis. Indicate (by attached table if appropriate) the current or anticipated prices or price ranges for the Company's products or services, or the formula for determining prices, and how these prices compare with those of competitors' products or services, including a description of any variations in product or service features. Name the principal competitors that the Company has or expects to have in its area of competition. Indicate the relative size and financial and market strengths of the Company's competitors in the area of competition in which the Company is or will be operating. State why the Company believes that it can effectively compete with these and other companies in its area of competition.*

The Company markets its products and services to two distinct, but closely related, markets. The first and traditional market consists of individuals who own or are purchasing a home away from utility company grid power and who want to produce their own electricity from alternative sources of energy. This market encompasses a wide range of humanity, ranging from people already living off the power grid, professionals who own second homes, suburban homeowners who are experimenting with independent energy, and even third world villages to whom independent power is a necessity. The largest geographic concentrations of this remote home market in the United States that the Company targets are in Northern California, Washington State, Colorado, Alaska, Hawaii, Oregon, upstate New York, and New England. There are also significant marketing opportunities in the South Pacific islands, East Africa, Indonesia, Central and South America, the Middle East, Mexico, and the Caribbean.

In this remote power market the Company competes primarily through its service capability and secondarily through competitive pricing. The Company writes and updates its Alternative Sourcebook frequently. The 500+ page Sourcebook is the primary education and marketing vehicle that the Company uses to present its products. The Sourcebook is recognized as a comprehensive source of information on alternative energy systems and products. The Sourcebook is complemented by the Company's technical staff, who are fully trained in energy system sizing and who specialize in designing solar systems of all sizes. In order to stay price competitive, the Company maintains competitive research, and periodically offers sales or discounts on selected merchandise. The Company generally sells its alternative energy products at a 30% profit margin in an effort to remain competitive.

The Company has several competitors in the alternative energy field. There are only two publicly traded alternative energy companies with which the Company competes. Photocomm, Inc. of Scottsdale, AZ, and Solar Electric Engineering of Santa Rosa, CA. Photocomm's revenues are approximately $10 million and Solar Electric's are approximately $1.7 million. Both are operating at a substantial loss. Other competitors include Alternative Energy Engineering of Redway, CA, with estimated retail sales of approximately $1 million, Backwoods Solar Electric, of Sandpoint, ID, with estimated retail sales of approximately $600,000 and Sunelco, of Hamilton, MT with estimated retail sales of approximately $1 million. The Company estimates the retail remote home market to be a $15-25 million per year business which is growing steadily at a rate of 10% per year. The Company now holds approximately an 18% market share. The Company believes that it enjoys a strong reputation within the industry.

The second market that the Company addresses is the energy conservation and ecological product market. These products include energy saving light bulbs, water conservation supplies, recycled and recycling products, water purification, toys, books, and gifts. This market is distinct from the previously discussed alternative energy market in that its purchasers primarily live in urban and suburban areas. The "Green Market Alert," an environmental trade publication, estimates that this is currently a $34 billion per year market, only a small portion of which ($45 million) is sold via mail order. The leading competitor, with catalog sales of approximately $7 million, is Seventh Generation of Colchester, VT. After several years of dramatic increases, their sales growth has slowed in the past two years. Other competitors include Save Energy Co., of San Francisco, CA with annual sales of approximately $1 million, and several other very small catalogers. Industry observers, as reported in the Green Market Alert, project that sales of conservation products via catalog channels will triple by 1996. The environmental segment is the more volatile of the two markets. A recent Roper Organization study on environmentalism commissioned by S.C. Johnson and Son pointed out that 78% of adults say that our nation must "make a major effort to improve the quality of our environment." At the moment, recycling appears to be the most rapidly growing pro-environmental behavior. Between March 1989 and February 1990, the share of Americans who say they regularly recycle bottles and cans rose from 41% to 46%, and the share who regularly recycle newspapers rose from 20% to 26%.

The Roper study broke down the American population into five basic segments: True-Blue Greens, Greenback Greens, Sprouts, Grousers, and Basic Browns. The first three market segments comprise the primary target for the environmental and energy conservation segment of the Company's market.

True-Blue Greens (11% of the adult population) have strong environmental concerns and are leaders in the environmental movement. 59% regularly recycle newspapers. *Greenback Greens* (11% of the adult population) are most will to pay more money for environmentally safe products. They will pay 20% more for environmentally safe products, compared with 7% for the general public. *Sprouts* (26% of the adult population) are the all important "swing" group that represent a future environmental target market. The Company competes in this market by using consumer education and quality service, as the market is not as yet overly price sensitive. The Company is widely considered one of the originators in what is known as the "socially responsible marketplace" and has the reputation of being thoughtful and environmentally responsible.

A number of new small competitors have emerged in the market place, as well as established companies newly selling into this market, such as the Sharper Image, Over 250 "green" stores, selling earth-friendly merchandise, have opened in the past two years. The Company believes that its strength lies in its complete array of alternative energy products, backed by full technical service and its full roster of communications vehicles, such as the Alternative Energy Sourcebook. As mentioned before, the Company sells alternative energy hardware products at a lower margin (approximately 30%) and sells its gift, educational, and energy conservation items at a higher margin (approximately 50%) as these items are typically sold at higher margins by the competition. The Company believes that most of its products are priced at or below the competition's price. The Company's average margin for the period of 1 April 1992 through 31 March 1993 was 45.3%, which is on the upper end of the mail order industry average, which (according to Robert Morris Associates' 1992 report on Retailers—Catalog & Mail-Order Houses) ranges from 38.5% to 43.0%. The Company has been averaging 39.74% gross profit margin (60.26% cost of goods sold), 18% for publicity expenses, 23% for operating expenses, and 1-5% pre-tax profit over the last several years. The range on the margin percentage varies between 38-43.6%, and the margin has improved in each of the past three years.

Note: Because this Offering Circular focuses primarily on details concerning the Company rather than the industry in which the Company operates or will operate, potential investors may wish to conduct their own separate investigation of the Company's industry to obtain broader insight in assessing the Company's prospects.

(d) *Describe specifically the marketing strategies the Company is employing or will employ in penetrating its market or in developing a new market. Set forth in response to Question No. 4 below, the timing and size of the results of this effort which will be necessary in order for the Company to be profitable. Indicate how and by whom its products or services are or will be marketed (such as by advertising, personal contact by sales representatives, etc.), how its marketing structure operates or will operate and the basis of its marketing approach, including any market studies. Name any customers that account for, or based upon existing orders will account for, a major portion (20% or more) of the Company's sales. Describe any major existing sales contracts.*

As one of the original "green" marketers, the Company believes it has an advantage in the market, but one that will become more fragile as the market becomes more saturated. The Company believes its position can be maintained and strengthened by enhancing its credibility and positive image in the alternative energy field by several marketing strategies.

The goals of these marketing strategies are to enhance the Company's position as an industry leader, to actively communicate the position to the consumer, and to convince the consumer that the Company can satisfy all of his/her energy saving equipment needs, thereby committing the customer to Real Goods by isolating him/her from other competitors.

The tactics that the Company will use to achieve its marketing goals are as follows:

1. Create educational vehicles that expose the consumer to the critical issues of energy and environment. These efforts have included.

    – The Declaration of Energy Independence, a document that the Company authored, that more than 20,000 consumers signed in conjunction with the first declared "Off the Grid Day," a national holiday when people were asked to disconnect from the power grid. This year for Off the Grid Day, the company is planning a National Home tour of alternatively-powered dwellings. This is scheduled for October 1993 and will give local media a convenient way of reporting on the application of energy independence in their particular region.

    – Establishment of the "Institute For Independent Living." The Institute provides interactive seminars in energy independence. Begun in 1992, each available session of the Institute is sold out, encouraging the company to expand its schedule for 1993, appoint a full-time "Dean," establish a more permanent campus, and to begin the creation of specifically designed educational materials. Institute students convene at the Company form all around the country to learn about all aspects of independent living. Students receive intensive hands-on training on the sizing and installation of photovoltaic systems. The Company has offered six weekend and one week-long seminars in 1993 to accommodate 140 students. As of the date of this Offering Circular, all workshops are nearly sold out. Since this is a new program for the Company, there can be no assurance that it will be successful.

    – Creation of a "Real Goods For Real Kids on Real Planets^{TM}" program to promote energy awareness among young people. This program enables local nonprofit, environmentally oriented organizations to raise funds by selling planet-friendly products and letting Real Goods handle the messy mechanics of order fulfillment. Four prototype organizations have signed on to date, and based on their experience the program will be fine-tuned and expanded in 1993. Preliminary discussions have already begun with several large children's organizations. Since this is a new program for the Company, there can be no assurances that it will be successful.

    – Co-publication (with Chelsea Green Publishing) of the *Real Goods Guide to Small Wind Systems* (*described previously*). Chelsea Green has published some of the nation's most-respected environmental books, including BEYOND THE LIMITS and THE MAN WHO PLANTED TREES. A roster of education titles related to independent living is planned for joint publication by the two companies, giving Real Goods new products to sell, exposure of its name in book stores, and educational properties that facilitate the case of independent living.

    – In addition to these activities Real Goods is an active participant in energy-related fairs, forums, and exhibitions. The Company sponsored the Tour de Sol (a race from Albany to Boston of solar-electric vehicles), displayed at Eco-Expose in Los Angeles, Denver, New York, and San Francisco, co-sponsored the Solar Energy Expo and Rally, and attended numerous conferences related to socially active businesses.

    – Real Goods acquired the direct marketing assets of a competitor, Rising Sun Enterprises of Boulder, CO. Among these was an informative booklet that the Company has renamed "The Book of Light" and re-issued under its own name. It is hoped that this piece can be further refined and used as the basis for a co-publishing project with the Chelsea Green Publishing Company.

2. Communicate directly to the consumer via:

– **The Real Goods Color Catalog**. This piece continued to improve in 1993, with new product, new photography, and a design "face-lift" to help clarify merchandise categories.

– **The Real Goods News**. This three-times-a-year publication is the Company's journal of independent living.

In addition to products for sale, the News contains editorial features, columns, staff and customer profiles, and the popular Reader's Forum, where Real Goods customers are given their turn on the soap box to express their views about the Company, the government, or the environment.

– **The Real Stuff Newsletter**. This simple newsletter is for subscribers and shareowners only and offers a behind-the-scenes look at what's going on at the Company. It also offers special buying opportunities on closeouts and overstocks and has proved to be extremely profitable and helpful to consumers.

– **The Alternative Energy Sourcebook**. This 500+ page book represents the core of the Company's offering. The Company believes that it is very well regarded in the industry as the definitive text on alternative energy systems. It offers guidance to the novice on conception, feasibility, and design of alternative power systems as well as a full compendium of accessories and products for every aspect of independent living. The Company prints up to 75,000 **Sourcebooks** annually, and distributes the book in over 100 countries. The book is updated more or less annually.

– **Media Advertising.** The Company offers its goods and services as well as its Alternative Energy Sourcebook to the general public via small space advertising in relevant periodical publications such as Garbage Magazine, Harrowsmith Magazine, the Utne Reader, E. Magazine, the Mother Earth News, Home Power Magazine and other avenues that reach prospective customers.

– **Public Relations Programs**. The Company sends regular press releases to its file of environmentally-oriented media. Two recent programs that have been successful have been the "Real Relief" program offering special discounts and priority shipment to victims of natural disasters like Hurricane Andrew and Iniki (in Florida and Hawaii). For Christmas a "Solar Sultan's" package, offering a complete package for independent living anywhere in the world, attracted great media interest.

– An experimental mailing, in the Fall of 1992, focusing on an expanded roster of educational materials related to environmental fields, is being tested to see if more targeted merchandising efforts hold promise for further segmentation of the customer population. More sophisticated segmentation of the market will be key to the Company's abilities to meet its growth objectives. It will allow the Company to mail more efficiently and environmentally responsibly and benefit its relationship with its customers.

3. Establish Owners' Programs that promote customer loyalty.

The Company's primary marketing vehicle for penetrating its market is its catalogs. The Company mails its main color catalog six times per year: January, April, June, August, September, and October. Typically, the October mailing is the largest and encompasses the holiday season, with this one catalog accounting for as much as 35% of annual revenues. The Company mails its "Real Good News" three times each year to its two-year buyer file and to its recent inquiries. The Company mails its "Real Stuff" newsletter four times each year to its shareowners and subscribers. In fiscal 1992-93 the Company mailed 2,547,750 catalogs, an average of 280,000 catalogs in each mailing, compared to 1.6 million in the previous fiscal year. Of these, approximately 1,588,000 went to the Company's own mailing list and the balance went to highly targeted prospective customers. The Company's mailing list consists of a 100,000 customer two-year buyer file (customers who have ordered within 24 months), 10,000 subscribers (explained later), and approximately 150,000 inquiries in the last 24 months. The Company mails to each subscriber a minimum of thirteen times per year, and to each buyer and inquirer a minimum of nine times per year. Prospective customers come from mailing lists rented from competitors and market segments that have been shown to be highly profitable in the past. The rate of return for the catalogs the Company has sent out far exceeds the average for direct mail companies. All Company marketing vehicles are used to aggressively promote sales of the Alternative Energy Sourcebook, which portrays the full range of the Company's products. The Sourcebook generally produces an average order over ten times that of the catalogs.

The Company also rents its mailing list to other non-competitive, responsible, and environmentally-conscious companies for mailings.

All shareowners on the Company's records receive 5% discounts on all purchases from the Company. The Company reserves the right to change or discontinue the program in the future.

The **Alternative Energy Sourcebook** is unique to the Company and is not easily duplicated by competitors. It enhances the overall credibility of the Company and is featured prominently in all catalogs and media ads. The Company distributes the Sourcebook through Ten Speed Press, of Berkeley, CA and will continue to aggressively promote the book through energy writers, environmental columnists, and other mail order catalogs that feature energy and environmental goods.

The Company is continuing its innovative Subscriber Program that it began in 1989 in response to the many very committed customers that it found in its customer base. These subscribers tend to take their energy independence more seriously. They're committed to the Company as their energy saving resource and the Company returns that commitment. The Company solicits a one-time fee from Subscribers, who receive the Company's Subscriber Newsletter, **The Real Stuff**, four times every year which contains special pricing, close out bargains, customer profiles, and lots of news. Subscribers get a free copy of the **Alternative Energy** Sourcebook and other benefits that return the initial investment in future savings. Subscribers have an average order 60% higher than the average customer and order at a frequency rate up to 50% greater. Subscribers tend to be loyal to the company and their support will be strongly targeted in the future. Expanding the Subscriber base and finding new ways to reward these customers for their loyalty will continue to be high priorities for the Company.

The Company conducted a customer survey of 2,000 of its customers (350 subscribers and 1650 general) in March of 1991 that confirmed its beliefs about the uniqueness of the subscriber customer base, as well as solidified its understanding of its general customer base. Some of the analyses from that survey are described in the charts on the next page. The average customer (non-subscriber and subscriber) purchased $169 worth of merchandise from the Company and placed an average of two orders. This average order is about three times higher than comparable direct mail companies which typically have an average order of $40 to $60. However the subscribers purchased an average of $469 with three orders and non-subscribers purchased an average of $121 with two orders. Further, subscribers showed the strongest interest and purchase intent for practical equipment-oriented product categories. The Company's customer survey revealed that the typical customer is 40.8 years old, has a median annual income of $38,450, (both fairly typical), but the Company's average customer has a far higher level of education than the

US average, with nearly 95% having attended college and a full 44% having attended graduate school.

The Company has collected its information on customer profile, customer demographics, past sales results, and industry trends into an in-house database. The information contained in this database guides the Company in its decisions regarding retail expansion, mail order strategies, and even creative design. The purpose of this intelligence-gathering effort is to lay the foundation for future growth.

Because the Company sells in the environmental marketplace, many of its customers are by nature counter-cultural in habits. They resist the proliferation of mail order materials and eschew traditional means of shopping (such as shopping malls). The Company hopes that from the creation of its database, the capabilities of its new computer system, and an intelligent strategic overview it will be able to reduce waste circulation by targeting its communications vehicles more precisely to the preferences of the specific audience.

Nine separate consumer profiles, each with corresponding strategy, have been created. In the coming year the communication vehicles will be altered so that content and style are suitable for a specific purpose, and will be phased into operation. Through the use of such database marketing, the Company hopes to be able to identify consumer segments that can then be grown through more traditional means of rental lists and media advertising.

Demographic Analysis From the Company's
March 1991 Customer Survey

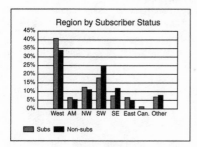

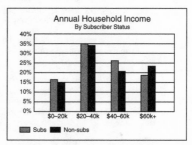

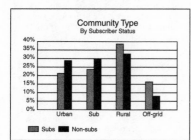

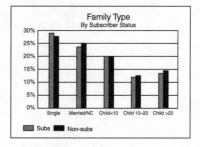

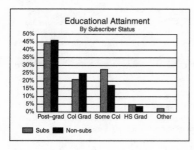

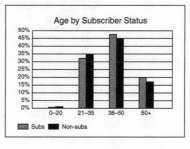

The Company's public relations efforts have been intensified in recent years, and will continue to be an important part of the overall marketing mix. The number of inquiries increased from 2,000 per month to over 10,000 per month from 1990 to 1993. This has been accomplished largely on the development of innovative programs that have been aggressively communicated to the environmental press.

The following programs are typical of the Company activities that have drawn attention from the media to the Company's overall mission of promoting independent living:

– **"Real Relief"** was spawned in the wake of natural disasters Hurricanes Andrew and Iniki, to provide alternative energy equipment to people living in federal disaster areas. In addition to promoting customer loyalty, the Company is experiencing positive feedback from the general public for its efforts during a time of need.

– **The Billion Pound Goal** describes the effort of the Company to reduce the production of greenhouse gases through the actions of its staff and customers. As of May 1, 1993, the Company believes that its customers have prevented the production of over 500 million pounds of carbon dioxide from being spewed into the atmosphere, putting it more than 50% ahead of schedule toward its billion pound goal.

– **The National Independent Home Tour** (planned for October 16, 1993) will give local journalists a chance to observe, personally, the way alternative energy lifestyles are being lived in their locale. Because this is a new program, there can be no assurance that it will be successful.

– **The Declaration of Energy Independence**, authored by the Company, was delivered to White House Officials by Presidential candidate, Jerry Brown.

These and many other efforts have kept Real Goods prominently in the public eye. Press coverage has included a segment on CBS's "This Morning," several mentions in INC. Magazine, the New York Times and The Wall Street Journal. Numerous radio interviews, including several on National Public Radio, and articles in smaller media have produced a continual flow of new inquirers interested in Real Goods. Most recently the Company was cited by a prominent consumer magazine as one of the best places to buy energy-efficient lighting. The Company believes it uses its small media budget efficiently. Magazines have been targeted by subject and circulation efficiency, with different creative aspects targeted for specific interest groups including alternative energy, counterculture, environment, and economic (energy savers). The Company is continually in the process of refining its marketing effort from both a strategic and tactical standpoint in order to better target its message to specific groups of customers.

(e) *State the backlog of written firm orders for products and/or services as of a recent date (within the last 90 days) and compare it with the backlog of a year ago from that date.*

As of: 3/31/93 $66,710

As of: 3/31/92 $41,882

Explain the reason for significant variations between the two figures, if any. Indicate what types and amounts of orders are included in the backlog figures. State the size of typical orders. If the Company's sales are seasonal or cyclical, explain.

Although backlogs are considered healthy in the manufacturing industry, in the mail order industry, backorders are generally a symptom of inefficiency and create additional costs and risks of lost sales. Backlogged orders in the mail order business are "backorders." The Company has over 200 vendors for the products that it carries in the catalogs. When a vendor fails to deliver as promised and the customer has paid for an order, a backorder is created. The Company's attempts to keep its backorders at any given time to less than 10% in total orders which is considered the industry standard. The Company is able to achieve this goal the vast majority of the time. The backorder figures above are within normal tolerance for the mail order industry.

(f) *State the number of the Company's present employees and the number of employees it anticipates it will have within the next 12 months. Also, indicate the number by type of employee (i.e., clerical, operations, administrative, etc.) the Company will use, whether or not any of them are subject to collective bargaining agreements, and the expiration date(s) of any collective bargaining agreement(s). If the Company's employees are on strike, or have been in the past three years, or are threatening to strike, describe the dispute. Indicate any supplemental benefits or incentive arrangements the Company has or will have with its employees.*

The Company currently employs 59 employees, of which 11 are administrative, 43 are in operations, and 5 are in clerical or data processing. Of the 43 operations employees, 31 are full time staff and 12 are part time or temporary. In peak periods of order activity such as the fall/Christmas season, the Company typically employs up to 25 additional temporary employees. The Company presently intends to increase its staff in the next twelve months, as necessary. At the end of that period, the Company has budgeted to have 69 employees; 16 in general and administrative positions, 47 in operations (of which 35 will be full time and 12 temporary or part time) and 6 in clerical or data processing. The Company's projections for increased staffing needs are somewhat dependent upon the success of this public offering, and if less than the maximum amount is raised, the Company would limit its staff increases accordingly. There can be no assurances that the Company's business will grow to require such a staffing increase. At present, the Company's benefit package consists of a medical plan, vacation, sick leave, 401-K retirement plan, a 125-S child care and medical flex plan, and employee discounts on merchandise for all full time employees. The Company has adopted a stock option plan which it intends to implement in the next 12 months for some of its key employees. The Company is not subject to any collective bargaining agreements at present, and no employees have been on strike, or threatened to strike since the Company's inception.

(g) *Describe generally the principal properties (such as real estate, plant and equipment, patents, etc.) that the Company owns, indicating also what properties it leases and a summary of the terms under those leases, including the amount of payments, expiration dates and the terms of any renewal options. Indicate what properties the Company intends to acquire in the immediate future, the cost of such acquisitions and the sources of financing it expects to use in obtaining these properties, whether by purchase, lease or otherwise.*

The Company currently leases both its operations facilities in Ukiah, an 8,000 square foot office/customer service/showroom/administration complex under a lease that expires at the end of March 1994, and a 7,500 square foot warehouse/distribution center facility, under a lease that expires at the end of September 1993. While the Company could continue renting the existing warehouse/distribution space, it has negotiated a lease of a 14,000 square foot warehouse/distribution space in Ukiah for one year beginning July 1, 1993, at which time the Company may elect to purchase it for fair market value of 15% of the original purchase price, which ever is lower. The lease on the warehouse racking and shelving system runs until October 1994, at which time the Company may elect to purchase the system for $1. The Company owns part of its current computer system, an IBM-compatible Novell network with 25 work stations and a 750 MB fixed disk, which runs the Company's communication, administrative, marketing, and accounting functions. The Company leases the balance of its computer hardware and software system that is used for order entry, inventory control, and back end catalog analysis for $3,700 per month. The lease runs until October 1, 1997, at which time the Company may elect to purchase the system for fair market value.

Although there is no assurance thereof, the Company believes that it will begin to strain its current facilities by the end of 1993 and will outgrow its facilities by the Spring of 1994. The Company's long term strategic planning calls for a consolidation of its current facilities (the warehouse is currently two blocks away from the main operation) into one large location. It has been determined that the Company requires 5-10 acres of land upon which it can build a 15,000 square foot warehouse with expansion capabilities to 75,000 square feet, a 10,000 square foot administrative/operations/training headquarters, and a 3,000 square foot showroom facility. The Company believes that this proposed Company Headquarters facility will be adequate for expansion of all the Company's plans for at least 10 years. The Company has determined that a good location for such a facility is adjacent to the U.S. Highway 101 corridor between Hopland and Willits, where maximum visibility is afforded to the 50,000+ vehicles that pass by daily. There can be no assurance that it can procure suitable land for an agreeable price or that it can obtain all necessary approvals and other resources to proceed with the plan described below.

The Company believes that it is in the best interests to build this "destination facility" as a showpiece of alternative energy and suitable, non-toxic building practices so that it can be a living monument to sustainability. The Company has begun its search for a suitable property site and has initiated discussions with several world-class environmentally oriented architects.

In choosing a building system, the Company believes it is important to consider the embodied energy of the materials. For instance, timber buildings require significantly less energy to produce than concrete and steel buildings. The Company would endeavor to design a project that could repay its embodied energy mortgage over time by generating more energy that it took to build it, providing a model for others to follow. Local materials as well as recycled materials would be utilized wherever feasible.

The current plan is to have the entire complex off-the-grid and powered by a photovoltaic array along with whichever other suitable renewable energy sources are available at the sight including wind and hydro power systems. Passive solar and subterranean cooling strategies would be employed to cool interior thermal mass at night and evaporative cooling in the day would be designed into the buildings to minimize or totally eliminate energy-hogging air conditioning loads. The contents of the warehouse could be used to help mitigate thermal loads and in-the-slab radiant heating could be further utilized for increased efficiency. Planting the roof to insulate against thermal loads and merging the building with the landscape would be considered and daylighting would be utilized for the entire warehouse. Appropriate eye-level views to the exterior to increase the sense of outdoors in the warehouse interior would further be employed.

The Company is considering a plan to treat all site-generated wastewater and perhaps other waste water (RVGs, local housing) on the site. This type of treatment system would provide for an onsite aquaculture system allowing the Company to grow heavy metal absorbing vegetation and shrimp for food. A well would be considered with a PV powered pump to maintain self-sufficiency and avoid city water hookup costs.

The Company's buildings at the new location will embody all the concepts espoused by its philosophy of sustainability, and safe and sane non-toxic building materials, The showroom will showcase all of the items within the Company's product line in actual use wherever possible. The Company will endeavor to make the entire site of its headquarters remarkable, unique, and slightly outrageous so as to develop the site as a demonstration farm. The development might well include an exterior "commons" or "Oasis" area with lush vegetation, sustainable agriculture, a possible aviary, and a solar greenhouse to accommodate agriculture in the winter months.

Outbuildings, currently sold by the Company such as geodesic domes, yurts, and earth-sheltered housing could be placed on the property for the dual function of showing the structures for sale as well as housing a segment of the "Institute for Independent Living." The Institute, which was highly successful in its debut sessions of 1992, endeavors to teach all aspects of independent living to interested students. The possibility of including a building as an alternative energy "bed and breakfast" is being discussed where interested customers could come to spend a night experiencing living off-the-grid. The Company believes that this project is so unique and educational and has the potential to be such a futuristic model of building and conducting business that it could very well become a tourist attraction and environmental center for Northern California.

By purchasing 5–10 acres, the Company would allow enough room for any expansion it foresees in the near future. The Company would target moving into the new warehouse, offices, and retail space by the spring of 1994. The Company estimates that a project of this scope would take nine months to plan and nine months to build. The following are estimates of costs for this project:

5–10 Acres of Land	$ 300,000
Warehouse Construction (15,000 sf @ $20/sf)	$ 300,000
Warehouse Equipment	$ 20,000
Office Construction (10,000 sf @ $65/sf)	$ 650,000
Office Furniture (50 people @ $300/person)	$ 15,000
Showroom Construction (3,000 sf @ $35/sf)	$ 105,000
Showroom Fixturing (3,000 sf @ $120/sf)	$ 360,000
Architect (@ 15% of Construction Costs)	$ 155,000
Energy System	$ 75,000
Parking & Paving	$ 20,000
Landscaping	$ 25,000
Relocation Expenses	$ 15,000

Total Expenses for Construction, etc. $2,040,000

The Company has been in contact with the Small Business Administration (SBA) about its construction packages for small businesses. The Company has received encouragement that it will qualify for a $1 million construction loan at the current rate of 8% amortized over 20 years. The Company would capitalize the building project with $1 million from the proceeds from this stock offering and would seek to borrow $1 million from SBA for the construction loan, although there can be no assurances that at the time of application the loan will be approved or that interest rates will remain at their current levels. See "Use of Proceeds."

(h) *Indicate the extent to which the Company's operations depend or are expected to depend upon patents, copyrights, trade secrets, know-how or other proprietary information and the steps undertaken to secure and protect this intellectual property, including any use of confidentiality agreements, covenants-not-to-complete and the like. Summarize the principal terms and expiration dates of any significant license agreements. Indicate the amounts expended by the Company for research and development during the last fiscal year, the amount expected to be spent this year and what percentage of revenues research and development expenditures were for the last fiscal year.*

The Company's **Alternative Energy Sourcebook** and its name are copyrighted and trademarked. The Company protects its customer list through limiting access to its computer system, proprietary information agreements with its employees, and appropriate list rental agreements. The Company keeps its vendor files under internal control. The Company is spending approximately $30,000 in the current fiscal year for research and development of new products. It intends to increase this amount to $75,000 in the next year and expend more energy and staff time into new product research. The Company sent its President, John Schaeffer, and its new product development manager, Jeff Oldham to the Guangzhou Trade Fair in China last year and has attended trade fairs in Europe this year. It plans to greatly expand its new product searches to keep its product offerings fresh and on the cutting edge.

(i)   *If the Company's business, products, or properties are subject to material regula-
      tion (including environmental regulations) by federal, state, or local governmental
      agencies, indicate the nature and extent of regulation and its effects or potential
      effects upon the Company.*

The Company is not subject to any material regulation beyond that generally
required for a retail catalog sales business.

(j)   *State the names of any subsidiaries of the Company, their business purposes and
      ownership, and indicate which are included in the Financial Statements attached
      hereto.*

The Company has no subsidiaries.

(k)   *Summarize the development of the Company (including any material mergers or
      acquisitions) during the past five years, or for whatever lesser period the Company
      has been in existence. Discuss any pending or anticipated mergers, acquisitions, spin-
      offs or recapitalization. If the Company has recently undergone a stock split, stock
      dividend or recapitalization in anticipation of this offering, describe (and adjust his-
      torical per share figures elsewhere in this Disclosure Document accordingly).*

The Company began operations in October, 1986 as a sole proprietorship owned
by John Schaeffer. The first mail order catalog was sent to 3,000 people at that
time and sales for the first three months ended 31 December 1986 were $29,831.
Three catalog mailings went out in calendar 1987 to approximately 30,000 people
with total sales of $250,397. Besides Mr. Schaeffer, one employee was hired in
1987. In 1988, the catalog expanded to 64 pages and the Company began renting
mailing lists from like minded companies. It sent out a total of 100,000 catalogs
and sales in 1988 were $726,407. By the end of 1988 there were three employees.
In 1989, mailing list rentals continued and three catalogs were sent to a total of
approximately 35,000 people. By the end of 1989 there were a total of 14 employees and sales were $1,933,008. In 1990, the Company continued to expand and
incorporate on 18 June 1990. Upon incorporation the Company employed 32 people and mailed 213,000 catalogs; sales prior to incorporation were $1,994,522.
Audited sales for fiscal 1991 (the period beginning June 18, 1990 and ending
March 31, 1991) were $3,993,451, 512,500 catalogs were mailed, and the Com-
pany had 45 employees at year end. In fiscal 1992 (April 1, 1991 through March
31, 1992) sales expanded to $6,178,476 and there were 46 employees. Fiscal 1993
sales were $7,778,282, catalogs mailed totaled 2,547,750, and there were 56
employees at year end.

Growth in the key elements of the business since its inception was as follows:

(Calendar years 1986 through 1990 are unaudited—Fiscal years 1991 through
1993 are audited)

Year	Revenues	Catalogs Mailed	Employees
1986*	$ 29,381	3,000	1
1987	$ 250,397	30,000	2
1988	$ 726,407	100,000	3
1989	$1,933,008	350,000	14
1990**	$1,994,522	213,000	32
1991***	$3,993,451	512,500	45
1992	$6,178,476	1,588,000	46
1993	$7,778,282	2,547,750	56

*   1986 figures include operations for 3 months
**   The Company incorporated June 18, 1990. Figures shown represent the
      period January 1, 1990 through June 17, 1990.
*** Revenues shown represent audited results of the period from June 18, 1990
      through the fiscal year ended March 31, 1991.

4. (a) *If the Company was not profitable during its last fiscal year, list below in chrono-
       logical order the events which in management's opinion must or should occur or
       the milestones which in management's opinion the Company must or should
       achieve in order for the Company to become profitable, and indicate the expected
       manner of occurrence or the expected method by which the Company will achieve
       the milestones.*

   Not applicable.

   (b) *State the probable consequences to the Company of delays in achieving each of the
       events or milestones within the above time schedule, and particularly the effect of
       any delays upon the Company's liquidity in view of the Company's then antici-
       pated level of operating costs. (See Question Nos. 11 and 12.)*

   Not applicable

   *Note: After receiving the nature and timing of each event or milestone, potential
   inventors should reflect upon whether achievement of each within the estimated time
   frame is realistic and should assess the consequences of delays or failure of achievement in making an investment decision.*

OFFERING PRICE FACTORS

*If the securities offered are common stock, or are exercisable for or convertible into
common stock, the following factors may be relevant to the price at which the securities
are being offered.*

5. *What were net, after-tax earnings for the last fiscal year?*

   Per share based upon average number of shares outstanding:
   In fiscal 1993 the company earned $43,470 in the aggregate or $.016 per share.

   *If the Company had profits, show offering price as a multiple of earnings. Adjust to
   reflect for any stock splits or recapitalization, and use conversion or exercise price in
   lieu of offering price, if applicable.*

   Offering price Per Share

   Net After-Tax Earnings   (price/earnings multiple) = 386
   Last year Per Share

7. (a) *What is the net tangible book value of the Company? (If deficit, show in parenthe-
       sis.) For this purpose, net tangible book value means total assets (exclusive of
       copyrights, patents, goodwill, research and development costs and similar intan-
       gible items) minus total liabilities.*

   $1,154,660 as March 31, 1993.
   Per share based upon number of shares outstanding as of March 31, 1993: $.406.

   *If the net tangible book value per share is substantially less than this offering (or exer-
   cise or conversion) price per share, explain the reasons for the variation.*

   In February 1992 the Company closed an offering of 200,000 shares of its common
   stock at $5.00 per share. Subsequently, in the very limited trading market, the Com-
   pany's common stock was bought and sold at $5.50 per share. Nevertheless, since
   there has been only a limited trading market in the Company's shares, the offering
   price is inherently arbitrary and is not necessarily related to any future value. Management believes that, since the Company is an ongoing retail business, tangible
   assets such as land, buildings and machinery are not as important in determining
   value as intangible assets such as customer relationships, employee team, reputation,
   and product knowledge.

(b) *State the dates on which the Company sold or otherwise issued securities during the last 12 months, the amount of such securities sold, the number of persons to whom they were sold, any relationship of such persons to the Company at the time of sale, the price at which they were sold and, if not sold for cash, a concise description of the consideration. (Exclude bank debt.)*

From the commencement of this offering through the date of this Offering Circular, the Company has sold 245,606 shares to 1,617 members of the public.

8. (a) *What percentage of the outstanding shares of the Company will the investors in this offering have?* (Assume exercise of options, warrants or rights and conversion of convertible securities.)

   If the maximum is sold: 17.7%
   If the minimum is sold: Not applicable[1]

(b) *What post-offering value is management attributing to the entire Company by establishing the price per security set forth on the cover page (or exercise or conversion price if common stock is not offered)? (Total outstanding shares after offering times offering price, or exercise or conversion price if common stock is not offered.)*

   If the maximum is sold: Approximately $20,382,960
   If minimum is sold: Not applicable[1]

(For above purposes, assume convertible securities are converted and outstanding options exercised in deterring "shares".)

Note: After reviewing the above, potential investors should consider whether or not the offering price (or exercise or conversion price, if applicable) for the securities is appropriate at the present stage of the Company's development.

---

[1]Note—The Company has established no minimum for this offering, however securities regulators in Mississippi and Texas have required the Company to establish an escrow account with respect to residents of their states until the proceeds exceed $1,800,000. Without an escrow requirement, securities regulators in Iowa and Massachusetts have established a minimum of $1,800,000 for residents of their states, and the Nebraska securities regulator has established a minimum of $2,160,000 for Nebraska residents.

USE OF PROCEEDS

9. The following table sets forth the use of the proceeds from this offering assuming $1,800,000 sold and if $3,600,000 is sold.

	If $1,800,000 Sold		If $3,600,000 Sold	
	Amount	%	Amount	%
Total Proceeds:	$1,800,000	100%	$3,600,000	100%
Less Offering Expenses				
Commissions & Finder's Fees*	$15,000	.8%	$115,000	3.2%
Legal & Accounting:	$90,000	5.0%	$90,000	2.5%
Printing & Advertising:	$50,000	2.8%	$50,000	1.4%
Other (specify) Consulting:	$39,000	2.2%	$66,000	1.8%
Postage:	$50,000	2.8%	$50,000	1.4%
Filing Fees:	$15,000	0.8%	$15,000	0.4%
Net Proceeds from Offering:	$1,541,000	85.6%	$3,214,000	89.3%

*If only the minimum is sold, a $15,000 commission is estimated assuming the Company will be able to raise $1,500,000 from its customers and will pay a 5% commission on the additional $300,000 to an outside broker/dealer. It is further assumed that if the Company succeeds in selling the entire $3.6 million worth of shares, a $115,000 commission will need to be paid to an outside broker/dealer. There can be no assurance that the assumptions will prove to be true.

As of June 21, 1993, the Company has raised $1,473,635 and has set no minimum necessary to close this offering. However the securities regulators from Mississippi and Texas have required the Company to establish an escrow account with respect to residents of their states until the proceeds exceed $1,800,000. Without an escrow requirement, securities regulators in Iowa and Massachusetts have established a minimum of $1,800,000 for residents of their states, and the Nebraska securities regulator has established a minimum of $2,160,000 for Nebraska residents. If less than $1,800,000 is received, the "Office/Warehouse/Showroom" complex will be scaled back to acquiring the land, but just building a destination retail/demonstration store and Real Goods will continue to lease office and warehouse space until such time as it can afford to build them.

"The payment for consulting is for services provided by Drew Field and Lorne Groe, including planning, scheduling and budgeting, drafting and reviewing materials; training staff; managing several parts of the process; preparing filings with the SEC and state securities administrators and responding to comments; coordinating with auditors and other service providers. The amount was negotiated by the Company to depend partially upon the amount of proceeds from this offering."

Use of Net Proceeds:

The Company presently intends to open a retail store in the San Francisco Bay Area (approximately 2,000 square feet), a second retail store in a smaller urban area (approximately 1,600 square feet), and a third store in a more rural area (approximately 1,200 square feet). The Company may alter its plans as necessary or appropriate. The Company's goal is to develop profitable retail models in three demographic locations that it can later evaluate and consider the possibility of further company stores or possible franchising.

The Company estimates that the Bay Area store would cost approximately $160,000 for renovation and displays ($80/square foot) and $200,000 for inventory. The Company estimates the second store (1,600 square feet) would cost $120,000 for renovation and $150,000 for inventory and that the third, more rural store (1,200 square feet) would cost $80,000 for renovations and $100,000 for inventory. The Company currently is a party to a letter of intent to purchase the more rural store in Wisconsin. There can be no assurance that such stores will be opened or that they will be successful.

If $1,800,000 Sold		If $3,600,000 Sold	
Amount	%	Amount	%
$360,000	20.0%	$690,000	19.2%

The Company presently intends to take steps to significantly increase its universe of mail order buyers. There can be no assurance that the Company will be successful. The Company currently has approximately 100,000 two-year buyers (customers who have purchased in the last two years). Each mail order buyer purchases on average $4 per catalog mailed for each of the 9 catalogs mailed per year, accounting for approximately $3,600,000 in annual revenues. The Company, through its test mailings to prospects, has determined that many more potential customers exist that would likely be receptive to its product offerings and philosophy. Through the rental of mailing lists, the Company is able to deliver a catalog to these new potential customers for approximately $0.36 each, including printing, mailing, and list rental. By mailing its catalog to 2,500,000 potential customers, the Company believes it can acquire 50,000 new buyers at a conservative 2% pull rate. The cost of such a mailing over the next year would be $900,000. At current buyer levels of purchase, these additional new 50,000 buyers would bring in an additional $1,800,000 in annual revenues at an average of $4 per catalog for 9 catalogs per year. Because it believes that these new customers would not perform as well as its long established "core" customers, the Company believes that new customers would experience an approximate 20% "fall-off" from its already established customers. This would amount to $3.20 per new customer per catalog for each of its 9 catalogs per year or a total increase in annual revenues of $1,400,000. The Company believes that expanding its universe of buyers would strengthen its position as the leading environmental cataloger and have the effect of significantly increasing revenues.

If $1,800,000 Sold		If $3,600,000 Sold	
Amount	%	Amount	%
$200,000	11.1%	$900,000	25%

The Company intends to purchase 5-10 acres of land and relocate its headquarters to this property. The Company plans to build a 15,000 square foot warehouse, a 10,000 square foot office complex, and a 3,000 square foot showroom facility to showcase its merchandise and provide a kinetic example of its products and philosophies in action (see section 3-G under Business and Properties). The Company intends to finance this proposed $2 million project with $1 million in capital from the offering and $1 million in debt from an SBA loan. There can be no assurance that the Company will locate appropriate land at an appropriate cost or that it will obtain the referenced debt financing.

If $1,800,000 Sold		If $3,600,000 Sold	
Amount	%	Amount	%
$700,000	38.9%	$1,000,000	27.8%

The Company sees great potential with its Institute for Independent Living following its successful debut season of 1992. If the offering is more than modestly successful, the Company intends to allocate $75,000 for the Institute's expansion, which would go for facilities improvements, educational materials, production of instructional videos, and the possible purchase of a school bus that would take the Institute on the road around the country. The funds would be used further to publish several books that would serve as textbooks for the Institute.

If $1,800,000 Sold		If $3,600,000 Sold	
Amount	%	Amount	%
$0	0%	$75,000	2.1%

The balance of funds will be used for additions to working capital that may be made (although actual allocations will depend upon management's judgment at the time cash becomes available):[1]

	If $1,800,000 Sold		If $3,600,000 Sold	
	Amount	%	Amount	%
Increase in average inventory	$100,000		$200,000	
Increase in annual payroll	$100,000		$150,000	
Other	$ 81,000		$199,000	
	$281,000	15.6%	$549,000	15.2%
Total Use of Net Proceeds:	$1,541,000	100%	$3,214,000	100%

[1]The amounts disclosed in this table are management's best estimate of the use of working capital. Actual allocations may vary depending on the circumstances at the time of expenditure. The increase in average inventory assumes a decrease in the number of turns per year from 8 down to 6.4, still more than double the industry standard (according to Robert Morris Associates). The Company intends to increase its average inventory from a current level of $700,000 to $900,000. The Company intends to hire within the next year a merchandising director, a buyer, retail store manager, and several clerical employees.

Note: After reviewing the portion of the offering allocated to the payment of offering expenses, and to the immediate payment to management and promoters of any fees, reimbursements, past salaries or similar payments, a potential investor should consider whether the remaining portion of his investment, which would be that part available for future development of the Company's business and operations, would be adequate.

10. (a) *If material amounts of funds from sources other than this offering are to be used in conjunction with the proceeds from this offering, state the amounts and sources of such other funds, and whether funds are firm or contingent. If contingent, explain.*

   If the Company is able to locate suitable land for its new headquarters, it plans to seek debt financing to improve the land as planned. While the company believes that an SBA loan would be the most suitable debt source, there can be no assurance that it will be forthcoming. In its absence, the Company would seek other funding sources and, if none is available, it might terminate the project.

   (b) *If any material part of the proceeds is to be used to discharge indebtedness, describe the terms of such indebtedness, including interest rates. If the indebtedness to be discharged was incurred within the current or previous fiscal year, describe the use of the proceeds of such indebtedness.*

   Not applicable.

(c) *If any material amount of the proceeds is to be used to acquire assets, other than in the ordinary course of business, briefly describe and state the cost of the assets and other material terms of the acquisitions. If the assets are to be acquired from officers, directors, employees or principal shareowners of the company or their associates, give the names of the persons from whom the assets are to be acquired and set forth the cost to the Company, the method followed in determining the cost, and any profit to such persons.*

See "Use of proceeds."

(d) *If any amount of the proceeds is to be used to reimburse any officer, director, employee or shareowner for services already rendered, assets previously transferred, monies loaned or advanced, or otherwise, explain:*

Not applicable.

11. *Indicate whether the Company is having or anticipates having within the next 12 months any cash flow or liquidity problems.*

No.

Whether or not it is in default or in breach of any note, loan, lease or other indebtedness or financing arrangement requiring the Company to make payments.

No.

Indicate if a significant amount of the Company's trade payables have not been paid within the stated trade term.

No.

State whether the Company is subject to any unsatisfied judgments, liens or settlement obligations and the amounts thereof.

No.

Indicate the Company's plans to resolve any such problems.

Not Applicable.

12. *Indicate whether proceeds from this offering should satisfy the Company's cash requirements for the next 12 months, and whether it will be necessary to raise additional funds. State the source of additional funds, if known.*

Proceeds from the current offering will satisfy the Company's cash requirements for the next 12 months. A line of credit from the bank will facilitate response to seasonal inventory demands and is required to be completely repaid for thirty days every year. However, if the company proceeds with the headquarters consideration described above, debt financing will be necessary to fund construction.

CAPITALIZATION

13. *Indicate the capitalization of the Company as of the most recent practicable date and as adjusted to reflect the sale of the minimum and maximum amount of securities in this offering and the use of the net proceeds here from:*

	Amount Outstanding	As Adjusted	
	As of March 31, 1993:	If $1,800,000 sold	If $3,600,000 sold
Debt:			
Short-term debt	$0	$0	$0
Long-term debt	$0	$0	$0
Total Debt	$0	$0	$0
Shareowners' equity:			
Preferred stock (without par value	$0	$0	$0
Common stock (without par value) (number of shares)	$921,602 (2,797,160)	$2,462,602 (3,097,160)	$4,135,602 (3,397,160)
Additional paid in capital	$0	$0	$0
Retained earnings	$76,758	$76,758	$75,758
Total shareowners' equity	$1,154,660	$2,539,360	$4,212,360
Total Capitalization	$1,154,660	$2,539,360	$4,212,360
Number of Shares Authorized:	10,000,000 Common 1,000,000 Preferred		

Number of preferred shares authorized: 1,000,000 shares without par value; none issued.

Number of common shares authorized: 10,000,000 shares, without par value.

Number of common shares reserved to meet conversion requirements or for the issuance upon exercise of options, warrants or rights: 600,000 are reserved for issuance under existing stock option plan. There are no options, warrants or rights outstanding.

DESCRIPTION OF SECURITIES

14. *The securities being offered hereby are:*

[x] Common Stock
[ ] Preferred or Preference Stock
[ ] Notes of Debentures
[ ] Units of two or more type of securities composed of:
[ ] Other:

15. *These securities have:*

Yes No
[x] [ ] Cumulative voting rights
[ ] [x] Other special voting rights
[ ] [x] Preemptive rights to purchase in new issues of shares
[ ] [x] Preference as to dividends or interest
[ ] [x] Preference upon liquidation
[ ] [x] Other special rights or preferences (specify):

Explain:

16. *Are the securities convertible?* [ ] Yes [x] No

17. (a) *If securities are notes or other types of debt securities:* Not Applicable.

    (b) *If notes or other types of debt securities are being offered and the Company had earnings during its last fiscal year, show the ratio of earnings to fixed charges on an actual and pro forma basis for that fiscal year. "Earnings" means pre-tax income from continuing operations plus fixed charges and capitalized interest. "Fixed charges" means interest (including capitalized interest), amortization of debt discount, premium and expense, preferred stock dividend requirements of majority owned subsidiary, and such portion of rental expense as can be demonstrated to be representative of the interest factor in the particular case. The pro forma ratio of earnings to fixed charges should include incremental interest expense as a result of the offering of the notes or other debt securities.*

    Not applicable.

    Note: Care should be exercised in interpreting the significance of the ratio of earnings to fixed charges as a measure of the "coverage" of debt service, as the existence of earnings does not necessarily mean that the Company's liquidity at any given time will permit payment of debt service requirements to be timely made. See Question Nos. 11 and 12. See also the Financial Statements and especially the statement of Cash Flows.

18. *If securities are Preference or Preferred stock:*
    Are unpaid dividends cumulative? [ ] Yes [ ] No
    Are securities callable? [ ] Yes [ ] No Explain:

    Not applicable.

19. *If securities are capital stock of any type, indicate restrictions on dividends under loan or other financing arrangements or otherwise.*

    The Company currently may not pay dividends on stock without the consent of the bank holding its $400,000 line of credit. The Company's Business Loan Agreement with its regular bank, National Bank of the Redwoods, requires the bank's written consent before any dividends may be paid (other than dividends payable in stock).

20. *Current amount of assets available for payment of dividends (if deficit must be first made up, show deficit in parentheses): $76,758 as of March 31, 1993, subject to approval of the bank.*

PLAN OF DISTRIBUTION

21. *The selling agents (that is, the persons selling the securities as agent for the Company for a commission or other compensation) in this offering are:*

American National Securities, Inc., Beverly Hills, CA, Walnut Street Securities, Inc., St. Louis, MO, and Progressive Asset Management, Inc., Oakland, CA.

22. *Describe any compensation to selling agents or finders, including cash, securities, contracts or other consideration, in addition to the cash commission set forth as a percent of the offering price on the cover page of this Offering Circular. Also indicate whether the company will indemnify the selling agents or finders against liabilities under the securities laws. ("Finders" are persons who for compensation act as intermediaries in obtaining selling agents or otherwise making introductions in furtherance of this offering.)*

Compensation will be paid only to any registered securities broker-dealer selected by the Company, and then only as a percent of the offering price. (The Company will pay 6% for shares sold by them to their customers and 3% for shares sold by them to the Company's customers.) An additional 1% will be paid on shares sold by Progressive Asset Management to the Company's customers for ongoing investor relations services if those sales exceed $200,000, and Progressive Asset Management will, at that time, be entitled to reimbursement of up to $5,000 in due diligence expenses. No compensation related to sales of shares will be paid to any employees of the Company. The Company will indemnify the selling agents against liabilities for claimed misstatements or omissions in this Offering Circular.

23. *Describe any material relationships between any of the selling agents or finders and the Company or its management.*

Not applicable.

Note: After reviewing the amount of compensation to the selling agents or finders for selling the securities, and the nature of any relationship between the selling agents or finders and the Company, a potential investor should assess the extent to which it may be inappropriate to rely upon any recommendation by the selling agents or finders to buy the securities.

24. *If this offering is not being made through selling agents, the names of persons at the Company through which this offering is being made:*

This offering is being made through selling agents (see question 21 above). In addition, this offering is being made directly by the company through written announcements, under the direction of John Schaeffer, the Company's president and CEO. The Company will publish announcements of the offering in its catalogs and newsletters, and will mail copies of the announcement to its shareowners and customers. The announcements will provide the very limited information permitted under applicable securities laws and will give the Company's telephone number for requesting this Offering Circular. Similar announcements will be published in other selected media and mailed to other selected individuals.

Offering Circular will be accompanied by a Share Purchase Agreement and a return envelope. Assistance in connection with the offering will be available from the selling agents and from John Schaeffer, President of the company, and Anne Mayes, its shareowner relations coordinator.

25. *If this offering is limited to a special group, such as employees of the Company, or is limited to a certain number of individuals (as required to qualify under Subchapter S of the Internal Revenue Code) or is subject to any other limitations, describe the limitations and any restrictions on resale that apply.*

The offering is being made only to persons for whom the amount invested does not exceed ten percent of the net worth of such persons (excluding principal residence and its furnishings and automobiles) including the net worth of spouse, if applicable.

Will the certificates bear a legend notifying holders of such restrictions? [ ] Yes [x] No

26. (a) *Name, address and telephone number of independent bank or savings and loan association or other similar depository institution acting as escrow agent if the proceeds are escrowed until minimum proceeds are raised:*

National Bank of the Redwoods (707)573-4800, 111 Santa Rosa Avenue, Santa Rosa, CA 95402. The states of Texas and Mississippi have requested that funds received from investors residing in these states be held in an Escrow Account until such time as $1,800,000 has been raised. Through June 21, 1993, the Company has received subscriptions for 245,606 shares and $1,473,636 in aggregate.

(b) *Date at which funds will be returned by escrow agent if minimum proceeds are not raised:*

November 30, 1993.

Will interest on proceeds during escrow period be paid to investors?
[ ] Yes [x] No

27. *Explain the nature of any resale restrictions on presently outstanding shares, and when those restrictions will terminate, if this can be determined:*

As a condition of registering shares in the initial public offering with state securities administrators, the Company's founders, John and Nancy Schaeffer, agreed to place 900,512 of their shares into an escrow. Those shares may only be released from escrow upon the occurrence of certain events such as the Company's earning at least $0.25 per share in each of two consecutive years, or earning an average of $0.25 per share for five consecutive years, or after the Company's shares have traded in certain stock markets at a price of at least $8.75 for at least 90 consecutive trading days. This requirement has been imposed by the Securities Division of the Department of Licensing of the State of Washington.

Sales by the Schaeffers of any non-escrowed shares are restricted by Rule 144 under the federal Securities Act of 1933, as amended. Generally, they may not sell more than 1% of the total shares of the Company outstanding within any three-month period, but if the number of shares being traded increases substantially, an alternative limit could apply, that is, the average weekly trading volume of the shares during the four calendar weeks preceding the date on which notice of the sale is filed. Rule 144 has additional requirements as to the manner of sale, notice, and availability of current public information about the Company.

DIVIDENDS, DISTRIBUTION, AND REDEMPTIONS

28. *If the Company has within the last five years paid dividends, made distributions upon its stock, or redeemed any securities, explain how much and when:*

Not Applicable.

OFFICERS AND KEY PERSONNEL OF THE COMPANY

29. *Chief Executive Officer:*   *Title*: President

Name: **John Schaeffer**   *Age*: 43

Office Street Address: 966 Mazzoni St., Ukiah, CA 95482

Telephone No.: (707) 468-9292

Names of employers, titles and dates of positions held during past five years with an indication of job responsibilities.

Founded the Company in 1986. Ran all aspects of organization for three years; after increasing management depth, has focused on Marketing and Merchandising departments.

Education (degrees, schools, and dates): B.A., Anthropology, University of California at Berkeley, 1971

Also a Director of the Company? [x] Yes [ ] No

Indicate amount of time to be spent on Company matters if less than full time: Full time.

30. *Chief Operating Officer.*

Title: Executive Vice president and Chief Operating Officer

Name: **David C. Smith**   *Age*: 50

Office Street Address: 966 Mazzoni St., Ukiah, CA 95482

Telephone No.: (707) 468-9292

Names of employers, titles and dates of positions held during past five years with an indication of job responsibilities.

Real Goods Trading Corporation, Ukiah, CA
Executive Vice president and Chief Operating Officer
1993–present
Responsible for all operational divisions of the company, including warehouse, distribution, phone agents, customer service, technical support, data processing, and retail store.

Self-employed writing, researching, and establishing a publishing company.
1993–1993

Medical Self Care, Inc.
President, Chief Executive Officer
1988–1991

Smith & Hawken, Ltd.
Co-Founder, President, Chief Operations Officer
1979–1988

Education (degrees, schools, and dates):

No formal degrees.

Also a Director of the company? [x] yes [ ] No

Indicate amount of time to be spent on Company matters if less than full time: Full Time.

31. *Chief Financial Officer*:

    Title: Controller and Chief Financial officer

    Name: **James T. Robello**　*Age*: 47

    Office Street Address: 966 Mazzoni St., Ukiah, CA 95482

    Telephone No.: (707) 468-9292

    Names of employers, titles and dates of positions held during past five years with an indication of job responsibilities.

    Real Goods Trading Corporation, Ukiah, CA
    Controller and Chief Financial Officer
    1991–Present
    Responsible for all financial and administrative functions including financial forecasting and planning, expense control, accounting, purchasing, human resources, banking relations, insurance, strategic planning, and facilities.

    Cray Research, Inc.; San Ramon, CA
    Business Manager II, Western/Asia Pacific Region
    1989–1991
    Responsible for all financial and administrative functions for 15 western states, Australia, and the Far East for this $250 + million division. Responsibilities included financial forecasting and planning, expense control, accounting, human resources, contract administration, strategic planning, and facilities.

    Cray Research, Inc.; San Ramon, CA
    Business Manager I
    1985–1989
    Responsible for all financial and administrative functions for 13 western states. Responsibilities included financial forecasting and planning, expense control, accounting, human resources, contract administration, strategic planning, and facilities.

    Cray Research, Inc.; San Ramon, CA
    Business Controls Manager, Western Region
    1983–1985
    Responsible for all financial functions for 9 western states. Responsibilities included financial forecasting and planning, expense control, accounting, strategic planning, and facilities.

    Education (degrees, schools, and dates): B.B.A., Finance & Business Environment; University of Oregon; 1967

    Also a Director of the Company? [ ] Yes [x] No

    Indicate amount of time to be spent on Company matters if less than full time:
    Full Time

32. *Other Key Personnel*:

    Title: Marketing Director

    Name: **Stephen Morris**　*Age*: 45

    Office Street Address: 41 South Main Street, Randolph, VT 05060

    Telephone No.: (802) 728-3180

    Names of employers, titles and dates of positions held during past five years with an indication of job responsibilities.

Sole Proprietor of Stephen Morris Associates, providing sales and marketing consulting service.
1990–Present

Prior: 1978–1990, Sales Manager; Director of Sales and Distribution; Vice President, Sales and Marketing for Vermont Castings, Inc. of Randolph, Vermont.

Indicate amount of time to be spend on Company matters if less than full time:
Minimum of 40 hours per month

The Company has a well-educated technical staff of six with over 100 years of combined experience with off-the-grid living products. These technicians are trained to do the sizing of alternative energy systems all over the world and produce competitive price quotations with solar sizing computer software.

DIRECTORS OF THE COMPANY

33. *Number of Directors*: 3

If Directors are not elected annually, or are elected under a voting trust or other arrangement, explain:

Not applicable

34. *Information concerning outside or other Directors (i.e., those not described above)*:

Name: **Michael Potts**   *Age*: 48

Office Street Address: 966 Mazzoni Street, Ukiah, CA 95482

Telephone No.: (707) 458-9292

Names of employers, titles and dates of positions held during past five years with an indication of job responsibilities.

Self employed consultant specializing in adapting computer technology and office automation to the needs of growing enterprises without losing sight of the human values involved; his special interest is in small, self-generated businesses working in socially responsible ways. Michael is a member of several mail order catalog networks.

1987–1992
Real Goods Trading Company
Manager of Information Services
1989–1991 (Less than full time)

Education (degrees, schools, and dates): BA degree in Irish Literature, Harvard College, 1967.

35. (a) *Have any of the Officers or directors ever worked for or managed a company (including a separate subsidiary or division of a larger enterprise) in the same business as the Company?* [x] Yes [ ] No

David C. Smith was formerly a director and president of Smith & Hawken, Ltd., a catalog retailer of garden products. In addition, he was formerly president and Chief Executive Officer of Medical Self Care, Incorporated, a catalog retailer of health products.

(b) *If any of the Officers, directors or other key personnel have ever worked for or managed a company in the same business or industry as the Company or in a related business or industry, describe what precautions, if any (including the obtaining of releases or consents from prior employers) have been taken to preclude claims by prior employer for conversion or theft of trade secrets, know-how, or other proprietary information.*

David C. Smith has no non-compete agreements or other legal restraints regarding proprietary business information from previous employers.

No proprietary information from former employers is applicable to the Company's business.

(c) *If the Company has never conducted operations or is otherwise in the development stage, indicate whether any of the Officers or Directors have ever managed any other company in the start-up or development stage and describe the circumstances, including relevant dates.*

Not applicable.

(d) *If any of the Company's key personnel are not employees but are consultants or other independent contractors, state the details of their engagement by the Company.*

Stephen Morris, of Stephen Morris Associates, serves as Marketing Manager for the Company on an hourly basis with a $1,500 monthly guarantee.

(e) *If the Company has key man life insurance policies on any of its Officers, Directors or key personnel, explain, including the names of the persons insured, the amount of insurance, whether the insurance proceeds are payable to the Company and whether there are arrangements that require the proceeds to be used to redeem securities or pay benefits to the estate of the insured person or to a surviving spouse.*

The Company has a life insurance policy for John Schaeffer in the amount of $1,000,000.

36. *If a petition under the Bankruptcy Act or any State insolvency law was filed by or against the Company or its Officers, Directors or other key personnel, or a receiver, fiscal agent or similar officer was appointed by a court for the business or property of any such persons, or any partnership in which any of such persons was general partner at or within the past five years, or any corporation or business association of which any such person was an executive officer at or within the past five years, set forth below the name of such persons, and the nature and date of such actions.*

Not applicable.

Note: After reviewing the information concerning the background of the Company's Officers, Directors and other key personnel, potential investors should consider whether or not these persons have adequate background and experience to develop and operate this Company and to make it successful. In this regard, the experience and ability of management are often considered the most significant factors in the success of a business.

PRINCIPAL SHAREOWNERS

37. *Principal owners of the Company (those who beneficially own directly or indirectly 10% or more of the common and preferred stock presently outstanding) starting with the largest common shareowner. Include separately all common stock issuable upon conversion of convertible securities (identifying them by asterisk) and show average price per share as if conversion has occurred. Indicate by footnote if the price paid was for a consideration other than cash and the nature of any such consideration.*

Name: John & Nancy Schaeffer

Office Street Address: 966 Mazzoni Street, Ukiah, CA

Telephone No.: (707) 468-9292

Principal occupation: President of the Company

Class of Shares: Common

Average Price Per Share: $.03. The consideration was the transfer of the assets of a going business.

No. of Shares Now Held: 2,569,109 including 900,512 shares held in escrow

% of Total: 91.8%

No. of Shares After Offering, if All Securities Sold: 2,569,109

% of Total: 75.6%

38. *Number of shares beneficially owned by Officers and Directors as a group*:

   Before offering: 2,571,909 shares (91.9% of total outstanding) including 900,512 shares held in escrow

   After offering: Assuming $3,600,000 sold: 2,571,909 shares (75.6% of total outstanding)
   Assuming $1,800,000 sold: 2,571,909 shares (83.0% of total outstanding)

   (Assume all options exercised and all convertible securities converted.)

   MANAGEMENT RELATIONSHIPS, TRANSACTIONS, AND REMUNERATION

39. (a) *If any of the Officers, Directors, key personnel or principal shareowners are related by blood or marriage, please describe.*

   John & Nancy Schaeffer are married.

40. *If the Company has made loans to or is doing business with any of its Officers, Directors, key personnel or 10% shareowners, or any of their relatives (or any entity controlled directly or indirectly by any of such persons) within the last two years, or proposes to do so within the future, explain. (This includes sales or lease of goods, property or services to or from the Company, employment or stock purchase contracts, etc.) State the principal terms of any significant loans, agreements, leases, financing or other arrangements.*

   The Company lent $47,609 to John Schaeffer on a demand basis. This promissory note which had a principal amount of up to $72,000, was executed on 1 July 1990 and bore an interest rate of 9% annually. The note was paid off in full on 25 August 1992 including $6,740 in accumulated interest. Any future loans to officers, directors, 5% shareowners, or affiliates will be for a bona fide business purpose and approved by a majority of the disinterested members of the Board of Directors. Any future transactions with such person will be on terms no less favorable to the company than could be obtained from unaffiliated third parties.

41. *If any of the Company's Officers, Directors, key personnel or 10% shareowners has guaranteed or co-signed any of the Company's bank debt or other obligations, including any indebtedness to be retired from the proceeds of this offering, explain and state the amounts involved.*

   John Schaeffer has signed personal guarantees to National Bank of the Redwoods in Santa Rosa for the Company's $400,000 line of credit.

40. (a) *List all remuneration by the Company to Officers, Directors and key personnel for the last fiscal year:*

   Chief Executive Officer: $70,061
   Chief Operating Officer: $58,963
   Chief Accounting Officer: $56,355

   Directors as a group: $0
   (Three persons)

(b) *If remuneration is expected to change or has been unpaid in prior years, explain*:

Remuneration is expected to be paid in Fiscal Year ending 31 March 1994.

Chief Executive Officer: $72,000
Chief Operating Officer: $83,000
Chief Accounting Officer: $60,000

Not applicable.

(c) *If any employment agreements exist or are contemplated, describe*:

John Schaeffer has an employment agreement with the Company providing a salary of $72,000 annually to be CEO and President of the Company. The contract is automatically renewed for an additional year.

41. (a) *Number of shares subject to issuance under presently outstanding stock purchase agreements, stock options, warrants or rights*:

None. The company will not grant options in excess of 10% of the outstanding shares for a one year period following the qualification date of this offering.

Indicate which have been approved by shareowners. State the expiration dates, exercise prices and other basic terms for these securities:

None. The exercise prices for any option must be at least 85% of the fair market value of the shares on the date the option was granted.

(b) *Number of common shares subject to issuance under existing stock purchase or option plans but not yet covered by outstanding purchase agreements, options or warrants*: 600,000

(c) *Describe the extent to which future stock purchase agreements, stock options, warrants or rights must be approved by shareowners.*

Shareowners approval would be necessary only to increase the authorized number of shares, not for any specific stock purchase agreements, stock options, warrants or rights.

42. *If the business is highly dependent on the services of certain key personnel, describe any arrangements to assure that these persons will remain with the company and not compete upon any termination*:

The business currently is highly dependent on the services of John Schaeffer, who will continue to be the majority shareowner of the Company. There is an employment contract with Mr. Schaeffer in effect. No other arrangements for retaining his services are considered necessary.

Note: After reviewing the above, potential investors should consider whether or not the compensation to management and other key personnel directly or indirectly, is reasonable in view of the present stage of the Company's development.

LITIGATION

43. *Describe any past, pending or threatened litigation or administrative action which has had or may have a material effect upon the Company's business, financial condition, or operations, including any litigation or action involving the Company's Officers, Directors or other key personnel. State the names of the principal parties, the nature and current status of the matters, and amounts involved. Give an evaluation by management or counsel, to the extent feasible, of the merits of the proceedings or litigation and the potential impact on the Company's business, financial condition, or operations.*

Not Applicable.

FEDERAL TAX ASPECTS

44. *If the Company is an S corporation under the Internal Revenue Code of 1986, and it is anticipated that any significant tax benefits will be available to investors in this offering, indicate the nature and amount of such anticipated tax benefits and the material risks of their disallowance. Also, state the name, address and telephone number of any tax advisor that has passed upon these tax benefits. Attach any opinion or any description of the tax consequences of an investment in the security by the tax advisor.*

The company is not an S corporation.

Name of Tax Advisor: Deloitte & Touche

Address: 50 Fremont Street
                       San Francisco, CA 94105

Telephone No.:   (415) 247-4000

Note: Potential investors are encouraged to have their own personal tax consultant contact the tax advisor to review details of the tax benefits and the extent that the benefits would be available and advantageous to the particular investor.

MISCELLANEOUS FACTORS

45. *Describe any other material factors, either adverse or favorable, that will or could affect the Company or its business (for example, discuss any defaults under major contracts, any breach of bylaw provisions, etc.) or which are necessary to make any other information in this Disclosure not misleading or incomplete.*

With rapidly increasing power company utility rates, which have been increasing at close to 10% every year, the market is expanding to the suburban sphere as the costs of solar-electric power approach the costs of power company rates on a 30-year amortized basis. If existing trends continue, electric rate analysts predict that in five to fifteen years solar-electric power will be cost competitive with electric grid power. Pacific Gas and Electric Company (P.G.&E), a Northern California utility company, has increased its rates at approximately 10% per year each of the last three years and has estimated that 10% of its power will be generated by photovoltaic modules in the next ten years.

MANAGEMENT DISCUSSION AND ANALYSIS OF CERTAIN RELEVANT FACTORS

47. *If the Company's financial statements show losses from operations, explain the causes underlying these losses and what steps the Company has taken or is taking to address these causes.*

Not Applicable.

48. *Describe any trends in the Company's historical operating results. Indicate any changes now occurring in the underlying economics of the industry or the Company's business which, in the opinion of Management, will have a significant impact (either favorable or adverse) upon the Company's results of operations within the next 12 months, and give a rough estimate of the probable extent of the impact, if possible.*

Real Goods has been profitable since its inception. The Company's rapid growth has been a result of investments in developing and growing its customer mailing list. Additionally, substantial investments have been made developing the Company's infrastructure to support a rapidly growing business. For the fiscal year ended March 31, 1992, the Company's Earnings From Operations were $22,078. The Company had Net Other Expenses of $12,075 which were primarily due to interest paid during the year. The Company's fiscal 1992 Earnings Before Income Taxes were $10,003, and Net Earnings were $5,603.

Net sales for the fiscal year ended March 31, 1993 increased 25.9% to $7,778,282 due to the increased circulation of catalogs. Cost of Goods Sold increased 22.2%, which represented a decrease as a percentage of sales from 56.4% to 54.7% because the Company was able to achieve certain purchasing economies and because of the continuing shift in the product mix toward high margin merchandise.

Selling, general and administrative expenses increased 29.4% to $3,459,927 due to the increased circulation of catalogs, accelerating the expense write-off period of catalogs from six months to four months, more accurately reflecting the catalog life, increased levels of sales activity, participation in trade shows, and establishment of the Institute for Independent Living.

The increase in sales and gross margin offset higher operating expenses and the Company's earnings from operations increased 173.9% to $60,469. The Company's interest expense decreased 86.4% to $3,463 due to the retirement of long and short term debt with the proceeds of the Company's first stock offering. Other income increased 29.5% to $2,242, while interest income decreased 13.7% to $10,024 due to lower interest rates and the retirement of the note receivable from stockholder. Income taxes of $25,802 were accrued in fiscal 1993, while just $4,400 was accrued the previous year.

As a result of the foregoing, the Company's net earnings for fiscal 1993 increased 675.8% to a profit of $43,470.

Note: At the end of fiscal 1993 the Company reclassified mail list rental income as an offset to mail list rental expense in accordance with generally accepted accounting principles. At that time, prior years statements were restated for reporting consistency.

Management believes that the Company's current infrastructure will support planned levels of growth. The Company plans to make selective additional investments in the future which may have short term negative effects.

In the longer term, the Company's plan is to increase its growth margin on sales as well as the dollar amount of sales. If achieved, this combination of better margin and higher sales volume would result in increased profits. There can be no assurance that the Company will increase either its gross margins or total sales.

See responses to Question 3(a), 3(c), and 3(d), above that discuss in detail the current market for the Company's products and industry trends. The Company's sales increased at a rate of 150–200% in the start up phase during our first three years of operations. The Company had sales growth of 33% in its fourth year of operations and growth of 25.9% in its fifth year. The Company is planning a sales increase of about 24.9% for the current fiscal year. There can be no assurance that sales will increase at all. Electric company rates are expected to continue to increase at the current rate of approximately 10% per year, with the result that the demand for the Company's alternative energy products should significantly increase. The Company has put significant attention toward increasing its gross profit margin which it expects will have a positive effect toward overall profitability in the next 12 months.

49. *If the Company sells a product or products and has had significant sales during its last fiscal year, state the existing gross margin (net sales less cost of such sales as presented in accordance with generally accepted accounting principles) as a percentage of sales for the last fiscal year:*

45.26%

What is the anticipated gross margin for next year of operations?

Approximately 46.5%, although there can be no assurance thereof.

If this is expected to change, explain. Also, if reasonably current gross margin figures are available for the industry, indicate these figures and the source or sources from which they are obtained.

The Company's gross profit margin for the fiscal year ending 31 March 1993 was 45.26%. The Company has budgeted its gross profit margin for the next fiscal year of operations to be 46.5%, although no assurances can be given that it will achieve this. According to Robert Morris Associates' 1992 report on Retailers—Catalog & Mail-Order Houses, the gross profit margin for the industry ranges from 38.5% to 43.0%. The Company expects gross profit margin to improve by 1.26% due to a change in mix of products sold favoring high margin products. This change in mix is expected as a result of the company increasing its mailings of color catalogs (with generally higher margin products), more than it is increasing the mailings of the Real Goods News catalogs and Real Stuff mailers (generally lower margin products). The fiscal 1994 mailing plan calls for mailing 3,347,000 color catalogs, 485,000 Real Goods News catalogs, and 46,000 Real Stuff mailers.

50. *Foreign sales as a percent of total sales for last fiscal year:*

2%

Domestic government sales as a percent of total domestic sales for last fiscal year: 2%. Explain the nature of these sales, including any anticipated changes:

Approximately 2% of the Company's sales for the last fiscal year were to foreign customers and approximately 2% of sales were to U.S. government agencies. These sales mostly involved photovoltaic modules and alternative energy systems. The Company expects these percentages to increase slightly, but not significantly, in the next fiscal year.

Appendix 6

Form U-7
(Contains
the SCOR Form)

FORM U-7

DISCLOSURE DOCUMENT

A manual has been prepared to help you complete this Disclosure Document. The manual contains instructions for completing each Item. If you do not have a SCOR Manual, contact your State or Provincial securities regulator or the North American Securities Administrators Association.
(www.nasaa.org)

THIS BOX IS NOT PART OF THE SCOR FORM AND SHOULD BE REMOVED BEFORE THE COMPLETED FORM IS GIVEN TO PROSPECTIVE INVESTORS

Cover Page - *Page 1*

Place Company Logo (if any) here or to left or right of Company Name

_____
(Exact name of Company as set forth in Articles of Incorporation or Organizational Documents)

Street address of principal office:

Company Telephone Number:

Person(s) to contact at Company with respect to offering:

Telephone Number (if different from above):

Type of securities offered:

Price per security: $

Sales commission, if any: _____%

Minimum number of securities offered:

Maximum number of securities offered:

Total proceeds: If minimum sold: $

                       If maximum sold: $

Investment in a small business is often risky. You should not invest any funds in this offering unless you can afford to lose your entire investment. See Item 1 for a discussion of the risk factors that management believes present the most substantial risks to you.

The date of this Disclosure Document is _____.

Small Company Offering Registration (SCOR) Form
Revised: September 28, 1999

Page - 1

Cover Page - Page 2

Executive Summary

The Company

Describe the business of the Company.

Describe how the Company plans to carry out its activities.

This Company:

[ ]   Has never conducted operations.
[ ]   Is in the development stage.
[ ]   Is currently conducting operations.
[ ]   Has shown a profit in the last fiscal year.
[ ]   Other (Specify):

        (Check at least one, as appropriate)

Jurisdiction and date of formation: _____   _____

Fiscal year end: _____   _____
                (month)   (day)

How the Company Will Use Your Money

Describe how the Company intends to use the proceeds of this offering.

For more information about how the Company will use your money, see Item 30.

The Principal Officers of the Company

The Principal Officers of the Company and their titles are:

Chief Executive Officer:

Chief Operating Officer:

Chief Financial Officer:

For more information about these Officers, see Item 77.

The Offering

Name of Sales Person(s):

Address:

Telephone Number:

Is there an impound of proceeds until the minimum is obtained?   [ ] Yes   [ ] No
(See Items 73 - 76)

Is this offering limited to certain purchasers?   [ ] Yes   [ ] No (See Item 72)

Is transfer of the securities restricted?   [ ] Yes   [ ] No   (See Item 53)

This offering is available for sale in the following states:

You should consider the terms and risks of this offering before you invest. No government regulator is recommending these securities. No government regulator has verified that this document is accurate or determined that it is adequate. It is a crime for anyone to tell you differently.

The Company has included in this Disclosure Document all of its representations about this offering. If anyone gives you more or different information, you should ignore it. You should rely only on the information in this Disclosure Document.

TABLE OF CONTENTS

Page

Risk Factors 6

Business and Properties 6
    General Description of the Business
    Suppliers
    Customer Sales and Orders
    Competition
    Marketing
    Employees
    Properties
    Research and Development
    Governmental Regulation
    Company History and Organization

Milestones 11

Use of Proceeds 13

Selected Financial Information 14
    General
    Capitalization
    Dilution

Management's Discussion and Analysis of Certain Relevant Factors 17

Description of Securities Offered 19
    General
    Preferred Stock
    Debt Securities
    Ratio of Earnings to Fixed Charges

How These Securities Will Be Offered and Sold 22
    Company Salespersons
    Other Salespersons and Finders
    Purchaser Limitations
    Impound of Offering Proceeds

Management 25
    Officers and Key Persons of the Company
    Directors of the Company
    Consultants
    Arrangements with Officers, Directors, and Key Persons
    Compensation
    Prior Experience
    Certain Legal Proceedings

Outstanding Securities...31
    General
    Dividends, Distributions, and Redemptions
    Options and Warrants
    Sales of Securities

Principal Stockholders..32

Management Relationships and Transactions 33
    Family Relationships
    Management Transactions

Litigation 35

Tax Aspects 35

Other Material Factors...36

Additional Information...36

Signatures 37

List of Exhibits 38

RISK FACTORS

1.   List in the order of importance the factors that the Company considers to be the most significant risks to an investor.

BUSINESS AND PROPERTIES

GENERAL DESCRIPTION OF THE BUSINESS

2.   Describe the business of the Company, including its products or services.

3.   Describe how the Company produces or provides these products or services and how and when the Company intends to carry out its activities.

SUPPLIERS

4.   Does the Company have any major supply contracts?   [ ] Yes   [ ] No
If yes, describe.

5.   (a)   Is the Company dependent upon a limited number of suppliers?
       [ ] Yes   [ ] No   If yes, describe.

5.   (b)   Does the Company expect to be dependent upon a limited number of suppliers?
       [ ] Yes   [ ] No   If yes, describe.

CUSTOMER SALES AND ORDERS

6.   Does the Company have any major sales contracts?   [ ] Yes [ ] No
     If yes, describe.

7.   State the total amount of the Company's sales of products or services for the most recent 12 month financial reporting period.

8.   State the dollar amount of a typical sale.

9.   Are the Company's sales seasonal or cyclical?   [ ] Yes   [ ] No
     If yes, explain.

10. State the amount of foreign sales as a percent of total sales for last fiscal year. _____%.
     Explain the nature of these sales, including any anticipated changes.

11. Name any customers that account for, or based upon existing orders will account for, a major portion (20% or more) of the Company's sales.

12. State the dollar amount of firm orders.

COMPETITION

13.   (a)   Describe the market area in which the business competes or will compete.

13.   (b)   Name the Company's principal competitors and indicate their relative size and financial and market strengths.

14.   (a)   Does the Company compete, or expect to compete, by price?
       [ ] Yes   [ ] No   If yes, describe its competitive strategy.

14.   (b)   Does the Company compete, or expect to compete, by service?
       [ ] Yes   [ ] No   If yes, describe its competitive strategy.

14.   (c)   Does the Company compete, or expect to compete, on some other basis?
       [ ] Yes   [ ] No
If yes, state the basis and describe the Company's competitive strategy.

MARKETING

15.   (a)   Describe how the Company plans to market its products or services during the next 12 months, including who will perform these marketing activities.

15.   (b)   State how the Company will fund these marketing activities.

EMPLOYEES

16.   (a)   State the number of the Company's present employees by type of employee (i.e., clerical, operations, administrative, etc.).

16.   (b)   State the number of employees the Company anticipates it will have within the next 12 months by type of employee (i.e., clerical, operations, administrative, etc.).

17.   Describe the Company's labor relations.

18.   Indicate any benefits or incentive arrangements the Company provides or will provide to its employees.

PROPERTIES

19.   (a)   Describe generally the principal properties that the Company owns or leases.

19.   (b)   Indicate what properties the Company intends to acquire or lease.

RESEARCH AND DEVELOPMENT

20.   Indicate the amounts that the Company spent for research and development during its last fiscal year.

21.   (a)   Will the Company expend funds on research and development during the current fiscal year?   [ ] Yes   [ ] No

21   (b)   If yes, how much does the Company plan to spend on research and development during the current fiscal year?

21.   (c)   How does the Company intend to fund these research and development costs?

GOVERNMENTAL REGULATION

22.   (a)   Is the Company's business subject to material regulation by any governmental agency?   [ ] Yes [ ] No

22.   (b)   Are the Company's products or services subject to material regulation by any governmental agency? [ ] Yes [ ] No

22.   (c)   Are the Company's properties subject to material regulation by any governmental agency?   [ ] Yes [ ] No

22.   (d)   Explain in detail any "yes" answer to Item 22(a), 22(b), or 22(c), including the nature and extent of the regulation and its effect or potential effect upon the Company.

23.   (a)   Is the Company required to have a license or permit to conduct business?
[ ] Yes [ ] No

23.   (b)   If yes, does the Company have the required license or permit?
[ ] Yes [ ] No

23.   (c)   If the answer to Item 23(b) is "yes," describe the effect on the Company and its business if it were to lose the license or permit.

23.   (d)   If the Company has not yet acquired a required license or permit, describe the steps the Company needs to take to obtain the license or permit. Estimate the time it will take to complete each step.

COMPANY HISTORY AND ORGANIZATION

24.   Summarize the material events in the development of the Company.

25. Describe any recent stock split, stock dividend, recapitalization, merger, acquisition, spin-off, or reorganization.

26. Discuss any pending or anticipated stock split, stock dividend, recapitalization, merger, acquisition, spin-off, or reorganization.

27. State the names of any parent, subsidiary, or affiliate of the Company. For each, indicate its business purpose, its method of operation, its ownership, and whether it is included in the Financial Statements attached to this Disclosure Document.

MILESTONES

28. Describe in chronological order the steps management intends to take to achieve, maintain, or improve profitability during the 12 months following receipt of the offering proceeds.

If management does not expect the Company to achieve profitability during that time period, describe the business objectives for that period and the steps management intends to take to achieve those objectives.

Indicate the probable timing of each step and the approximate cost to complete it.

29. (a) State the anticipated consequences to the Company if any step is not completed as scheduled.

29. (b) Describe how the Company will deal with these consequences.

NOTE: After reviewing management's discussion of the steps it intends to take, potential investors should consider whether achievement of each step within the estimated time frame is realistic. Potential investors should also assess the consequences to the Company of any delays in taking these steps and whether the Company will need additional financing to accomplish them.

USE OF PROCEEDS

30.   Show how the Company intends to use the proceeds of this offering:

	If Minimum Sold		If Maximum Sold	
	Amount	%	Amount	%
Total Proceeds	$	100%	$	100%
Less: Offering Expenses				
Commissions and Finders Fees				
Legal & Accounting				
Copying & Advertising				
Other (Specify):				
Net Proceeds from Offering	$_____	___%	$_____	___%
Use of Net Proceeds				
	$	%	$	%
	$	%	$	%
	$	%	$	%
	$	%	$	%
	$	%	$	%
Total Use of Net Proceeds	$_____	100%	$_____	100%

31.   (a)   Is there a minimum amount of proceeds that must be raised before the Company uses any of the proceeds of this offering?   [ ] Yes[ ] No

31.   (b)   If yes, describe how the Company will use the minimum Net Proceeds of this offering.

31.   (c)   If the answer to Item 31(a) is "yes," describe how the Company will use the Net Proceeds of this offering that exceed the amount of the minimum offering proceeds.

31.   (d)   If the answer to Item 31(a) is "no," describe how the Company will use the Net Proceeds of this offering.

32.   (a)   Will the Company use other funds, together with the offering proceeds, to fund any project or activity identified in Item 31?   [ ] Yes[ ] No

32.   (b)   If yes, state the amounts and sources of the other funds.

32.   (c)   Indicate whether the availability of the funds is firm or contingent. If contingent, explain.

NOTE: See the answer to Item 70 for information about proceeds used to compensate sales agents. See the answer to Items 108 and 109 for information about proceeds used to purchase assets from Officers, Directors, key persons, or principal stockholders or their associates or to reimburse them for services previously provided or moneys borrowed.

SELECTED FINANCIAL INFORMATION

NOTE: The Company has adjusted all numbers in this section to reflect any stock splits or recapitalizations.

GENERAL

33.   What were net, after-tax earnings for the last fiscal year? (If losses, show in parenthesis.)

Total $
Per share $

34.   If the Company had profits, show offering price as a multiple of earnings.

Offering Price Per Share   =   (price/earnings multiple)
Net After-Tax Earnings Per Share for Last Fiscal Year

CAPITALIZATION

35.   Indicate the capitalization of the Company as of the most recent balance sheet date, and as adjusted to reflect the sale of the minimum and maximum amount of securities in this offering and the use of the net proceeds from this offering.

	Amount Outstanding		
	As of: _// (date)_	As Adjusted Minimum	Maximum
Debt:			
Short-term debt (average interest rate ___%)	$	$	$
Long-term debt (average interest rate ___%)	$	$	$
Total debt	$	$	$
Stockholders equity (deficit):			
Preferred stock - par or stated value (by class of preferred – in order of preferences)			
_____	$	$	$
_____	$	$	$
_____	$	$	$
Common stock - par or stated value	$	$	$
Additional paid in capital	$	$	$
Retained earnings (deficit)	$	$	$
Total stockholders equity (deficit)	$	$	$
Total Capitalization	$_____	$_____	$_____

Number of preferred shares authorized to be outstanding:

Class of Preferred	Number of Shares Authorized	Par Value Per Share
		$
		$
		$

Number of common shares authorized: shares.
Par or stated value per share, if any: $

Number of common shares reserved to meet conversion requirements or for issuance upon the exercise of options, warrants or rights: shares.

DILUTION

36. (a)   The price of the securities in this offering has been arbitrarily determined.
     [ ] Yes   [ ] No

36. (b)   If no, explain the basis on which the price of the securities was determined.

37. (a)   The net tangible book value per share before offering is: $

37. (b)   For the minimum offering:

The net tangible book value per share after the minimum offering will be: $

The amount of increase in net tangible book value per share as a result of receipt of cash from purchasers in this offering will be: $

The dilution per share to purchasers will be: $

37. (c)   For the maximum offering:

The net tangible book value per share after the maximum offering will be: $

The amount of increase in net tangible book value per share as a result of receipt of cash from purchasers in this offering will be: $

The dilution per share to purchasers will be: $

38. For each share purchased in this offering a purchaser will pay $ _____ but will receive a share representing only $ _____ in net tangible book value, if the minimum offering is achieved, or $ _____ , if the maximum offering is achieved.

The difference between the amount a purchaser pays for a share and the amount of net tangible book value that share represents is the dilution to the purchaser.

39.   In a table, compare the existing stockholders' percentage ownership in the Company and the consideration paid for that ownership with that of purchasers in this offering.

| | Shares Purchased | | Total Consideration | | Average Price |
	Number	Percent	Amount	Percent	Per Share
Existing holders					
New Purchasers:					
Minimum offering					
Maximum offering					

40.   Using the offering price of these securities, what value is the Company's management attributing to the entire Company before the offering?

$ _____

NOTE: You should consider carefully whether the Company has this value at the present time. Some issues you should think about include: (1) the risks to which the Company is subject before it achieves success (see Item 1, Risk Factors); (2) the exercise prices of outstanding options (see Item 101); and (3) the prices that the Company's Officers, Directors, and principal stockholders paid for their shares (see Items 104 and 105).

MANAGEMENT'S DISCUSSION AND ANALYSIS OF CERTAIN RELEVANT FACTORS

41.   Is the Company having or does the Company anticipate having within the next 12 months any cash flow or liquidity problems?   [ ] Yes   [ ] No   If yes, explain.

42.   (a)   Is the Company in default of the terms of any note, loan, lease, or other indebtedness or financing arrangement requiring the Company to make payments?
        [ ] Yes   [ ] No
42.   (b)   If yes, explain. Identify the creditor, state the amount in default or the term that the Company has not complied with, and describe any consequences to the Company resulting from each default.

43. Are a significant amount of the Company's trade payables more than 90 days old?
     [ ] Yes   [ ] No

44. Is the Company subject to any unsatisfied judgments, liens, or settlement obligations?
     [ ] Yes   [ ] No   If yes, state the amounts.

45. Describe how the Company will resolve the problems identified in Items 41 - 44.

46. (a)   Do the Company's financial statements show losses from operations?
     [ ] Yes   [ ] No

46. (b)   If yes, explain the causes underlying these losses and what steps the Company has
taken or is taking to address these causes.

47. (a)   Describe any trends in the Company's historical operating results.

47. (b)   Indicate any changes now occurring in the underlying economics of the Company's
business which, in the opinion of Management, will have a significant impact upon the Company's
results of operations within the next 12 months.

47. (c)   Describe the probable impact on the Company.

47. (d)   Describe how the Company will deal with this impact.

48.   (a)   Will the proceeds from this offering and any available funds identified in Item 32 satisfy the Company's cash requirements for the 12 month period after it receives the offering proceeds?   [ ] Yes   [ ] No

48.   (b)   If no, explain how the Company will satisfy its cash requirements. State whether it will be necessary to raise additional funds. State the source of the additional funds, if known.

DESCRIPTION OF SECURITIES OFFERED

GENERAL

49.   The securities being offered are:

        [ ]   Common Stock
        [ ]   Preferred or Preference Stock
        [ ]   Notes, Debentures, or Bonds
        [ ]   Limited Liability Company Membership Interests
        [ ]   Units of two or more types of securities, composed of:

        [ ]   Other (specify):

50.   These securities have:

Yes	No	
[ ]	[ ]	Cumulative voting rights
[ ]	[ ]	Other special voting rights
[ ]	[ ]	Preemptive rights to purchase any new issue of shares
[ ]	[ ]	Preference as to dividends or interest
[ ]	[ ]	Preference upon liquidation
[ ]	[ ]	Anti-dilution rights
[ ]	[ ]	Other special rights or preferences (specify):

Explain any yes answer.

51.   Are there any restrictions on dividends or other distributions?   [ ] Yes   [ ] No
If yes, describe.

52.   Are the securities convertible?   [ ] Yes   [ ] No
If yes, state conversion price or formula.

        Date when conversion becomes effective: __/__/__
        Date when conversion expires: __/__/__

53.   Describe any resale restrictions on the securities and when the restrictions will terminate.

PREFERRED STOCK

If the securities being offered are Preference or Preferred stock:

54.   Are unpaid dividends cumulative?   [ ] Yes   [ ] No

55.   (a)   Are the securities callable?   [ ] Yes   [ ] No   If yes, describe.

55.   (b)   Are the securities redeemable?   [ ] Yes   [ ] No
If yes, describe, including redemption prices.

DEBT SECURITIES

If the securities being offered are notes or other types of debt securities:

56.   What is the interest rate on the debt securities? _____%
If the interest rate is variable or there are multiple interest rates, describe.
57.   What is the maturity date? __/__/__

If the securities will have serial maturity dates, describe.

58.   Is there a sinking fund?   [ ] Yes   [ ] No   If yes, describe.

59.   Is there a trust indenture?   [ ] Yes   [ ] No
If yes, state the name, address, and telephone number of Trustee.

60.   (a)   Are the securities callable?   [ ] Yes   [ ] No   If yes, describe.

60.   (b)   Are the securities redeemable?   [ ] Yes[ ] No
If yes, describe, including redemption prices.

61.   Are the securities secured by real or personal property?   [ ] Yes   [ ] No
If yes, describe.

62.   (a)   Are the securities subordinate in right of payment of principal or interest?
[ ] Yes   [ ] No   If yes, explain the terms of the subordination.

62.   (b)   How much currently outstanding indebtedness of the Company is senior to the securities in right of payment of interest or principal? $

63.   How much currently outstanding indebtedness ranks equally with the securities in right of payment? $

64.   How much currently outstanding indebtedness is junior (subordinated) to the securities?
      $

RATIO OF EARNINGS TO FIXED CHARGES

65.   (a)   If the Company had earnings during its last fiscal year, show the ratio of earnings to fixed charges on an actual and pro forma basis for that fiscal year.

	Actual		Pro Forma	
	Last Fiscal Year	Interim Period	Minimum	Maximum
"Earnings" =				
"Fixed Charges"				

65.   (b)   If no earnings, show "Fixed Charges" only

NOTE: See the Financial Statements and especially the Statement of Cash Flows. Exercise care in interpreting the significance of the ratio of earnings to fixed charges as a measure of the "coverage" of debt service. The existence of earnings does not necessarily mean that the Company will have cash available at any given time to pay its obligations. See Items 41 - 48. Prospective purchasers should not rely on this ratio as a guarantee that they will receive the stated return or the repayment of their principal.

HOW THESE SECURITIES WILL BE OFFERED AND SOLD

COMPANY SALESPERSONS

66.   Provide the following information for each Officer, Director, or Company employee who intends to offer or sell the securities:

66.   (a)   Name:

            Title:

            Address:

            Telephone Number:

67.   Describe any compensation that the Company will pay each person in addition to his or her customary salary and compensation.

OTHER SALESPERSONS AND FINDERS

68.   Provide the following information for each salesperson who is not an Officer, Director, or employee of the Company:

68.   (a)   Name:

              Company:

              Address:

              Telephone Number:

69.   Provide the following information for each person who is a finder:

69.   (a)   Name:

              Company:

              Address:

              Telephone Number:

70.   Describe all compensation that the Company will pay to each person identified in Items 68 and 69.

71.   Describe any material relationships between these sales persons or finders and the Company or its management.

PURCHASER LIMITATIONS

72.   (a)   Is the offering limited to certain purchasers? [ ] Yes   [ ] No

72.   (b)   Is the offering subject to any other purchaser limitations?   [ ] Yes   [ ] No

72.   (c)   If the answer to either 72(a) or 72(b) is yes, describe the limitation.

IMPOUND OF OFFERING PROCEEDS

73.   (a)   Will the Company impound the proceeds of the offering until it raises the minimum offering proceeds?   [ ] Yes   [ ] No

73.   (b)   If yes, what is the minimum amount of proceeds that the Company must raise and place in an impound account before the Company can receive and use the proceeds?
         $

73.   (c)   If the answer to Item 73(a) is "yes," state the date on which the offering will end if the Company has not raised the minimum offering proceeds.   _____
                                                                                                date

74.   (a)   Does the Company reserve the right to extend the impound period?
         [ ] Yes   [ ] No

74.   (b)   If yes, describe the circumstances under which the Company might extend the impound period.

75.   State the name, address, and telephone number of the bank or other similar depository institution acting as impound agent.

76.   If the offering proceeds are returned to investors at the end of the impound period, will the Company pay any interest earned during the impound period to investors?
         [ ] Yes[ ] No

MANAGEMENT

OFFICERS AND KEY PERSONS OF THE COMPANY

77.   Provide the following information for each Officer and key person. The term "key person" means a person, other than the chief executive officer, chief operating officer, and chief financial officer, who makes a significant contribution to the business of the Company. Identify who performs the functions of Chief Executive Officer, Chief Operating Officer, and Chief Financial Officer.

77.   (a)   Name: Age:

        Title:

        Office Street Address:

        Telephone Number:

        Names of employers, titles, and dates of positions held during past five years, with an indication of job responsibilities.

        Education (degrees, schools, and dates):

        Also a Director of the Company   [ ] Yes   [ ] No

        Indicate amount of time to be spent on Company matters if less than full time:

DIRECTORS OF THE COMPANY

78.   (a)   Number of Directors:

78.   (b)   Are Directors elected annually?   [ ] Yes   [ ] No   If no, explain.

78.   (c)   Are Directors elected under a voting trust or other arrangement?
        [ ] Yes   [ ] No   If yes, explain.

79.   Provide the following information for each Director not described in Item 77:

79.   (a)   Name: Age:

        Office Street Address:

        Telephone Number:

        Names of employers, titles, and dates of positions held during past five years, with an
indication of job responsibilities.

        Education (degrees, schools, and dates):

CONSULTANTS

80.   (a)   Are all key persons employees of the Company?   [ ] Yes   [ ] No

80.   (b)   If no, state the details of each contract or engagement.

ARRANGEMENTS WITH OFFICERS, DIRECTORS, AND KEY PERSONS

81.   Describe any arrangements to ensure that Officers, Directors, and key persons will remain
with the Company and not compete with the Company if they leave.

82.   (a)   Describe the impact on the Company if it loses the services of any Officer, Director,
or key person due to death or disability.

82.　(b)　Has the Company purchased key person life insurance on any Officer, Director, or key person?　　　[ ] Yes　　[ ] No

82.　(c)　Has the Company made any arrangements to replace any Officer, Director, or key person it loses due to death or disability?　　　[ ] Yes　　　[ ] No

82.　(d)　If the answer to either Item 82(b) or 82(c) is "yes," describe.

COMPENSATION

83.　List all compensation that the Company paid to its Officers, Directors, and key persons for the last fiscal year:

	Cash	Other
Chief Executive Officer	$	$
Chief Operating Officer		
Chief Financial Officer		
Key Persons:		
Total:	$_____	$_____
Officers as a group (number of persons ___)	$	$
Directors as a group (number of persons ___)	$	$
Key Persons as a group (number of persons ___)	$	$

84.　(a)　Has compensation been unpaid in prior years?　　[ ] Yes　　[ ] No

84.　(b)　Does the Company owe any Officer, Director, or employee any compensation for prior years?　　　[ ] Yes　　[ ] No

84.　(c)　Explain any "yes" answer to Item 84(a) or 84(b).

85.   Is compensation expected to change within the next year?   [ ] Yes   [ ] No
If yes, explain.

86.   (a)   Does the Company have any employment agreements with Officers, Directors, or
key persons?   [ ] Yes   [ ] No   If yes, describe.

86.   (b)   Does the Company plan to enter into any employment agreements with Officers,
Directors, or key persons?   [ ] Yes   [ ] No   If yes, describe.

PRIOR EXPERIENCE

87.   Has any Officer or Director worked for or managed a company (including a separate
subsidiary or division of a larger enterprise) in the same type of business as the Company?
        [ ] Yes   [ ] No   If yes, explain in detail, including relevant dates.

88.   (a)   If the Company has never conducted operations or is otherwise in the development
stage, has any Officer or Director managed another company in the start-up or development stage?
        [ ] Yes   [ ] No

88.   (b)   If yes, explain in detail, including relevant dates.

CERTAIN LEGAL PROCEEDINGS

Insolvency

89.   Has a petition for bankruptcy, receivership, or a similar insolvency proceeding been filed by or against any Officer, Director, or key person within the past five years, or any longer period if material?   [ ] Yes   [ ] No

90.   Was any Officer, Director, or key person an executive officer, a director, or in a similar management position for any business entity that was the subject of a petition for bankruptcy, receivership, or similar insolvency proceeding within the past five years, or any longer period if material?   [ ] Yes   [ ] No

91.   Explain in detail any "yes" answer to Item 89 or 90.

Criminal Proceedings

92.   (a)   Has any Officer, Director, or key person been convicted in a criminal proceeding, excluding traffic violations or other minor offenses? [ ] Yes   [ ] No

92.   (b)   Is any Officer, Director, or key person named as the subject of a pending criminal proceeding, excluding traffic violations or other minor offenses?   [ ] Yes   [ ] No

92.   (c)   Explain in detail any "yes" answer to Item 92(a) or 92(b).

Civil Proceedings

93.   (a)   Has any Officer, Director, or key person been the subject of a court order, judgment or decree in the last five years related to his or her involvement in any type of business, securities, or banking activity?   [ ] Yes   [ ] No

93.   (b)   Is any Officer, Director, or key person the subject of a pending civil or action related to his or her involvement in any type of business, securities, or banking activity?
     [ ] Yes   [ ] No

93.   (c)   Has any civil action been threatened against any Officer, Director, or key person related to his or her involvement in any type of business, securities, or banking activity?
     [ ] Yes   [ ] No
93.   (d)   Explain in detail any "yes" answer to Item 93(a), 93(b), or 93(c).

Administrative Proceedings

94.   (a)   Has any government agency, administrative agency, or administrative court imposed an administrative finding, order, decree, or sanction against any Officer, Director, or key person in the last five years as a result of his or her involvement in any type of business, securities, or banking activity?   [ ] Yes   [ ] No

94.   (b)   Is any Officer, Director, or key person the subject of a pending administrative proceeding related to his or her involvement in any type of business, securities, or banking activity?
            [ ] Yes   [ ] No

94.   (c)   Has any administrative proceeding been threatened against any Officer, Director, or key person related to his or her involvement in any type of business, securities, or banking activity?
            [ ] Yes   [ ] No

94.   (d)   Explain in detail any "yes" answer to Item 94(a), 94(b), or 94(c).

Self-Regulatory Proceedings

95.   (a)   Has a self-regulatory agency imposed a sanction against any Officer, Director, or key person in the last five years as a result of his or her involvement in any type of business, securities, or banking activity?   [ ] Yes   [ ] No

95.   (b)   Is any Officer, Director, or key person the subject of a pending self-regulatory organization proceeding related to his or her involvement in any type of business, securities, or banking activity?   [ ] Yes   [ ] No

95.   (c)   Has any self-regulatory organization proceeding been threatened against any Officer, Director, or key person related to his or her involvement in any type of business, securities, or banking activity?   [ ] Yes   [ ] No

95.   (d)   Explain in detail any "yes" answer to Item 95(a), 95(b), or 95(c).

        NOTE: After reviewing the background of the Company's Officers, Directors and key persons, potential investors should consider whether or not these persons have adequate background and experience to develop and operate this Company and to make it successful. In this regard, the experience and ability of management are often considered the most significant factors in the success of a business.

OUTSTANDING SECURITIES

GENERAL

96.   Describe all outstanding securities.

97.   Describe any resale restrictions on outstanding securities and when those restrictions will terminate, if this can be determined.

98.   Describe any anti-dilution rights of outstanding securities.

DIVIDENDS, DISTRIBUTIONS, AND REDEMPTIONS

99.   (a)   Has the Company paid any dividends on its stock, made any distributions of its stock, or redeemed any securities within the last five years?   [ ] Yes   [ ] No
If yes, describe each transaction.

99.   (b)   Does the Company have any plans or commitments to pay dividends on its stock, make distributions of its stock, or redeem its outstanding securities in the future?
[ ] Yes   [ ] No   If yes, explain.

OPTIONS AND WARRANTS

100.   (a)   State the number of shares subject to issuance under outstanding stock purchase agreements, stock options, warrants or rights.   _____ shares

100.   (b)   The shares identified in Item 100(a) are ____% of the total shares to be outstanding after the minimum offering.

100.   (c)   The shares identified in Item 100(a) are ____% of the total shares to be outstanding after the maximum offering.

101.   In a table, describe these stock purchase agreements, stock options, warrants, and rights. State the basic terms of these securities, including the expiration dates, the exercise prices, who holds them, whether they are qualified or non qualified for tax purposes, and whether they have been approved by stockholders.

102.   State the number of shares reserved for issuance under existing stock purchase or option plans but not yet subject to outstanding purchase agreements, options, or warrants.
_____ shares

103.   Does the Company have any plans or commitments to issue or offer options in the future?
[ ] Yes   [ ] No   If yes, explain.

SALES OF SECURITIES

104.   (a)   Has the Company sold or issued securities during the last 12 months?
[ ] Yes   [ ] No

104.   (b)   If yes, in a table, provide the following information for each transaction: the date of the transaction; the amount and type of securities sold or issued; the number of purchasers to whom the securities were sold or issued; any relationship of the purchasers to the Company at the time of sale or issuance; the price at which the securities were sold or issued; and a concise description of any non-cash consideration.

PRINCIPAL STOCKHOLDERS

105.   In the following table, provide the name and office street address of each person who beneficially owns at least 10% of the common or preferred stock of the Company.

Class of Shares	Average Price Per Share	No. of Shares Now Held	% of Total	No. of Shares Held After Offering if All Securities Sold	% of Total

106.   Number of shares beneficially owned by all Officers and Directors as a group:

106.   (a)   Before offering: _____ shares   (_____% of total outstanding)

106.   (b)   After offering: Assuming minimum securities sold:_____ shares
(_____% of total outstanding)

106.   (c)   After offering: Assuming maximum securities sold: _____ shares
(_____% of total outstanding)

       NOTE: These calculations assume that all outstanding options have been exercised and all convertible securities have been converted.

MANAGEMENT RELATIONSHIPS AND TRANSACTIONS

FAMILY RELATIONSHIPS

107.   Is there a family relationship between any Officer, Director, key person, or principal stockholder?   [ ] Yes   [ ] No   If yes, describe.

MANAGEMENT TRANSACTIONS

108.   (a)   Will the Company use any offering proceeds to acquire assets from any Officer, Director, key person, or principal stockholder?   [ ] Yes   [ ] No

108.   (b)   Will the Company use any offering proceeds to acquire assets from an associate of any Officer, Director, key person, or principal stockholder?   [ ] Yes   [ ] No

108.   (c)   If the answer to Item 108(a) or (b) is "yes," provide detailed information about each transaction. Include the name of the person, the cost to the Company, the method used to determine the cost, and any profit to the seller.

109.   (a)   Will the Company use any offering proceeds to reimburse any Officer, Director, key person, or principal stockholder for services already rendered, assets previously transferred, or moneys loaned or advanced, or otherwise?   [ ] Yes   [ ] No

109.   (b)   If yes, provide detailed information about each transaction. Include the name of the person, the cost to the Company, the method used to determine the cost, and any profit to the person.

110.   (a)   Has the Company made loans to any Officer, Director, key person, or principal stockholder within the last two years?   [ ] Yes   [ ] No

110.   (b)   Does the Company plan to make loans to its Officers, Directors, key persons, or principal stockholders in the future? [ ] Yes   [ ] No
If yes, describe any policies the Company has adopted to deal with the conflicts of interest in these transactions:

111.   (a)   Has the Company done business with any Officer, Director, key person, or principal stockholder within the last two years?   [ ] Yes   [ ] No

111.   (b)   Is the Company currently doing business with any Officer, Director, key person, or principal stockholder?   [ ] Yes   [ ] No

111.   (c)   Does the Company plan to do business with its Officers, Directors, key persons, or principal stockholders in the future?   [ ] Yes   [ ] No
If yes, describe any policies the Company has adopted to deal with the conflicts of interest in these transactions:

112.   Explain any "yes" answers to Items 110(a), 111(a), or 111(b). State the principal terms of any significant loans, agreements, leases, financing, or other arrangements.

113.   (a)   Has any Officer, Director, key person, or principal stockholder guaranteed or co-signed the Company's bank debt or other obligations?   [ ] Yes   [ ] No

113.   (b)   If yes, explain the terms of each transaction and describe the Company's plans for repayment.

LITIGATION

114.   Describe any recent or pending litigation or administrative action which has had or may have a material effect upon the Company's business, financial condition, or operations. State the names of the principal parties, the nature and current status of the matters, and the amounts involved.

115.   Describe any threatened litigation or administrative action that may have a material effect upon the Company's business, financial condition, or operations. State the names of the principal parties, and the nature and current status of the matters.

TAX ASPECTS

116.   Describe any material tax consequences to investors in this offering.

OTHER MATERIAL FACTORS

117.   Describe any other material factors, either adverse or favorable, that will or could affect the Company or its business or which are necessary to make any other information in this Disclosure Document not misleading or incomplete.

ADDITIONAL INFORMATION

118.   (a)   Describe the types of information that the Company will provide to security holders in the future.

118.   (b)   Describe the schedule for providing this information.

118.   (c)   Attach the Company's financial statements to the Disclosure Document.

SIGNATURES:

    The Company's Chief Executive Officer, Chief Financial Officer, and its Directors must sign this Disclosure Document. When they sign this Disclosure Document, they represent that they have diligently attempted to confirm the accuracy and completeness of the information in the Document.

    When the Chief Financial Officer signs this Disclosure Document, he or she represents that the financial statements in the Document have been prepared in accordance with generally accepted accounting principles which have been consistently applied, except where explained in the notes to the financial statements. He or she represents that the financial statements fairly state the Company's financial position and results of operations, or receipts and disbursements, as of the dates and periods indicated. He or she also represents that year-end figures include all adjustments necessary for a fair presentation under the circumstances.

Chief Executive Officer: Directors:

Title: _____   _____

Chief Financial Officer: _____

Title: _____   _____

LIST OF EXHIBITS

INDEX

Accountants, 14, 44, 47, 146, 176
  cold comfort letter, 79
  disagreements with, 96
  due diligence requirements, 65–67
  fees, 63
Accounting standards, Foreign
  Corrupt Practices Act of 1977,
  199–202
Accredited investors, 112–119
  NASAA model exemption, 121–125
Acquisitions, growth through, 4–5,
  22, 96
Advertisements. *See also* Publicity
  general, 112–114, 118, 141,
  143–144
  Regulation A, 128–130, 136–137,
  139
  restricted securities, 212
  tombstone, 40–42
Advisory committee, 27–28
Aftermarket, 39, 50, 107–108,
  141–142
Aiders and abettors, 204–206
All-hands meetings, 72
American Bar Association State
  Regulation of Securities
  Committee, 142
American Depository Receipts
  (ADRs), 177, 178
American Institute of Certified
  Public Accountants, 111, 146
American Stock Exchange, 74, 157,
  170
  fees, 172–173
  initial public offerings on, 171
  listing requirements, 159, 166–167
  newspaper listing, 176–177
Andreessen, Marc, 13
Anti-takeover defenses, 10–11,
  25–27
Appraisal, 15–16
ASAF Janus SmallCap Growth, 77
Asked price, 108, 152, 158, 168
Assets
  acquisition of, 4–5, 22, 96
  companies classified by, 21
Attorneys, 44, 47, 71, 185, 206

due diligence requirements, 65–67
fees, 62–63
SCOR form preparation, 143
selection of, 14
for self-underwritten offerings, 111
underwriter's counsel, designation
  of, 60
Audit committee, 27, 174–175, 185,
  201–202
Audited or auditable financial
  statements. *See* Financial
  statements
Auditors
  independent, 71, 176
  qualifications, 111
  selection of, 14

Backlog orders, 88
Bad boy disqualification, 116,
  130–131
Bankruptcy Act, 173
Barksdale, Jim, 13
Bear, Stearns & Co., Inc., 18–19, 34
Bear raids, 172
Best-efforts underwriting, 38, 61–62,
  99, 103–104
  limited dollar amount offering,
  117–118
  types of offerings, choice of,
  111–121
  unlimited dollar amount, 116–117
Bid price, 108, 152, 158, 168
Blackrock Micro-Cap, 77
Blockbuster Video, 102
Bloomberg LP, 77
Blue sky laws. *See* State securities
  laws and regulations
Board of directors. *See* Directors
Book, 168–169
Book manager, 39
Boston Stock Exchange, 177
Box, sales against, 184, 190–191
Broken IPO, 2
Broker-dealers, 36, 105–108, 110,
  168
  Rule 144 transactions, 213
  shell mergers, 151, 152

Bulletin Board, 159, 168
Business plan, 44
Business section, prospectus,
    86–89

Cancellation of IPO, 7, 46–47. *See
    also* Underwriters, withdrawal
    from offering by
Capital
    cost of, 1–2
    internally generated, 22
    needs, 58
    prior to IPO, 75
    resources, 22, 90, 92–93, 102
    working capital items, 88
Capitalization
    market, 18–22
    stock, 59
Cash reserve, use of, 4
Charter, 10–11, 174–175, 183
Cheap stock, 74–75
Chicago Board Options Exchange,
    Inc., 74, 177
Chicago Stock Exchange, 177
Chief executive officer, 13, 71
    compensation, 97
    competency of, 44–45
Chief financial officer, 13–14, 71
Chinese Wall, 35
Cincinnati Stock Exchange, 177
Class action lawsuits, 11–12
Classes of stock, 10, 25–26, 46, 75,
    176
Closing, 46, 71, 80
Cold comfort letter, 79
Commission, underwriter. *See*
    Underwriters, compensation
Common stock, restrictions on issue
    of, 176
Compensation
    broker-dealers, 36, 106, 145–146
    directors, 28
    management and professional
        team, 23, 96–97
    underwriters (*See* Underwriters)
Competition, 88–89, 102. *See also*
    Similar companies
Competitive position, enhancement
    of, 3
Conspirators, 204–206
Control, loss of, 10–11, 37, 102, 175
Control securities. *See* Restricted or
    control securities
Controlling persons, 204–206

Corporate governance requirements,
    174–176
Costs of IPO, 7–8, 50
    accounting fees, 63
    examples, 64–65
    filing, listing, and entry fees, 63,
        158–159, 172–173, 177–179
    Internet, direct IPOs using, 108
    legal fees, 62–63
    ongoing costs of public company,
        7–8, 51
    out of pocket, 7, 46, 60, 62–63
    printing costs, 63
    SCOR registration, 141, 143
    traditional IPO, 62–65
    underwriters, incurred by, 64
    underwriter's compensation (*See*
        Underwriters)
Counsel. *See* Attorneys
Credit Suisse First Boston
    Corporation, 34
Customers, dependence on, 88
Cyberonics, 19

Day traders, 4
Debt. *See* Loans
Debt-to-equity ratio, 5
Deutsche Banc Alex. Brown, 34
Developmental companies, 75
Dial Corp., 154
Directed shares, 80
Directors, 96
    compensation, 28
    corporate governance
        requirements, 174–176
    due diligence requirements, 65–67
    independent, 27–28, 174–175
    relationships, disclosure of, 97–98
    short sales or sales against the
        box by, 184, 190–191
    short-swing profits of, 184,
        187–190
    terms, 11
Disclosure of information, 8–10,
    84–85. *See also* Prospectus,
    statutory; Registration
    statement; Reporting
    requirements
    due diligence, 65–67, 71
    Regulation A, 132–133, 137–138
    Rule 10b-5, 204–206
    Rule 144, sales of
        restricted/controlled securities
        under, 212

self-underwritten offerings,
109–111
Discount
underwriter (*See* Underwriters,
compensation)
valuation, 58
Distribution
breadth of, 39, 46
trading during (Regulation M),
198–199
Dividends, 23, 28–29, 154–155
Dollar Time Group, Inc., 149
Donaldson, Lufkin & Jenrette, Inc.,
34
Drkoop.com, 18–19, 64–65, 89, 94,
98
Due diligence, 65–67, 71

Earnings
pooling-of-interest to increase,
5
pre-IPO, 22–24
eBay, Inc., 4
EBITDA, 58, 77
Employees. *See also* Management
and professional team
attracting and retaining, 6
as self-marketing spokespersons,
107
stock option plan as incentive, 14,
15
termination, effect on stock
options of, 16
Entry fees, 63
Environmental laws, effects of, 89
Equity
dilution of, 1–2, 14–15, 22, 49, 75,
102
enhanced ability to raise, 6
*Escott v. Bachris Construction
Company,* 66–67
Escrow, 147
Estate planning, 6–7, 12
Experienced and sophisticated
investors, sales to, 112–113,
116–117

Fads, 29–30, 101
Family and friends shares, 80
Filing fees, 63
Financial disclosures. *See* Disclosure
of information
Financial statements. *See also*
Prospectus, statutory

audit committee and, 175
audited or auditable, 24, 132–133,
146
SCOR registration, 146
Firm-commitment underwriting,
61–62
Fisher Price, 154
Float, 50, 59
Follow-on offering. *See* Secondary
offering
Foreign bribes, 202–204
Foreign Corrupt Practices Act of
1977, 185, 199–204
Form 3, 184–187
Form 4, 184, 186–187
Form 5, 184, 186–187
Form 8-K, 182, 204
Form 10-K, 182
Form 10-Q, 182
Form 144, 213–214
Form D, 144
Form S-1, 82–98, 114, 116
Form SB-1, 83–85, 114, 117,
133
Form SB-2, 82–85, 114, 116
Form U-7. *See* SCOR registration
Founders Discovery, 77
Fraud, rules against, 84–85,
109–110, 142, 143

General advertisement and
solicitation. *See* Advertisements
General Motors Corp., 154
GFC Financial Corp., 154
Goldman, Sachs & Co., 34
Good faith compliance defense,
139–140
Green shoe, 79
Growth
plan, 44
potential for, 20, 100
pressure to maintain, 8–9
strategies, 22
"Gun jumping" publicity prohibition,
67–69

Hambrecht & Quist, 19
Hancock SmallCap Growth, 77
Hostile takeovers, 10

Illiquidity discount, 2, 102, 149, 152,
153
Immediate family, 97–98
Industry segments, 86–87

Information. *See* Disclosure of information; Reporting requirements
Initial listing requirements, 159–167
Insider bailout opportunities, 28–29, 45
Insider debt, 29, 75
Insider information, 185, 191–196
Institutional sales, 34–37, 76–77, 103
  anti-takeover provisions and, 10–11
  institutional bias of underwriters, 35–37
Insurance
  liability, for directors/officers, 12, 27–28
  life, 7
Internal Revenue Code, 16, 28
International offerings, 114, 164–165, 167
Internet
  direct IPOs over, 108–109
  road shows on, 77
  Web sites, 109, 147–148, 174
Internet companies, IPO offerings of, 19, 20, 30
  earnings, 23, 58
  revenue, 24, 58
Investment advisors, 44
Investment banking, 34–35
Investment Dealer's Digest, 40
IPO Plus Aftermarket, 77
IPO Reporter, The, 30
IPO windows, 29–30, 101

J. Michaels, Inc., 150–151

Kidder, Peabody & Co., 19
Known uncertainty, 91, 93–94

Leakage provisions, Rule 144, 210–212
Legal proceedings, 96
Letter of comment, SEC, 73
Letter of intent, 59–61, 72
Levitz Furniture, 102
Liabilities
  legal, 11–12, 24–25, 65–67, 81, 84–85, 109–111, 142, 143, 155
  personal, 65–67, 142, 143, 184–185, 191–196, 204–206
  of shell corporation, 153

Liability insurance, for directors/officers, 12, 27–28
Life insurance, 7
Limit orders, 168
Liquidity, 6, 50, 90–92, 153. *See also* Illiquidity discount
Listing fees
Loans, 22
  enhancing ability to obtain, 5–6
  insider, 29, 75
  IPO proceeds used to discharge, 58, 95–96
  personal guarantees of, 6
  repayment to insiders, 29
Local underwriters. *See* Underwriters, local
Lock-up period/agreement, 3, 79

Maintenance criteria, 172–174
Management and professional team, 96–97
  compensation, 23, 96–97
  development of, 13–14
  due diligence requirements, 65–67
  quality of, 44–45, 100–101
  relationships, disclosure of, 97–99
  as self-marketing spokespersons, 107
  short sales or sales against the box by, 184, 190–191
  short-swing profits of, 184, 187–190
Management discussion and analysis, prospectus, 89–95
Managing underwriters, 38–39, 43
Manipulation of stock, 50
Market capitalization
  companies classified by, 21
  size of, 18–22
Market makers, 46, 50, 168–170, 213. *See also* Underwriters
Market price fluctuations, using, 4
Market value. *See* Valuation
Marketing, 71–72. *See also* Advertisements; Publicity
  attracting an underwriter, 44–45
  prospectus used for, 81–82
  SCOR, 143–144
  selecting an underwriter, 45–47
  self-underwritten offerings, 105–106
  steps, 33–34
Martha Stewart Living Omnimedia, Inc., 25–26

Mergers, 22. *See also* Shell corporations, mergers with
Merrill Lynch & Co., 34
Momentum investing, 4
Morgan Stanley, Dean Witter, 19, 25, 34
Muriel Siebert Capital Markets, Inc., 150–151
Mutual funds, 76–77. *See also* Institutional sales

NASAA Web site, 109, 147–148
NASD Corporate Financing Rule, 52–56
NASD Regulation, Inc. (NASDR), 52–56, 106
NASDAQ Bulletin Board, 80, 107, 158
NASDAQ National Market (NM), 74, 152, 157–159, 169
  fees, 63, 159, 172–173, 177–178
  float requirement, 59
  listing requirements, 159–160
  maintenance criteria, 173
  short-sale rule, 172
NASDAQ SmallCap Market, 157, 159, 169
  fees, 63, 159, 172–173, 177–179
  listing requirements, 159, 161
  maintenance criteria, 173–174
  publicity for, 170
NASDAQ Stock Market (NASDAQ), 49, 80, 107, 157–179
  corporate governance requirements, 174–176
  fees, 63, 158–159, 172–173, 177–179
  initial public offerings on, 171
  maintenance criteria, 172–174
  newspaper listing, 176–177
  stock exchanges compared, 169–170
NASDAQ Stock Market Web site, 174
National Association of Securities Dealers (NASD), 52–56, 63
National Quotation Bureau, Inc., 158
National underwriters. *See* Underwriters
Net worth, increasing, 5
NetRoadshow, 77
Netscape, 13
Neuberger & Berman Millennium, 77

New York Stock Exchange, 74, 157, 170
  fees, 159, 172–173
  initial public offerings on, 171
  listing requirements, 159, 162–165
  newspaper listing, 176–177
Newspaper listings, 176–177
Niche businesses, 18, 44
Niche underwriters, 37
Nontraditional IPOs, 38, 99–104. *See also* Best-efforts underwriting; Self-underwritten offerings
  advantages of, 103–104
  aftermarket trading, 107–108
  reasons for, 101–103
  types of, 99
North American Securities Administration Association (NASAA), 109
  model accredited investor exemption, 121–125
Northstar Special, 77
Numerex Corp., 152

Offering statement and circular, 132–133, 137–139. *See also* Prospectus, statutory
Offers to sell. *See also* Prospectus, statutory
  defined, 68
  "gun jumping" prohibition, 67–69
  written offers, 69
Officers. *See* Chief executive officer; Chief financial officer; Management and professional team
Operations, results of, 90–91, 93
Oppenheimer Enterprise, 77
Overallotment option, 79
Overpriced stock, sale of, 4
Over-the-counter market, 159, 168–169. *See also* NASDAQ Stock Market

Pacific Stock Exchange, Inc., 74, 177
PaineWebber, Inc., 34
Participants, IPO, 71, 204–206
Patents, 87
Penny stock, 59, 107–108
Personal assets
  enhancement through IPO, 2–3
  protection of, 111

Personal holdings, sales of, 2–3, 45, 46. *See also* Stock option plans
  insider bailout opportunities, 28–29, 45
  lock-up period, 3, 79
  public reports of, 3
Philadelphia Stock Exchange, Inc., 74, 177
Phoenix SmallCap, 77
Pink Sheets, 158, 159, 168
Planning for IPO, 13–31
  anti-takeover defenses, 25–27
  attracting an underwriter, 44–45
  audited or auditable financial statements, obtaining, 24
  earnings or revenue, demonstrating, 22–24
  independent board members, selection of, 27–28
  insider bailout opportunities, 28–29, 45
  management and professional team, development of, 13–14
  public market place, awareness of, 17–22
  questionable practices, eliminating, 24–25
  selecting an underwriter, 45–47
  stock option plan, 14–17
  windows and fads, using, 29–30, 101
Pooling-of-interest accounting, 5
Posts, 168
Preferred stock, 25–26
  as anti-takeover defense, 10
  "blank check," 75
  issued after IPO, 176
Press releases. *See* Publicity
Prestige of public company, 3–4
Price of stock. *See* Valuation
Price/earnings multiples, 18, 57–58, 77
Price/revenue multiples, 58, 77
Pricing meeting, 57, 77–78
Prins Recycling Group, 149
Printing costs, 63
Private placement, 1–2, 48, 49, 56, 102, 117, 120–121
  exemptions for, 207
  SCOR compared, 144
  shell corporation mergers and, 149, 152, 153
Private Securities Litigation Reform Act of 1995, 205

Proceeds, use of, 44, 58, 95–96
Products, principal, 22, 85, 87–89
Promotional companies, 75
Prospectus, statutory, 69–73
  amendments, 73
  Form S-1 prospectus, sections of, 85–98
  objectives, 81
  plain English requirement, 98
  preparation, 81–98
  risk in, 81–82
  SEC forms and rules, 82–98
Proxies, 175
Prudential Securities, Inc., 34
Public market place, awareness of, 17–22
Public offering
  advantages of, 1–7
  disadvantages of, 7–12
  planning for (*See* Planning for IPO)
  price (*See* Valuation)
  private placement compared, 48, 49
  self-underwritten/best-effort choices, 118–120
  steps in process, 71–72
  total number of shares in, 58, 59
Publicity, 11–12, 50, 61, 67–70, 170, 176–177. *See also* Advertisements; Prospectus
  after effective date of registration statement, 70
  after filing registration statement, before effective date, 69
  prior to filing registration statement, 67–69
  Regulation A offerings, 69
  road shows, 69, 71, 76–77
  supplemental sales literature, 70

Quaker Oats, 154
Questionable practices, eliminating, 24–25
Quiet period, 70, 73

Raw materials, 87
Real estate investment trusts, 63
Reconciliation note, 146
Red herrings. *See* Prospectus, statutory
Regional underwriters. *See* Underwriters, regional
Registrant's securities, description of, 96

Registration statement, 46, 112, 132, 182. *See also* Prospectus, statutory
amendments, 73
drafting of, 71, 72
due diligence and, 66
effective date of, 78
exemptions from, 207
filing, 73
publicity prior to filing, 67–69
publicity after filing, before effective date, 69
publicity after effective date of, 70
SEC forms and rules, 82–98
SEC letter of comment, 73
suspension of, 79
Regulation A, 108, 112–114, 117–119, 127–140
bad boy disqualification, 130–131
good faith compliance defense, 139–140
investor interest, determining, 128–130
issuer and offering requirements, 130, 134–135
maximum money available from, 131–132
offering statement and circular, 132–133, 137–139
offers prior to and after filing and qualification of offering statement, 128–130, 136–137
overview, 133–134
publicity, 69
reports, 139
sales, timing of, 139
test-the-waters rule, 128–130, 136–137
Regulation M, 198–199
Reporting requirements, 7–9, 11–12, 139, 181–206, 204. *See also* Disclosure of information
Repurchase of stock, 4
Research and development, 89
Restricted or control securities, 207–210
adequate public information, 212
amount saleable under Rule 144, 210–212
exemption if held two years, 214
Form 144, filing of, 213–214
manner of selling, 213
one-year holding period for, 209–210
Retail businesses, 102

Retail sales of stock, 34–37, 104
Revenues
companies classified by, 21
pre-IPO, 22–24, 86
price/revenue multiples, 58, 77
product sales, disclosure of, 85, 87
Risk, 44–45, 81–82
Road shows, 69, 71, 76–77
Rubio's Restaurants, Inc., 64
Rules, SEC. *See* Securities and Exchange Commission (SEC)

Safe harbor provisions, 116–117, 135
Sale of company prior to IPO date, 60–61
Sales against the box, 184, 190–191
Salomon Smith Barney, 34
Schedule 13D, 184, 196–198
Schedule 13G, 184, 196–198
SCOR registration, 113–115, 119, 141–148
commissions or fees for sales, 145–146
eligibility to use, 144–147
escrow, 147
federal registration exemption, 143–144
instructions and forms, 147–148
offers and sales, 147
Seasonality of business, 88
Secondary offering, 2–3, 6, 51, 58, 60
Securities Act of 1933, 207–215
due diligence, 65–67
"gun jumping" publicity prohibition, 67–69
offer to sell, definition of, 68
registration statements, requirements for, 84–85, 110, 117
Section 3(b), 108 (*See also* Regulation A)
Securities and Exchange Commission (SEC), 49, 118
accounting charges for stock options, 17
comments from, 71
confidential treatment of documents by, 9
filing fees, 63
filing with, 71
letter of comment, 73
mandated disclosures, 9–10, 84–85
market capitalization report, 20–22
prospectus, rules and forms for, 82–98

Securities and Exchange
    Commission (SEC) *(continued)*
  Regulation S, 114
  reporting requirements *(See*
    Reporting requirements)
  Rule 3a4-1, 107
  Rule 10b-5, 191–196, 204–206
  Rule 144, 3, 6, 207–215
  Rule 408, 84
  Rule 501, 113
  Rule 504, 113–120, 141–148
  Rule 505, 117–118, 120–121
  Rule 506, 112–113, 116–117,
    120–121, 153
  SCOR, Form D filing for, 144
  suspension of registration
    statement effectiveness by, 79
Securities Exchange Act of 1934,
    183–206
  Foreign Corrupt Practices Act,
    amendments to act by, 199–204
  Regulation M, 198–199
  Rule 10b-5, 191–196, 204–206
  Section 12, 80, 150, 158, 181–182
  Section 13, 182
  Section 13(d), 196–198
  Section 13(g), 196–198
  Section 14, 182
  Section 15(d), 182
  Section 16(a), 185–187
  Section 16(b), 187–190
  Section 16(c), 190–191
Self-underwritten offerings, 99,
    103–104
  aftermarket trading, 107–108
  Internet, direct IPOs over,
    108–109
  legal considerations, 109–111
  limited dollar amount, 117–118
  marketing, 105–107
  types of offerings, choice of,
    111–121
  unlimited dollar amount, 116–117
Selling agreements, 110–111
Selling groups, 39
Shareholder approval of securities
    issues, 175–176
Shareholder lawsuits, 11–12
Shareholder meetings, 175
Shareholders, reporting
    requirements based on number
    of, 181–183
Shell corporations, mergers with, 99,
    103, 149–153

Short sales, 170–172, 184, 190–191
Short-swing profits, 184, 187–190
Similar companies
  capitalization of, 102
  IPOs of, 29–30
  performance of, 101
  price/earnings multiple of, 18,
    57–58
  underwriters used by, 47
Size of company, 18–22
Size of IPO, 19–22
Small businesses. *See also*
    Nontraditional IPOs
  registration statement forms for,
    82–98
  SCOR for, 142
Solicitation, general. *See*
    Advertisements
Sophisticated investors. *See*
    Experienced and sophisticated
    investors, sales to
Specialists, 168–169
Spin-offs, 99, 153–155
Spring Street Brewing Company,
    108–109
Startup companies, 20
State securities laws and
    regulations, 26, 73–76, 118
  intrastate offerings, 113, 114, 116,
    119, 141
  merit review laws, 76
  personal assets, protection of, 111
  private placements, 117
  Rule 504/accredited investor
    exemptions, 115–116
  SCOR registration, 141–148
  self-underwritten offerings, 107
  underwriter compensation, 56
Stock, classes of, 75
Stock capitalization, 59
Stock exchanges, 157. *See also*
    American Stock Exchange; New
    York Stock Exchange
  dealer market compared, 169–170
  fees, 158–159, 172–173
  listing on, 80, 107, 159–167
  maintenance criteria, 172–174
  SEC reporting requirements, 182
  tick rule and short selling,
    170–172
Stock option plans
  adopting, 14–17
  "call provision," 16
  cheap stock, 74–75

dilution of equity, reducing, 14–15
duration of stock options, 16
employee termination, effect of, 16
excessive number of options, 75
exercise prices, setting, 14
as incentive, 14, 15
market value, determination of, 15–16
no IPO, effect of, 15
proximity to public offering, effect of, 16–17
shareholder approval requirement, 175
Stock splits, 59, 78
Stockholders' meetings, 7
Stop orders, 168
"Story" of company, 44
Subchapter S corporations, 23, 28–29
Subsidiary spin-offs, 153–154

Tacking provisions, Rule 144, 210
Takeovers, hostile, 10. *See also* Antitakeover defenses
Technology companies, 102
Test-the-waters rule, 128–130, 136–137
Tick rule, 170–172
Timetable, IPO, 71–72
Tipping of material, 185, 195–196
Tombstone advertisements, 40–42
Tracking stock, 154
Traditional IPOs. *See also* Planning for IPO; Underwriters
companies not qualifying for, 100–101
costs of, 62–65
cyclical market for, 101
nontraditional IPOs compared, 103–104

Unaffiliated companies, spin-offs of, 154–155
Underwriters, 71
anti-takeover provisions and, 10–11, 25–28
attracting, 44–45
compensation, 7, 35–36, 50, 52–56, 60–62, 64, 65, 106, 145–146
costs incurred by, 64
counsel, designation of, 60
distribution capability, 46
due diligence requirements, 65–67

experience, 46
flexibility of, 46
local, 38, 106, 110
low company valuation, underwriters for, 48–51
managing, 38–39, 43
market-making capability, 46
national, 34–35, 62
niche, 37
nonprestigious, 39–42
prestigious, 39–42, 47, 48, 51, 101
prospectus and, 72–73
references for, 47
regional, 37–38, 62, 106
reputation, 45
selection of, 45–57, 103
shell corporation mergers handled by, 149–150
statutory underwriter, spin-off sponsor as, 155
third-tier, 49–51
track records, 42–43
withdrawal from offering by, 60–61, 63–64, 79
Underwriting agreement, 46, 78–80
Underwriting syndicates, 38–39
Underwritings
number per year of, 30–31
types of, 61–62

Valuation, 6, 57–59, 71, 77–78, 103
below $20 million, 48–51
cheap stock, 74–75
determination of, 15–16
discounting, 58
post-IPO, 100
SCOR stock offering price, 145
shell merger, 150
splitting of pre-IPO shares, 59, 78
stock options and, 16–17
underpricing, 58, 78
Venture capital, 22, 56, 102. *See also* Private placement
Voting rights, 10, 75, 176

Wall Street Journal, The, 40–42, 176–177
William Blair Value Discovery, 77
Wire houses, 34
Wit Capital Corporation, 19
Working capital items, 88

Yahoo! Inc., 77

ABOUT THE AUTHOR

Frederick D. Lipman is a partner with the nationally prominent Philadelphia law firm of Blank Rome Comisky & McCauley LLP, with offices in Pennsylvania, New York, Connecticut, New Jersey, Delaware, Maryland, Washington, D.C., and Florida. He has appeared as a television commentator on initial public offerings for both CNN and CNBC. Mr. Lipman has participated in numerous public offerings over his forty-year career and helps guide companies through the IPO process. A graduate of Harvard Law School, Mr. Lipman lectures on corporate finance in the MBA program of the Wharton School of Business and has taught at the University of Pennsylvania Law School. He is the author of *Financing Your Business with Venture Capital, Venture Capital and Junk Bond Financing, Audit Committees,* and *How Much Is Your Business Worth?* The previous edition of this book, *Going Public,* was named one of the ten favorite business books by *Your Company* magazine, a publication of American Express.